OUR LAND AT WAR

OUR LAND AT WAR

A Portrait of Rural
Britain 1939–45

DUFF HART-DAVIS

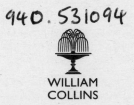

WILLIAM
COLLINS

William Collins
An imprint of HarperCollins*Publishers*
1 London Bridge Street
London SE1 9GF
WilliamCollinsBooks.com

First published in Great Britain by William Collins in 2015

1

A catalogue record for this book
is available from the British Library

ISBN 978-0-00-751653-7

Printed and bound in Great Britain by
Clays Ltd, St Ives plc

Contents

Prologue

They shut the road through the woods
Seventy years ago.
Weather and rain have undone it again,
And now you would never know
There was once a road through the woods …
Rudyard Kipling, *The Way Through the Woods*

I was too young to understand what people meant when they said that war had broken out on 3 September 1939; and as our home was some forty miles west of London, we escaped most of the hazards that harassed rural people closer to the enemy. But I do remember occasional fighter aircraft streaking overhead, searchlight beams flicking about the night sky, and, one afternoon, the rough roar of a V-1 flying bomb – like a malfunctioning motorbike engine – which suddenly cut out above us, leaving the doodlebug to crash and explode a mile away.

I was lucky enough to be brought up in an isolated farmhouse in the Chiltern Hills, and images of rural England at that time remain vivid in my mind. My family were not farmers: we merely rented the house. But we lived deep in the countryside, surrounded by the woods and fields of a large estate, and joined in many of the farm activities. With five bedrooms, the Victorian house was quite large, and perhaps had been built for a farm manager; but its facilities were primitive, and much the same as those in the cottages round about. We had no mains water, and our supply had to be pumped up by hand from one of the brick-lined underground cisterns built around the farm to collect rain for animals and humans. Our electricity – fit only to light feeble bulbs – came from a temperamental generator in one of the sheds.

With my father away in the army, my mother must have had a tough time managing our household. She cooked on an ancient, coal-fired iron range, boiled up the laundry in a copper heated by wood and coal, and wrung out the washing through a mangle before hanging it on a line slung between two old apple trees. She heated her iron on the range, and the only means of keeping the other rooms warm were small open fires. How she did her shopping, I do not know – but as our little Morris Eight was off the road for lack of petrol, I can only assume that she walked the mile to the main road and caught the bus into town, or else that a van from the local grocer made occasional deliveries.

We were seldom short of food, for we had rabbits from the game-keeper, eggs from our own chickens, vegetables from the garden and any amount of fruit – apples for cooking and eating, currants black and red, blackberries in the autumn and huge white-heart cherries from two splendid trees in the paddock. My mother preserved everything she could lay hands on – eggs in earthenware tubs of slimy waterglass, fruit in Kilner jars with clipped-on lids. In good seasons another vener-able tree showered down hundreds of walnuts, and in autumn mead-ows turned white with mushrooms.

We children had wonderful freedom outdoors. Petrol rationing meant that my sister and I had to make our own way to school, pedal-ling our bikes along farm lanes or wheeling them through woodland rides to the point on a minor road where a school bus picked us up. Dense laurel thickets and towering beech trees held no terrors, even in the dark of winter afternoons, for the way through the woods was as familiar to us as our garden paths. No sign or building marked our rendezvous on the public highway: the only shelter for our machines was the hollowed-out trunk of a huge beech tree which stood beside the road – and in that fire-blasted cavern we left them, unlocked and unprotected, until the bus brought us back and we recovered them to ride home.

Having been born with a hunter's instinct, I spent every available minute out of doors. Spring was the time to search for birds' nests and augment my collection of eggs, which I emptied, in time-honoured fashion, by making a pin-hole at either end and blowing out the contents. I was under strict orders from my parents not to take more than one egg from any nest I found – but the temptation was always strong, and in any case for species deemed harmful, like crows and magpies, the prohibition was waived. Twice I hurt myself quite badly and was carried home with my head covered in blood after falling from a height in attempts to reach the stinking, domed structures built by magpies in the tree-tops. I shall never forget landing face-first in a patch of brambles and ripping my hands to shreds as I crawled desperately through the thorns in an attempt to get breath into my lungs.

Accidents notwithstanding, the nesting season was always a time of miracles. How did a pair of long-tailed tits manage to rear a dozen or fifteen babies inside their tiny, vertical oblong of wool and moss and grass? How did wood pigeons stop their bright-white eggs rolling off their platforms of dry sticks, from which they were constantly departing with a great clatter? How did green woodpeckers interpret the messages they sent each other in the bursts of gunfire – *brrrrrp, brrrrrp* – which they generated when hammering out nest-holes in the trunks of trees?

Wandering about the woods, I often made for a clearing in which a gnarled and grizzled ancient, with a filthy pork-pie hat crammed down on his head, sat upright on a section of tree trunk, cutting tent pegs from hazel branches. One, two, three jabs against a long blade fixed upright in front of him – and almost before the chips had landed on the ground another peg went onto the pile. He hardly ever spoke; but as he did not seem to resent my presence, I used to stand and watch him, fascinated by the precision and economy of his movements. I see him now, chipping away in a sea of bluebells every spring.

Other choice destinations were the dew ponds scattered about the woods – small, circular pools ten or fifteen yards across, all perfectly round and enclosed by trees or bushes. It was clear from their shape that they had been dug by humans, but there was something mysterious about the way they always contained water. In that high chalk country there were no springs or streams to replenish them, yet they never dried out. Was it rain that filled them, or, as their name suggested, condensing dew? One pool was so thickly covered with algae that we called it the Green Slime – and it was there that I witnessed the magical sight of a woodcock carrying chicks, one at a time, between its thighs. The bird flew low and heavily for about fifty yards, before depositing its freight at a point which it obviously thought safe.

On the farm most of the power came from heavy horses, which did the ploughing and drilling, and hauled the wooden-wheeled harvest wagons into the rickyard behind the barns. They were driven and looked after by old Dave Collis, a small, bent man with one rheumy eye, who was reputed to be deaf only when he wanted to be. The farm also boasted one veteran blue tractor – a sign of things to come; but, like the horses, life moved at a leisurely pace.

The two great events of the year were harvest and threshing. As the corn ripened in July, everybody available joined forces to bring in the barley, wheat and oats: children, office workers, shop girls, boys from school camps organized by the Government – all came out to help. Our harvesting machine was a binder, drawn by two horses – a weird looking contraption with spinning wheels and unguarded drive belts, topped by a skeletal rotating flail which swept the crop backwards onto a reciprocating knife. Round and round the field it crawled, cutting the stalks, ingesting them and binding them into bundles with heavy twine, the knife chattering and the release mechanism giving a loud *clack* every time it ejected a sheaf.

Great was the excitement as the area of standing corn gradually diminished and rabbits trapped in it began to panic, weaving tell-tale trails of ripples through the ears as they dashed back and forth in search of a safe exit. Boys with sticks and, further out, old farmhands with guns, surrounded the shrinking patch, eager for the quarry to break cover. With the light failing and their shelter almost gone, the rabbits had no option but to run for it – and suddenly all was action: the men firing, the boys yelling, lashing out with our sticks and diving onto individual sheaves as we tried to pin down fugitives which had taken temporary cover. Nobody was squeamish in those days: we knew how to kill a rabbit by chopping it on the back of its neck with the edge of a hand, and how to paunch it by slitting open the skin over its stomach and scooping out the warm entrails with our fingers.

Cutting the corn was only the start of the laborious harvesting operation. The sheaves had to be picked up by hand and stood in pairs to make stooks – three pairs for a wheat or oat stook, four for barley, with a neat tunnel along the middle so that air would flow through and dry the grain in the ears. Boys could make good pocket money from stooking – and we earned it, for wheat sheaves were heavy, and the prickly hairs on barley stalks lacerated the inside of our wrists and fore-arms, as did the spines of thistles.

Threshing, which took place in winter, was heralded by the arrival of a majestic steam engine, which gave a couple of saucy hoots as it crawled down the last stretch of the lane, crunching gravel under its steel wheels and towing the great drum or barn worker – the threshing machine itself. In the rickyard the two had to be precisely aligned, so that a long canvas belt could transmit power from the flywheel of the traction engine to the drive wheel on the drum. When all was set, work began.

A man, woman or boy on top of the rick pitched sheaves down, one at a time, to a man on the drum, who cut the strings and dropped the loose stalks into the maw of the greasy monster. Standing aloft on the rick, lifting the sheaves with a pitchfork, was exciting work, for every movement might lay bare a nest of mice or rats, which would erupt and make a dash for the edge, launching themselves into space – only to meet their doom among the dogs and boys below. Experienced workers tied twine round the bottoms of their trouser legs to deny mice access, but often a yell or a shriek meant that their defences had been penetrated.

As the sheaves were beaten out in the drum, the air filled with dust, sending hay-fever sufferers into paroxysms of sneezing. Wheat was bad enough, but barley was worse, as the spiky ears set floating in the air left faces red and raw. From a tube on the side of the drum golden corn came pouring out into sacks, and these had to be lifted by hand and carried away for storage. The noise was intoxicating: the steam engine hissing, the drum roaring and rattling, the canvas belt flapping, boys shouting, terriers yapping, whippets and collies barking.

In spite of the war, everything about the farm seemed comfortably old and settled – the eighteenth-century barns, with their huge beams, red-tiled roofs, walls of blackened feather-edge planks and their fusty smell of rats and mice; the carthorses and their stable hung with leather harness; the wooden wagons, some of them gaily painted; the cast-iron hand pumps, mounted on little brick pillars, for bringing up water from the underground cisterns; the hand-turned mangold-cutter; the huge hay knife, three feet long, for chopping slices from the stacks; the heavy platform scales with their 56-lb iron weights. Yet my favourite emblem of perpetuity was not on the farm at all.

Far out in one of the woods was an ancient shepherd's caravan, with a hooped roof and steps leading up to the door. It stood in a clearing, and although it was still on its wheels in my imagination it had been there for ever: long grass had grown over its axles, and the planks along its walls had weathered to a shade of soft, pale grey furred with lichen. Once a shepherd's mobile summer home, it was used in my day by the gamekeeper as a store for pheasant food, rabbit traps and so on. But it also had another, more subtle role.

In the middle of one board on its south face was a knot-hole, and anyone peering through it, as though through a pin-hole camera, could see a small area of the opposite wall. At dusk on winter evenings the keeper would light an oil lamp, hang it from the ceiling, and, at the point on which any nocturnal snooper's eye would fall, prop up a crudely written notice proclaiming in big letters painted on cardboard, BACK IN HALF AN HOUR. Whether or not this enigmatic device had the effect of deterring poachers, none could say; but now, seventy years later, I feel it epitomized the simplicity of country life in those far-off days.

I was not old enough to realize that change was coming apace. Blocks of woodland were being clear-felled, one after another, to help meet the nation's desperate need of timber – softwood like larch for pit props, hardwood like beech (for which the Chilterns are famous) for building Mosquito fighter-bombers. Another tractor arrived on the farm. Fields that had always been meadows were ploughed for corn, throwing up flints by the million. Long Field, Marlins, Amos – even Shanty Meadow, traditionally sheep ground – down they all went to wheat. Another field was renamed Searchlight, from the installation built there early in the war, and at night slender, incandescent beams blazed from it, raking the sky for intruders. Centuries-old work patterns were being shaken apart by the growing crisis, and gradually life had to change.

One

The Old Ways

Oft did the harvest to their sickle yield,
Their furrow oft the stubborn glebe has broke.
How jocund did they drive their team afield!
How bowed the woods beneath their sturdy stroke!

Thomas Gray, *Elegy Written in a Country Churchyard*

The First World War had taken thousands of young men from the land. Farmers paid them such miserable wages that they were virtually slaves, so when they saw a chance of escape from drudgery they jumped at it. In *Akenfield*, his classic evocation of a Suffolk village, Ronald Blythe recorded that in March 1914 one nineteen-year-old, Leonard Thompson, was earning 11s a week, and later told the author: 'The village people in Suffolk in my day were worked to death. It literally happened. It was not a figure of speech. I was worked mercilessly.'

When the farmer stopped his pay because it was raining and the men couldn't thresh,

I said to my seventeen-year-old mate, 'Bugger him. We'll go off and join the army …' We walked to Ipswich and got the train to Colchester. We were soaked to the skin but very happy. At the barracks we kissed the Bible and were given a shilling … In my four months' training with the regiment I put on nearly a stone in weight and got a bit taller. They said it was the food, but it was really because for the first time in my life there had been no strenuous work ... We were all delighted when war broke out on August 4th.

Leonard survived the horrors of Gallipoli, the Somme and German prison camp, but thousands of his contemporaries did not. When he returned to Suffolk, for a while things were better on the land. The Corn Production Act of 1917, which guaranteed cereal growers good prices for wheat and oats, enabled farmers to pay higher wages, and hundreds of men joined the Agricultural Labourers' Union. But then a severe drought in the summer of 1921, and a repeal of the Act in August, precipitated a decline which led to a prolonged agricultural slump.

In 1938 Britain was growing only 30 per cent of its food, and only nine million acres of arable land were under cultivation, compared with eleven million in 1914. The Government saw that if war came the nation's essential supplies of wheat travelling by ship from North America and Canada would be threatened by Germany's U-boats. It was imperative that more corn should be grown at home.

Life in the countryside was still largely feudal. Many of the great estates had remained intact, and even if the proprietors no longer flaunted the size of their possessions in their *Who's Who* entries ('Owns 22,000 acres'), they still presided over very substantial areas of the country. Yeoman farmers had their own relatively modest houses and land-holdings, but most farm workers lived in tied cottages – that is, in houses owned by their landlords which went with their jobs. If a man lost his job, he lost his house as well – a system which gave owners an absolute grip of their employees.

By the middle of the 1930s huge areas of the countryside had fallen into a state of dereliction. Landowners had lost heart and let their acres go to ruin; tenant farmers, unable to make a living, had simply given up and gone away, leaving houses to decay or fall down and fields to rot. In the absence of grazing animals or cultivation, thousands of acres had been overrun by weeds, brambles and shrubs. In the high Cotswolds huge tracts had been taken over by thorn bushes and stunted trees. In low-lying areas drain clearance had been abandoned, with the result that hawthorn and bramble had spread so far outwards from the hedges that the undergrowth almost met in the middle of soggy fields.

Farming was decidedly old-fashioned. Mechanization was creeping in, but heavy horses still provided most of the power, outnumbering tractors by thirty to one. At the Centenary Royal Show held in Windsor Great Park early in July 1939 and attended by the King and Queen, the entries included 150 Suffolk Punches, along with 100 Percherons, eighty Shires and fifty Clydesdales.

As Ronald Blythe recorded, the horsemen were always the 'big men' on the farm:

> They kept in with each other and had secrets. They were a whispering lot. If someone who wasn't a ploughman came upon them and they happened to be talking, they'd soon change the conversation! The horses were friends and loved like men. Some men would do more for a horse than they would for a wife. The ploughmen talked softly to their teams all day long, and you could see the horses listening.

Since, in 1939, most tasks were still tackled by hand, farm workers needed to be strong, fit and hardy. A ploughman plodded over ten or eleven miles of ground every day, guiding his team, as did a man broadcasting seed or fertilizer by hand. A tractor driver had no protection from sun, wind, rain and snow except for his coat and hat: winter and summer he sat in the open on a steel seat, sprung on a flat steel tongue, and maybe slightly padded with an old hessian sack. He had no cab to shield him from the elements, still less any ear-defenders. His only air conditioning was provided by nature.

Starting one of those old bangers was a labour in itself, especially in winter. Having primed the fuel pump, the driver had to turn the engine over by swinging the crank handle at the front – a procedure that might drag on for ten minutes or more in cold weather. If he failed to keep his thumb on the same side of the handle as his fingers, and the engine kicked back, his thumb could be dislocated or broken. Some farmers had trouble progressing from old equipment to new: one in Cornwall tried to get his new machine to stop by shouting 'Whoa!' – and in consequence drove straight through the wall of a shed.

A tractor with rubber tyres was rare. The majority had all-steel rear wheels fitted with angled cleats or protruding lumps called spade-lugs. These gave a grip on fields, but made driving along hard roads impossibly rough – on the surface, the machine and the driver – so whenever a farmer wanted to move his machine any distance along a highway, he had to go through the laborious process of fitting protective metal covers round each wheel, bolting two semi-circular sections together. Rubber tyres were much coveted; they gradually became more available, in effect making a tractor a dual-purpose vehicle, equally at home on field or road; but early in the war any tractor passing along a road attracted attention.

In March 1940 the law was amended to allow boys of twelve and upwards to drive tractors on roads. But boys of eleven or twelve, who had never taken a test, were already working unsupervised on the land. Francis Evans, son of a Gloucestershire farmer, was eleven in 1941 and frequently went ploughing on his own all day. 'My father would come with me along the road to the field being worked, and then go home on his bicycle, leaving me to carry on.'

At hay-time, in June, everyone turned out to help make the most of good weather: wives and children as well as men. Round the edges of fields, where the grass might be wet and choke a mechanical knife, the

hay was still mown with scythes. The mechanical cutter was a reciprocating knife with jagged teeth, powered by gears from the axle, and (in
the absence of a tractor) it was pulled by two horses walking slowly.

The cut grass was evenly spread with pitchforks until it had begun
to dry in the sun, giving off a delicious smell like that of biscuits cooking; then it was turned and left until it was ready to be collected, either
by hand or by a horse-drawn rake with long, curved, downward-facing
tines, which could be lifted clear of the ground by pulling a lever. A boy
riding jockey on the rake had to pay attention, for if he fell off he might
be impaled on the tines before he could stop the horse.

Every available person and every available vehicle joined in. In the
summer of 1940 the actress, singer and monologist Joyce Grenfell
turned out to help at Cliveden, the Astors' home in Buckinghamshire,
driving a twelve-year-old, two-seater Chrysler. 'Now it is entirely paint-
less, bonnetless, brakeless, roofless, floorless and hornless,' she wrote of
the car,

> but still it goes in bottom gear. It is equipped with a giant
> wooden comb-like device that is fixed on in front. You drive
> the car along rows of raked hay and this arrangement collects it
> up. When you have enough you steer off the row into the open
> and deliver your load in a part of the field near the rick. To
> unload you merely reverse; in fact, that is the only means of
> stopping anyway!

Loaded onto horse-drawn wagons, the hay was transported to the
farm, where, again, pitchforks lifted it onto a rick. The entire process
was labour-intensive, and greatly dependent on the weather: for good
hay, dry days and hot sun were essential. As one reader of *The Farmers'*
Weekly remarked, 'Of course, the ideal is to have ideal weather, but only
in the fields of Elysium is the ideal continuous.' In the rick, during
autumn and winter, the hay gradually solidified, so that when it was

needed for feeding horses and cattle, slices of it had to be cut as if from a loaf of bread with a knife three feet long.

After haymaking, the busiest time of year was harvest, from July to September, when everybody again joined forces to bring in the corn. Cutting and stooking were only the start. The next step was to load the sheaves onto a cart, passing them up one at a time with a pitchfork to a man who had the skill to lay them in overlapping layers so that they bound each other in and did not slip off as the cart lurched towards the farmyard on its wooden wheels. Once there, the process had to be repeated: an elevator ferried the sheaves up onto a rick, and again a skilled operator built them up so that they would hold together and not slide outwards.

By the beginning of the war a few early combine harvesters were working, but these were large, inefficient contraptions and needed tractors to pull them – which meant that a good deal of the corn was flattened ahead of the cutter. The first self-propelled prototype, the Canadian Massey-Harris M-H 20, which appeared in 1938, travelled at four miles per hour without running down any of the crop, and cut, threshed and delivered a continuous stream of grain into sacks. Two men were needed to operate it – one to drive, and one to stand on a platform at the back, changing the sacks and sliding them off onto the ground when they became full. As each of them weighed 200 lb or more, and they were scattered about the field, collecting them up and lifting them onto a wagon was no easy task – and then at the farmyard they had to be carried up a long plank or flight of steps and tipped into the barn.

Other farm tasks were less dramatic. Ploughing was one of the slowest, demanding skill, patience, strength and stamina. Although even early tractors could plough far faster than horses, many people clung to the old ways. Angus Nudds, who started work on a farm in Wiltshire when he was fourteen, and later became a gamekeeper, remembered, 'Not many people have had the pleasure of ploughing with horses.'

Instead of the roar of the tractor, there was just the occasional gentle cough of one of the horses, the sound of the soil coming off the plough-share, the jingle of the harness and the constant cry of the seagulls which competed for the worms that were turned up out of the ground. I loved working with horses; they are such noble animals, not asking much out of life, just a warm stable, some good food and a bit of kindness, and they repay you by working for you eight hours a day.

No one endorsed those feelings more warmly than John Stewart Collis, an intellectual who worked as a farm labourer in Sussex and Dorset from 1940 to 1946. Already almost forty when the war broke out, he opted for work on the land and wrote two classic books about it, *While Following the Plough* and *Down to Earth*, which he later combined into a single volume, *The Worm Forgives the Plough*. Precise, accurate and never for a moment boring, he described the ancient rituals of farming in a marvellously lucid narrative of day-to-day tasks and events.

He scarcely mentioned his wife Eirene and two daughters, whom he packed off as evacuees to America: he referred but rarely to Bindo, the devoted dog which always accompanied him. His whole narrative was dedicated to describing work on the land, and he wrote about the most basic tasks with lyrical grace. Like Angus Nudds, he loved ploughing with a horse:

> Your feet are upon the earth, your hands upon the plough. You seem to be holding more than the plough, and treading across more than this one field: you are holding together the life of mankind, you are walking through the fields of time.

Most farm workers' language was as old-fashioned as the plough. In many counties 'w's were dropped – for example, the word 'woman' was pronounced 'ooman', and grammar was all over the place. When an old gamekeeper agreed that one of the park deer looked poorly, and said, 'Arr, I seed one up there crope about fairish', it was clear that he meant the animal looked pretty sick. No point in telling him that 'seed' was not the past tense of 'see', nor 'crope' that of 'creep'. One day Jack Hatt, who farmed at Checkendon in Oxfordshire, returned from market to see Olive, his Shire horse, lying prostrate on the field, with the ploughman, Danny, standing disconsolately beside her.

'Danny! Danny!' cried Jack, running up. 'What's wrong with Olive?'

'Blamed if er didn't go and die on me,' Danny answered, 'and I've never knowed she do that afore.'

Two

All Hands to the Plough

His way is still the obstinate old way,
Even though his horses stare above the hedge,
And whinny, while the tractor drives its wedge
Where they were wont to serve,
And iron robs them of their privilege.

The Yeoman, from Vita Sackville-West's *The Land*

The Emergency Powers (Defence) Act, passed on 1 September 1939, gave the Ministry of Agriculture drastic powers to intervene in the countryside. When the Government announced that it would pay £2 for every acre of old grassland ploughed up, there was a stampede of applications. By the middle of September 12,000 farmers had applied, and 220,000 acres had qualified for the grant. On 15 September *The Farmers' Weekly* declared:

Within the last ten days the whole face of British farming has been transformed. The industry … has been brought under a degree of Government control which has never been experienced before, and which only a few weeks ago would have been unthinkable. Maximum prices have been fixed for many of the things the farmer has to buy or sell. Within certain limits he will be told what he may or may not grow. Many of his younger employees will be taken away and replaced by labour which, in many cases, will be less efficient.

In a national farm survey owners and tenants were required to record the condition of their land – the nature of the soil, the acreage of arable crops and grass, the areas that were derelict, the state of their cottages, buildings, tracks, fences, ditches and water. They also had to declare if their property was infested with rats or rabbits, and to suggest ways of improving land in poor condition. The survey, which took more than two years, was an enormous undertaking: there were 300,000 farmers in England and Wales, and as one expert pointed out, 'No two farms were identical in soil, in layout, in buildings or in climate; no two farmers, in temperament, training and experience.'

The agents created for achieving results were the County War Agricultural Executive Committees (commonly known as 'War Ags'), reincarnations of similar bodies set up during the First World War. There was one War Ag committee for each of the fifty-two counties, made up of seven to ten unpaid local men, experts in various fields, principally farming. These then appointed sub-committees to deal with individual areas. Whenever they were photographed for one of the agricultural journals, attending demonstrations of new machinery or going out to inspect a farm, committee members turned out in uniform of suits and bowler hats or trilbies – although often the Chairman can easily be identified as a landed gentleman from his tweed jacket and plus-fours as he sits in the centre of the front row.

The officials were empowered to walk anybody's land and prescribe what needed to be done, even down to decreeing which crop was to go in which field, and the dates by which crops must be planted. If a farmer agreed to be helped, the Committee would loan him machinery from a pool, and extra labour whenever it could be found. If he refused to plough as directed, or his land was in too bad a state for him to tackle it, the War Ag could take over his whole operation and run it with their own men and machinery, or offer the tenancy to someone else.

A leader in the *The Farmers' Weekly* warned readers that the Minister might also 'authorise persons to enter upon land for the purpose of preventing or minimising injury to crops or wastage of pasture by birds, hares, rabbits, deer, vermin or pests, for the purpose of increasing the supply of food to the United Kingdom'.

> In other words, the Minister of Agriculture has more or less complete power over the farming of this country … County authorities will have a difficult and thankless task. They will be servant and whipping-boy, adviser and master. They will do their best to be friend as well.

To men with strong territorial instincts, whose families had always managed their own land, at their own pace, for generations, such draconian intervention came as a shock. Many resented being given orders by strangers, and were suspicious of officials who, having walked their fields in city suits, then told them what to do. Still worse, if a difficult decision had to be taken, the whole of the War Ag committee might turn out in force to assess the position – a posse of interlopers tramping over the fields, and an even greater insult. Yet it was no use arguing. Anyone who rejected the Committee's suggestions was liable to be fined, and, if he still refused to cooperate, to be evicted from his house and holding.

One such was Merriam Lloyd, owner of Dove Farm at Akenfield, in Suffolk. The story was told to Ronald Blythe by Lloyd's grandson Terry:

> He was a bachelor who walked about with a gun – you know the sort. He was very independent, and nobody could tell him anything. He knew it all. His farm wasn't much when he bought it, by all accounts, but it was a sight worse when the

Second World War broke out. He hadn't done a thing except walk round it. Of course the War Ag told him to plough up his meadows – told him! Of course, he wasn't having that. He took no notice. So they pushed him out. Some men came and literally pushed him out of his own front door. Then they brought some bits of furniture out and stood it round him on the lawn. They wanted the house, you see, for administration. Well, he went to live in a shepherd's hut in the orchard, where he stayed all through the war, and doing absolutely nothing, of course, and the Dove was given to Jolly Beeston to farm.

In a still more extreme case a farmer refused to plough his land, as directed, then ignored an eviction order. In the words of the historian Sadie Ward,

> The police were sent in, only to find the farmhouse secured against them and the farmer armed with a shotgun. After an exchange of shots and the unsuccessful use of tear gas, the police, backed up by troops, forced an entry. Continuing to resist arrest, the farmer was shot dead.

Even minor infringements of the Tillage Act were mercilessly punished. Two poor old farmers in Northern Ireland, both in their seventies, and with tiny holdings of ten and eleven acres, were fined £20 and £18 for falling short with their ploughing. The Ministry of Agriculture rejected their appeal, saying that the Act had been introduced in the national interest, and that no breaches of its provisions would be tolerated.

Between 1939 and 1945 some 15,000 farmers were forcibly dispossessed – a figure that sounds distressingly high, until one takes account of the fact that it represented only about 5 per cent of the agricultural holdings at that time. A great many farms changed hands: some were sold at auction in the normal way, but at the end of the war land would be offered back to an evicted owner, and if for any reason he did not want it, or if he had died, it would go on the market.

Most farmers were glad of help, and many were grateful to be relieved of responsibility. As one former official put it, 'They looked upon us as saviours.' When, after struggling with years of deficits, they saw money begin to roll in, they often became positively enthusiastic.

In the experience of Derek Barber (later Lord Barber), who was a student at the Royal Agricultural College in 1938, and then a member of the Gloucestershire War Ag committee, 'the war made everyone realise how important food production was. Simple people were introduced to more sophisticated ways of working the land.' Seventy years later he was still haunted by the memory of finding a young man dragging dung out of a horse-drawn cart with a pitchfork. The farm was a mass of weeds, and the mother sat in the house all day while her son did what he could to keep things under control. The farm had 'got into a terrible muddle', and Barber managed to persuade the family to accept help. The War Ag took over, paid some rent and lifted the family out of their despair.

Derek Barber's mentor was Professor Robert Boutflour, Principal of the Royal Agricultural College at Cirencester since 1931, and Chief Executive Officer of the Gloucestershire War Ag. Son of a farmer in Northumberland, he was short, stocky and boiling with energy – a tremendous man-manager: his ability to generate enthusiasm spurred countless farmers into far more effective action than they had thought possible, and he became a symbol of the war effort, in that he made the best of everything given him. One night he telephoned Barber and said, 'There are a hundred tons of potatoes arriving at Moreton-in-Marsh station at six tomorrow morning. Plant 'em.'

'We haven't got any land to plant them,' Barber protested.

'Plant 'em,' said Boutflour, and put the receiver down. 'A patch of ground was found on the side of a hill, the spuds were planted, and it became known as "Barber's folly".

Boutflour was nothing if not outspoken. One of his well-known observations was that 'a farmer with 150 acres is equal to a brigadier-general in the army'.

When people started complaining about bacon rationing, he wrote in *Country Life*: 'One British habit is causing a great deal of worry, and that is the demand for bacon for an Englishman's breakfast. Why should we worry? No other man in the world asks for such a breakfast, not even in countries where most bacon is produced.' He went on to say that the oatmeal from a field of oats would produce 'eight times as many good breakfasts in the form of porridge as would the same oatmeal converted into bacon ... Bacon for breakfast is a habit, almost a vice.'

Ploughing was accelerated by the issue of tractors, of which the Ministry had a pool. Through the War Ags it distributed them all over the country according to the nature of the land: fifty went to Devon, where grassland predominated, but only ten to Essex, much of which was already down to cereal crops. Progress was hampered by violent changes in the weather. The summer of 1939 had been gloriously hot (bringing out a plague of adders in the New Forest), but it left the ground baked hard and difficult to break up. Then October turned cold and wet, and in November frosts set in – the first of a bitter winter which brought cultivation to a halt and, in several places, froze the Thames from bank to bank, so that ice-breakers were working in the river.

When the weather eased, and March 1940 came in with two blessedly dry weeks, farmers began ploughing at night as well as during the day: a special amendment of the blackout regulations allowed them to use headlamps, provided they were screened so that they could not be seen from above – and in any case, on moonlit nights they could work with no lights at all. Phenomenal progress was made, and by the middle of the month 1,370,000 acres had been brought under the plough. In Scotland alone, by the beginning of June, farmers had notified the

Ministry of their intention to plough 252,000 acres of old grassland, and the War Ags had taken almost 2000 acres from nine farms 'which were not being cultivated in accordance with the rules of good husbandry.'

Wheat, for bread-making, was the principal crop; but another promoted by the Ministry was flax, or linseed, which was needed to replace the supply of cotton from abroad, cut off by the war. The plants had almost gone out of cultivation in England, though they were still grown in Northern Ireland for their tough fibre; but now, for the coming season, the Government ordered a fourfold increase in English production, from 4000 to 16,000 acres. One advantage of flax – whose flowers open and turn a glorious pale slate-blue when the sun comes on them – is that it grows fast: a crop sown in March should be ready by July. Another bonus is that rabbits do not like it, and will eat almost anything in preference.

In the old days flax used to be pulled by hand, but by 1940 pulling machines could be hired; the seed heads were crushed for oil, and the tough stalks processed to make cloth. Earl de la Warr, Chairman of the Flax Board, called flax one of the main munitions of war: when used in the manufacture of wing fabric for aircraft, it was claimed to add five miles per hour to the speed of certain bombers. Potatoes also came under the control of the Ministry, which ordered a far larger acreage to be planted.

According to Derek Barber 'the impact of the war effort on the character of the countryside was quite incredible'. He cited the example of a 2000-acre block of land close to Cheltenham, on the edge of the Cotswolds, which half a dozen farmers had been using as a huge ranch. One of them had a flourishing trade in pit ponies, which he bred, but none did any cultivation, and the ground had degenerated into bush, 'just like in Africa'. With the thorns ripped out by tractors and winches, the land ploughed and sown, it turned into 2000 acres of wheat, and the change wrought on the appearance of the landscape was as drastic as that caused by Dutch elm disease fifty years later.

Similar transformations occurred all over Britain. Every possible piece of ground was ploughed: not just meadows and the lower slopes of mountains in Wales and the Peak District, but cricket fields, commons and golf courses. The parkland surrounding large country houses excited much irritation. Farmers argued that the parks were a conspicuous waste of land, lost to agriculture for the sake of mere display. 'Private parks,' wrote one, 'are now the exercising ground of deer and pheasants ... Much of it would grow cereals well. The deer and pheasants could be killed to augment the meagre [ration of] 1s 2d worth of meat a week, which is by no means enough for heavy manual workers.' Golf courses, he added, 'should be made to produce food for man or beast ... I say we are fighting a life-and-death struggle, and money does not enter into it.'

On 4 July 1940, in the House of Commons, Mr J. J. Tinker, Labour MP for Leigh, in Essex, asked if a survey could be made of the Royal Parks in London, 'to see whether some parts of them could be used for growing foodstuffs, and in particular, whether the stretch of ground known as Rotten Row, in Hyde Park, could be utilised for this purpose'. The answer was that sixty-three acres had already been devoted to allotments, and eighty acres to the cultivation of oat and root crops. 'In addition, two-thirds of the greenhouse space normally used for the production of flowers is being used for the cultivation of vegetables.' As for Rotten Row: 'It consists of sand up to a depth of six inches on a brick floor about a foot thick, and, further, for a great part of its length it is lined by tall trees.'

The War Ags were certainly proud of what they achieved. A makeshift notice stuck up in a field proclaimed:

War Agric
47 Acres
Debushed – Drained – Reclaimed
WHEAT
52,000 Loaves?

Growing more food was essential for the nation's survival, but so was the harvesting of the crops; and farmers were soon severely handicapped by the shortage of labour, particularly for potato-picking in late autumn. The list of reserved occupations which exempted men from call-up included agricultural workers; but many farm boys, eager to escape the drudgery of life on the land, volunteered for the army, navy or air force, or went to earn better money on the building sites springing up all over the country in the rush to construct new military camps and airfields. All this created a serious deficiency, exacerbated by the fact that the seasonal influx of migratory workers from Ireland had been cut off.

In one issue after another *The Farmers' Weekly* bewailed the fact that farmers were losing stockmen, milkers, dairymen. 'From all over the country they are asking for skilled women to fill the abruptly-emptied places. If you have daughters who are clever with stock, or in the dairy, or are good milkmaids, urge them to think quickly about responding to this call.' The Situations Vacant columns were packed with advertisements seeking 'foreman cowman … girl calf rearer … young man to work horse … intelligent young Lady or Girl for milk round … cheesemaker man or woman … Respectable youth wanted, improver, general farm work … Strong woman wanted … Strong girl wanted for milk delivery in the City of Oxford. Horse vans used.'

In summer civil servants were given special leave to do farm work, and many rose to the challenge. But a still more valuable source of extra labour lay in the harvest camps for schoolchildren, organized by the Government. At first, in 1941, only boys were allowed to take part, but in 1942 girls joined them, and the number of camps rose sharply from 335 in the first year to a peak of 1068 in 1943, putting 68,000 young workers into the field, for an average stay of four weeks. Boys earned between 6d and 8d an hour, but they had to pay for travel to and from the site, and contribute towards the cost of their food – which left little in hand at the end of a three-week stint.

Although the work was tough, the camps were much enjoyed by most of the inmates, who remembered 'the pleasures of tent life, camp food, fireside sing-songs, the camaraderie with older farm workers and, in particular, the fact that campers found a new freedom and gained a sense of independence denied to many at the time'. Even so, pea-picking was regarded as a 'horrendous' job by the girls of Manchester High School, who were sent out to tackle the crop near Ormskirk in 1943, and worked with hessian sacks over their heads to protect them from the rain. Their miserable lot was to move along the rows, pulling up plants with their left hand, and with their right stripping the pods, which they dropped into a skip that held 40 lb when full.

That freedom of the fields often extended to the complete absence of safety precautions. Gerald Pendry, who went from a London school to a harvest camp in Warwickshire in 1941, was set to work with another boy on a flax-pulling machine, which had to be constantly unblocked, as the tough fibres kept jamming the rubber belts. Drive-shafts and belts had no form of protection, and the lads were supervised by a Polish tractor driver who spoke no English.

With still more harvesting hands needed, in 1943 camps for adults were introduced, and after a series of appeals by Robert Hudson, the Minister of Agriculture, thousands of men and women applied to join.

Perhaps it was a sense of achievement, coupled with hope that the war might not last long, which lent buoyancy to the sale of farms early in the war. Estate agents cheerfully reported good business, 'and plenty of eager applicants for good holdings, either for investment or occupation'. Prices seem ridiculously low. In March 1940 a freehold, 'highly farmed' holding of 163 acres in Suffolk, including an 'excellent residence' with five bedrooms, 'splendid premises' and two 'superior cottages', was advertised at £2500. A 170-acre grass farm in Nottinghamshire, including a cottage, could be had for £1750. In July *Country Life* reported that 'The investor's quest for first-rate farms goes on with increasing vigour'. The Yews Farm, near Rugby, with 215 acres, went at auction for £4800. On the other hand, with cement scarce, and bags of it described as 'precious as gold dust', repairs were difficult and farm buildings were tending to fall into decay.

Three

Exodus

It's dull in our town since my playmates left,
I can't forget that I'm bereft
Of all the pleasant sights they see,
Which the piper also promised me.

Robert Browning, *The Pied Piper of Hamelin*

Even as ploughshares bit into virgin turf, people everywhere were bracing themselves for war. On Saturday, 2 September thunderstorms rumbled and crashed over the south of England; but Sunday, 3 September was gloriously fine and warm. Hardly had the Prime Minister, Neville Chamberlain, made his fateful wireless broadcast at 11.15 a.m., declaring that the country was at war with Germany, when air-raid sirens wailed out, rising and falling over London. Worshippers in St Paul's Cathedral were ushered down into the crypt, and everywhere in the city householders hastened, as instructed, to stick crosses of brown paper on their windows, to minimize the risk from flying glass. Others hung wet blankets over doorways as a precaution against gas attack, which was many people's worst fear.

On a blustery morning in Banff, far off on Scotland's north-east coast, young David Clark saw his father, the minister, running up and down the streets in search of a wireless powerful enough to broadcast the news in St Mary's Church – and when Chamberlain came on:

'Tommy, my wee brother, and I immediately looked to the skies. Not for heavenly persuasions of any sort, but simply because we thought that German Stukas would immediately appear.' At Four Elms, a village in Kent, a boy rushed into the church during the service and handed the vicar a message, saying the war had begun – whereupon the congregation stood and sang the National Anthem. On their way home people collected wood from a spinney, assuming that coal would soon be unavailable.

Out in the country farmers covered hay and corn stacks with tarpaulins, to prevent gas sprayed by low-flying German aircraft, or dropped in bombs, from contaminating the precious stored crops. Over cities and large industrial sites barrage balloons floated in the clear sky like silver whales tethered by steel cables.

The threat of air attack seemed so real that on Friday, 1 September the Air Ministry had ordered a countrywide blackout, in the hope that the suppression of all lights on the ground would make identification of targets harder for the German air force, the Luftwaffe. The new regulations laid down that after dark all windows and doors must be covered by heavy material, cardboard or paint. The rules were strictly enforced by Air Raid Precaution wardens (ARPs) – easily identified by the white W painted on the front of their steel helmets – who adopted an aggressive approach during their rounds, and if they spotted a chink of light would come hammering on the door. Persistent defaulters could be reported to the police and heavily fined.

Anyone showing a light was liable to be besieged by neighbours, angry that one selfish or idle person was endangering everyone else. Total darkness was considered so essential that one night Sergeant D. M. Hughes of the Caernarvon police felt obliged to put out a light left on in an office building by shooting it with a .22 rifle. Outside, street lights had to be switched off, or screened so that they shone downwards. Traffic lights were fitted with slitted covers which filtered signals towards the ground. Car headlamps at first had to be blacked out entirely, but so many accidents occurred that restrictions were soon relaxed, and shielded headlights were allowed.

The blackout was exceedingly tiresome, indoors and out. Unless householders were prepared to live in permanently darkened caves, they had to take down the window covers in the morning and fix them up again in the evening – a time-consuming chore, especially in large houses with multiple windows. Outside, the restrictions put pedestrians in danger, not only of tripping over drain covers and pavement edges, but of being run down by vehicles feeling their way through the streets. White lines were painted along the middle of roads, but even to walk along them was dangerous, when drivers could hardly see ahead of them.

Townspeople were terrified by the threat of air raids. Householders hastened to fill sandbags to protect their properties from blast, or put finishing touches to the Anderson air-raid shelters in their gardens. More than a million and a half of these sturdy little huts, each of which could hold six people, had already been distributed across the country, free to those with an annual income of less than £250, £7 to others. Made of corrugated steel sheets bolted together in hoops, and covered with a fifteen-inch layer of soil, they could withstand the impact of shrapnel, but not a direct hit from a high-explosive bomb. Indoors, Morrison shelters – in effect reinforced steel tables – gave protection against falling masonry.

Country people were less alarmed by the idea of bombs, which they imagined would fall mostly on industrial centres. For farmers, a worse scenario was that of invasion. They could hardly believe that Germans would take over their land or slaughter their livestock. Nevertheless, some of them took precautions – like one man in Dorset who said to a friend: 'Bloody old 'itler's coming. I'm going to start saving money. I've got one churn buried, full of half-crowns and two-shilling pieces, and I've started to fill up another one.'

Five years earlier Winston Churchill had predicted that, in the event of war, three or four million people would be driven out into the open country around London. The exodus of 1939 was not as drastic as that: nevertheless, it was a huge movement, planned with skill and care, which drained the cities and deluged the countryside with a flood of urban children.

'The scheme is entirely a voluntary one,' the Government's Public Information Leaflet No. 3 had announced, 'but clearly the children will be much safer and happier away from the big cities where the dangers will be greatest.' The leaflet struggled to reassure everyone that the scheme would be for the best:

> The purpose of evacuation is to remove from the crowded and vulnerable centres, if an emergency should arise, those, more particularly the children, whose presence cannot be of assistance. Everyone will realise that there can be no question of wholesale clearance. We are not going to win a war by running away.

Safer – yes. But happier? That was wishful thinking. The diaspora began on the morning of Friday, 1 September, the day Germany invaded Poland. Children streamed out of London – and not only from the capital, but from other cities that were potential targets for the Luftwaffe – Bristol, Birmingham, Glasgow, Liverpool, Manchester, Newcastle, Sheffield. From Manchester alone 66,000 unaccompanied children dispersed to farms, villages and towns in the surrounding country.

On the morning, in London, outside schools all over the city pupils lined up with an escort of teachers and marched off to the nearest bus stop or Underground station. Each child had a brown identity label pinned to its jacket and carried a case containing a change of clothes, as well as a cardboard box holding a black rubber gas mask. For security reasons – and to prevent them following – the parents had not been told where their children were going: they would not know until a message came back to say that the travellers had arrived. Mothers, in tears, waved from behind iron railings, and most of the evacuees were sunk in misery – torn from home, and mourning their cats, dogs, mice, guinea pigs, canaries and parrots, which had either been exterminated or, on Government orders, left behind.

Some of the children from Central Park School in the East End of London were elated, but most were frightened and downcast. The carriages of the Underground on the old Metropolitan line to Paddington were so packed and stifling that some of the young passengers were sick over their neighbours, and when they reached the mainline station they collapsed, slumping to the floor of the concourse, which was thick with noise, black smoke and steam. Others put down their pathetic luggage and cried. In spite of the crowds, one boy felt 'very alone in a world going horribly mad'.

While the children of ordinary citizens waited on station platforms, better-off families were pouring out of London by car, in such numbers that roads became, in effect, one-way. Every vehicle was packed with people, luggage and pets, heading for safety in the west or north.

A train took the Central Park contingent of children to Shrivenham, then in Berkshire, where buses ferried them through the town to a school, for dispersal. After a sandwich lunch and a period to recover, they all had to strip and stand in line, for inspection by an elderly nurse, to make sure they were clean and free from head lice. Later, as they laid out mattresses for the night in neat rows on the floor of an assembly hall, two small girls appeared wearing headscarves. One stopped and stood with her head hanging, but the other turned round and ran, overcome by the shame of having had her hair shaved to get rid of nits.

To city children the country at first seemed hostile and alarming. One batch from London, taken to a Welsh mining village, arrived in the blackout-intensified dark of a wet, foggy night. Billets were found for most of them, but the last eight had nowhere to go, and their teachers were forced to knock on door after door, beseeching people to take one in. The same thing happened to twelve-year-old Eileen Ryan, sent from

London to Weymouth with her three-year-old brother Gerard in tow. Groups of children were led along the streets, with their leader knocking on doors and asking if the occupants would take any evacuees. 'I can't have the little boy,' said one householder after another – but because Eileen's mother had told her never to let Gerard go, they had to persevere until somebody let them both in.

Billeting officers, appointed by the Government, tried to rely on friendly approaches, but when persuasion failed they had the authority to compel householders to accept children if they had space enough. An eight-year-old Jewish girl called Sylvia was taken from Liverpool to Chester, but at first no householder would have her. She and her mentor walked round the city for hours before, at about midnight, a family took her in – but they put her into a storage room with no light, and left her there alone and terrified.

In Scotland 120,000 children left Glasgow within three days, spreading out into Perthshire, Kintyre and Rothesay. From Edinburgh some 50,000 headed north for the safety of the Highlands or down to the Border country. From Merseyside 130,000 dispersed into North Wales and northern England. As in the south, some fared better than others. Sara Cockburn, a young teacher from Glasgow, volunteered to accompany a group of evacuee children to Lochmaben, in Dumfriesshire, where they lived on a farm and were royally fed:

> We had what I will have in heaven if I am spared – pin-head porridge with cream every morning. Usually I weigh about eight-and-a-half stone. When I went back to Glasgow, I weighed ten-and-a-half stone. I was spherical, and I couldn't get into any of the clothes. All that was due to the boss's cream.

Good food remained a lasting memory in the minds of many evacuees. Eleven-year-old Ray Fletcher was sent with his two sisters from Margate, in Kent, to the Staffordshire mining village of Landywood.

The families on whom they were billeted were 'kindness itself', even though at first Ray could not understand a word of what they were saying, as their 'broad Midlands accent' seemed like a foreign language. But he never forgot the first meal he had with them – 'the most enormous plate of egg and chips I had ever seen', or the little potatoes which he fished out of a boiler as he sat in a barn, cooking up vegetable scraps for the pigs: 'There were a lot of *Oohs! Arghs! and Hars!*, for they were hot – but that didn't matter: they tasted delicious.'

In many villages the sudden arrival of extra children overwhelmed the facilities. At Orwell, near Cambridge, there was no room for new pupils in the school, so the evacuees sat on the floor and were kept separate from local children. 'We were not accepted by them as friends, and we were often bullied by them,' remembered James Kilfoyle. 'As there were no teachers, my sister, aged thirteen, used to teach the younger ones.'

At Badminton, a small village near Bristol, on 11 September 1939 the school roll leapt in a single day from ten to seventy-seven – the result of an influx from Birmingham. A shift system had to be adopted: indigenous children were taught by their own teachers from 12.15 to 4.15, but had to surrender their classrooms at other times. The immigrants inevitably brought unwelcome fellow travellers with them, and a week after their arrival a local report recorded that 'Nurse Brown visited and examined the heads of the seventy-two children present'.

Many urban children were already used to simple ways of life, but of a different kind. Some were poorly house-trained, if at all. Refusing knives and forks, they ate with their hands. Rather than use a lavatory, with which they were unfamiliar, they persistently relieved themselves in a corner of the room. One boy sent to the middle of Wales landed at an old-fashioned farm 'with a two-seater loo over the edge of the hillside, and when you looked down, it was like a giant precipice'. When Bangor, in North Wales, was invaded by 2000 children and their teachers, most of the evacuees could not understand a word or read the notices in schools, for half the population spoke only the native language. Landing in a strange environment could be highly alarming. A five-year-old girl placed with a mining family near Doncaster screamed when the man of the house returned from work 'all black, covered in soot, with just his eyes peeping out'.

Some city dwellers found the country 'a place of vast loneliness and fearsome terrors'. There was too much open space in the fields, and too many big animals which might bite or kick or knock little people down. Cows were particularly frightening – their size, their horns, the loud bellows they emitted, to say nothing of the mess they left behind them. One six-year-old girl's nightmare was having to walk home from school along a village street thronged every afternoon by a jostling, shoving milking herd on its way to the parlour (she never shed her fear of cows, and many years later her son recalled 'some pretty strange evasions over hedges and once along a railway line to avoid herds in fields while we were walking'). To a five-year-old from Walthamstow, a seventeen-hand carthorse was a threatening monster, and the screams that pigs gave out were blood-curdling. Another London girl sent into the country felt she was going 'on a journey to oblivion', convinced that all the people at her destination would be 'thick and dirty'.

In Kent the writer H. E. Bates ferried families to their appointed destinations in a huge, old, borrowed Chrysler, and was dismayed to discover that all they wanted was 'shops, cinemas, pubs, buses, pavements to walk on … It was incredible to find that a huge section of our population were producing children who did not know how potatoes grew'.

The sudden arrival of evacuees sent many a rural community into a spin. The leading lights of Tolleshunt d'Arcy, a village on the Blackwater Estuary in Essex, had made elaborate preparations, including a census of houses with space to spare. Among the organizers was the thriller writer Margery Allingham, who recorded how they had carried out a survey, making comments on various properties and proprietors: 'Good for nice girls', 'Good for tough boys', 'Good at a pinch', 'Would, but not keen', 'Could, but wouldn't without a row', 'Impossible', 'Never on Your Life'.

The villagers had been promised, and had prepared for, ninety children – so they were appalled when eight London double-decker buses rolled in, 'as foreign-looking as elephants', and disgorged 300 exhausted, irritable women and babies. Frantic efforts were made to place as many of them as possible that evening, but it was only the arrival of another bus, sent to take some to another destination, that solved the immediate crisis. In another village, suddenly landed with seventy more children than expected, one of the organizers commandeered an empty house and herded the whole lot into that for the night.

Officials charged with the task of dispersing evacuees had a nightmare job. Twenty-three-year-old Alan Stollery, a traffic trainee, was sent to Norfolk to arrange the reception of 16,000 children coming from London, about 1000 (including their attendants) on every train:

> My job was to assess the number of coaches required to meet each train, then to check the receiving villages to which each coach should be routed … For a train carrying 1,000 children, probably a minimum of thirty coaches was needed [but] for each train there were probably a hundred or more villages, each to receive a differing number of children.

As a retired army officer testily remarked, 'We have all got to realise that the Englishman's home is no longer his castle'; but many householders were dismayed by the idea of being required to act as foster-parents – and the higher up the social scale they were, the greater the difficulties they created about taking in urban children, shamelessly pleading lack of servants rather than lack of space. It was the poorest families, especially those with no children of their own, who were readiest with hospitality.

Children sent to the country were liable to be treated like the cattle they dreaded. When a bunch from Liverpool arrived by train at Ellesmere, in Shropshire, they were indeed put into cattle pens in the market, where people came and chose the ones they liked. Five-year-old Audrey Jones was similarly humiliated at Bletchington, near Oxford, along with her sister and two younger brothers, when locals looked them over critically in the village hall, selecting and rejecting. Her brothers James and Bernard were chosen quickly, as they were big boys, aged twelve and ten, and would be able to work for the farmer who picked them, but the two small girls were left until last. Many local people fancied Edna, who was six and a half, blonde-haired, blue-eyed and sweet looking; but they were put off by Audrey, who by her own account was a plain redhead with protruding red cheeks, and crouched under a table wetting herself.

In the end the Jones girls were taken by a Mrs Denton, with whom they spent their time 'reading the Bible and being very clean'. When their mother came down to see them, she was denied access to the house and had to speak to her daughters on the doorstep. 'Mummy could not believe her eyes on seeing me,' Audrey remembered, 'as when I left London I had long ringlets, but Mrs Denton had cut them off, saying long hair was sinful.'

The girls went to the village school, which they enjoyed, and after enduring only a month of Mrs Denton's cruel eccentricities they were moved to another house in the village – but this turned out to be even more unpleasant. Insecurity still made them wet their beds, and for this they were 'continually thrashed' by their new guardian, Mrs Taylor, sometimes with holly branches. Small wonder that when they found some brown paper and string, Edna tried to roll her little sister up in a parcel and find a post box big enough to post her back to London.

Later they were moved again, this time to a Mrs Harris, who had a backward daughter, Christine, and lived at the end of the village in an old house with no running water or sanitation. The girls' daily job was to walk to a well a quarter of a mile away, to bring back buckets of water for the house. When Audrey was nine she decided to run away – but of course she was found and brought back.

Out of doors, things were better, and gradually they learned about the country. One winter day they came across a dead sheep: it was stiff as a board with frost, but they took off their coats and covered it, hoping to bring it back to life.

Years later they realized that Mrs Harris was not really the demon she had seemed. The strain of coping with Christine (who ended up in a mental institution) and two London girls was more than she could handle – but, like other householders, she was paid 7s 6d per evacuee per week, and in those poverty-stricken days she desperately needed the money. After the war she showed that she must have had some affection for her young visitors, by always wanting to keep in touch.

The occasional child was insufferably bumptious. One six-year-old from London confronted her foster-mother at first meeting with the words, 'Who's boss here, Auntie?' The woman, taken aback, replied, 'I am the boss of the house, and Uncle (my husband) is boss of the garden.' To which the child retorted, 'Well, God and me are the boss of the lot.'

Little horror! But it is hard to believe that any evacuees were as poisonous as the three Connolly children who, in Evelyn Waugh's novel *Put Out More Flags*, are found 'lurking under the seats of a carriage' when their train is emptied at a country station. Acknowledging no parents, they speak only of 'Auntie' in London, to whom, it seemed, 'the war had come as a godsent release', and in the country they prove so rebarbative that they are passed from hand to hand by increasingly desperate householders – none less scrupulous than the smoothly dishonest Basil Seal, who, with his power as billeting officer, resorts to bribery and extortion to move them on.

Most new arrivals presented less of a problem – and many positively welcomed a move to the country. A youth sent from Surrey to the Yorkshire moors was delighted by his new environment: 'One begins to realise after frequent moves from one place to another that all town is monotonous and boring and that every strip of country has its collection of vital interests.' He was thrilled by the speed with which the mountain becks rose into rushing torrents after rain, and by the sight of snipe 'flying off in their peculiar corkscrew motion'.

Bob Browning was similarly delighted to exchange the inner suburbs of Birmingham for the Gloucestershire village of Uley, on the western edge of the Cotswolds. With fifty other children, including his sister, he travelled by train to Dursley, and thence by coach to the village hall in Uley. There he was met by a smart twenty-five-horsepower Wolseley, driven by the local garage owner, Chris Bruton, and taken up a steep hill to Lampern House. High above the valley, the two Misses Lloyd-Baker, daughters of a land-owning family, lived in style, and for Bob it was astonishing to be waited on at table in a house with stone-flagged floors, oil heating and lighting.

This sybaritic existence lasted only a few days; but when he moved down to the village and lived with the Bruton family because their modest house was closer to the school, he was just as happy. To him the countryside was a revelation. The beech woods which cloaked the flanks of the valley were turning to copper and gold, and to be able to go straight out into green fields was 'a miracle'. Mad as he was on football, he did not care if the grass was plastered with cowpats. The woods were ideal for hut-building, and Uley Bury – the biggest Iron Age hill fort in England, surrounded by a Roman race-track on an outlying ridge of the escarpment – made a thrilling natural playground for army games: boys would disappear up there after breakfast and not come back until lunchtime, having had a glorious, adult-free morning.

A system of barter helped fill gaps in the food supply. Since Birmingham enjoyed soft water, and people there had more soap than they needed, parcels of washing materials would come down to Gloucestershire, and freshly killed rabbits packed in moss would go the other way. Besides, there was pocket money to be made. Bob delivered milk from a churn on a round with a pony and trap, and with his friend Bill Bruton hunted cabbage white butterflies, of which there was a plague, swatting them with tennis rackets and filling jam jars to earn rewards at school.

The only member of the community who had a car was the doctor. Some houses had gas, but there was no electricity and people used oil lamps. Nevertheless, the village was lively: shortage of petrol (which limited visits to the nearest cinema) combined with the blackout to stimulate community life. There was a whist drive once a week, and a dance in the village hall on Friday night, from eight to one.

Dennis Swann, who lived near the Elephant & Castle in London, 'where all was buildings and pavements and street noise', landed at a farm near Colyton, in east Devon. Aged eleven, he had 'never seen cows, nor even a green hill', so he had never considered where milk came from, and found the sight of a cow being milked 'astonishingly exciting'. John Swallow wrote from Kidderminster, in Warwickshire: 'I broke my record by eating eight pieces of bread'; but then, asking if he might come home, he went on gloomily: 'If we have to go, we might as well all go together – you have got to die sometime, and it might as well be painlessly by the bomb as by a long illness or something.'

Some city-based mothers, unable to bear the separation from their children, forged out into the country to reclaim them, only to find that the foster-parents had become so fond of them that they were reluctant to let them go. Most children were too far out for regular visits, but one father who worked for the Post Office in London sometimes cycled seventy miles in each direction to see his son in Northamptonshire.

When several evacuees landed in the same place, they tended to stick together, to protect themselves from gangs of village boys. This happened at Ditchling, in Sussex, and Diana Ansell still has all too vivid memories of being posted, as a five-year-old scout, to keep watch while her companions scrumped apples in orchards and gardens, among them that of the Forces' Sweetheart, the singer Vera Lynn. Being a shy, quiet girl, Diana did not relish her role, but was forced into it with threats of dire tortures by her elder brother and his friends. A legitimate activity was working in the fields, for which they were paid pennies, and one day, as they were raking up hay, they were machine-gunned by a hit-and-run German pilot. By flinging themselves to the ground and burrowing under the hay, they escaped unhurt.

London and the northern industrial centres were by no means the Luftwaffe's only targets. Belfast was also evacuated – and Emily Cathcart, who ran a small country store and post office in the village of Bellanaleck in Co. Fermanagh, vividly remembered newcomers arriving:

> These city people were completely disorientated in the country. It was difficult to look after them. They rolled themselves in any bedding they could find. Although there was water laid on, some of the mothers made no effort to wash themselves or the children or provide for them in any way. Some of the evacuees wandered off to make their own way home. Altogether it was a terrible experience for anyone trying to help. One young lad was discovered with a stick in his hand, beating ducks around a house in a yard at his billet … Children in many cases couldn't get used to the food provided. You would find food stashed away in a bedroom or maybe in flowerpots – anything to avoid admitting they didn't like it.

Evacuees found the intense darkness of a country night alarming; but for country people the blackout brought little change. It may have encouraged them to stay indoors at home after nightfall, but it also stirred deep feelings, evocatively described by the poet and novelist Vita Sackville-West, who lived in Kent:

The moon has gone, and nothing but stars and three planets remain within our autumn sky. Every evening I go my rounds like some night-watchman to see that the black-out is complete. It is. Not a chink reveals the life going on beneath those roofs, behind those blinded windows; love, lust, death, birth, anxiety, even gaiety. All is dark; concealed. Alone I wander, no one knowing that I prowl. It makes me feel like an animal, nocturnal, stealthy. I might be a badger or a fox …

I think of all the farms and cottages spread over England, sharing this curious protective secrecy, where not even a night light may show from the room of a dying man or a woman in labour … I wander round, and towards midnight discover that the only black-out I notice is the black-out of my soul. So deep a grief and sorrow that they are not expressible in words.

One magazine commentator inadvertently made himself ridiculous to later generations by remarking that 'the countryman is accustomed to going about in the dark, and, alternatively, to staying in at nightfall', then adding:

Townsmen at present may still be, on the whole, a race of gropers after nightfall; but they are undaunted gropers, and will develop the sense which enables them to find their way in the dark.

Even undaunted gropers found nocturnal sounds disturbing. The mellow hoots of a tawny owl were enough to scare East Enders witless, and, as winter came on, the dry triple bark of a dog fox on his nuptial round, or the scream of a vixen mating, might terrify anyone who did not know what creature was creating the disturbance. The boy from Surrey who found delight in the wilds of the Yorkshire moors remarked on 'the weird, cackling laugh' of grouse: 'Had I been a stranger walking on the moor at night, I might have thought it was some evil spirit leering from the darkness.' There was an awful lot to learn. One boy who had never been in a car before was driven up to his foster-home by the vicar, and noticed a strange diagram on the knob of the gear lever. When he reached the house, he reported that the driver had a swastika in his car – with the result that the local bobby was alerted, and went round to interrogate the priest.

Hardly any cottages or farms had telephones, and soon communication became even more difficult, for, under the guise of maintenance, General Post Office engineers began cutting subscribers off so that most of the system, such as it was, could be reserved for essential purposes of defence. Householders who lost their line were compensated, but had no right of appeal. Telegrams were much used, and boys could earn useful pocket money by conveying them to their destinations – 7d for a bicycle trip out to a distant farm, 2d for a shorter ride. If a message contained bad news, the postmaster (who, of course, had read it) would tell the boy not to wait for an answer. Besides the difficulties of communication, another annoyance was the suspension of weather forecasts, which were suppressed indefinitely for fear that they might somehow help the enemy.

Many boys turned out to be natural country lads. One, from Finsbury Park, in north London, and from what he described as 'the sort of street people lived in when they couldn't afford a slum', was translated to the head gardener's house on an estate in Essex, where he and two friends quickly attached themselves to the gamekeeper 'like leeches'.

Rough shooting in the mornings, rabbiting in the afternoon, we learned more about the countryside in six months than we ever learned before or since. Can you imagine an eleven-year-old kid from a London slum recognising the flight of a snipe, feeding pheasants and partridges on their nests, handling a .410 shotgun, gutting and skinning rabbits, moles or anything else that came within range?

Few wartime children can have been luckier than the boys of Dulwich College Preparatory School, in south London, which was closely allied to the college of the same name; for their headmaster (and sole proprietor of the school) John Leakey was a man of exceptional resource and determination. In 1938, expecting London to be heavily bombed the moment war broke out, he decided to construct an evacuation camp of his own in the grounds of a manor house owned by his father-in-law at Coursehorn, near Cranbrook in Kent. There he built six big wooden huts and put up bell tents.

The boys, aged from eight to fourteen, loved being in the country. They helped farmers, rode around the lanes on bicycles and learned to read Ordnance Survey maps. Soon they became extremely fit, and Leakey 'felt a great surge of life and activity pulsing through the camp'. In spite of flu and German measles, they survived one of the coldest winters in living memory, and then revelled in the lovely summer weather of 1940 – until the fall of France suddenly rendered Kent unsafe.

In an urgent search for another site, Leakey's wife Muff explored possible houses in the West Country, but all were too expensive or had already been requisitioned by the Government. Hearing of a hotel in the far north-west of Wales, at Betws-y-Coed, among the mountains of Snowdonia, she sped thither, only to find that it too had been requisitioned. Then her luck changed, and she hit on the Royal Oak Hotel, in the same village, which she managed to rent for £1000 a year, the landlord to retain the bar.

On a baking hot day a special train brought the whole school from Kent to Betws, only to find the hotel still partially occupied – but as soon as each room became vacant, the boys stripped it to make space for their own furniture. When a new scare flared up – that the Germans would seize Ireland and invade England from the west, through the Welsh passes – bloodhounds were trained for tracking parachutists or other infiltrators. Joining the defence initiative, the Leakeys worked with the Home Guard to hide caches of emergency rations in remote caves, and the boys were briefed to make for prearranged rendezvous in the mountains.

Between lessons, they lived a wonderfully free outdoor life, walking, cycling, fishing, going for picnics and rock-climbing on Tryfan (one of Snowdon's neighbouring 3000-foot peaks). Parties went out into nearby Forestry Commission plantations to brash the lower branches of young conifers; they also dammed a stream to make a pond for fire-fighting, and themselves put out two forest fires. So useful was their work that at the end of the war the Commission named a new plantation after the school.

They helped the war effort even more directly by collecting sphagnum moss (which is four times as absorbent as cotton wool and contains iodine, making it ideal for use at forward dressing stations, as it can be applied to wounds without being sterilized). One of the boys reported, 'We are collecting stagnant moss for use in the hospitals'. Their foraging also brought in male fern, foxgloves and nettles (useful for medicaments and dye), and rose hips for the production of syrup rich in vitamin C. One evening Leakey took some of the boys into the graveyard of St Mary's Church and, as they sat among the ancient tombstones, continued his reading of Gray's *Elegy Written in a Country Churchyard*: an experience they never forgot. Many of the poet's rolling cadences – 'Each in his narrow cell for ever laid,/The rude forefathers of the hamlet sleep' – stayed with them all their lives.

As in Kent, the boys became self-reliant and tremendously fit (even though contaminated now and then by new evacuees from Liverpool), and Leakey derived enormous satisfaction from comparing the 'splendid specimens' which he had at Betws with the white-faced children with dark lines under their eyes who had remained in London. Later in the war, when the threat of invasion had evaporated and the Blitz on London had died down, the Betws boys went south on overcrowded trains for their holidays, but always rejoiced when they returned to the mountains.

The Government had realized that, in the event of war, it would not be possible to evacuate all schoolchildren to private homes, and the Camps Act of April 1939 prompted the creation of the National Camps Corporation. The aim was to build fifty camps in attractive, wooded country, but in the event only thirty-six were completed, thirty-one of them in England and Wales, five in Scotland. Designed by the distinguished Scottish architect T. S. Tait, each could accommodate 350 children in huts made of Canadian red cedar.

One of the first was at Colomendy, near Mold in North Wales, where construction began on two sites, upper and lower, in April 1939, on the side of a lovely valley. Known to its inmates as 'Collo', the camp was created as a safe refuge for 170 boys and 125 girls from schools in Liverpool, some twenty miles to the north. Many of the inmates were scared by tales of Peg-Leg, the resident lame ghost said to haunt a particular bed in one of the huts; but agreeable recreations included exploration of the local caves and ascents of Moel Famau, the highest hill in the area, whose bare slopes were alleged to be alive with snakes, and from whose summit the fires raging in Liverpool after big air raids were clearly visible, lighting up clouds all over the sky. One girl remembered the peace and quiet of Colomendy as 'absolute bliss', but she was terrified for her family who had remained in the city, and she kept writing letters home without knowing if the house was still standing.

Another successful camp, in a less dramatic setting, was Kennylands, near Reading in Berkshire, which took in the 300 boys of Beal Grammar School from Ilford. The camp's setting, in twenty acres of land, gave scope for gardening, pig-rearing, potato-picking and bee-keeping, as well as for adventures in the surrounding woods, which the boys loved. At school many of them were inspired by the teaching of William Finch, a talented artist and writer who came from Lowestoft and created a unique pictorial record of the east coast fishing industry. On 30 September 1940 good reports of Kennylands attracted a visit from King George and Queen Elizabeth, during which the King startled his retinue by scratching a pig's back.

Many schools moved out en bloc, among them the girls of the Royal School in Bath, who were welcomed to the grandeur of Longleat by the owner, Lord Bath, and given the run of the Elizabethan house, including the library, with its priceless collection of books and manuscripts. The boys and staff of Malvern College, whose buildings were requisitioned in September 1940, also landed on their feet, for the Duke of Marlborough offered them the use of his vast home, Blenheim Palace, on the edge of Woodstock, in Oxfordshire. Indoors, screens were built round the walls to protect precious tapestries, and the state rooms, together with the 180-foot-long library, became dormitories. In a splendidly sustained burst of energy, the masters dug a half-mile trench to accommodate a new gas main from Oxford.

Did any prep school have worse luck than St Peter's at Broadstairs? When Kent became too dangerous, the boys were evacuated to the relative safety of Shobrooke House, near Crediton in Devon; but during the night of 23 January 1945 the building caught fire, and pupils and staff alike, trapped on balconies, were forced to abseil down makeshift ropes made from torn-up sheets and blankets into six inches of snow. One of the boys, Peter de la Billière, then eight, never forgot that nightmare:

> The sheets were so old that the strips kept tearing through. As every third or fourth boy went over the edge, there would come a yell, followed by a dull thud – and another rope was needed … As we waited on the balcony, the sound of the blaze rose from a muted crackling to a roar, and suddenly the whole

[central] dome, with its little bell cupola above it, collapsed downwards into the well of the stairs, sending a fantastic eruption of sparks into the sky.

One matron and three boys were killed, and another, who lived, fell onto an iron spike which speared his throat. Peter survived physically unscathed, but was left with a horror of fires, and for the rest of his life has made it his first priority, on arriving at a hotel, to check the escape facilities.

Altogether the evacuation from cities and towns displaced nearly four million people. In the first three days of the official exodus one and a half million left London – 827,000 schoolchildren, 524,000 mothers and children under five, 103,000 teachers and other helpers, 13,000 pregnant women and 7000 disabled persons. It is thought that another two million people made their own arrangements: some settled with relatives or in safely situated hotels, and thousands emigrated (or at least sent their children) to the United States, Canada, South Africa or Australia. Under 'Plan Yellow' more than 20,000 civil servants were moved to hotels in seaside resorts and spa towns.

When the expected massed air attacks failed to materialize, foster-families complained vociferously that they were giving sanctuary to people whose houses or flats were standing intact and empty. Thousands of city-dwellers returned to their homes – and none were keener to go back than the mothers who had accompanied their children into the sticks but had been disgusted by the lack of facilities (mainly shops and picture houses) that the countryside offered. During the relatively calm period that became known as the Phoney War, which lasted into the spring of 1940, it seemed that the whole upheaval had been unnecessary – a huge waste of time and effort, and the cause of untold anxiety. Yet many evacuees took root where they had landed, and grew up to be country people. Martin Wainwright, later Northern Editor of the

Guardian, reckoned that 'for all the initial scares about vermin, disease and incomprehensible Cockney or Geordie, the close-knit world of Britain's villages benefited from this fresh blood'. Others agreed that the great migration brought positive social benefits. A leader in *Country Life* entitled 'Converting the Townsman' declared:

> The old drift to the cities has not only been stemmed but
> reversed … It is a vital matter that we should make it
> impossible, when the immediate crisis of the war is past, either
> to relapse again into indifference or to resume the old antipathy
> between town and country.

The least fortunate victims of the mass evacuation were domestic pets. Alarm about the possibility of immediate air attack gripped people so fiercely that during the four days after 3 September 1939 a colossal number of pets were put down. Some were killed by their owners, who brought them to the Royal Society for the Prevention of Cruelty to Animals for burial; others were destroyed by vets or welfare organizations such as the Canine Defence League and the PDSA, the People's Dispensary for Sick Animals. The slaughter – by captive bolt, gas, electricity or lethal injection – was appallingly rapid; corpses of dogs and cats were soon piled high in and around the killing premises. Thousands of carcasses were incinerated, others dumped and buried on wasteland. The RSPCA gave the total as 200,000, but one later estimate was 750,000, and another 2.5 million – a vastly greater number than that of British civilians (60,000) killed in the whole of the war.

The panic seems to have had multiple causes. A rumour had gone round that it was compulsory to get rid of all domestic animals; but this was officially denied – and the idea was refuted by many newspapers, including *The Times*. Another rumour suggested that Hitler would try to introduce rabies into England, in the hope that the disease would spread from domestic animals to farm stock – but even at the time this must have seemed far-fetched. The immediate trigger was a notice, *Advice to Animal Owners*, given out by the National Air Raid Precautions Animals Committee (a unit of the Home Office), which recommended that, 'if at all possible', animals should be taken out into the country 'in advance of an emergency', but if they could not be placed in the care of neighbours, 'it really is kindest to have them destroyed'. Memorial notices, feline and canine, began to appear in newspapers. Bereaved cat-lovers immediately predicted a disastrous increase in the rat and mouse population.

Determined efforts were made to save as many pets as possible – and pre-eminent among the rescuers was Nina, wife of the 13th Duke of Hamilton, who led a crusade to provide animals with alternative accommodation. First she opened her house north of Regent's Park as a clearing station; then she created a sanctuary at her country home, Ferne House in Wiltshire, where 200 dogs settled in the coach house, and 200 cats pitched up in the hangar on the private aerodrome. Such was her energy and compassion that she became known as 'that lady of the dogs'.

Four

Braced for Invasion

This fortress built by Nature for herself,
Against infection and the hand of war.
Shakespeare, *Richard II*

Big, black capitals stand out starkly from the Ministry of Information's poster: 'If the INVADER Comes'. When the Phoney War ended, with the evacuation of the British Army from Dunkirk at the end of May 1940 and the capitulation of France in June, fear of a German invasion increased sharply. Within days of the fall of Paris on 14 June Hitler's armies were on the Channel coast and starting to mass for Operation *Seelöwe* (Sealion), the assault on Britain. In his Directive No. 16, issued on 16 July, the Führer stated his intentions with characteristic subtlety:

As England, in spite of her hopeless military situation, still shows no willingness to come to terms, I have decided to prepare, and if necessary to carry out, a landing operation against her. The aim of this operation is to eliminate the English mother country as a base from which the war against Germany can be continued, and, if it should be necessary, to occupy it completely.

His Army Commander, Field Marshal Walther von Brauchitsch, who was to take charge of Britain if the invasion succeeded, had clear ideas about his treatment of the conquered people. In his Directive No. 5 he proclaimed: 'The able-bodied male population between the ages of seventeen and forty-five will ... be interned and dispatched to the Continent with a minimum of delay.' There were also rumours that all young British men were to be sterilized. In his *Proclamation to the People of England* von Brauchitsch stated: 'I warn all civilians that if they undertake active operations against the German forces, they will be condemned to death inexorably.'

After the first evacuation of the cities in September 1939, many people had trickled back to their homes; but as Hitler's forces massed across the Channel, fear reasserted itself and another emigration took place. Driving about the south coast, the American reporter Vincent Sheean got the impression that it was the better off who went first, boarding up their houses and moving further inland. In St Margaret's, near Dover, a woman whom he had known before the war stood in the door of her cottage and told him 'how it was':

> 'The gentry's all gone away,' she said, her eyes twinkling with some enjoyable malice. 'It was the same in the last war. I never did 'old with going away the minute there's a bit of trouble.'

'For the second time the war is coming nearer, looming up large and threatening,' wrote the author Frances Partridge (a pacifist and conscientious objector) in her diary on 3 April.

> Air raids, invasion, refugees. One's whole body reacts with a taut restlessness, as though one had a lump of lead for stomach and sensitive wires from it reaching to toes and fingers.

As a second exodus from cities took place, villages were flooded once more. Between 13 and 18 June about 100,000 children were evacuated from London and 'invasion corner' – the towns on the south coast. Some 17,000 went to the West Country and South Wales, in blazingly hot weather, and by the time one trainload reached Plymouth the young passengers were gasping for water. When drinks were administered by sailors waiting on the platform, some quick-witted young fellow called out, 'Blimey, we must be near the sea!'

Frances Partridge was one of a reception committee in Hampshire, standing by in a village:

> The bus came lumbering in ... As soon as they got out, it was clear they were neither children nor docksiders, but respectable-looking middle-aged women and a few children, who stood like sheep beside the bus looking infinitely pathetic. 'Who'll take these?' 'How many are you?' 'Oh well, I can have these two but no more,' and the piteous cry, 'But we're *together*.' It was terrible. I felt we were like sharp-nosed housewives haggling over fillets of fish. In the end we swept off two women of about my age and a girl of ten ... Their faces began to relax. Far from being terrified Londoners, they had been evacuated against their will from Bexhill, for fear of invasion, leaving snug little houses and 'hubbies'.

By the end of June another 100,000 people had left the South East, and the population of some towns in Kent and East Anglia had shrunk by 40 per cent. The north country author and broadcaster J. B. Priestley recalled a visit to the ghost town of Margate:

> In search of a drink and a sandwich, we wandered round, and sometimes through, large empty hotels. The few signs of life only made the whole place seem more unreal and spectral.

Once an ancient taxi came gliding along the promenade, and we agreed that if we hailed it, making a shout in that silence, it would have dissolved at once into thin air.

With this second influx, the rural population again rose sharply. The village school at Thurgarton, in Nottinghamshire, which had taken in twenty-two children from Sheffield the previous autumn, now received another eighteen from Southend. The school became so crowded that some lessons took place in a barn next to the pub, the Coach and Horses. Among the evacuees was Gladys Totman, then seven, who remembered her foster-home, Hill Farm, as 'sheer paradise'.

There was always something going on – new calves and lambs, pink silky piglets in an old galvanised bath in front of the kitchen range, hunting free-range eggs and picking plate-sized field mushrooms or blue buttons on late autumn mornings. We were all included in the farm activities such as hay-making, harvest, potato-picking, gathering blackberries, sloes and hazelnuts. At harvest time there was a school holiday, and we all joined in; we rode on the huge carts ... we carried big baskets of bread, cheese, apples and cold tea in quart beer bottles up to the men who worked in the fields well into the dusk. Acorns were collected by the sackful to supplement the pigs' diet, and rose hips to make syrup for vitamin C.

This time hundreds of people brought their domestic animals with them, so that the countryside was freshly inundated with cats and dogs which had survived the initial massacre; many dogs were destabilized by the sudden change of habitat, or by loud noises, and bolted when let out. Their arrival exacerbated the problems of farmers, who accused them of worrying sheep or killing chickens. Some were recovered after frantic hunts by their owners; others disappeared for good, and a few demonstrated uncanny powers of direction-finding, making their own way home over long distances. Later, there were reports of dogs sensing the distant approach of enemy aircraft and beginning to whine or bark long before humans picked up any audible warning of an air raid.

Spy fever became ubiquitous. It was assumed that if enemy agents were dropped by parachute, they would surely aim for the countryside, where they might come to earth unseen, rather than urban areas, where they would be spotted and apprehended. For this reason the land became rife with suspicion. Official orders issued to country people, should a parachutist be discovered, included the instruction: 'DO NOT GIVE ANY GERMAN ANYTHING. DO NOT TELL HIM ANYTHING. HIDE YOUR FOOD AND YOUR BICYCLES. HIDE YOUR MAPS.'

Challenges at road blocks caused travellers untold irritation, for nobody could move across country at night without being stopped and questioned; rumours spread like fire, and there were countless false alarms – none more ridiculous than one which started when a young man with a furtive manner and a strange accent was discovered wandering about in Oxfordshire. Because the Canadian soldiers who found him could not understand what he was saying, they arrested him. When questioned, he gave an address that quickly proved false; and when taxed with being a German agent who had descended by parachute, he said he was exactly that. Moreover, he gave the name of a well-known local farmer, claiming that this man was the chief German agent in the area, to whom he had been ordered to report. To the chagrin of the farmer, and the disappointment of the authorities, the entire story proved a fabrication: the stranger was Welsh, a parson's son who had once worked for the farmer, but now had deserted from his anti-aircraft unit – a crime for which he was sentenced to two years in gaol. It was purely his accent that had foxed the Canadians.

In that febrile atmosphere spy mania flourished. All strangers were suspect. A man walking along a lane with a pack on his back was obviously a spy – until he turned out to be a farm worker on his way to a distant field. Scratches which appeared on telegraph poles were waymarks incised by agents to guide the German infantry when they invaded. Arrow-shaped flower beds in cemeteries had been deliberately planted with white flowers so that they pointed towards ammunition dumps. A farmer who covered a field with heaps of white lime was suspected of deploying them in a pattern that would indicate the direction of a railway junction to a pilot overhead.

The population was warned against impostors. 'Most of you know your policemen and your ARP wardens by sight,' ran an official pamphlet. 'If you keep your heads, you can also tell whether a military officer is really British or is only pretending to be so.'

Particular suspicion attached to nuns – or to people dressed like them – who were almost certainly enemy spies in disguise, with weapons hidden under their habits. Amateur sleuths followed black-clad figures eagerly, only to be disappointed when the fugitives turned round and revealed themselves as elderly women. One day on a train the writer Virginia Woolf insisted to her husband Leonard in a stage whisper that a woman who had got into their carriage was a German spy. In fact she was an embarrassed and innocent nun.

In fact a few spies *were* arriving, some by parachute, some by ship or submarine. In the autumn of 1940 twenty-odd German agents came to Britain, but all were so incompetent or amateurish that they were quickly rounded up, mainly because the cryptanalysts at Bletchley Park had cracked the wireless code used by the Abwehr (the German military intelligence service) and were reading messages between Berlin and its outstations. Forewarned and forearmed, the British arrested the new arrivals one after another – all except one man who escaped and shot himself. After interrogation, five of the prisoners were executed, fifteen were gaoled and four were taken on to become double agents.

A leaflet issued by the Ministry of Information gave civilians detailed instructions on how to behave if the Germans arrived. Just as in 1803, when fear of invasion by Napoleon's armies was widespread, the inhabitants of Hastings had been advised to stay at home 'for the preservation of their lives and property which would be much endangered by any attempt to remove from the Town', so now people were told: 'You must remain where you are. The order is to "stay put" to avoid clogging up the roads and being exposed to aerial attack ... Think always of your country before you think of yourself.'

Individual motorists were ordered to immobilize their cars by taking the rotor arm out of the distributor whenever they left them; the police were empowered to remove some essential part of the mechanism from any vehicle they found inadequately crippled, and to leave a label on the car saying that the part could be recovered from a police station. Another Government order prohibited the use of 'wireless receiving apparatus' in all road vehicles.

A leaflet reminded farmers that their first duty was to 'go on producing all the food possible ... Unless military action makes it impossible, go on ploughing, cultivating, sowing, hoeing and harvesting as though no invasion were occurring.' 'Plough now! By day and night' exhorted one of the Ministry's posters. Farmers also received instructions for putting their tractors out of action if there was a danger that the enemy might capture them.

Parish Invasion Committees were formed 'to draw up precise inventories of things available likely to be of use – horses, carts, trailers, wheelbarrows ... crowbars, spades, shovels ... paraffin lamps etc'. The Ministry of Information issued a short film, *Britain on Guard*, only eight minutes long, with script and narration by J. B. Priestley, which included an excerpt from Churchill's 'we shall fight on the beaches' speech, and the stirring declaration that Britain was responsible 'for the future of the civilised world'. Along the south coast farmers made plans to move their cattle and sheep inland, their overriding aim being to ensure that neighbours did not manage to annex any of their animals during a sudden, unseasonable transhumance.

With nerves on edge, people began to agitate for permission to take up arms to defend themselves. From their redoubts in the Home Counties superannuated colonels dropped hints in letters to the press: 'Retired men over the age limit are of course a confounded nuisance in wartime, but' … 'Parachutists? The great army of retired-and-unwanted at present … can all use the scatter-gun on moving objects with some skill.' The newspaper tycoon Lord Kemsley suggested to the War Office that rifle clubs should be formed as the basis of a home defence force, and the *Sunday Pictorial* asked if the Government had considered training golfers in rifle shooting, to pick off German parachutists as they descended. The Home Office, worried that private defence forces might start to operate outside military control, issued a press release laying down that it was the army's task to engage enemy parachutists: civilians were not to fire at them. In the House of Commons an MP asked the Secretary of State for War, Anthony Eden, whether, 'in order to meet the imminent danger of enemy parachute landings', he would sanction the immediate formation of a corps of older, armed men 'trained for instant action in their own localities'.

Together with senior military officers, the Government had been putting together a plan, and on the evening of 14 May, after the nine o'clock news, Eden came on the radio with a stirring announcement:

> We want large numbers of such men in Great Britain as are
> British subjects, between the ages of seventeen and sixty-five to
> come forward now and offer their services in order to make
> assurance doubly sure. The name of the new force which is now
> to be raised will be the Local Defence Volunteers. The name
> describes its duties in three words. You will not be paid, but
> you will receive uniforms and will be armed.

Anyone might join, said Eden, simply by handing in his name at the local police station. The result was phenomenal. Men were heading for their nearest station before he had finished speaking, and within seven days 250,000 too old or too decrepit to fight in the armed services, or already in reserved occupations, signed up for the LDV. On the day after Eden's broadcast the War Office announced that volunteers would be issued with denim uniforms and field service caps – and these had to suffice until serge khaki battledress and armbands became available.

Such was the enthusiasm that in July the number of volunteers rose to 1.5 million, but at first the organization of the new force was chaotic, as different factions had different ideas about its role. Almost at once it became known by its alleged motto: Lie Down and Vanish. Was its purpose merely to act as an armed constabulary, observing the movements of any German troops who landed, or was it to be more aggressive, and attack invaders whenever possible?

Within days the embryonic organization had a new title. Churchill, disliking 'Local Defence Volunteers', which he found uninspiring, changed its name to the Home Guard. Enthusiasm was particularly strong on the south coast, where any invasion force was most likely to land. When a company was formed in Worthing, with platoons in the town and outlying villages, two local benefactors each offered £1000 for the purchase of arms and equipment, and a theatre was taken over as a headquarters.

One of its first units was established at Storrington, a village north of Worthing, where recruits set up their headquarters in an evacuated monastery and began to patrol the South Downs on the lookout for paratroopers, besides guarding a railway tunnel against sabotage. Little did they know how quickly they might have become engaged with German forces – for in the final version of Hitler's invasion plan, after a landing between Brighton and Eastbourne some units would have swung westwards along the line of the Downs, and Storrington would have lain directly in their path.

If anyone sought to ridicule the new organization, there were plenty of spokesmen to defend it. 'It is no mere outlet of patriotic emotion that we are endeavouring to recruit,' said Lord Croft, the Joint Parliamentary Under-Secretary of State for War, in the House of Lords, 'but a fighting force which may be at death grips with the enemy next week, or even tomorrow.'

Another leading advocate of the need for a people's army trained in guerrilla warfare was Tom Wintringham, the Communist writer and editor who had visited Moscow in the 1920s and commanded the British Battalion of the International Brigades in the Spanish Civil War, during which he was twice wounded. In the summer of 1940 he set up a private training school in Osterley Park, Lord Jersey's stately home in Isleworth, teaching street fighting and the use of explosives; but because of his Communist background, the War Office did not trust him. Having first tried to close the school, they took it over in September 1940, setting up training establishments of their own. Wintringham himself was never allowed to join the Home Guard, since membership was banned to Communists and Fascists.

Twenty-eight years later the Home Guard would be immortalized (and ridiculed) by the BBC television series *Dad's Army*, which became one of the nation's favourite programmes. At the outset in 1940 much about the organization *was* ridiculous, not least its weapons, which included wooden rifles, pitchforks, pick-handles, ancient revolvers, swords, daggers, stilettos, clasp knives and coshes made from garden hosepipe filled with lead. The force's initial low rating derived partly from a remark by Churchill, who told the War Office that 'every man must have a weapon of some kind, be it only a mace or a pike'. Taking him at his word, the War Office ordered 250,000 metal poles with surplus rifle bayonets welded to the ends – a move much resented by the volunteers, as it made them sound idiotic, and no more use than bystanders in the production of a Shakespeare comedy.

Other objects of mockery were their ill-fitting denim overalls, which had a revolting smell when new. When squads started marching about on their evening parades, little boys would run after them, derisively calling out the sizes from the tickets on their backs and trousers, and comparing them unfavourably with the physique of the wearers.

A good deal about the nature of the organization is revealed in *The British Home Guard Pocket-Book*, a small volume which first appeared in October 1940. Its author, Brigadier General Arthur Frank Umfreville Green, had fought in the Boer War and First World War. In 1940 he was sixty-one, and his rank and seniority made him an obvious choice for the commander of some Home Guard unit; but he preferred to let junior officers exercise control, while he went round teaching his own special subject, musketry. He was also something of a writer, with two published novels to his credit, and clearly had a robust sense of humour. His pocket-book, though primarily an instruction manual, was so engaging that it sold 22,000 copies in its first year and was reprinted five times before going into a second edition in 1942.

The text – 150 pages of detailed advice on leadership, training, weapons, battle drill, reconnaissance, patrolling, digging trenches, creating obstacles, handling explosives and many other topics – was both outspoken and intensely practical, and his first chapter set the tone:

> As I see it, our only excuse for existence is to look out for
> Germans and to help the military to kill them, or – better still –
> kill themselves.
>
> *Discipline* does not consist merely in smartness on parade –
> it consists in all working as a team and obeying a permanent or
> temporary *Leader* promptly, vigorously and intelligently ...
>
> *Duds, Dead-Weight and Passengers* – are they of any use to
> H.G.? What are we to do with malcontents and subversive

individuals and inefficient men? The answer is easy. As Mr Middleton [the radio gardener] teaches us to prune roses, so can we prune our duds. 'Ruthlessly' is the operative word. We are at war, and there is no time to spare. If you see dead wood or anything unhealthy – cut it out.

Rank. Are we to salute or not? Whom shall we salute? If, for example, a tradesman with no military prestige … has in his unit an Admiral and a couple of Generals, the question they ask is 'Who salutes whom?' My answer is clear. If I am a Volunteer in a section or a patrol commanded by a General or a Blacksmith or my own Gardener, I do what he orders to the best of my ability. And on parade I salute him.

Stirred up by General Green and others, many countrymen handed in their shotguns for use by the Home Guard, and these were tested by experts for their ability to fire single-ball ammunition. Later the volunteers were properly armed with British .303 rifles and American P17 .300 Springfields, and they quickly became less of a joke then than now. Captain Mainwaring and his ramshackle crew provoked great hilarity in the television audiences of another generation, but it is easy to forget that 1600 members of the Home Guard were killed on duty during the war.

Many absurd incidents did take place. One moonlit night there was a call-out in Shropshire, when somebody claimed to have seen a parachute descending. Norman Sharpe, gamekeeper on the Apley Hall estate, remembered how he and his fellow volunteers rapidly took up prearranged positions:

The night wore slowly on, with everyone becoming increasingly bored and tired. Suddenly a shot rang out! Action at last! Everyone was electrified. Complete with escort, the Company Commander strode away in the direction of the shot.

A sentry had been posted along a narrow lane, and he was asked, 'Did you fire that shot?'

'Yes Sir.'

'What at?'

'A rabbit, Sir.'

'You absolute so-and-so.'

'Yes Sir. But I did as you instructed. I said halt but he came on. I said halt again and he took a few more hops forward. I challenged a third time and still he came on, so I shot him.'

Much of the recruits' time was spent training. Nineteen-year-old Charles Bond, at forestry school in the Forest of Dean, beyond the Severn in Gloucestershire, was actively involved, and many an entry in his diary recorded Home Guard activities: 'HG exercise in morning … HG parade … rifle range drill, distance judging … HG lecture on Sten gun, practice at moving in extended order through woods … Posting night sentries.' But a questionnaire issued by headquarters in Inverness to all Zone Commanders, Group Commanders and Battalion Commanders, and kept under lock and key, suggests that in March 1941 instruction was still at an early stage: 'How do you distinguish between enemy and friendly (a) parachutists (b) troop carriers? … Do you and your men understand map references? Have you a map? … Have you fired your rifle? If so, what result?'

The amateur soldiers studied maps, gave orders to the platoon in drill halls and went on exercises at weekends, often in pairs, guarding railway lines and bridges, and defending beaches against practice attacks by units of the regular army. Indoors, they stripped their rifles with the lights on and reassembled them in the dark. For live firing on the ranges, they were supervised by regular soldiers. At first ammunition was so scarce that men were allowed to fire only five rounds a day. All the same, target practice took place not just on designated ranges but also in old quarries and chalkpits, where any vertical wall or cliff-face served as a stop-butt and minimized the chance of casualties among the local population.

For country boys on the loose, such places were a delight, for they yielded treasures such as empty cartridge cases, fragments of grenades and even the occasional live round. Spent .22 bullets were highly prized, even if crumpled up by impact on metal or stone, for they could be melted down, fashioned into arrow-heads and fitted to home-made shafts of hazel or willow. Better trophies still were intact heavy-calibre machine-gun bullets found dumped, presumably because they had failed to fire; and thunderflashes, which simulated grenade explosions. Sometimes these big, thick fireworks were accidentally dropped during night exercises and could be found lying about in the morning – but they needed careful handling, for a premature detonation could easily blow off fingers. Even bits of bomb casing were much valued.

Ian Hacon and Peter Lucas, two boys who lived near Ipswich, were much given to riding around the countryside on their bikes. When they discovered an ammunition dump which was guarded during the day but not at night, they several times climbed over the barbed wire and helped themselves to cartridges, which they sold to school friends for 2d each. Schools, of course, made it illegal to collect such desirable souvenirs, and boys found secreting them were punished, usually with the cane; nevertheless, collectors keenly swapped and traded items, not least the silver paper dropped by enemy aircraft to confuse radar.

In the words of the historian Geoffrey Cousins, 'Although defence was the stated object of the exercise, every man who answered the appeal [to join the Home Guard] was captivated by the idea of being on the offensive.' That opinion was seconded by Captain Clifford Shore, an expert on guerrilla warfare and sniping, who reckoned that the creation of the force had a marked effect on morale: quite apart from its practical use, it gave men a positive way of serving their country. To him it was 'a marvellous organisation', and did a tremendous amount of good. 'I am sure it prolonged the life of many men, taking them away from a life of total sedentary [sic] and lack of healthy interest. Thousands of men discovered the delights of shooting for the first time.'

Among the part-time soldiers was Eric Blair, better known as George Orwell, author of *Animal Farm* and *1984*. Having failed an army medical, he joined the Home Guard and became a sergeant in the St John's Wood platoon – only to be incensed by closer acquaintance with the army, and in particular by the futility of a lecture from some general:

> These wretched old blimps, so obviously silly and senile, and so obviously degenerate in everything except physical courage, are merely pathetic in themselves, and one would feel rather sorry for them if they were not hanging round our necks like millstones … The time has almost arrived when one will only have to jump up on the platform and tell them [the rank and file] how they are being wasted and how the war is being lost, and by whom, for them to rise up and shovel the blimps into the dustbin.

Soon after the creation of the Home Guard – and as a protest against the exclusion of women – the Amazon Defence Corps was set up by ladies with hunting, shooting and deer-stalking experience. In Herefordshire the redoubtable Lady Helena Gleichen took the lead. British, but the daughter of Prince Viktor of Hohenlohe-Langeburg (and so a grand-niece of Queen Victoria), she had abandoned her German titles during the First World War and worked with distinction for the British Red Cross in Italy. Later she became a well-known painter, particularly good at depicting horses. Then in 1940, aged sixty-seven, she formed her estate workers and tenants into an unofficial observation corps, the Much Marcle Watchers, eighty-strong and armed with their own weapons. But when she applied to the Shropshire Light Infantry for rifles, 'plus a couple of machine guns, if you have any', she received a dusty answer.

Her initiative reflected the tension gripping England by the middle of May 1940: it seemed possible that the invasion might start at any moment. Hitler's forces had stormed through France to the coast only twenty miles from Dover at such a speed that it was easy to imagine their momentum propelling them on across the Channel. Particularly in the country, where paratroops were most likely to land, everyone was on edge. Margery Allingham described how many people in her village were overcome not by any particular grief, but by cumulative emotional strain.

Government posters were plastered up everywhere: 'Dig for Victory', 'Lend a hand on the land', 'Keep calm and carry on.' 'BEWARE' shouted one of the 'Careless Talk Costs Lives' series, with a crude caricature of half Hitler's face in the top corner:

> Whether alone or in a crowd
> Never write or say aloud,
> What you're loading, whence you hail,
> Where you're bound for when you sail.
> ABOVE ALL NEVER GIVE AWAY
> THE MOVEMENTS OF H.M. SHIPS

Although most members of the Home Guard lived in towns, their real role was on the land, where they felt they were defending their own territory. As J. B. Priestley put it in one of his immensely popular Sunday evening *Postscript* broadcasts in June 1940, describing a night vigil:

> Ours is a small and scattered village, but we'd had a fine response to the call for volunteers … I think the countryman knows, without being told, that we hold our lives here, as we hold our farms, upon certain terms. One of these terms is that while wars still continue, while one nation is ready to hurl its

armed men at another, you must if necessary stand up and fight for your own … As we talked on our post on the hill-top, we watched the dusk deepen in the valleys below, where our women-folk listened to the news as they knitted by the hearth … I felt too up there a powerful and rewarding sense of community, and with it too a feeling of deep continuity. There we were, ploughman and parson, shepherd and clerk, turning out at night, as our fathers had often done before us, to keep watch and ward over the sleeping English hills and fields and homesteads.

Of course, rivalry sprang up between neighbouring units, each hell bent on defending its own patch, and reluctant to help anyone else. In Devon a man whom the poet Cecil Day-Lewis tried to recruit came back with the retort: 'We don't want to fight for they buggers at Axmouth, do us?'

Small detachments were posted to man lookouts, some of them on the tops of church towers; they struck aggressive poses when photo-graphed, but, in spite of the all-round enthusiasm, recruits were often scared of their own weapons, and numerous accidental discharges took place. One man put an M 17 round through the flat roof of a golf club-house which had been identified as an ideal Home Guard observation point. The bullet tore a large exit hole in the roof, missing the watch-man above by inches. Another stray round went through the driver's door of an Austin Seven, deflated the cushions in both front seats and passed out through the passenger door, leaving a neat hole.

People supposed that if German parachutists landed they would try to hide in woods, where, at close range, a shotgun would be a handier weapon than a rifle. Unofficial experiments were therefore conducted to make shotguns more lethal – for instance, by opening up cartridges and pouring molten wax into the pellets to form a heavier and more solid single missile, with greater killing power. There was a risk that the procedure would bulge or even split the barrel of the gun; but its efficacy was proved when someone fired a doctored 12-bore cartridge at an old barn, and the whole door collapsed in a cloud of dust and splinters.

In their attempts to grow more corn, farmers were seriously impeded by military plans for protecting the countryside against the possibility of enemy airborne landings. All over the South East fields were disfigured by new defences. Anti-tank lines of reinforced concrete cubes, each weighing a ton or more and cast *in situ*, were strung out across fields, often two or three rows deep. Where firing lines were cleared through woodland, the trees were felled across each other and the stumps were left high.

In June the Ministry of Agriculture encouraged farmers to build their hayricks in the middle of fields – especially flat fields suitable for glider landings. All open spaces should be obstructed (the directive said), and some fields should be trenched diagonally. In Wiltshire and Gloucestershire broken telegraph poles were dug into the ground upright and festooned with networks of wires. In other fields trees were felled and laid across a glider's most likely line of approach. To protect standing corn from incendiaries, farmers were advised to cut ten-yard-wide strips across any large field, aligning the firebreaks with the prevailing wind, while the crop was still green. The immature cut corn could be used as fodder or made into silage, and when harvest approached and the remaining crop was dry the danger of a major blaze would be reduced.

Along the coast entanglements of barbed wire, with one coil laid on top of two others, blocked the beaches, which were also protected by minefields and miles of anti-tank scaffolding. Some possible landing places were stocked with barrels of pitch, which could be set on fire to incinerate troops trying to come ashore, and in other bays oil was pumped out underwater so that it could be released to form pools on the surface, which could be ignited. Concrete pillboxes sprouted on the cliffs and vantage points, some sunk into the ground, some showing above it. Areas of Romney Marsh were flooded, in the expectation that they might be used for a landing, and thousands of sheep were driven inland to deny the enemy any chance of seizing them. Swarms of barrage balloons swung in the sky, not only above and on the outskirts of conurbations, but round individual factories.

In the rush to collect scrap metal for munitions, iron railings round parks disappeared. Churchyard gates and railings – many of them beautifully designed – went the same way. Metal objects – even hair-pins and combs – vanished from the shops. To confuse enemy trying to travel by road, signposts were removed from junctions, railway crossings and stations. Old milestones with names carved on them were dug up and taken into safe keeping. If the names of towns and villages appeared on shop fronts, they were painted over. All this was irksome for country people and anyone trying to move around on legitimate business: if a motorist pulled up at a crossroads to ask for directions, locals were forbidden to answer his questions. As the American Vincent Sheean remarked, 'The barricading of roads was going on all through the country, and you did not have to travel far down any one of them to see the sudden feverish construction of tank traps and airplane obstacles … The threat of invasion had suddenly risen like a dark cloud over the whole island.'

The aim was not so much to stop an enemy advance as to delay it until strong British forces could muster further inland, and ships of the Royal Navy could steam down from Scapa Flow, where they had been sheltering, to knock out the German fleet in the Channel and cut off the invaders' supplies of fuel, ammunition and food.

On shore, the general plan was to move vital assets away to the west, as far as possible from likely landing points and lines of advance. The King and Queen – the jewels in the crown – were furnished with a personal bodyguard consisting of one company of the Coldstream Guards, known, after its commander, Lieutenant Colonel J. S. Coats, as the Coats Mission. With their four armoured cars and some civilian buses, the little force stood by to whisk the royal family out of danger, particularly in the event of an airborne landing by enemy forces.

Their initial rendezvous would have been Madresfield Court, a huge, redbrick house, part-Jacobean, part-Victorian Gothic, with more than 130 rooms, standing out in the plain at the foot of the Malvern Hills in Worcestershire. The home of the Lygon family for eight centuries, the house is now inextricably associated with Evelyn Waugh's novel *Brideshead Revisited*, which was inspired by his fascination with the Lygon girls, Lettice, Maimie, Coote and Sibell, with their brother Hugh, whom he knew at Oxford, and their notorious father, the homosexual Lord Beauchamp, whose excesses eventually forced him to live abroad (his brother-in law, the Duke of Westminster, who loathed him, referred to him as 'my bugger-in-law').

Brideshead and its landscape, as Waugh described them in 1945 – the house set in a valley above a lake, among rolling hills – bore no physical resemblance to 'Mad' and its pancake surroundings; but the author had been entranced by another immense house, Castle Howard, near York, and made that his model for the home of the Flyte family. On that and his love of the Lygons he built a dream world, and there is no doubt about the twin sources of his inspiration: Brideshead is a version of Castle Howard, but Sebastian Flyte, the central figure in the novel, is Hugh Lygon in all but name.

In 1940 Madresfield, with its sixty acres of gardens, its carp-haunted moat and four glorious avenues, would never have been remotely defensible, furnished though it was with a token guard force. Nevertheless, large quantities of non-perishable food were imported and stored in the basement, and much of Worcestershire was fortified as a kind of redoubt. The Severn, Avon and Teme rivers were designated 'stop lines', with crossing points defended by camouflaged gun emplacements, tanks parked in copses, pillboxes, road blocks and lines of trenches. Worcester itself, Kidderminster and Redditch were marked out as anti-tank islands, to act as centres of resistance, and the aim was to retard any German advance until regular home forces could regroup.

On the eastern side of Worcester another great house – Spetchley Park – was earmarked as a refuge for Churchill and his Cabinet if the invasion took place or London became too dangerous. The grand Palladian building belonged (and still belongs) to the Berkeley family, and before the war was a haunt of the composer Edward Elgar, who often stayed in the Garden Cottage and told his hosts that parts of *The Dream of Gerontius* were inspired by pine trees in the park.

If the Germans had landed, the transfer to the west would have taken place in two phases: in Yellow Move, non-essential staff from Whitehall would have led the way, followed, in Black Move, by the Prime Minister, the Cabinet and the royal household. The city of Worcester would have been invaded by armies of civil servants, and the Royal Shakespeare Theatre at Stratford-upon-Avon would have housed Parliament. Luckily for the owners, in the event neither Madresfield nor Spetchley was needed for senior evacuees from London; but later in the war the US Eighth Air Force took Spetchley over as a recuperation centre for pilots, and added to its amenities by building a squash court.

Two other grand houses, further north, were also considered as possible royal retreats. One was Pitchford Hall in the wilds of Shropshire, a wonderfully romantic, black and white Tudor mansion in which the King and Queen had stayed (while Duke and Duchess of York) in 1935. The other was Newby Hall, home of the Compton family, an eighteenth-century redbrick house set in splendid gardens at Skelton-on-Ure in North Yorkshire.

While the King and his Government stood fast, Nazi propaganda took to the air by way of the New British Broadcasting Station, which sent out messages intended to intimidate the population of the United Kingdom. The broadcasts, purporting to emanate from dissident elements within the country, sought to portray a nation in disarray and ripe for takeover. 'Disunity, demoralisation, hatred of its leaders and a passionate yearning for peace were the distinguishing characteristics of this cloud-cuckoo land,' wrote one historian.

> Everybody knew that not only Churchill and his friends but even Socialist Cabinet Ministers were being bribed by Jews to continue the war. Sabotage was rife, and so were foot-and-mouth disease, faked Treasury notes and tins of meat poisoned by German agents in the Argentine.

More concrete attempts were made to unnerve the population. On the night of 13/14 August 1940, German aircraft staged an *Abwurfaktion* (throwing-down or dropping action), in which 'pack assemblies' were released by parachute over various parts of the Midlands and lowland Scotland. The packs contained maps, wireless transmitters, explosives, addresses of prominent people and instructions to imaginary agents about their roles in the imminent invasion. The aim was to suggest that the attack would come from the east coast, and that a Fifth Column of Fascists and Nazi sympathizers eager to undermine the regime was established all over the country, ready to receive the invaders. Farmers, in particular, were sceptical: they pointed out that documents purporting to be those of parachutists who had landed in standing corn, but had left no trails when they moved out of the field, must have been carried by men with exceptional powers of levitation.

There was much talk of Fifth Columnists, but most people thought that, if any existed, they were harmless. On the contrary: in the words of the historian Ben Macintyre, 'There was an active and dangerous Fifth Column working from within to hasten a Nazi victory … motivated in large part by a ferocious hatred of Jews.' Not for seventy years did the release of secret files reveal that during the war a large network of crypto-Fascist spies in Britain had been run – and neutralized – by one extraordinarily skilful and courageous agent working for MI5, who posed as a member of the Gestapo. He was known as Jack King, until, in 2014, his real name was revealed as John Bingham. His contacts thought he was working for the Nazis, and happily revealed their treachery to him, but none of them was ever prosecuted, partly because they were doing no real harm, and partly because any action taken against them might have broken Jack King's cover.

On 13 June 1940 the Government imposed a ban on the ringing of church bells, except to warn of imminent air raids or invasion – in which case they would play the role of the beacon fires which signalled the approach of the Spanish Armada in 1588. Even in an emergency they might be rung only by the military or the police. Senior clerics protested, and the restriction caused displeasure among many villagers, who felt that an important part of their lives had been suppressed, and that, in the event of an attack, the invaders might single out churches for retribution, on the grounds that they were part of the defenders' warning system. Prophesying doom, *The Ringing World* denounced the ban as 'a stunning blow to ringing, from which, even when the war is over, it will take a long time to recover'. On the other hand, some people who lived near churches were delighted, and hailed the silence on Sunday mornings as one of the few blessings brought by the war. As the threat of invasion waned, the restrictions were gradually lifted, but not until VE Day in May 1945 were full peals allowed again.

Country priests and members of congregations did what they could to protect their churches from bomb damage. At Fairford, in Gloucestershire, the vicar, the Revd Francis Gibbs, supervised the removal of the outstanding medieval stained glass from the windows of St Mary's Church and had thousands of pieces buried in a vault beneath a large memorial cross in the grounds of Fairford Park, outside the village. In a similar but even bigger undertaking, the twelfth-century stained glass was removed from the great window in the south-west transept of Salisbury Cathedral. Three effigies from the Cathedral were wrapped up and taken to East Quantockshead in Somerset, where they were hidden in the cellar of St Audrey's School; the transfer was supposed to be deadly secret, but pupils in the school saw the bundles arriving, thought they were bodies, and alarmed their parents with lurid stories about casualties or plague victims.

As the bells fell silent, new airfields were being laid out all over the country, especially in East Anglia, some with grass strips good enough for fighters and light bombers, others with asphalt or concrete runways for heavier aircraft. Hangars and Nissen huts made from curved sheets of corrugated iron (for accommodation and storage) sprouted at their edges. To the irritation of people living close by, footpaths across these new bases and other military areas were closed for the duration.

Besides the genuine airfields, numerous decoys were created in the hope of luring Luftwaffe pilots away from vulnerable targets. Daylight airfields, known as K sites, were furnished with inflatable or wooden aircraft, usually with wings but only a skeleton fuselage. To add verisimilitude, redundant training aircraft, old bomb tractors and other service vehicles were parked in the open and moved around to new positions during the night. On dummy night airfields, known as Q sites, there was often a runway flare path made from small burning lamps, and lights that went on and off at various points to give the impression of vehicles moving. Experiments were made with various kinds of fires, including drums of burning creosote, designed to simulate activity in railway yards or factories.

The decoy fields began to attract attention immediately after the withdrawal from Dunkirk. One successful K site was at East Kirkby in Lincolnshire, where wooden Whitley bombers were trundled around from day to day by the local RAF contingent: their efforts evidently paid off, for German planes bombed the airfield several times. The Q sites in East Anglia and Lincolnshire were the most frequently targeted, and during June thirty-six Q raids were recorded in England as a whole.

All farming became more difficult and dangerous, especially in the south and east of the country as, out of sheer spite, stray German aircraft began to attack obviously civilian targets before they headed for home. One Luftwaffe pilot provoked a volley of sarcastic comments on the ground in Kent when he bombed a hayrick and then came in on another low pass, riddling the stack with his machine guns. As the farm workers had already taken shelter, the only casualties were a few sheep.

Some countrymen went to extraordinary lengths to safeguard their property. Colonel Charles Owen, who had been involved with the development of camouflage during the First World War, lived in a house called Tre Evan on a hill outside the Herefordshire village of Llangarron, near Ross-on-Wye. There he went up and down a ladder to paint the building's white, stuccoed front with splodges of green and brown, both to make it a less conspicuous target, and to disguise a landmark that might be useful to the enemy pilots on their way to or from Coventry or Cardiff. Neighbours – mostly First World War veterans – considered the exercise mildly eccentric, and the Colonel's family found it rather embarrassing; but he – head of the local ARP squad – was serious about it, and organized regular fire drills, during which his grandchildren stood to with stirrup pumps and pails of water.

Five

Going to Ground

The rabbit-hole went straight on like a tunnel for some way,
then dipped suddenly down, so suddenly that Alice had not a
moment to think about stopping herself before she found
herself falling down what seemed to be a very deep well ...
First she tried to look down and make out what she was
coming to, but it was too dark to see anything: then she
looked at the sides of the well and noticed that they were
filled with cupboards and bookshelves: here and there
she saw maps and pictures hung upon pegs.

Lewis Carroll, *Alice's Adventures in Wonderland*

Captain Peter Fleming was an unconventional figure, to say the least. An Old Etonian aged thirty-two at the start of the war, he was well known to the public as the author of two runaway bestsellers published in the 1930s, twenty years before his younger brother Ian thought up James Bond. *Brazilian Adventure* – funniest of travel books – sent up a quest for the explorer Percy Fawcett lost in the Mato Grosso, and *News from Tartary* described how the author had walked 3500 miles from Peking to Kashmir in the company of Ella Maillart, lesbian captain of the Swiss women's hockey team, without telling his fiancée, the actress Celia Johnson, that he was accompanied by a woman. Yet, in spite of his renown, Fleming was essentially a private person, and one main qualification for an unusual wartime commission was his first-hand knowledge of the English countryside.

At home in the woods and fields of his 2000-acre estate in Oxfordshire, he could distinguish the sett of a badger from the earth of a fox; he could read the tracks left by animals and interpret the calls made by birds and animals both in daylight and in the dark. As a means of confusing the enemy, he would sometimes advocate the Victorian poacher's trick of walking backwards through mud or snow, to make it look as if the passer-by had been moving in the opposite direction.

As the threat of invasion intensified, General Andrew Thorne, Commander of XII Corps, was given the task of defending south-east England along a front that stretched from Greenwich, on the Thames, round the coast of Kent and Sussex to Hayling Island, in Hampshire. Remembering how, six years earlier, he had seen peasants in East Prussia digging last-ditch defence positions in the hills and stocking them with food, weapons and ammunition, in the hope that they would be able to disrupt the supply lines of an invading army, Thorne appointed Fleming to do much the same in England: to raise and train a body of men whose role would be to go to ground behind any German advance and harass the invaders from the rear, while the main line of defence was organized nearer London.

Armed with a letter of authority, and operating in the strictest secrecy, Fleming set up his headquarters in a brick and timber farmhouse called The Garth on a hill at Bilting, between Ashford and Faversham. The true identity of his organization was buried under the meaningless title 'The XII Corps Observation Unit', and individual patrols were assigned an equally uninformative name, the 'Auxiliary Units'.

Together with Captain Mike Calvert, a Royal Engineer, Fleming first went about his area setting up booby traps by stuffing ammonal explosive into the churns in which dairy farmers set out their milk for collection – but even though these home-made bombs were never fitted with detonators, they made people nervous and were soon removed. He and Calvert also mined a whole belt of bridges, in the hope of slowing any German advance, and booby-trapped country houses which the enemy might use as headquarters by cramming the cellars full of explosives. As Calvert put it, their task was 'to make Kent and Sussex as unsafe and unpleasant as possible for the Germans if ever they got that far'. They also blew out the centre sections of the piers at Brighton, Worthing and Eastbourne. Then, in absolute secrecy, they began recruiting gamekeepers, poachers, foresters, gardeners and farmers – men with intimate knowledge of the area in which they lived. All were hand-picked, after apparently casual approaches, and all were vetted for security by their local police – even though the police did not know what role the candidates were going to undertake.

Meanwhile, Colonel Colin Gubbins (a specialist in guerrilla warfare, and later head of Special Operations Executive) established a training base in Berkshire at Coleshill House, a relatively small but elegant seventeenth-century mansion bristling with tall chimneys, home of the Pleydell-Bouverie family, well isolated by its own park, shrubberies, fields and woods. Recruits were told to report to Highworth village post office, where the elderly postmistress, Mabel Stranks, would check their identity papers, disappear for a few minutes, then return and say 'Someone's coming to fetch you'. A vehicle would appear to ferry the newcomer to the house. Training weekends took place in the house and grounds, and three manuals were produced, each succeeding the earlier one as guerrilla activity became more refined. Some predictions were blissfully optimistic: 'In districts where the war is intense and enemy troops thick on the ground, it will not be necessary to go far to find a target.'

Men chosen to be auxiliaries were set to work building subterranean lairs which they stocked with ammunition, explosives, sabotage equipment, rations and cooking stoves. One of these dens in Kent was in the cellars of a ruined house that had been destroyed by fire years earlier, but most of them lay in dense woods, and at least one was excavated from on old badger sett in a derelict chalkpit: the long, winding tunnels – a foot or so in diameter – were enlarged into a reasonably comfortable hideout, which Fleming himself later described:

> They [the men] took a pride in their place. They schemed endlessly and worked hard to improve it. Ventilation shafts, alarm signals, dustbins, lights, clothes pegs, bookshelves hollowed out of the chalk, washing up arrangements – all these tactical problems they tackled with enthusiasm.

In his book *A Very Quiet War* Ralph Arnold, ADC to General Thorne, gave an idea of how cleverly the den was concealed. In the middle of a thick belt of woodland on the hillside above Charing, the General was led into a clearing and challenged to find the entrance to the local unit's hideaway:

> We poked about unsuccessfully for a few minutes, and then our guide casually kicked a tree stump. It fell back on a hinge to reveal a hole with a rope ladder dangling into a cavern that had been enlarged from a badger's sett. In this cave, sitting on kegs of explosive, and surrounded by weapons, booby-traps, a wireless set and tins of emergency rations, were some Lovat Scouts and half-a-dozen hand-picked Home Guards ... It was pure *Boys' Own Paper* stuff, and the Corps Commander, whose brainchild the Auxiliary Units had been, simply loved it.

Another distinguished visitor was General Bernard Montgomery, who took over from Thorne as Commander of XII Corps, and early in 1941 was escorted out onto a Kent hillside by Captain Norman Field, Fleming's successor as the Auxiliary Units' Intelligence Officer. When the walkers reached a battered old wooden trough, Field suggested they should sit on it to enjoy the view. They did just that, but a few moments later Montgomery was startled to find that, without a sound or any apparent movement, his companion had vanished. Only when he saw Field's head appear beside him, sticking up through a rectangular opening in the bottom of the trough, did he realize that he had been perching on top of a perfectly concealed hideout. When the young officer told him that this was one of XII Corps' two-man observation posts, he was furious, because no one had let him know that such lookouts existed; but when he wormed his way down into a small chamber hacked out of the earth, he could not help admiring the way in which two authentic looking rabbit holes leading out through the steep bank beneath the trough had been adapted to give a view of the A20.

In the construction of such dens, the disposal of excavated soil was a problem, not least because it usually had to be done in the dark. The diggers would carry away earth and rocks in buckets, and either dump them elsewhere in the wood (having first scraped back the leaves and earth on the forest floor), or tip them into streams strong enough to wash new deposits away. If the site was on sandy ground, the spoil could be loaded into hessian bags, thousands of which were being piled up all over the country to protect buildings or gun sites from blast.

Many of the larger bases were built by the Royal Engineers or by civilian contractors, who told inquisitive locals that the holes being dug in the woods were to house emergency food stores. These professionally made dens were lined with sheets of corrugated iron, and had access and escape tunnels made of wide-diameter concrete pipes. Later in the war one, near the Northumberland village of Longhorsley, caused huge excitement among a gang of boys, vividly remembered by Bill Ricalton:

We climbed up the wooded hill from the burn side for perhaps fifty or sixty yards. Beside the base of a large tree our leader stopped and cleaned away decayed grass and leaves with his hands, which exposed a wooden door with a handle on it. When the door was opened it revealed a concrete shaft, about two to three feet square. A metal rung ladder was attached to the side, and disappeared into the darkness below ...

We all descended the steps and into the tunnel below. The bottom of the iron ladder must have been eight feet or more below the trap door. Leading from the bottom was a concrete tunnel, large enough for a grown man to stand up. We were to visit this place many times over the next few years, sometimes just to sit and talk and wonder why it was there and what it was for.

Years later shivers went down his spine when he discovered that it had been one of the Auxiliary Units' lairs, and that the locked rooms (which he and his friends never penetrated) had been stocked with food, water, the new plastic explosive (known as 'PE') and weapons, among them Piat anti-tank grenade launchers and the first Thompson sub-machine guns imported from the United States.

During the war Boy Scouts were taught to carry verbal messages from one place to another, using roundabout routes to dodge other Scouts sent to intercept them: back gardens, passageways, ditches, orchards, fields – all became familiar undercover approaches. Few, if any, of the boys realized that what seemed an amusing game might, in the event of invasion, suddenly become an important messenger service.

Because the role of the Auxiliary Units would be mainly nocturnal, most of their training was done at night, or wearing dark goggles during the day. 'Make a patrol march past and listen for avoidable creaks,' Fleming noted in his diary. 'Even at his stealthiest the British soldier emits a sound as of discreet munching.' In his own headquarters officers sat on packing cases of explosives and ate off a table formed from boxes of gelignite; but because of his social standing, the diners might sometimes include a brace of generals or even a Cabinet Minister.

Fleming himself was almost comically cack-handed, but he took delight in devising esoteric methods of attacking the enemy, such as training his men to shoot with bows and arrows. Archery, he thought, might come in useful, either for silently picking off individual German sentries, or for causing confusion in their camps if arrows carrying small incendiary devices could be shot over perimeter defences, to cause inexplicable fires or explosions within. Posterity credited him with the ability to bring down a running deer at 100 yards, but in reality he could not be sure of hitting a barn door at twenty-five paces.

If the invasion had taken place, the auxiliaries would have immediately left their homes and gone to ground, emerging at night. No one will ever know how much the troglodytes could have achieved if the Germans had come. Fleming himself doubted if his force could have been 'more than a minor and probably short-lived nuisance to the invaders': he feared that his men would have been hunted down as soon as autumn stripped leaves from trees and hedges, and that reprisals against the civilian population would soon have put the teams out of business. Besides, he noticed that among his own recruits 'it was not long … before claustrophobia and a general malaise set in, because they were civilised men who had suddenly executed a double somersault back into a cave existence'. His colleague Mike Calvert was more optimistic:

> If it had been called to action, the Resistance Army of Kent and Sussex would have had at its core some of the toughest and most determined men I have ever met. Their farms and their shops and their homes would have been highly dangerous places for any enemy soldier to enter.

No doubt the defenders would have killed quite a few Germans, had the invasion taken place; but, judging by the brutality shown by the Nazis to French resistance fighters, of the two estimates Fleming's seems the more likely. (As an illustration of this, in July 1944 the Germans massacred hundreds of Maquis in an all-out attack on their stronghold in the Vercors massif, in the south-east of France.)

Fleming's counterpart in Essex, Captain Andrew Croft, a former head boy of Stowe, felt the same as Calvert, and believed that his units could have held out indefinitely by stealing food, weapons and ammunition from the invading forces. In any case, under Colonel Gubbins's direction resistance cells came into being all over the country, not only in Kent, but in the South West, in East Anglia and up the coasts of Yorkshire, Northumberland and Scotland, as far as Cape Wrath in the far North West. Scotland certainly needed them, for regular troops were thin on the ground, and there was always a chance that the Germans might invade up there.

The man chosen to create Auxiliary Units north of the border was Captain Eustace Maxwell, nephew of the Duke of Northumberland and brother of the writer Gavin. His aristocratic connections made it easy for him to recruit, as did the fact that he was an Argyll and Sutherland Highlander; and the terrain in which he went to work – miles upon miles of scarcely populated moors, mountains and coastline – was ideal for guerrilla warfare. So were the inhabitants: farmers, foresters, deer-stalkers, ghillies – all used to living and working in the open air.

Melville House, a huge, square, four-storey building, the Palladian home of the Leslie-Melville family at Monimail in East Fife, became the Coleshill of the north – a training centre, surrounded by woods and farmland, approached by a beech avenue and equipped with all the facilities needed for firing weapons, setting demolition charges and learning hand-to-hand combat. Behind the house a gentle slope made an ideal background for a small-arms range, and rail tracks were laid in the woods so that budding demolition experts could practise blowing them up. When a German prisoner-of-war camp was established at Annsmuir, near the railway station at Ladybank, Wehrmacht uniforms found their way into Melville House to add verisimilitude to the training.

As recruits went through the mill there, hideouts were being dug or built all over Scotland. Ruined castles made ideal sites: caverns were dug out beneath heaps of stone at the foot of collapsed walls, with access via a single, spring-loaded slab. Once a few rainstorms had swept over the rubble, there was no sign that anyone had been there for centuries. Other dens were made beneath houses in villages and entered through cellars – but always with an escape tunnel leading to a disguised exit some distance away. By the end of 1940 about a hundred units were fully established, and Maxwell himself had driven 70,000 miles overseeing their creation. In Britain as a whole some 3000 men were trained to go to ground, and they were issued with liberal amounts of ammunition and explosives. They remained ready for action throughout the war; but so deeply secret was the organization that its existence was not officially admitted until the middle of the 1950s.

Later in the war a parallel clandestine organization was formed, under the cover name of the Special Duties Section of the Auxiliary Units. This was a secret radio network staffed mainly by women, who went to ground with transmitters in hideouts of their own, charged with the task of keeping communications open in the event of an invasion. Like the operational bunkers, every den was elaborately concealed: if there was no building at hand tall enough to carry a forty-foot aerial, men from the Royal Corps of Signals would climb a tree, cutting grooves in the trunk, laying the wire in them and filling them with plaster of Paris painted to resemble the bark.

During the Phoney War Fleming at times thought uneasily of *Rogue Male*, a thriller by Geoffrey Household set in the 1930s. In the novel an anonymous British sportsman, 'who couldn't resist the temptation to stalk the impossible', is at large in central Europe, bent on personally assassinating a loathsome dictator. The target's name is never mentioned, but clearly it is Hitler whom the rifleman has in his sights.

Before he can fire a shot, he is seized by security men and beaten up, but escapes and flees back to England. Even there, however, he is not safe. Enemy agents pursue him so tenaciously that he is forced to go to ground in an old badger sett, with the entrance tunnel disguised as an 'apparent rabbit hole' in the side of a sunken lane. His only ally is a feral cat which he calls Asmodeus – the legendary king of the demons – and in the end it is this animal, or, rather, its skin, that saves him. The chase is immensely exciting, and the claustrophobic atmosphere of the dank hideaway is powerfully evoked. The timing of the novel's publication, in 1939, was extraordinarily apt, and the book foreshadowed many of the elements – the claustrophobic subterranean redoubts, the nocturnal forays – with which the Auxiliary Units became familiar.

Above ground there was at first no place for female talent in the Home Guard; but in 1942 the Women's Home Guard Auxiliaries were formed, and girls were allowed to join the men, both in the office and in the field. At St Ives in Huntingdonshire a small team dealt with telephone and radio equipment in the local headquarters, and also took part in night exercises. One of them remembered how disconcerting it was to find 'well-respected businessmen from the town crawling along ditches in camouflage, with blackened faces', and another gave herself a nasty fright when she blundered on all fours into a big, solid, warm lump, which turned out to be a recumbent cow. In the office they whiled away spare time by sending each other frivolous radio messages – until some of them were intercepted by staff at Wyton Airfield, three miles away, who thought the traffic was coded signals transmitted by enemy agents, and the girls were severely reprimanded.

Yet another agency at work in town and country was the Royal Observer Corps, whose members spotted, identified and tracked any aircraft that appeared in the sky and reported its details to group head-quarters, whence the message was swiftly passed to the RAF. The organization's motto was 'Forewarned, Forearmed' – and success depended on continuous vigilance backed by speedy reaction. During the Battle of Britain the volunteer observers, stationed in posts about ten miles apart, furnished the only means of tracking enemy aircraft once they had crossed the coast; and so valuable was their work that in April 1941 the King awarded the Corps the prefix 'Royal'.

The two-man crews devised any number of comfortable lairs from which to keep watch: wooden huts, little brick buildings, concrete boxes on prominent mounds, penthouses on the roofs of factories. One outpost was beautifully captured by the war artist Eric Ravilious, whose delicate watercolour portrayed two watchers standing in a kind of grouse butt, protected by sandbags and a canvas screen, with a single telephone wire disappearing through the air above a wintry landscape. Still more elaborate was a contraption in Ayrshire which consisted of a heavy metal post sunk into the ground, topped by a revolving cross-piece, on either end of which was a padded seat made from a car's steering wheel. Each seat revolved individually, and one of the team was always aloft, binoculars at the ready.

Although able to operate only in daylight, and often blinded by fog, the Observer Corps provided a vital service throughout the war. But in the autumn of 1940 the enormous, all-round effort of the Auxiliary Units in going to ground proved unnecessary – for the time being, at any rate. It has never become clear why, on 17 September 1940, Hitler ordered the postponement of Operation Sealion until the spring, or why in the end he abandoned his invasion plan altogether. Instead, he unleashed the full fury of the Luftwaffe in the Blitz on London.

Six

Adapting to War

Necessity is the mother of invention

Traditional proverb

When petrol rationing came into force on 19 September 1939, only 10 per cent of the population had cars; and now each owner was limited to seven gallons – or about 200 miles – a month. The result was that many people put their vehicles into storage, mounting them on blocks in shed or garage to take the weight off the tyres. After November 1940 no new cars were built for civilian use, and those that were available (about 400 in the whole country) were allocated for use by doctors, police and so on. Buses ceased to run, leaving many country people marooned, and most rural roads were almost free of traffic.

Restrictions brought out a rash of new bicyclists, who often discovered that travel on velocipedes is hard going: as someone pointed out, 'A bicycle finds out the uphill gradients in a remarkable manner.' Because they lacked both practice and confidence, and rode machines bedevilled by lack of maintenance, these novices were a menace to other road-users; but boys soon mastered the trick of catching hold of the back of a slow-moving lorry and getting a tow uphill. Children lucky enough to own bicycles rode to and from school as a matter of course.

Old pony traps and governess carts were dragged out of sheds in surprising numbers: dusted down and polished up, they commanded two or three times the price that any owner would have dared ask before the war: £30 or £40 instead of £10 or £12. The writer Penelope Chetwode (wife of the poet John Betjeman) described how she taught Mrs John Piper, wife of the artist, to ride. Myfanwy had never been near a horse before, but now she sold her car, bought a 14.1 hands black gelding, and after minimal instruction was riding twenty or thirty miles a day around her home near Henley-on-Thames.

Farmers were allowed an extra ration of fuel. Even so, lack of petrol often meant that they had to move their sheep and cattle to market on foot, sometimes walking ten or twenty miles a day. Because the police began to stop private cars and ask drivers to justify their journey, many farmers took to carrying a decoy sack of wheat, or the punctured front tyre of a tractor, which remained on board indefinitely as a decoy to allay suspicion.

Fuel shortages put new life into another transport medium: the canals. The Grand Union Canal from London to Birmingham was a key route for shifting heavy loads: boats carried fifty tons of steel, aluminium and cement northwards to the industrial Midlands and brought back coal. When some of the barges were laid up for lack of crew, a scheme was launched to recruit women, and more than sixty took up the offer. One, Emma Smith, found that the experience changed her life. Having grown up in a privileged background, the daughter of a banker, she felt that in joining the dockers, the boatmen and the regular boaters who travelled with their families, she had 'crossed over a boundary line, and never went back. I became a working-class girl.'

On the land, every effort was being made to increase food production. In a message to *The Farmers' Weekly* the Minister of Agriculture, Sir Reginald Dornan-Smith – a popular figure, who had served with a Sikh regiment in India, and was a former President of the National Farmers' Union – offered the magazine's readers some stirring thoughts:

The fresh-turned furrows are our trenches: the added blades of grass are our bullets, and every extra sheaf of corn is a shell in this war of resources ... The war is here in earnest, and two opposing ideas, freedom versus a ruthless tyranny, are locked in a grip in which one or other must die ... The farmer is a key man in the events which now shake Western civilisation.

In response to the Government's urgent appeal, agricultural machinery began pouring into the country: from America, under the Lend-Lease agreements made in the spring of 1941, came big Allis-Chalmers and Minneapolis-Molines tractors, but also small Ford Fergusons, built in Detroit under a contract signed in 1938 between the Irish engineer-inventor Harry Ferguson and Henry Ford Senior. Ferguson's key innovation was the revolutionary three-point linkage, which attached the tractor to an implement (for instance a plough) with hydraulically operated arms, and in effect made the pair a single unit, instead of one pulling the other. During the war thousands of Ford Fergusons were made in America and shipped to Britain, and the three-point linkage has been taken up all over the world.

Besides tractors, Massey-Harris combine harvesters came in from America, Sunshine combines from Australia, and various types of drill for sowing seed. Crawler tractors went high up hillsides in the north of England and in Wales, ripping out bracken, which had invaded over two million acres and was useless as fodder, being poisonous to ruminants. A study by the Oxford Agricultural Research Institute worked out that ploughing with a horse and a single-furrow plough cost 12s per acre, whereas a two- or three-furrow tractor cost just over 9s per acre – and the tractor could cover at least four times as much ground in a day.

With American imports pouring in, the number of tractors available to farmers increased so fast that in 1941 190 Oxford undergraduates (a third of them girls) were given instruction in the basics of driving and maintenance and sent to a hundred public and secondary schools to pass on their skills to older boys. Each instructor was detailed to take on twenty-four boys of sixteen or over, who would learn to drive 'dead straight', and to back a two-wheel trailer between stakes (no easy task). They were also to learn about servicing, 'the meaning and use of the grease gun and nipples'. The idea of fitting tractors with cabs was still so new that a photograph of a man ploughing steep ground at Almondbank in Perthshire was captioned: 'The cab on this caterpillar tractor makes the driver independent of good weather.'

Some farmers invented methods of their own for speeding production. One was Jack Hatt, who hitched four implements in line behind a powerful tractor and proclaimed the virtues of PPDH – Plough, for turning the furrows over, Press, for levelling, Drill, for sowing the seed, and Harrow, for working it in. By this means he was able to cover enormous acreages, saving time and fuel.

On waterlogged land, especially in the clay of East Anglia, ploughing had to be preceded by the restoration or creation of drains – and here again astonishing results were achieved. By February 1943 the Government had sanctioned 10,380 mole-drainage schemes, 19,725 tile-drainage schemes, 66,011 farm-ditch schemes and 5338 schemes for small areas. The land improved extended to more than four and a half million acres. One outstanding success was the reclamation of 400 acres on Ferrymoor Common in Yorkshire, which until then had been used as a camping ground by gypsies, but after treatment yielded huge crops of potatoes, wheat, oats, rye, clover and turnips.

The frenzy of ploughing led to some unforeseen results. One was that on upland farms the pastures on which dairy cattle had been grazing disappeared under corn, and the cows had to move to higher ground. Up there, however, there was often no water, so that the Government had to offer farmers 50 per cent grants to install piped systems.

So urgent was the need to increase food production that the Government declared war on all species which it reckoned were inhibiting farmers' efforts. The first and foremost enemies were rabbits; thousands of acres round the edges of fields close to woods and spinneys were being eaten to the ground, yielding only a quarter of their potential output. Norman Sharpe, gamekeeper on the Apley Hall estate in Shropshire, attributed their proliferation to the fact that control measures had been abandoned during the Great War, and remembered how some of the fields bordering the Spring Copse at Apley Hall 'simply appeared to be moving of an evening'.

On a farm at Linkenholt in Hampshire four guns killed 940 rabbits in a morning, but that made little difference, and the owner became so desperate that he decided to wire in his whole estate. This drastic solution took fourteen miles of rabbit netting, four feet tall, with a mesh of 1⅝ inches, and with the bottom turned outwards horizontally so that rabbits outside the pale could not burrow underneath. Those that remained inside were exterminated by gun, dog, trap, snare and gas; and although fiendishly expensive, the experiment was reckoned to have paid off in the amount of crops saved.

If live rabbits were a menace, dead ones were very popular. On one farm near Newton-by-the-Sea, on the Northumbrian coast, the assembled villagers killed 250 out of a single field of corn, whereupon the chief vermin-catcher gave one to everybody present and loaded the rest into his Austin Seven. He and the farmer then drove to the Ship Inn to celebrate their record bag, but got so drunk that when they reached home they failed to empty the car – only to find, in the morning, that most of their cargo had disappeared.

As for rats – the annual damage done by them was estimated at £12 million (over £600 million in today's terms), and Mr E. C. Read, later technical adviser to the Ministry, quoted the cost of every rat as 30s a year. The Ministry commissioned a study to determine the cost of rat-proofing corn stacks with circular walls of corrugated-iron sheets, sunk two feet into the ground and protruding four feet above it. Estimating that 411,000 stacks would have been needed to store the 1939 harvest, researchers concluded that the cost of corrugated iron for 1940 would be £2,719,000. Since this was clearly prohibitive, the Ministry urged farmers to use every means to destroy the vermin: 'Spring traps, wire traps, snares, sunk pit traps, barrel traps, break-back traps and varnish traps, known as sticky boards.'

In October 1940 the Minister, invoking the Rats and Mice (Destruction) Act of 1919, announced that the annual Rat Week should be held, 'notwithstanding the war'. Everyone in the country was asked to 'take concerted action against these vermin'. The success or failure of the initiative was not recorded – but the Pied Piper himself could hardly have matched the performance of Louth Rural District Council, in Lincolnshire, which in the previous November had begun paying 2d for each rat's tail handed in. By 31 March 1940 almost 42,500 rats had been destroyed. This astonishing cull must have reduced the local population substantially; but as *Country Life* declared, 'A combined effort is necessary for their extermination. Every method must be brought to bear simultaneously – rat-hunts, gassing, poisoning, trapping, and particularly the surrounding of ricks before thrashing.' The Government was doing its best. 'Kill that rat!' cried one of its posters. 'Rats rob us of food. Rats spread disease. Rats delay our victory.'

The Ministry also turned its fire on the poor house sparrow. A pamphlet emphasized the bird's destructive habits – pecking blossoms of currants and gooseberries, eating whatever seedlings it could reach, and, at harvest time, flocking to the fields to devour huge quantities of corn. A 'wanton pest', the sparrow was said to destroy fledglings of other species. The campaign was welcomed by many War Ags, including that of Lancashire, which encouraged people to destroy nests and eggs; and *Country Life* suggested that the best way to deal with the menace might be to recruit village boys in spring and pay them a small sum for every dozen eggs collected. Vermin bounties paid by the War Ags varied from place to place, but were generally 2d for a rat's tail, 3d for a grey squirrel's tail and a halfpenny for a sparrow's head.

Another detested species was the wood pigeon, described as the 'food growers' enemy No. 1', which was notorious for plundering newly planted crops of peas, beans and corn. One experiment seemed to justify the farmers' hostility. A sweepstake was held on the number of grains of barley a single bird had swallowed: the highest guess was 722, and investigation of its crop showed that the answer was 711. In November, when flocks had begun their seasonal migration from north to south, *Country Life* was again in an aggressive mood: 'It is more than ever necessary this winter that an attack should be made on the flocks of migrant wood pigeons which have already begun to come in.' The best method, the article recommended, was for the National Farmers' Union to organize country-wide shoots in the afternoons, when the birds were flighting into the woods to roost. Even the starling ('a most unpleasant bird') attracted the magazine's wrath: by January 1940 flocks were said to be making an unprecedented assault on holly berries, and were almost as great a threat to agriculture as other 'feathered pests'.

As always, from time to time curious incidents were reported in farming journals. On one grass airfield a swarm of bees settled on a wheel chock underneath a fighter. The mechanics working on the plane panicked and started the engine, trying to scare them off; but when they found that the bees remained unmoved by the noise, they calmed down, switched off and continued their maintenance. In the middle of March a calf was 'born underground' in Cornwall. A terminally pregnant cow had been standing in the farmyard when the ground beneath her gave way, and she fell fifty feet into an old mine working. Next day she was found partially buried, with a newborn calf by her side, and neither of them any the worse.

Life on a wartime farm was brilliantly evoked by Xandra Bingley in her memoir *Bertie, May and Mrs Fish*, a headlong narrative of the author's early days, almost all in the present tense, set in a decrepit smallholding high on the Cotswolds above Cheltenham. Bertie is her father – explosive, loving, mostly away in the army; May is her mother

– wonderfully capable and compassionate, as ready to release gas from a bloated cow by driving a needle into its stomach as she is to shoot pigeons or comfort Xandra when she breaks an arm; Mrs Fish, with her orange ringlets and an ungovernable thirst for gin, is a neighbour who comes in to help. Crisis follows crisis. Horses escape; the farm-hand cuts off two fingers with the circular saw; the police arrive hunting a murderer. One extract must suffice to give an idea of May's character:

She has an accident when her car hits a black bull on a narrow road near Guiting Power … She drives into the bull head-on and breaks his front legs. She gets out of the car and kneels by him, and her hands feel his broken bones as he tries to stand up and falls.

She sits on the tarmac and rests his heavy head in her lap and she strokes and strokes his face and says … I'm sorry … I'm so sorry … In the dark I didn't see you … Why were you in the road? Where were you coming from at nearly midnight? Try to lie still my darling. Before long someone will find us. Sooner or later the pain will go. She sings … There is a green hill far away … without a city wall … Where our dear Lord was crucified … he died to save us all.

Just before sunrise a lorry stops and the driver stands over her and says … Those Yanks do him … all over the shop they are, going like the clappers.

My mother says … No … I did. I saw him too late … Will you go to a telephone box and dial the Hunt Kennels … Andoversford 248 … they'll be up and about … tell them where I am and tell them to send a winch lorry and a kennelman with a gun.

The milkman says … You'll be half dead of cold … and my mother says … He keeps me warm … be as quick as you can.

The kennel lorry arrives and the kennelman in black rubber boots and a brown overall says … You can slip out from under him … then I'll get to work.

My mother says … I'll stay put where I am … he's been through a lot tonight … he's very brave.

The hunt kennelman says … He's carrying a mountain of flesh … and kneels and puts the gun to the bull's black curly-haired forehead.

My mother says … May his spirit for ever rest in peace … for the sake of the Father and the Son and the Holy Ghost.

The gun fires and the kennelman says … I'll lift his head … Out you come … You going far?

She says … Only another seven miles … I thought at first he must be Zeus … He was a god and a black bull.

The kennelman says … Master will be pleased … hounds can live off his flesh for a week.

For May, and for all the other country housewives working day in, day out to sustain their households with primitive equipment, there was little entertainment to be had. But one great morale-booster was the radio. In the mornings and afternoons the half-hour programmes of continuous *Music While You Work* had the same soothing effect on rural housewives as on women toiling in factories, where productivity increased sharply for a while after each broadcast. Another infallible solace was the voice of Vera Lynn, the nation's best-loved singer, who received a thousand letters a week begging her to sing 'We'll Meet Again', 'The White Cliffs of Dover', 'You'll Never Know' and other favourites. (When rationing began to bite, 'We'll Meet Again' was sometimes parodied as 'Whale meat again'.)

Children's Hour, broadcast from 5 to 6 p.m., was also immensely popular. Under the direction of Derek McCullough – 'Uncle Mac' – the programme achieved an audience of four million in 1939, and young listeners eagerly awaited his invariable valediction, 'Goodnight children, everywhere'. In the evenings people out in the sticks crowded round their Bakelite sets to hear BBC news bulletins. The readers always identified themselves, to prove that Lord Haw-Haw or some other obnoxious interloper had not taken over the microphone: 'Here is the news, and this is Bruce Belfrage reading it.'

A farmer's wife living at Thornton-le-Moor in Lincolnshire, eight miles from one town and nine from another, gave a dispassionate account of how she adapted to wartime exigencies and was, as she put it, 'plodding away very happily'. She sent postcards to order her groceries, which were delivered once a fortnight by van, along with her allowance of paraffin. A baker left bread at a neighbour's house. Newspapers arrived by post, at least one day old. Movies were 'out of the question', but she got books from the local library, and belonged to a club with twelve members, each of whom bought one book a year and passed it on after a month, so that at the end of a year all volumes came back to their original owners.

Village halls became hives of activity, used for numerous purposes. At Trumpington, near Cambridge, the hall was let to the local Education Committee as a canteen for school dinners. Evacuee children from St James's School in Muswell Hill, north London, had a classroom there and held a Christmas party in the building. The British Legion and Women's Institute opened a canteen for soldiers from nearby camps. Outside the hall was a National Savings indicator, with a moveable seagull showing how much the village had raised. In 1941 the ARP unit set up a feeding centre in the hall, in case of enemy attack, and the Brigade Headquarters at Anstey Hall, near Trumpington, used the building for dances, causing (as a local report put it) 'inevitable problems'. Dances were held on Saturday nights (tickets 1s), and on 18 November 1944 (the day street lights were turned on again) a reception was held after the wedding of Percy and Mabel Seeby – she having come to the village as an evacuee.

The passion for dancing spread all over the country. Frank Mee, who grew up during the war in Norton-on-Tees in Co. Durham, and 'lived for dancing', was told by his father that, given some music, he'd 'dance on the roof of the pigsty'. He remembered how 'every town and village had a hall where dancing could take place', and reckoned that later generations had 'no idea what part the dance halls played in keeping up morale'. The bigger halls had orchestras, the smaller ones three-piece bands, a gramophone, or sometimes only a piano.

> In the small halls it was plank floors with nails sticking up or concrete with linoleum squares glued down … Any kind of footwear would do, but some people had dancing pumps and others wore what they had, down to hob-nail boots. The lights, the music and the company let you forget the misery, austerity and danger of the war … You could live your dreams for a few sweet hours. Escapism? Yes, but we came out of those places light of heart and uplifted to another planet for a short while. We would come back down with a crash when someone asked whose turn it was to buy the fish and chips.

Music and singing played an important part in village life, as at Spondon, near Derby, where a choral group formed in 1941 grew rapidly until it became a well-balanced choir of eighty. In the words of one member, Gwendolyn Hughes, 'It gave people something different to think and talk about, instead of surmising and worrying about the war.' But the war was constantly on every villager's mind, and event after event – dog show, pony show, garden show, baby show, whist drive, fête – was organized to raise money for some sector of the armed forces. In the summer and autumn of 1941 the village of Foxholes, near Driffield, raised £212 for the Red Cross Agricultural Fund – part of a total of £48,000 collected in Yorkshire.

Seven

Rain of Death

Through many a day of darkness,
Through many a scene of strife,
The faithful few fought bravely
To guard the nation's life.
Hymns Ancient & Modern, No. 256

Forecasts of German airpower made in the early 1930s soon proved to have been wildly inaccurate. The Government had assumed that even if war opened with a blitz on London, the limited range of Luftwaffe aircraft would mean that destruction would be confined to the south and east of the country. The rest of England, north of a notional line from the Wash north of East Anglia to the Solent on the south coast, was reckoned to be relatively safe from bombardment.

Perhaps that was true in 1939; but with the fall of France in the summer of 1940, the picture suddenly changed. Taking off from captured airfields closer to England, German bombers could reach targets much farther inland, and to the north and west. One of the first daytime raids on the United Kingdom was an attack on Wick, at the extremity of Caithness – about as far from the Channel coast as any point in Britain. The object of the attack may have been to disable the RAF fighter squadron based on the airfield just north of the town, which was there to defend ships in the anchorage in Scapa Flow. The

Luftwaffe raiders came in at teatime on 1 July, a fine summer's day, and whether they meant to hit the airfield or the harbour, a stick of bombs fell in the middle of Bank Row, a narrow road alongside the port, killing fifteen people, including eight children (the youngest not quite five) who were playing on the bank. After its first run one aircraft turned and came back, machine-gunning along the river. In all Wick was raided six times, the last on 26 October, when three Heinkels dropped twenty high-explosive bombs on and around the airfield.

All summer the Luftwaffe carried out sporadic raids on convoys in the Channel and on south coast ports, from Dover in the east to Swansea in the west in what Hitler called the *Kanalkampf* – the Battle of the Channel. Key targets were Weymouth (which suffered forty-eight raids in all during the war) and Portland, home of the Whiteways Royal Naval torpedo works. On 9 July twenty-seven people were killed in Norwich. Southampton and Coventry were also heavily bombed.

People soon learned to identify the marauders, especially when they attacked at low level. The Heinkel 111 – a twin-engined medium bomber – was easily recognized by its bulbous cockpit with curved, clear panels through which the crew were visible. Also all too familiar was the Junkers JU 88, a fast and versatile twin-engined fighter-bomber with low-mounted wings, and the JU 87, also called a Stuka, or dive-bomber, distinguished by its upwardly bent wings and fixed undercarriage (with wheels permanently down). The Dornier D-17, known to the Germans as *der fliegende Bleistift* (the Flying Pencil), was recognizable by its slim body and twin tail, especially in its low-level role. Even schoolboys could soon identify fighters like the Messerschmitt Bf 109 and the twin-tailed Bf 110 by the noise of their engines alone.

On 16 July Hitler issued Directive No. 16, which authorized detailed preparations for Operation Sealion, the invasion of England. Three days later he proclaimed his 'Last Appeal to Reason', still pretending that he did not want war with Britain, and demanding that the nation surrender. When this rant failed to produce the required result – even after leaflets of the text had been dropped over England – he changed tactics and in Directive No. 17 ordered the destruction of the entire RAF – aircraft, airfields, supply organizations, factories – a task which the Commander-in-Chief of the Luftwaffe, the sybaritic, elephantine Hermann Goering, assured him could be accomplished in four days.

On 24 August bombs fell on central London for the first time, killing nine people. In fact the docks had been the target, and the German navigators had lost their bearings. But Churchill was so outraged by the strike on the heart of the capital that the War Cabinet countermanded Bomber Command's plan to hit Leipzig in retaliation, and on the night of 25 August a force of seventy aircraft went out to bomb Berlin.

Hitler, infuriated in turn, set in motion *Adlerangriff* (Eagle Attack), his attempt to destroy the RAF and its bases. Preliminary raids were launched on 12 August, and heavier ones on the 13th (*Adlertag* – Eagle Day); but all else paled before the mass assault on 15 August, when 2000 aircraft attacked. Seventy-six of them were shot down, but the raids continued and many key fighter airfields – Biggin Hill, West Malling, Croydon, Kenley – were badly damaged.

As battle raged in the sky, of all the counties Kent was at the greatest risk. Any Luftwaffe raid made life in the countryside hazardous, for the danger area extended far beyond the perimeter of whatever airfield the Germans were attacking, with stray bombs falling, aircraft crashing and shrapnel cascading down. One farm lost forty sheep to bombs and bullets, and its pastures were pitted with ninety-three craters, the biggest forty feet across and more than twenty deep. With such dangers prevailing, it was hardly surprising that many Londoners decided not to take their annual holiday hop-picking. To fill their places 2000 soldiers were drafted in, and local schools waived normal rules so that children could help with the harvest. Elaborate precautions had been made to protect those taking part: shelter trenches had been dug, casualty stations built and camouflaged. One of the most evocative images of the whole war is a photograph of a dozen small children crouching in the bottom of a freshly dug slit trench, gazing upwards at a dogfight in progress high overhead.

Farmers naturally wanted compensation for damage to their crops, and to their land. If the army could provide labour to carry out repairs, there was no problem; but if no military help was available, farmers often called on rural solicitors to make their case to the War Department. A 250kg bomb created a sizeable crater and scattered earth for hundreds of yards, which made filling in the hole a laborious and expensive business. Damaged trees also gave rise to disputes. Branches blown off of an oak (for instance) could be burnt *in situ*, but if bomb splinters were embedded in the trunk, no timber merchant would look at it, for fear of wrecking his saws. Market gardeners – especially those with big greenhouses – were particularly vulnerable, and often had an entire crop destroyed by a single explosion.

Northern farmers were hit as well. 'Eh! Just fancy! Bang in the middle of Ford's clover root,' wrote the Mancunian diarist Arnold Boyd. 'These Jerries will stick at nothing.' Another diarist, identified only by the initials M.A., reported the effect of a bomb which fell in a woodland copse in the winter of 1940:

> The small symmetrical crater was ringed round by the now-familiar mound of earth, and the surrounding bracken and grass was mown close to the soil. About thirty yards away from the crater a large number of beech saplings had had their heads cut cleanly off with a cut that ran parallel to the earth and not, as one would have supposed, at an angle to it. The larger trees that had the misfortune to find themselves in the path of the shell splinters received deep, clean cuts often six inches deep and the width of the bole.

In spite of the obvious danger, country people going about their work soon became phlegmatic, tending to call a siren a 'cyrene', or just to refer to it as 'that thing'. 'There goes that thing again', they would say, before getting on with the job in hand; and distant dogfights were regarded as a form of free entertainment. 'They were just like butterflies flying round each other', said a woman of two tussling aircraft. 'Lovely to watch.' Children felt the same. Twelve-year-old Eileen Ryan, who had been evacuated from London to Weymouth, was walking with friends on the promenade one day and stopped to enjoy the spectacle of Spitfires wheeling in pursuit of ME 109s – until a warden roared at them, 'You bloody kids – GET IN THE SHELTER!'

There was huge excitement one day in Essex when a lone parachutist was seen swinging down out of the sky over Dagenham. Nine-year-old Richard Hunt was messing about with a gang of friends when somebody shouted that the invasion had begun, and a great crowd of people poured into the boys' lane, armed with every kind of makeshift weapon, from garden forks to butchers' knives, making for the fields. Richard had his airgun, and his friend Reggie some other weapon. Joining the rush, they ran through allotments, scattering the crops and breaking down fences in their way. At one stage they heard shots, and later learned that some member of the Home Guard, ignoring all the rules, had opened up on the parachutist and wounded him. The boys reached the scene in time to see an army van drive off with the man inside, and found out that, far from being German, he was one of the Polish or Czech pilots flying Spitfires with the RAF.

Between 19 and 24 August bad weather enforced a lull and gave the RAF fighter squadrons some respite, but then Goering decided to concentrate attacks on 11 Group, which was defending London and the South East, and by the end of August Fighter Command had been drastically weakened: in the last week of August and the first of September 112 pilots and 256 aircraft were lost. Damage to ground stations was so severe that the fighters had to use small civilian airfields.

Fortunately Goering never realized how close the RAF was to collapse. Instead of keeping up the pressure on fighter stations, he switched to the bombing of London – and so the Blitz proper began late in the afternoon of Saturday, 7 September 1940.

Just after eight o'clock that evening the Chiefs of Staff issued the code word CROMWELL to military units, signifying that invasion was imminent. The warning put the whole country on alert: church bells rang out, the Home Guard stood to, and remained on post all night. Many people believed that German troops had already landed. What Hitler had launched, in fact, was Operation *Loge*, a mass attack on London, in which more than 1000 aircraft took part. Between then and the end of May 1941 the capital was attacked seventy-one times; a million houses were destroyed, and more than 40,000 civilians were killed.

H. E. Bates was fishing on a lake in Kent when he witnessed one of the big raids coming in:

> Up to that day we had seen as many as eighty, a hundred, a hundred and fifty planes flying over at one time. Now we saw a phenomenon. It was like the inland migration of hundreds of black and silver geese. They came in steadily and unceasingly, not very high, the black geese the bombers, the silver the fighters. The fighters made pretty circling movements of protection above the bombers. They went forward relentlessly. The air was heavy with moving thunder and the culminating earthquakes of bombs dropped at a great distance. All that had happened before that day now seemed by comparison very playful.

On 15 September – which became known as Battle of Britain Day – Fighter Command achieved its most spectacular success, breaking up raid after raid over London and the south coast. Such was Hitler's frustration that two days later he shelved Operation Sealion indefinitely and turned his attention eastwards to Russia. It is estimated that during the Battle of Britain the RAF had lost just over 1000 aircraft, and the Luftwaffe nearly twice as many.

When Hitler realized that his attempt to demoralize England had failed, attacks on London dwindled. But all Britain had been battered by bombs. After the capital, the city most heavily raided was Liverpool, where nearly 4000 people were killed. Bristol also came under persistent attack: on the night of 3–4 January 1941 a single raid lasted for twelve hours. Birmingham, Glasgow, Liverpool, Manchester, Plymouth, Swansea and Southampton were also prime targets.

Of all the outrages perpetrated by Hitler, none caused greater anger and grief than the attack on Coventry, on the night of 14 September 1940. The city was, in a sense, a legitimate target, for its factories were making cars, aircraft engines and munitions; but nothing could have prepared it for the devastating raid, which began at 8 p.m. and lasted until midnight, killing 560 people, destroying most of the city centre and leaving the fourteenth-century cathedral a ruined shell.

Almost as emotive was the series of attacks that became known as the Baedeker raids. In April and May 1942, in revenge for Bomber Command's laying waste the Baltic port of Lübeck, Hitler ordered reprisals against Exeter, Bath, York and Norwich – historic towns of no strategic importance. The raids killed 1600 civilians and wrecked many notable buildings, including the Assembly Rooms in Bath and the Guildhall in York. Baron Gustav Braun von Stumm, a Nazi propagandist, announced that the Luftwaffe would hit every town in Britain marked with three stars in the Baedeker tourist guide. His threat was never carried out; but in another burst of retaliation Hitler responded to Bomber Command's mass attack on Cologne (in May 1942) with three raids on Canterbury.

* * *

In all the air raids throughout the war, human casualties were inevitably by far the most numerous in cities and towns, but the countryside suffered as well, mainly from bombs jettisoned by crews who had accomplished their principal mission and were on the way home, or were being hard pressed by fighters and sought extra speed to escape.

In the early days of the battle a rumour went round that the Germans were dropping magnetic mines, and people wearing steel helmets were warned not to approach them in case they set off an explosion. But in fact almost everyone *did* wear steel helmets when out of doors, including ladies playing tennis, because during dogfights shrapnel and spent bullet cases were constantly raining down out of the sky. Vera Lynn wore a helmet in the car while driving to her shows.

There were some astonishing survivals, such as that of Mr Withers and his neighbours in their Essex village, described by Margery Allingham:

Their stick of bombs fell neatly between their bungalows, one bungalow, one crater, and so on … In the actual spot where Mr Withers's own bomb fell he had a shed containing a pony and trap, a cat, some budgerigars, a jackdaw and a ton of coal. They got the pony out from under the trap in the crater and held it up for a minute or two until, to everyone's amazement, it wandered off and began to eat. The cat ran away for nearly a fortnight. The budgerigars were none the worse. Most of the coal was retrieved, and the jackdaw died three days later, more from rage than anything else, Mr Withers said. No one in the houses was hurt.

Between raids, life carried on. At Cranbrook School anti-aircraft guns were installed on the cricket field, and, whenever they opened up during a game, the boys had to sprint for cover. For minor crimes committed, an alternative to detention was a spell hoeing the sugar beet planted on one of the rugger pitches.

Later in the war the *Kent Messenger* published a map showing where high-explosive bombs of 50kg or more had fallen on Sevenoaks Rural District between the end of July 1940 and the end of February 1944. Even though some 50,000 incendiary bombs were not included, the chart looked as though it had been blasted with a charge of No. 5 pellets from a shotgun, so thickly was it spattered with dots. One particularly dense cluster, running north-west to south-east, lay close below Chartwell, as if the Luftwaffe had been aiming for the Prime Minister's country home.

Efforts were made to lure German pilots to false targets. One decoy town was laid out by Shepperton Studios on Black Down, north of Bristol. Bales of straw soaked in creosote were set alight to simulate the effects of the incendiary bombs dropped at the start of a raid, and drums of oil were ignited to represent buildings on fire. Dim red lights, powered by petrol generators, were switched on in a pattern based on the streets and railways of the city. But these initiatives seem to have been fruitless, for no bombs landed on or around the site.

The Germans went so far as to attack the Republic of Ireland – even though the country was officially neutral, and the Government had embellished the south coast with signs made from white-painted concrete blocks proclaiming EIRE in huge letters. People were nervous of German intentions, fearing that Hitler might use the Republic as a springboard for invading England from the west – and the saying went that if the Führer wanted to take Ireland at 13.00 hours, it would be his by 16.00.

Even so, nobody was prepared for the attack at lunchtime on 26 August 1940, when four bombs fell on the Shelburne Cooperative Dairy factory at Campile, in Wexford. The first landed in the canteen, killing three young women; the second came through the roof and started a fire; the third hit the railway line and the fourth landed in a field. The Germans claimed that the pilots had become separated from the rest of their formation, and had jettisoned their bombs over open country. To the people on the ground it seemed that they had made a precision raid. No convincing reason for the attack was ever established, but great was the fury of witnesses who saw the German Ambassador come from Dublin to the women's funeral sporting a top hat and a scarlet sash emblazoned with a swastika.

In England animal losses on farms mounted rapidly: in the nine months to December 1940 the National Air Raid Precautions Animals Committee – a voluntary body – reported 3000 air-raid casualties, mostly cattle and sheep. Of these, 843 were killed outright, 706 had to be put down and 440 were given first aid treatment. Many of the deaths and injuries resulted from the Nazi fighter pilots' deplorable habit of machine-gunning herds in low-level attacks – more for target practice and their own amusement than from any hope of reducing English food supplies. From the dead stock, 30 per cent of the meat was bought by the Ministry of Food and sent for human consumption – but the salvage of a carcass depended on prompt action immediately after the animal had been killed. Unless some competent person – farmer, butcher or vet – tackled the victim within a few minutes, it would be useless; and the easiest method of disposal would be to bury it at the bottom of a bomb crater. The Ministry had its own arrangements for salvaging useable livestock, but told farmers that they themselves should be prepared 'to slaughter, bleed and disembowel any animal injured beyond hope of recovery'.

By no means all carcasses passed through official channels. One night, when a stick of bombs fell among cattle in a field near Upton House in Gloucestershire, locals sallied forth to assess the damage; but they went armed with knives, hacksaws, sacks and buckets, and by morning there was nothing left of the single casualty – a Friesian cow – except its horns and a few scraps of skin.

The Luftwaffe had targets all over Britain, and people living under the bombers' flight path had many alarming nights, wherever they lived. Stray bombs fell in the wilds of Wales and Shropshire, in the Lake District and on the North York moors. Legitimate targets like the Royal Ordnance Factory at Pembrey in Carmarthenshire inevitably attracted the Luftwaffe and endangered communities near them. At Brynamman, at the head of a mining valley, twenty miles north of Swansea, one morning in July 1940 two bombs landed next to the school and blew the roof off the church, but by a miracle none of the children was seriously hurt. During raids on the Liverpool docks shrapnel from the shells of anti-aircraft batteries rained down on the houses of Bromborough, ten miles away across the Mersey. The guns must have scored some hits because, for a fee of 3d, boys in the area could sit in the cockpit of a shot-down German plane.

For country lads in Devon there was nothing to beat the lure of a downed enemy aircraft. On the morning of 4 May 1942 Dennis Moss and his twin brother Alan were out on their bikes near the village of Northleigh when they came on a place where the hedges on either side of the road had been breached, and the ground was littered with roots and branches.

> We dropped our bicycles on the grass and ran towards what was left of the crashed German plane [a JU 88]. Jagged pieces of the fuselage and wings were strewn over the field where it had come to violent rest … A policeman stood guard over the wreckage. An RAF airman hovered too. They didn't seem to mind the morbid curiosity of thirteen-year-old boys as we inspected the remains … An arm severed at the shoulder was all that connected this sprawl of metal with the men who the previous night had been aiming to fly back over the Channel.

The difficulties of rural life stand out in the diary of Doreen Kippen, who was twenty-one in 1941 and living in Cinders Cottage, a rented house with no running water and an earth closet in the garden, three

miles out of Tenbury Wells in Worcestershire, some fifty miles west of
Birmingham. Lively minded, brave, stoical and slightly irreverent, with
a strong sense of humour, she endured the privations of war and winter
with indomitable spirit. One main comfort was her boyfriend, Bert;
another the wireless, with its news bulletins reporting the progress of
the war, and *Workers' Playtime* endlessly repeating songs like 'Coming
In on a Wing and a Prayer' and 'Run, Rabbit, Run'. A third escape was
the cinema in town, where she watched films like *Rulers of the Sea*, with
Margaret Lockwood, Douglas Fairbanks and Will Fyffe, *Geronimo* ('the
Indian who massacred American settlers. Thrilling!'), and *Pride and
Prejudice*, starring Greer Garson and Laurence Olivier.

January 1, 1941. Wed. Very dark and cold. Last year was
dreadful but I met Bert and fell off bike in mud and was kissed
in bomb crater, so not as bad as it might have been. Meat ration
down to half again and Lord Woolton asks us not to eat cheese
but to save for miners.

2 Thurs. Light fall of snow. First of year and Uncle and I went to
evening pictures. Halfway through, whistle and lights up for
'alert'. Nobody moved and show went on. Terrific noise on way
home and barrage over Hereford and Birmingham.

4 Sat. Saw Bert and found he likes me as much as ever although
I had been wondering. Don't want him to rave over me but do
want him to go out with. Bristol raided very badly. Incendiaries
and high explosives, casualties fairly heavy.

8 Wed. Bert proposed. Refused on grounds of non-saving.
Enjoyed it immensely and parted on best of terms. Lord
Baden-Powell, founder of scout movement, reported dead.
King and Queen visited bombed Sheffield and were very upset.

9 Thurs. Nice frosty day and Grandma's newly-washed blankets
froze stiff, to her fury. Uncle came over and played cards. I
never win. Butcher gloomily prophesies no joint this weekend,

as his meat so far amounts to 6d per head. No bird seed,
onions, lemons, cabbages.

11 Sat. Eight o'clock news says severe raid on West Country
town with heavy casualties. Tobruk is reported to be
surrounded. All offal now rationed.

13 Mon. Very cold, sunny and thick frost.

14 Tues. Market day. No cheese, fish or anything for dinner.

16 Thurs. Snow frozen like glass and roads very dangerous. Had
quite effective reconciliation with Bert. Wonderful how a week
without a kiss sours you … [We] gave Germany a pasting last
night.

18 Sat. Snowing fast this morning but cycled through blizzard
to library in Tenbury, just on two hours and had to walk all way
back, snow was so deep. This evening it is two foot shallowest
and heavy going.

20 Mon. Absolutely bunged up with snow. No bread, papers or
letters. Shovelled path but soon lost it. Definitely a day for
miseries. No news on wireless, but heard President Roosevelt
sworn in for third term of office, first time in history. Duchess
of Kent as C-in-C WRNS broadcast an appeal for recruits.
They'll never get many with those hats.

So Doreen's life went on. On 1 February she reported 'Invasion
expected any fine day now', and thought that an attack by 'gas in waves'
was almost a certainty. Having watched a war film, *Convoy*, she went
home 'very quietly and felt so small after seeing what the Merchant
Navy is doing'.

As spring came on, she planted vegetables in the garden and tried
to find war work, but was frustrated because no buses were running.
Shortage of food was a constant preoccupation: 'Cheese rationed now,
1 oz. per week. Little cocoa, no sweets, razor blades, fish paste, suet,
raisins etc., honey, onions, lemons.'

On 19 April 1941 she was 'requisitioned for National Service under Conscription for 1920 Class Women', and passed medical tests. But a devastating raid on London made her feel very low: 'Please God I will never forget what wars mean to the little people who stay at home and yet are bombed, killed and made homeless refugees.'

On 4 July she got 7 lb of old potatoes intended for pig food. As the shopkeeper said, 'They look a bit old-fashioned at you', but they turned out not too bad. Then came the triumph of digging the first of the new potatoes that she herself had planted. When, in chapel, a 'revivalist sort of young man, red-haired, freckled and most competent', kept pointing at her and saying, 'Will you come to Jesus?', her reaction was typically direct: 'I thought of the new potatoes for dinner and hoped I could have them first.' Next day she went to the cottage hospital and gave a pint of blood, praying that it would save the life of somebody injured in the air raids.

By the middle of 1941 the whole country was alive with military activity. One night Frances Partridge was woken by 'crunching sounds on the gravel' outside her house in Wiltshire. Her husband Ralph looked outside and said, 'The Army is everywhere, lorry-loads of it.'

> By breakfast time a sense of drama had possessed the house
> and its inmates. Our house was, in fact, no longer our own.
> Processions of soldiers drew water from the tap; others went to
> the lavatory or to telephone. [Later] While I was planting
> snapdragons along the drive a Scotch Army cook came up and
> said, 'Missus, could you sell me a few spring onions to give a
> taste to a stew?'

Much the same was happening in the far north. A farmer's wife living near Scapa Flow described how tradesmen's and fried fish vans had disappeared from the roads, along with commercial travellers and holiday-makers' cars:

> In their place came army lorries, trucks, ambulances, lorry-loads of workmen from a' the airts to work on the dromes and dumps which are springing up everywhere. Gradually all of us came to have our quota of soldier-visitors who so gladly spent their half days and holidays on the farm ... and how welcome these boys were to me.
>
> Then came 'schemes' and 'stunts', and how exciting for everyone they were. It should have been alarming to see cookhouse, duck-house, garden wall suddenly sprout bayonet and helmet, and then to have the granary 'besieged' and the house surrounded by creeping, silent, stalking figures, but I only kept the kettle on the boil, lest I had grimy, tired, thirsty warriors asking in vain for a cup of tea.

By that stage of the war parachutists *were* descending on England, but, rather than German spies, they were more than likely to be air crew who had baled out of stricken bombers or fighters. Most of them, when they landed, were either injured or terrified or both, fearful that they would be shot on sight, and wanting only to give themselves up. Even so, they were liable to alarm civilians by their abrupt appearance.

Early one morning five-year-old Susie Procter and a young school-friend went out of the house on the edge of Milverton, a village in Somerset, and ran down the long passage to the garden, which was bordered by fields. There they found a slight, dark-skinned man dressed in black, and wearing a belt with loops on it, gathering up what looked like a parachute. When the girls appeared he stood still, looking frightened. *They* weren't frightened, because he seemed friendly; but then it occurred to them that he might be a German, and when he moved, they did, too. They ran back to the house and reported what they had seen. At first the grown-ups did not believe them, and when at last they went to investigate, there was no sign of any stranger. Had Susie imagined him? Her memory of him is absolutely sharp. She remains convinced that he was flesh and blood, a real airman who had just come to earth, and quickly absented himself.

There was no doubt about the arrival of another parachutist, witnessed by young Jeff Woods, who was seven when the war broke out. His family was among the thousands of expatriate Britons who fled from France when the German armies invaded in the spring of 1940. Jeff had been born and brought up in France, where his father George, a professional jockey, rode racehorses for the owner-trainer Marcel Boussac; and the family had enjoyed a comfortable life at Chantilly, near Paris. Then, suddenly, Hitler's forces were advancing towards them, and, like millions of other people in Europe, they were engulfed in chaos.

To their aid came Frances Phipps, wife of Sir Eric Phipps, the British Ambassador in Paris, who had a large house on the Boussac estate. Through her benevolence, George Woods, his wife Beryl and their six children escaped to England in a fishing boat and found sanctuary at a pub in Wiltshire. The Raven, a half-timbered hostelry in the village of Poulshot, near Devizes, became their home, and they settled there for the rest of the war.

Although Poulshot, seventy-odd miles west of London, was not affected by the Blitz on the capital, it lay beneath the flight path of Luftwaffe aircraft heading for Bristol, and bombs occasionally landed close to the village, especially when the attackers, fleeing for home, dumped the remains of their loads. Young Jeff and his brothers became expert at interpreting the sound of engines overhead: a thudding *whumf, whumf, whumf* meant planes on their outward journey, heavily laden, whereas a higher, thinner whine signified Heinkels or Dorniers returning. All members of the family slept in their clothes, ready to make a dash for the deep ditch behind the pub, where they had a shelter fashioned from railway sleepers and corrugated iron topped with earth. Whenever they heard the sirens start wailing in Devizes, three miles away, they would pile into it until the all-clear sounded.

Jeff's father George was very small – at about five foot two inches small even for a jockey – but he was tough and aggressive, and much given to chastising his sons, who called him 'the Old Man'. When the Government sent him a dozen sets of uniform, along with a dozen Lee-Enfield .303 rifles, a dozen mouth organs and a bell for summoning his troops, he lost no time in forming a squad of Local Defence Volunteers, to secure his part of the realm against any German spies who might drop in. Relishing his new role, he held a drill parade every Sunday morning, marching his recruits up and down in front of the pub. The dignity of the proceedings was not enhanced by the antics of old Dick Perrett, who lived across the road, illiterate but always laughing, and owned only one lot of clothes – filthy great boots, gaiters up to his knees and baggy corduroy trousers. He was quite unable to march in time, and his gait was so erratic that the Old Man would not entrust him with a rifle, but got him armed with a pitchfork, with which he paraded back and forth.

One summer evening brought this doughty band a chance of glory. Jeff and his mates were playing cricket on the common when they heard an aircraft approaching. Quickly they saw that it was a German plane that had been hit: it was trailing smoke and on its way down, about to crash. There came a clatter of machine-gun fire as, in a final gesture of defiance, the pilot emptied his last rounds into the ground ahead of him. The bullets kicked up spurts of turf all round the boys, but hit none of them. On went the doomed plane, down, down, until it smashed into a hay barn in the distance. But Jeff, looking up, saw that one of the crew had baled out high up and was floating away beneath a parachute.

With a yell he ran to summon his father from behind the bar. Outside, the survivor was drifting off on the wind to the north-west. The Old Man rang the bell to summon his worthies, grabbed a rifle and set off in pursuit, racing up the lane that led to the village of Seend. Of course the boys went after him, about twenty of them. Every hundred yards or so he stopped, turned round and roared at them to go home, but they were far too lit up to obey and carried on, passing older volunteers who sat gasping for breath on the sides of the road.

When at last the airman touched down in the outskirts of Seend, the hounds were on him in a flash, with the Old Man and Reg Collett, the blacksmith (an enormous hulk), first on the scene, levelling their rifles at him. He drew a pistol from his belt and threw it towards them, then raised his hands and cried '*Kamerad!*' He looked terrified, especially when Old Dick hove up with his pitchfork. Obviously he had no intention of trying to escape, but the Old Man and Reg started arguing about how they should tie his hands: in front of him or behind? Although Reg prevailed, and knotted the man's thumbs together in front, it was the Old Man who led the prisoner in triumph through the village before depositing him at the police station. When the posse returned to Poulshot, they found that a second crewman had been killed in the crash, but this did not dampen their celebrations. George became a bit of a hero, and for the next few days trade in the pub was brisk.

Jeff was soon enjoying life in England, but he was puzzled by the official attitude to prisoners. He and his mates were told never to trust them – after all, they were Huns, who might easily do you a mischief – and to spit on them whenever they got a chance; but in his view they were decent enough people – and they were certainly hard workers. Every day in autumn a truck-load of them was brought out from the camp at Devizes to dig potatoes on land which the Old Man had rented. Jeff was dismayed to see that all that the men had for lunch was some porridge-like gruel, which they made by boiling coarsely ground oats in a big copper.

Presently his mother took pity on them, and got him to collect a bucketful of pig spuds, the tiny potatoes normally left on the field as being too small to be worth picking up. These she boiled, sometimes putting a smear of butter on the top, and Jeff took them down to the prisoners, who received them ecstatically.

Scrump apples and gather mushrooms though he might, young Jeff never had enough to eat. The Woods clan of two parents, six children and a grandmother had a weekly allowance of six sausages, which seemed to be stuffed mainly with sawdust. Yet they were better off than most, for the Old Man was licensed to rear six pigs at a time, and occasionally purloined one for his own use.

He would wake Jeff and one of his brothers in the middle of the night, creep out into the stable and bolt the door on the inside. In the sty a helper would lasso the victim's nose with rope to prevent it squealing, and the men would carry it into the stable, where one of them slit its throat so that the blood ran down the drain. The boys' job was to light a small straw fire and singe the bristles off the skin before the animal was butchered and shared out among the villagers in the know. Another task assigned to Jeff was to clear out the main intestine by forcing water through it: his mother would then coil the gut into a dish and bake it in the oven until it came out like a meat loaf, which all ranks ate with relish.

The pigs themselves were on wartime rations. Feed wheat was unobtainable, so they got no mash, but lived on potatoes and the lees from empty beer barrels: the boys would extract the bungs, drink any dregs that remained (disgusting though they were) and fish out the spent hops with sticks. The mixture was alcoholic enough to knock the pigs sideways: their legs and eyes would cross, and they would fall about the sty in such ridiculous fashion that Jeff could charge his mates from the village a penny a head to come and watch.

So, with courage, ingenuity, a bit of harmless cheating and a sense of humour, the Woods family survived the war. But, as with millions of other Britons, the conflict had dragged them out of their former environment, and changed their lives for ever.

Just as a bad air raid killed humans and wrecked their houses, so it left pets at large on the streets or lanes. The Manchester diarist Arnold Boyd wrote a charming account of how wanderers quickly attached themselves to persons wearing khaki:

A devastating air raid brought the homeless in by platoons. An attractive mongrel (a fox bull terrier) walked in that night and was taken at once on the strength for rations and discipline. He answers to the name of Blitz and is friend to all the world. He and Buchanan, a black and white kitten, sleep side by side and eat from one dish, and he was sadly affronted when one cat rejected his advances with a masterly right hook to the nose. The sirens alone make him bark. We also have Nellie, a little yellow bitch with a smug expression, and Nellie Wallace, another mongrel … All these animals, and I have mentioned only a few, scorn civilians. For them khaki is the only wear, and their trust is never misplaced.

Eight

Food from Everywhere

'Oh, where are you going to, all you Big Steamers,
With England's own coal up and down the salt seas?'
'We are going to fetch you your bread and your butter,
Your beef, pork and mutton, eggs, apples and cheese …

For the bread that you eat and the biscuits you nibble,
The sweets that you suck and the joints that you carve,
They are brought to you daily by All Us Big Steamers,
And if anyone hinders our coming, you'll starve.'

Rudyard Kipling, *Big Steamers*

Whale and snoek were the twin horrors of wartime food. Whale meat, tough and fishy tasting however it was cooked, came into the country frozen; snoek came in cans from South Africa, where the long, slim fish were caught off the south-west coast. Both were imported by the Government to ease food shortages, but even when times were at their leanest, neither found favour.

Rationing was nothing new. It had been imposed towards the end of the First World War, in 1917, and it had been threatened (though not applied) before the General Strike of 1926. But in 1939 Hitler was determined to starve Britain into submission: U-boats began taking heavy toll of merchant ships in the Atlantic, cutting off essential food supplies, and early in 1940 the threat of invasion made some measure of control essential.

The need had been anticipated: ration books, printed in advance, were issued to the public on 8 September 1939. Everybody had a book – even the King and Queen – and rationing was announced on 1 November. The news unleashed volleys of protest in the popular press, the *Daily Mail* claiming that Dr Goebbels himself could not have devised 'a more harmful piece of propaganda for Great Britain'.

Most ordinary citizens accepted that restrictions were inevitable. All the same, it was an unpleasant shock when rationing of bacon, butter and sugar came into effect in the depths of the freezing winter on 8 January 1940. Other staples were soon on the list, and adults were restricted to minuscule weekly amounts: bacon and ham (4oz), cheese (2oz), milk (three pints), butter (2oz), margarine (4oz), tea (2oz) eggs (one in a shell, if available), dried eggs (one pack per month, if available, and looking like custard powder), cooking fat (4oz), jam (1 lb every two months) – as well as tea, breakfast cereal, biscuits and canned and dried fruit. Meat was rationed by price rather than by weight. In May 1940 an adult was allowed 1s 10d worth a week, which would buy almost 3 lb of beef, pork or mutton – *if* they were available; but in June 1941 these amounts were almost halved. The financial constraint was designed to encourage people to go for cheaper cuts such as beef skirt or breast of lamb.

Fresh fish, though not rationed, became progressively more expensive as the Admiralty requisitioned trawlers for mine-sweeping and closed some fishing grounds for security reasons. Trawlermen were reluctant to endanger their boats and themselves by going to sea, even in coastal waters, and as supplies fell to 30 per cent of pre-war levels, the price of a stone of haddock rose from 4s to 18s (£9.50 to £43 in today's values), that of cod the same. In November 1939 the Ministry sought to improve life for fish-fryers by importing frozen cod fillets from Norway; and fish and chips – before the war regarded as a working-class meal – rose rapidly in public estimation to become universally popular.

At the beginning of the war fish was going literally in all directions. Catches landed at Cardiff, for instance, were being sent cross-country to Grimsby, on the east coast, and Cardiff was getting regular supplies from Fleetwood in Lancashire. As one expert recorded, 'The journeys of fresh fish about the country presented a fantastic and intricate network.' Government attempts to rationalize distribution by means of the White Fish Zoning Scheme caused 'the most violent uproar' in the trade, and it took a personal intervention by the Minister of Food, Lord Woolton, in December 1942 to calm things down.

Even in wartime, there was room for private enterprise. People living on the coast could catch sea fish, and along rivers like the Tweed or the Wye there was always the chance of a salmon, caught legally or otherwise: explosives were stored everywhere, not always in secure depots, and a hand-grenade was much deadlier than a fly or a worm when dropped into a pool.

Bread, the staff of life, was never rationed during the war, but it was made with flour described as 'an eighty-five per cent extraction from the wheat', and the ubiquitous National Loaf turned out grey rather than white. Fastidious housewives crumbled the bread and sieved it in old silk stockings, which left the flour white; and one woman wrote to Lord Woolton saying, 'I got all your vitamins out and gave them to the pigs.'

Measures were passed to control the consumption of bread, because, in spite of the huge expansion of arable farming, wheat was still short. Bakers were not allowed to sell loaves until they were a day old – in the hope that people would eat less if the bread had lost its delicious freshness, and that if it were slightly stale they would be able to slice it more thinly. But in any case it was so much disliked that it was soon known as Hitler's Secret Weapon.

Fresh fruit and vegetables were not rationed, but quickly became scarce in cities and towns. Apples, for instance, were few and far between out of season, and greengrocers often limited shoppers to one at a time. Exotic fruit like lemons and bananas disappeared for most of the war. Although some greengrocers had bunches of dummy bananas hanging outside their shops, the real thing could not be found, and one lad was downcast when he got his first banana – but that was because he ate it with the skin on. After the Allied victories in North Africa in 1943 oranges reappeared, reserved in the first instance for children. One boy, seeing a picture in a school book, conceived a yearning for a grape-fruit – but when he eventually got one after the war, he was dreadfully disappointed to find how bitter it was.

Onions also almost vanished when supplies from the Channel Islands and Brittany were cut off. In 1939 90 per cent of the onions eaten in Britain had been imported, many of them slung in chains over the handlebars of salesmen's bicycles; but over the next four years the amount fell drastically. Imagine the chagrin of a merchant seaman on leave who brought home a sackful from North Africa. Having docked at Hull, he had to travel to Lancashire in a crowded train; because the onions smelled so strong, he left them in the corridor – only to find, whenever he changed trains, that more and more of them had been pilfered, and by the time he reached his destination hardly any were left.

Before the war few people had grown onions for themselves, as importers provided plenty; but now gardeners realized that the vegeta-ble was easy to grow and started to produce their own crops. Onions were also grown on farms with suitable soil, and Land Girls spent days crawling along the rows with sacking round their knees, hand-hoeing or turning over the stalks; but there were still not enough to go round, and a single good specimen was sometimes given as first prize in a village whist drive. In spring wild garlic made an acceptable substitute for onions, and in summer country cooks had an extra green vegetable in the form of stinging nettles – of which there was never any shortage. People compared their taste with that of rather sharp spinach, and nettle soup was often on the menu. Nettles were also used to dye camouflage material.

Shopping for food became a tedious business. Every citizen was issued with an identity card and a ration book: a buff-coloured general book, a blue one for children under six, and others for travellers, service personnel on leave and seamen. Armed with their books, shoppers had to register with a supplier for each of the rationed items, and stay with that supplier indefinitely – which made it important to cultivate good relations with one or two shopkeepers, who might be prepared to slip extra portions across the counter.

Queuing became endemic. 'Queue, queue, queue,' one girl remembered. 'What patience and stamina we must have had!' Housewives grew so addicted to queuing that they would join a line merely if they saw one forming, without even knowing what lay at the end of it – but fish, which was never rationed, attracted longer queues than anything else. When invasion seemed a distinct possibility, the Government advised housewives in rural areas to keep enough food in their homes for at least three days. Among the stores suggested for four people were twelve Oxo cubes, two tins of salmon, two tins of Irish stew or other meat, 14 lb of potatoes, oatmeal, flour and macaroni. 'Arrange now to join up with near neighbours in the event of invasion.'

Ground down by shortages, people became depressed by the lack of variety but grateful for anything they could get. Cheese was typically boring. Only one National Cheddar was available, and the production of any other cheese was banned (although of course it continued in out-of-the-way farm dairies).

At first restaurants were free from controls, but the exemption caused much resentment, as well-to-do people could always supplement their rations by eating out. To make things fairer, new rules rendered it illegal for restaurants to charge more than 5s for a meal, or to provide meals of more than three courses, or to serve meat and fish at the same sitting. The restrictions led to the establishment of

Community Feeding Centres, soon (at Churchill's suggestion) renamed British Restaurants, run by local authorities and volunteers, set up in schools, town halls and church halls to provide midday meals for all comers. Customers paid 9d at the entrance and were given tokens for soup, a main course – maybe minced beef with parsnips and greens – and a pudding. Basic though they were, these places were extremely well patronized, and by September 1943, 2160 of them had come into being. The food was not to everyone's taste. 'British to me means Barbarian,' roared the portly Scottish MP Sir William Darling. 'They are brutal in their cooking, brutal in their presentation of food. One needs to be British to "take it" in a British Restaurant.'

Any establishment selling cooked food did well: in the summer of 1942 a pie station was opened in the men's reading room at Hever, in Kent. The cost of the equipment was met from donations and the sale of horse chestnuts collected by schoolchildren, and the pies, made three days a week by members of the Women's Voluntary Service, proved highly popular. By the autumn over 7000 had been made – at first for farm workers only, but later for general sale.

The man universally identified with rationing was Lord Woolton. A cheerful north countryman, with an easy, outgoing personality, he came from Salford, in Lancashire, and went to Manchester Grammar School. Born Frederick Marquis, in 1935, for his work as Managing Director of Lewis's department stores in Liverpool, he was knighted, and in 1939 he was raised to the peerage for services to industry. He would have liked to become Baron Marquis, but was told that this was impossible, as his own name denoted another grade of nobility; so he took the title Lord Woolton, after the Liverpool suburb in which he had lived.

In April 1940 he was appointed Minister of Food. In spite of the fact that the entire population deplored rationing, and the boring nature of the wartime diet, he put such energy and good sense into press conferences, broadcasts and positive advertising campaigns that he quickly became known as 'Uncle Fred', and often received 200 letters a day, many bringing thanks and congratulation from grateful citizens. Part of his success was due to his habit of warning people in advance when some shortage was in the offing. Whenever he and Lady Denman (Founder and Queen of the Land Girls) visited a farm together, they were received like royalty. His reputation survived even the creation of the dreaded Woolton Pie to which he gave his name – a concoction of potatoes, parsnips, turnips, carrots and oatmeal, seasoned with herbs and awash with brown gravy, under a crust of pastry or potato, created at the Savoy Hotel in London by the master chef Francis Latry.

Woolton understood not only the intricacies of the food supply, but also the need to put over the necessity for rationing to the public. One of his most successful inventions was *The Kitchen Front*, a five-minute radio programme which came on after the eight o'clock news six mornings a week and encouraged housewives to greater efforts of economy and imagination in the use of whatever ingredients they had. In his memoirs he recorded how, having decided that 'the public was either going to laugh or to cry about food rationing, and that it was better for them that they should laugh', he summoned two professional entertainers to his assistance:

> I asked two ladies named Miss Elsie and Miss Doris Waters – who were more widely known as 'Gert and Daisy' – if they would come to see me. I told them that I wanted their help in making people see that food rationing – which was increasingly inevitable – was not necessarily a matter for perpetual gloom … They said to me, 'But, Lord Woolton, we don't think you understand: we are music hall artistes.' I did understand, and told them in greater detail the sort of things I had in mind. To my intense joy, one of them said, 'Do you mean something like this?' and they proceeded, quite impromptu, to do a little turn.

The lively Gert and the dim Daisy – described by one fan (Ralph Arnold) as 'looking like every man's favourite aunts' – became immensely popular, and people loved repeating their jokes, especially when they were spiced with a little smut.

Gert, or it may have been Daisy, had overslept, because her alarm clock had stopped. She hopped out of bed in her nightdress, put her head out of the window, and saw a man delivering milk. 'Have you got the time?' she shouted. 'Yes,' was the eager reply, 'but what shall I do with my horse and cart?'

Woolton had an endearing readiness to record encounters with members of the public. Staying one night in the Cotswolds, he was accosted by a woman who said that her small daughter became confused when she recited the Lord's Prayer, and after the line 'Give us this day our daily bread', frequently asked, 'Why do we have to have both God and Lord Woolton?'

His book reveals how fair-minded he was, and what a magnificent grip he had on a task of immense complexity; but – perhaps for propaganda reasons – he told a big white lie when he claimed that corruption scarcely existed. He certainly did his best to suppress illegal transactions, and recalled that, 'unknown to everybody in the Ministry of Food except the Chief Permanent Secretary', he 'housed in a separate building a group of men very skilled in tracing defaulters: they were ever on the look-out for organised attempts at dealing in the black market'. He also introduced severe penalties for infringing the food regulations – a fine of £500 with or without two years' imprisonment, and an additional fine of three times the value of the capital involved in the transaction. These measures may have deterred serious criminals, but any amount of minor breaches of the rules were committed, every day and everywhere, especially in the country.

Woolton had a marvellously direct way of addressing housewives. 'Many of you must have a very good stock of canned foods,' he said in one broadcast. 'Make it last. Go easy with the tin-opener and regard all your tinned food as an iron ration.' Economy with cheese was another of his themes:

> Don't eat cheese unless you need it. Don't eat it as an extra. Some people must have cheese, such as miners and farm-workers, and if it were rationed, it would make it short for everybody. I know it is a question of changing the habits of a lifetime, but war makes us do that.

He was right about cheese, which had been the staple fare of farm workers for generations. One old shepherd of sixty-five said that cheese had been his 'regular fare' for seven days a week. He had always depended on it for energy, and now he was obliged to eat onions with his bread and margarine, which wasn't the same at all. Another veteran labourer echoed him: he used to eat a pound and a half of cheese a week, for lunch, dinner and tea – but now he had only bread and margarine.

Besides exhorting cooks to be imaginative in their use of scarce ingredients, Woolton also urged them to hand in surplus aluminium utensils and even milk-bottle tops for reuse in aircraft parts. Lord Beaverbrook launched an appeal, promising to 'turn your pots and pans into Spitfires and Hurricanes'. In one village alone – Arborfield in Berkshire – nine and a half tons of scrap metal were collected, as well as eight sacks of aluminium. The campaign was hardly needed, as scrap aluminium was already abundant, but it evoked one spirited response:

My saucepans have all been surrendered,
The teapot has gone from the hob,
The colander's leaving the cabbage
For a very much different job.

So now, when I hear on the wireless
Of Hurricanes showing their mettle,
I see in a vision before me
A Dornier chased by my kettle.

The Ministry of Food became an enormous organization, eventually employing 15,000 people, many of them based in Colwyn Bay, on the north-west coast of Wales, where they took over hotels, boarding houses and the premises of Penrhos College, the girls' school which had been evacuated to Chatsworth. Scattered round the country were 1300 Local Food Offices, which distributed ration books, and licensed shopkeepers to handle them. Unknown to most of the population, the Ministry also stockpiled food in secret warehouses, against the threat of invasion. Woolton himself travelled huge distances, rallying his troops, and often broke the long haul to Colwyn Bay by staying a night at the Lygon Arms, a coaching inn at Broadway, in the Cotswolds.

The best antidote to rationing was the Dig for Victory campaign, launched by Sir Reginald Dornan-Smith when Minister of Agriculture and Fisheries in October 1939, and taken over by his successor Robert Hudson in 1940. 'Let Dig for Victory be the motto of everyone with a garden,' he exhorted in a radio broadcast. The phrase entered the national vocabulary and conscience – yet 'Dig for Victory' was not the Minister's invention. It was coined by the London *Evening Standard*, and the real architect of the crusade was the Scottish economist Professor John Raeburn, head of the Agricultural Plans Branch at the

Ministry of Food, who was only twenty-eight in 1940 but had already worked at Nanking University, fascinated by all things Chinese.

'Dig, dig, dig,' went the campaign song, 'And your muscles will grow big ... Just keep on digging/Till we give our foes a wigging/Dig, dig, dig for Victory!' The Ministry's Leaflet No. 1 made gardening sound easy: 'Grow for Winter as well as Summer,' it urged:

> Vegetables for you and your family every week of the year.
> Never a week without food from your garden or allotment. Not
> only fresh peas and lettuce in June, new potatoes in July, but all
> the health-giving vegetables in winter when supplies are scarce
> – SAVOYS, SPROUTS, KALE ...

The leaflet gave a year-round cropping plan, but made no mention of slugs, wireworm, blackfly, birds, frost or any of the other hazards that dismay amateur horticulturalists.

Especially in London and the large northern cities, a high proportion of houses lacked gardens; but the Cultivation of Lands (Allotment) Order of 1939 empowered councils to take over unused land, and so enticing were the Ministry's posters, encouraging countless people to have a go, that the number of allotments provided by local authorities rose from 815,000 in 1939 to 1,400,000 at the end of the war. The increase was due in no small part to the advocacy of the National Allotments Society, which claimed that plots 'are of immense service to the nation in times of peace, and are indispensable in times of war, and that the contribution which they make to personal and public health are [sic] immeasurable'.

The Indian professor N. Gangulee, a research scholar at Rothamsted Experimental Station, who toured Britain and wrote a series of articles which were published in a small book, *The Battle of the Land*, was impressed by the increase in numbers, and by the work people were putting in. In 1943 he calculated that home production of vegetables and fruit amounted to 600,000 tons a year, and concluded that allotment holders were 'making a valuable contribution to the war effort'. He also praised the enthusiasm of gardeners in RAF camps, especially one barrage-balloon crew who had built a greenhouse out of old car windscreens.

Even the most unlikely patches of land – tennis courts and railway embankments, the moat of the Tower of London, the ground beside the runway at Manchester Ringway parachute-training base (now Manchester airport) – were dug up and planted. Bomb sites were cleared of rubble – with enormous labour – and brought back to productive life. The wrecked roof garden of Selfridge's emporium in Oxford Street was cleared and restocked. Schools sacrificed their playing fields for growing vegetables, which the pupils were allowed to take home. Children of five or six were taught to recognize good and bad plants, and were set to pulling up weeds. Boys were excused lessons to go and work on farms. 'The [Education] Committee have given permission for ten senior boys to pick up potatoes in school hours,' said the record of the school at Akenfield in autumn 1941. 'The school has been closed for the salvage drive, blackberrying, wartime cookery demonstrations and meetings.'

The effort made gardeners feel they were contributing to the national cause – and Woolton urged them on. 'This is a food war,' he announced in 1941. 'Every extra row of vegetables in allotments saves shipping … The battle on the kitchen front cannot be won without help from the kitchen garden.'

Bright, boldly coloured posters and leaflets put out by the Ministry encouraged housewives to be economical and inventive, and to cook healthy food. 'Doctor Carrot, the Children's best friend', said one, with a drawing of the good, carrot-shaped physician carrying a little case marked 'Vit. A'. People were assured that carrots would help them see better in the dark, and so negotiate the hazards of the blackout more safely. Carrots achieved unprecedented importance in the national diet and appeared in numerous guises: curried carrot, carrot cake, carrot jam, carrot lollies. A national competition announced in December 1941 was won by Marjorie Casey of Palmer's Green with her Carrot Savoury Pudding, chosen from a huge entry by 'a mixed committee of tasters at the Ministry of Food'.

'Food is a munition of war', said another official poster. 'Don't waste it.' One of the Ministry's major aims was to make people eat less bread and to increase the consumption of potatoes, hence a seductive leaflet proclaiming 'There is no vegetable more useful than the homely potato. It is a valuable yet cheap source of energy, and one of the foods that help protect us from ill health. It contains the same vitamins as oranges ...' Spuds were a central element of wartime food, and their nutritional value was so successfully promoted – not least by the bouncy cartoon character Potato Pete, who had his own song – that at the end of the war consumption had gone up by 60 per cent. No doubt the Minister would have been delighted to learn that some people's dogs developed a passion for baby potatoes, and made for the fields when the crop was being lifted.

Of course there were disasters – as when a bomb landed among the vegetables lovingly grown by Herbert Brush, a pensioner in Forest Hill, south London. 'I went round to look at the allotment,' he recorded in his diary for 26 October 1940, 'but it was a case of looking *for* the allotment. Four perches out of the five are one enormous hole, and all my potatoes and cabbages have vanished.'

One class of gardeners was dismayed by the Ministry of Agriculture's drive to grow food: the owners of nurseries which raised ornamental plants and flowers for the market. Compelled by the War Ags to switch many of their greenhouses and much of their land to vegetable production, they found their incomes tumbling. Harry Wheatcroft, the celebrated grower and breeder of roses – he of the outrageous handlebar moustache – spoke for dozens of his fellow nurserymen when he lamented:

We put the plough through a field of some hundred thousand [rose] trees – a heartbreaking job. We tore from the greenhouses the bushes that were to give us blooms for the spring flower shows, and so made room for the more urgent bodily needs of the nation.

Pigs now wander about where our Polyantha roses bloomed. There's wheat and barley where acres of Hybrid Teas coloured the land – even the humble cabbage stands where standard roses once held majestic sway. The odour of our glasshouses has changed too. Here half a million onion plants have taken the place of the roses. They, in turn, will be succeeded by tomato plants and fruit; then lettuce, while the light still holds, and afterwards the humble mustard and cress.

Besides the craze for vegetables, there was such a tremendous drive for collecting herbs that hedges and gardens must have been stripped nearly bare. Before the war almost all the plants used in the manufacture of medicines had come from Europe and the Far East. With the supply cut off, the Government created a body of experts who appealed to the public to gather wild herbs. Every county set up a herb committee, and the Women's Institutes, the Women's Voluntary Service, Scouts, Girl Guides, schools – all joined in. An official guide, *The Hedgerow Harvest*, sent thousands of people out foraging, and the result was enormous: in the five years of the war, more than 4000 tons of herbs were collected. Rose hips – the fruit of the dog rose, a traditional remedy for exhaustion and stomach upsets – were gathered in huge quantities to make ruby-red syrup packed with Vitamin C. In 1944 the Knockholt WI earned a special commendation for picking 97 lb of hips, but their efforts were far exceeded by those of Doris Frecknall, of Woodhouse Eaves in Leicestershire, who alone collected a quarter of a ton. Meanwhile, the Monks Risborough WI sent nine sacks of belladonna stalks to the Islip Herb Centre for the production of pain-killing drugs.

Country dwellers were far better supplied with food than people in towns, not only because they had more space to grow vegetables and fruit, but because they could also keep chickens, ducks and geese. Chickens, being easily managed, fitted well into urban gardens or back-yards, but ducks and geese were more suitable for the country, as they generate a daunting amount of mess, either by paddling the ground into mud or by prodigious defecation. Khaki Campbell ducks were (and are) indefatigable layers, each female producing up to 300 eggs a year, and geese, which feed themselves entirely on grass, yielded valu-able extra meat.

Few smallholders can have been more dedicated than George Orwell. In his diaries he meticulously recorded successes and failures on his patch at Wallington, in Hertfordshire, where he kept chickens, sold eggs and grew many varieties of vegetables and fruit. The outbreak of war quickly made life more difficult – 'Impossible to get iron stakes for wire netting,' he wrote on 24 October 1939. 'Timber also almost unprocurable' – yet he went doggedly ahead with long-term plans, collecting sacks full of fallen beech leaves for compost and planting new currant bushes.

The sale of eggs, at 3s a score, was an important element in his economy, and he kept details of production with almost obsessive precision. Returning to Wallington after a fortnight in London at the end of 1939, he tried to reconstruct the performance of the hens during his absence:

> In the time we have been away – i.e. since 22.12.39 – there have apparently been 101 eggs – a falling-off, but not so bad as I expected. Shall have to make the weeks up by guesswork but can get the actual numbers right … The total number of eggs,

including those laid on the 2 (unentered) days before we went away, and today's, is 120. I have entered the last two weeks at 45 a week, which leaves 30 to be added to those of Friday-Sat of this week: i.e. this week's eggs will equal Friday-Sat's eggs + 30. This will make the total right even if the weeks are incorrect.

Orwell loved his chickens, his fruit bushes and vegetables; but in May 1940 he left the smallholding for the time being when he and his wife Eileen moved to a house in the centre of London, near Regent's Park. Back at Wallington a year later, he sowed 40 or 50 lb of potatoes, hoping that they would yield a crop of 200 to 600 lb in the autumn.

It would be queer – I hope it won't be so, but it quite well may – if when this autumn comes those potatoes seem a more important achievement than all the articles, broadcasts etc. I shall have done this year.

For farmers, smallholders, or people with big gardens, pigs were another standby. Anybody was allowed to keep one, with the proviso that another had to be reared at the same time for the Ministry of Food. But many a pig-keeper privily added a third animal to his retinue, and when it had been slaughtered he would salt some of it (maybe in the bath) for his own use. Children were later haunted by ineradicable memories of being sent down to the cellar in the evening to rub salt into slimy joints, and Frances Partridge recalled how she and her household at Ham Spray, their home in Wiltshire, tackled other grisly tasks:

We sat up till midnight making the brawn. Head, heart, trotters etc were all boiled in a cauldron till they became a grey, glutinous mass, and then, seated round our kitchen table with our visitors, like the witches in *Macbeth*, we hand-picked it and chopped it, removing first an eye and then a tooth, or detaching the fat from an ear. After the first horror it was quite fascinating … [A week later her husband Ralph] rendered down the lard of our pig – a heroic act, for it made a sickly-sweet, hot, oily smell of such fearfulness that it drove me out of the kitchen.

Hams and sides of bacon would hang out of sight in cellar or loft, and when the meat was cured it would be shared out with local friends. Some people went so far as to bury their half-pig in a bath of salt at the end of the garden, or in a field, and a farmer in Shropshire, known to be operating the black market, was caught secreting his pork down a well. Distribution of joints was best done after dark, and one man decided that the ideal form of clandestine transport was a baby's pram. Unfortunately on his round he met the local policeman, who stopped for a chat and remarked that he was out late with the baby – to which he replied that he was walking the infant to lull it to sleep.

Local bobbies seemed to attract pig rustlers. A girl living near Hull regularly escorted her father when he walked out on a round: pushing her doll's pram, which was full of meat under the blanket, she made a perfect decoy – not that one was needed, as they often delivered to the policeman's house. In Yorkshire a farmer, on an illicit run in his van with a load of parcelled meat in the back, came on a policeman whose bicycle tyre had punctured. He gave the man a lift, with the bike on the roof, but his passenger could smell the cargo, and at journey's end he simply held out a hand, into which one of the parcels was pressed. Did these rural coppers know that the Metropolitan Police operated a piggery of their own in Hyde Park?

Pigs were instrumental in the efforts being made to cut down the waste of food, which was estimated at 200,000 tons a year. A Member of Parliament reminded the House that during the later stages of the First World War every camp in England and France kept pigs to dispose

of waste efficiently. 'Beating food waste beats the U-boats' ran an advertisement from Silcocks, merchants of feeding stuffs. Swill from air
stations and military camps was already going to pigs, but now the
regulations were tightened, and all reject food had to go through
companies authorized to process it. Shortage of meal led to some odd
questions. A man who had been offered 'a regular supply of bananas'
– by whom? one would like to know – asked if it would do harm if he
fed them to pigs. The answer was that peeled bananas contained practically the same amount of dry matter as potatoes – so the reply was 'No'.

In towns heavy, galvanized pig bins chained to lamp posts were
stationed at strategic points for the collection of potato peelings and so
on, and local authorities installed plants for treating kitchen waste. 'The
war has brought the swill-tub itself into its own,' declared *The Times* –
and the first plant was at Tottenham, in north London: hence the creation of Tottenham Pudding, a compound of all rejects converted into
food for pigs and poultry. Another early exponent was Cheltenham
Corporation, which used three old tar boilers to cook up fifty tons of
excellent pig food every month.

In the country recourse was had to medieval methods: come
autumn, people living among oak or beech woods went out and gathered acorns and beech mast which, in the old days of pannage, the
animals would have foraged for themselves. The Ministry of Agriculture
advised farmers to arrange with schools to collect acorns, and claimed
that dried acorns compared well with locust beans in food value. But
Gwen McBryde, who farmed in Herefordshire, suffered a severe disappointment through following official advice:

> There was a large, fatted pig ready to kill; her sty was under a
> spreading chestnut tree. Into her trough we emptied acorns,
> which she ate greedily, and we added some horse chestnuts to
> those already fallen into her sty. In the morning the pig was
> dead. Inflammation caused by acute indigestion, said the vet.

Community pig clubs were encouraged, especially in Scotland, where 900 were set up. Some of them were at schools; the animals, when fattened, went off to a butcher, and came back as bacon and joints of pork, for sale to the parents of pupils. Resourceful cooks used every bit of the animal: the head, the trotters, even the tail – 'all parts of the pig except the squeal'. Even the bladder could be converted into a serviceable football.

Fresh eggs were highly valued and much sought-after. From June 1941 the ration was one per person per week, but during the winter, when production naturally slowed, it went down to one a fortnight – and most people considered that dried egg, though tolerable in cakes, was horrible if scrambled. Demand for home-produced eggs was therefore keen. Evacuee boys who worked on farms might be given one or two, or a few ounces of home-made cheese, in return for their efforts. At harvest time suburban householders who kept hens in their back gardens (a hobby encouraged by the Ministry) would take a bus out into the country and venture onto the fields to glean ears of corn, often to the rage of farmers, who did not like strangers tramping about their territory.

When chickens were laying well, people preserved surplus eggs by immersing them in earthenware crocks full of isinglass, or waterglass, a glutinous substance made from the swim bladders of fish, that looked like dirty water. Another method was to smear the palms of the hands with a dry preservative – Oteg or Gep-ek – and roll the eggs between them until the shells were coated. The aim was to exclude air by sealing the shells, and generally it worked well; but there was always a chance that the next egg out of the crock would be a rotter, with a devastating smell.

Woolton's reminiscences reveal that he once had to deal with this kind of problem on a gorge-raising scale, when a vast consignment of eggs went bad in sea transit from America:

By the time they arrived and the hatches were opened, the stench was unbearable. Extra money had to be paid to the dockers to get the eggs out of the ships … I arranged in Liverpool to transport truck-loads of these eggs secretly from the docks to a place called Skelmersdale [some twenty-five miles to the north] where there was a disused mine; I was told that quietly – and irreverently – they were dropped down the mine.

Country cooks would have loved a little book called *They Can't Ration These* by an eccentric, peripatetic French nobleman, Georges, le Vicomte de Mauduit de Kervern. Of distinguished lineage – his great-grandfather had escorted Napoleon to St Helena in 1815, when the British imprisoned Boney on the island – the author was born in 1893, went to school in England and travelled widely: he called his autobiography, *Private Views*, 'the reminiscences of a wandering nobleman'. He flew fighter aircraft in the First World War and worked on irrigation projects in Egypt: he had lived in France, America and England, and wrote three other cookery books. With his dapper appearance, and a monocle settled firmly in his right eye, he hardly looked a hunter-gatherer – but that is what he was, and his wartime recipes embraced many species 'from Nature's larder' not often seen on British plates: roasted sparrows, stewed starlings, squirrel-tail soup and hedgehogs baked in clay, gypsy fashion. Even amid the stringencies of wartime some of his suggestions may not have appealed to British housewives. 'The frog,' he remarked, 'common on the Continent, is encountered in many parts of England.'

Edible frogs are caught in ponds, lakes and streams in the day-time by means of a red rag hooked to a line, and after sun-down with a red lantern and a hand-net … Their legs when cooked in different ways (roasted, stewed etc.) are a delicacy, the flesh tasting somewhat like chicken, only more tender ... In cookery all four legs are used, whilst the rest of the body is discarded or used for feeding poultry.

The Vicomte's movements in 1939 and 1940 are hard to reconstruct. It is clear from his book, which was published in 1940, that he had been in England shortly before the war broke out; his aim, he wrote, was 'to show where to seek and how to use Nature's larder, which in time of peace and plenty people overlook or ignore'. But he then disappeared, and he was said to have been executed by the Nazis in Germany or occupied France.

It is a pity that he gives no indication of where he had foraged in England. Whatever his hunting ground, he secured the support of no less a figure than David Lloyd George, who had met his father during the First World War. Unfortunately, in contributing a foreword to his book, the former Liberal Prime Minister, who owned a fruit farm at Churt, in Surrey, gave no hint of the author's whereabouts or fate; but he did make some good points. It had long been his own ambition (he wrote) to help in restoring a 'juster balance between town and country'. For years he had tried in vain to persuade the Government to 'bring back to the empty fields and villages of Britain' some of the people who had migrated into towns.

But what reason and peaceful persuasion have been unable in long years to accomplish, war is now bringing to pass. Under its stern compulsion, scores of thousands of our children have been thrust hurriedly into the country-side for safety, and very many of them are now learning for the first time the lore of Nature which ought to be the birthright of all. Not a few, let us hope, will form a purpose to seek there a permanent home and career.

Lloyd George went on to praise the Vicomte for his skill in describing how to turn 'even unpromising weeds of the hedgerow into dainty dishes', and called his book 'a valuable contribution towards our national defence'. That was a generous assessment – but who knows how many housewives tried, and benefited from, Mauduit's recipe for dealing with slippery elm bark ('first discovered by the early colonists of America'), or took comfort from his assertion that 'carrageen moss is a splendid food for invalids'? How could they make his special chestnut soufflé if they had no fresh eggs?

Maurice Barnes, thirteen-year-old son of a farmer in Dorset, used to feel sorry for the town people, because 'they couldn't get much food, you see, only what was in the shops'. His father, who kept three or four hundred chickens, sold eggs freely – and neighbours always had surpluses of something else. One day a friend turned up and said,

'I got a fair bit of cheese. Would you like a bit of cheese?'
'Yes,' Father said, and he [the friend] brought round a thirty, forty pound cheese!
'How much for 'e?'
'Oh – five bob!'

Young Maurice supplemented the family's rations by shooting a couple of rabbits every week – and the supply was inexhaustible. Other village lads would come home early on summer mornings after a round of their snares with dozens, paunched, hocked and paired, hanging over the handlebars and frames of their bikes. Whether or not they had been poaching was a moot point. If they had been shooting and ferreting on land over which they had permission, they were within their rights; but even if they had strayed onto neighbours' territory, no one was likely to object, because in reducing the number of rabbits they were performing a useful service.

On another level, the demand for rabbits was strong enough to turn some men into professional poachers. A lorry driver in Northamptonshire habitually went out at night with a long net, which he would set up on stakes along one side of a field, while his son trekked round the opposite boundary, trailing a line to drive the rabbits in. As the boy remembered,

> Now that doesn't sound much, but to a ten-year-old, walking round a field at midnight or later, when you shouldn't be there, is a different thing altogether. Your imagination works overtime, and a bush in the field can turn into a keeper or another poacher, so you close your eyes for a few seconds and it becomes a bush again.

One night the pair were out so late that dawn was approaching, and the father thought they had better lie low until full daylight, for to be seen abroad in the early hours would arouse suspicion. So they shared an orange which he had somehow acquired and went to sleep in a haystack. The boy was woken by what he thought was hay blowing gently over his hands and around his mouth, but when he opened his eyes he found that four rats, two on each side, were licking the remains of the orange juice off his lips, and a whole lot more were nuzzling his hands. One rabbit fetched 2s 6d, and another 3d for its skin.

People who did not know how to cook the meat soon gave it up: as a testy commentator in *Country Life* remarked, 'The rabbit is not sufficiently rich and succulent to survive being boiled furiously in half a gallon of water with a couple of onions.' But for many countrymen it was an absolute staple. As one farmer recalled, 'Nice young rabbit, three parts growed. Par-boil 'im, then put 'im in the oven with a slice of bacon on top – beautiful!' In autumn and winter a pheasant could sometimes be got from a poacher or friendly gamekeeper, and a joint of venison made a noble supplement to the meat ration.

Sugar was a luxury in much demand. In one of many amusing anecdotes Woolton recalled how he managed to borrow a million tons from Abboud Pasha, a wily Egyptian merchant who had a Scottish wife and, when he came to England in the middle of the war to negotiate, said he greatly hoped Hitler would be defeated. Woolton handled him with masterly skill, and when the Egyptian offered to *give* the sugar (which in fact belonged to his daughter) as a contribution to the war effort, the Minister said he would prefer to borrow it, and pay back later – almost certainly because he knew of Abboud's dubious reputation (it was said that the Pasha, known as the richest man in Egypt, once paid King Farouk to appoint the Prime Minister of his choice).

Even an extra million tons was not enough for housewives in the country whose enthusiasm for making jam with gooseberries, strawberries, raspberries, blackcurrants, redcurrants and blackberries was prodigious. Before the days of freezers, fruit was preserved by bottling it in glass Kilner jars sealed with a rubber ring and a lid held in position by a spring; but the jam-makers needed extra sugar, and during the fruit season they would amass stocks by bartering away unwanted tea coupons.

The most powerful fruit-preserving force in the country was the National Federation of Women's Institutes, which launched a tremendous effort. By harvest time in 1940 – a phenomenal year for plums – over 1000 'preservation centres' had been established in farm kitchens, outbuildings, private houses, village halls and schools, and a Government grant enabled the NFWI to buy £1400 worth of sugar. As a result, members of the organization made 1631 tons of jam that year – and the passion for preservation extended to all corners of the kingdom. On 21 October 1942 a report by the WI at Abberley, a village in Worcestershire, showed that 1600 lb of jam, 220 bottles of fruit, 150 lb of chutney and 1044 cans 'had been completed in the fifty-two days on which the kitchen had been opened'. (It was a poor reward for all this

effort when the parish hall was requisitioned for the making of munitions, and the workers ruined the dance floor.)

During the war the eight jam-makers of Rosedale, a village on the
North Yorkshire moors, produced three and a half tons: they brought
the fruit to the reading room of the village hall in market baskets, and
because they had no electricity or gas, they had to boil up their vats on
an oil stove with water carried by hand from a source a quarter of a mile
away. They had help from children, who picked blackberries and
topped and tailed gooseberries, but by any measure theirs was a
phenomenal achievement.

Elsewhere, some of the jam-makers' sugar came from pilfering in
offices, which were allocated a certain amount for the inmates' tea: at
mid-morning the official tea-maker would put a spoonful into each
cup, and another into a tin. Once the tin was full, it was taken home by
one of the working women – and managers who knew about the little
racket paid no attention.

People in East Anglia, where the Government encouraged the
growing of sugar beet, made their own sugar substitute. Chopped up,
boiled for twenty-four hours and squeezed in a home-made press
powered by a car jack, the beets yielded juice, which was then boiled
again to thicken it, and the result was pungent black treacle.

Better by far was honey: beekeepers could sell every drop they did
not need for themselves, and a special dispensation allowed them to
buy sugar for feeding their bees in winter. Whether or not they *had* any
bees was another matter. According to the records of the British
Beekeepers' Association, the number of registered hives rocketed
during the war, but many of them stood empty – and many were home-
made or patched up with odd bits of wood, for permits were needed to
buy timber, and people had to make do with what they could scrounge.
With keepers away at the war, hives were less well managed than usual,
but bees seem to have been more self-reliant then than now, and pests
and diseases were fewer, so that colonies probably survived without

much attention. There were also more feral colonies, and, when these swarmed, they were likely to occupy any hive they found uninhabited, thus keeping up numbers.

The war encouraged apiarists to close ranks. At a monthly meeting of the British Beekeepers' Association in 1940 it was decided, after discussion, that 'psychologically' it was time for beekeepers to get together, even if physical reasons made it difficult just at that moment. In spite of the problems, enough cohesion was achieved for county associations to send generous gifts of honey to submarine crews: in December 1940 Sussex sent 500 lb, and by February 1941 the total had risen to 802 lb. In March 1941 another minor success was recorded by *The Farmers' Weekly*:

> The shareholders of the Market Rasen School Beekeeping Company, under the direction of Peter Hesslewood, its 13-year-old chairman, have achieved a dividend of 150 per cent. The company, with a capital of £10 in shilling shares, has sold honey to the value of £28 9s 11d during the year.

Experience soon showed that the fumes of German high explosive were particularly obnoxious to bees, and this made them an extra hazard for ARP workers who were liable to be stung when they went into action, rescuing people and clearing up after a bomb had fallen. Beekeepers tried to minimize the danger by storing a bottle of chloroform in the top of a hive, together with pieces of rag that could be soaked in the spirit and stuffed into hive entrances as soon as possible after an explosion had taken place, to stupefy the inhabitants and keep them at home.

Like honey, beer was never rationed. Complaints about beer being deliberately weakened were generally unfounded: statistics in *The Brewers' Almanack* show that during the six years of the war its strength went down marginally, from 1040.93 specific gravity to 1034.54, but that the amount produced every year rose from 25,532 barrels to 32,667.

Sometimes beer did run short, and publicans shut their front doors, adorned with notices saying 'Closed', so that they would not disappoint their regular customers who knew the way into the bar round the back. One publican, at least, was determined that agricultural workers should get their fair share:

> A man that's working in the fields needs his beer, 'specially with the food they got to eat nowadays. But I rations 'em. I says to 'em, 'Now look here, you want your beer regular, don't you? Wouldn't you rather have a pint with your dinner every day than four pints one day and three the next?'

In the great drive to grow vegetables one of the leading figures was Cecil Henry Middleton, the first radio celebrity to talk about gardening on the BBC. In 1939 'Mr Middleton' was already familiar to millions of listeners, for he had been broadcasting fifteen-minute talks called *In Your Garden* ever since 1931. His early talks had gone out at 7.10 on Friday evenings, but in the autumn of 1936 his slot was moved, by popular request, to 2.15 p.m. on Sundays. He also made some pioneer appearances on television, broadcasting from a specially built plot at Alexandra Palace; but when the BBC abruptly closed down its television service on the outbreak of war (in the middle of a Mickey Mouse cartoon), he extended his wireless series to embrace the Dig for Victory campaign, which he was chosen to launch.

There was something immensely reassuring about his voice and manner. He addressed listeners as if they were close friends, and so comforting was his seamless flow of advice and anecdote, of common sense and gentle humour – like that of a benevolent uncle droning on in a Northamptonshire accent – that he attracted three million listeners. His habit of pronouncing 'herbaceous' 'herbyceous' was much mimicked by music hall comedians; but research carried out in 1940 revealed that *In Your Garden* was easily the most popular programme of its kind. He also contributed an influential gardening column to the *Daily Express*, and when he appeared as Roy Plomley's guest on *Desert Island Discs* in November 1943, he revealed a remarkable range of musical tastes, from *Ständchen* in Schubert's *Schwanengesang* to the snorts, grunts and whistles of Albert Richardson in 'The Old Sow' ('Susannah's a funniful man', etc).

Horticulture was in Mr Middleton's genes, for his father was Head Gardener at Weston Hall, the Sitwell family's house in Northamptonshire, where he grew up with that formidable trio of intellectuals Edith, Osbert and Sacheverell. He began work in 1899 as a seed-boy, aged thirteen, in the Sitwells' garden, and after a spell in the seed trade and studying at Kew Gardens, he developed a particular love of flowers; in the words of one contemporary, 'he could not love an onion where a dahlia might grow'. But in wartime he recognized that the need for vegetables was paramount, and hoped that his regular listeners would not desert him:

> In happier days we talked of rock gardens, herbaceous borders and verdant lawns; but with the advent of war and its grim demands, these pleasant features rapidly receded into the background to make way for the all-important food crops … Presumably most of my old friends still listen when I hold forth on Leeks, Lettuces and Leatherjackets, instead of Lilac, Lilies and Lavender … These are critical times, but we shall get through them, and the harder we dig for victory, the sooner will the roses be with us again.

Cosy as he could be, he also tried to push Government policy in the right direction by suggesting that too much of the Dig for Victory effort was being concentrated on people in towns and cities, whereas country-dwellers had far more space in which to expand their output. He also acted as an adviser and writer for Boots, which then promoted itself as 'The Gardener's Chemist'. For the most part, his radio talks were a mixture of practical advice and accounts of his own recent experience, burbling gently on from one subject to another:

> I wonder how many of you have sprayed your potatoes this year? I'm afraid we didn't get much suitable weather for the job after early July, and a good many of the crops must have been missed. It's no use talking about it now, of course … I have noticed a good many white butterflies about and you know what that means – caterpillars on the brussels and other greens if something isn't done about it. I find a tennis racket a very good thing for swatting white butterflies. I'm getting quite expert at it and developing quite a good overarm stroke, but even so, you can't swat them all.

When a small book of his talks was published in 1942, it faithfully preserved the ambling gait of the broadcasts. Page after page went by without a new paragraph, which made things rather tiring for the reader; but this did nothing to deter his fans, and the book has been reprinted several times. What shines through it is the author's inexhaustible enthusiasm for all aspects of garden work, his attention to detail, and his willingness to describe even the most basic processes. His instructions for digging new ground remain precise and perfect:

> Cut each spadeful out neatly, not more than six inches at a time, drive the spade in vertically to its full length and turn it completely over, leaving it like that without chopping it up or trying to leave a neat surface; the rougher you leave autumn digging the better, with plenty of holes and spaces for the frost and snow to get into it.

It seems sad that he was shabbily treated, first by Hitler and then by the BBC, for whom he worked. His house in Surbiton was destroyed by a bomb, forcing him to go and live with relatives in Northamptonshire. When he fell ill with bronchitis, and a stand-in had to read his script, his fee was reduced; and when he put in a claim for extra petrol coupons, necessitated by his constant travelling, the BBC dismissed it as 'grabbing'. The Corporation also prevented him from taking part in the radio *Brains Trust* on the grounds that he was 'an amateur expert'. In contrast, millions of citizens were grateful for his unfailingly cheerful and practical advice – but he only just survived the war. When he died of a sudden heart attack outside his home in London on 18 September 1945, tributes, written and floral, poured in from all over Britain. The historian Philip Ziegler considered that 'he did as much as anyone to convince doubters that running an allotment was a pleasant and profitable pursuit'.

Lord Woolton's time as Minister of Food ended in November 1943, when, to his great disappointment, Churchill moved him on to become Minister of Reconstruction. But his skill in feeding the nation for three such difficult years was demonstrated by the fact that, in spite of rationing – or perhaps because of it – the population ended the war in better health than they had enjoyed before. Children were taller and heavier, and their teeth were in better condition, mainly due to the shortage of sugar and sweets. Infant mortality rates had fallen, and civilians were living longer. Hitler killed 60,000 Britons by bombing, but the war left the survivors in better shape than ever.

Nine

Girls to the Fields

End, in the language of a farm, is another word for
beginning. Work without end. Amen.

Rachel Knappett, Land Girl

Even before the onset of hostilities, the urgent need for more labour
on farms spurred the Government to resuscitate the Women's
Land Army, originally founded in 1914. In spite of its title, the WLA was
an army only in the sense of it being a large force, and its unarmed
soldiers were known as Land Girls. When the Ministry of Agriculture
put out a call for 10,000 women to work on the land, there was an
enormous response: by September 1939 more than 17,000 women had
applied. Many old rustics were sceptical, if not downright antagonistic.
Women working on the land? The idea was ridiculous, and entirely
inappropriate. Women, they said, could manage light farm work like
milking or feeding chickens or weeding crops, but they were simply not
strong enough to pitch sheaves onto a cart or control a bull or haul a
tractor out of a bog.

Ignoring insults, girls applied to join in droves – and at first there
were far more than the county committees could place: the
organization was overwhelmed by sheer numbers, and many of the
applicants had to wait months before finding a post. By November
only 1000 had gone to jobs on farms. Nevertheless, the WLA was in

being, and the army climbed rapidly to a peak strength of 80,000 in 1943.

The honorary head of the organization – its Commander-in-Chief – was the formidable Lady Denman (generally known as Trudie), pioneer of birth control, passionately keen hunting woman, first President of the National Federation of Women's Institutes, and wife of Lord Denman, former Governor-General of Australia (it was she who had named the capital of Australia Canberra at a ceremony in March 1913). The WLA was organized on a county basis, but its administrative headquarters were at the C-in-C's home, Balcombe Place, a substantial early Victorian house in Sussex.

When the fifty-strong staff arrived for the first time at Balcombe station, their train was met by a fleet of cars, including Trudie's Rolls-Royce, ready to ferry them to their new quarters; and at the house, while they waited for bedrooms to be allocated, they were refreshed with cocktails. 'Never did staff enjoy pleasanter surroundings or a friendlier atmosphere for their work,' wrote Trudie's biographer Gervas Huxley. They could swim, play tennis, darts and ping-pong, pick flowers in the garden and dance in the music room. Not surprisingly, ten days after they had arrived, Lord Denman moved out and took up residence in a hotel. But if Trudie pampered her headquarter staff, she also, like a mother hen, adopted a fiercely protective attitude towards the huge army which she had helped to create, defending the girls against attacks from misogynistic farmers on the land and hostile bureaucrats in Whitehall. She herself moved freely around the country, lending moral and administrative support to the county branches, and in 1941 she wrote to the Queen asking if she would become the Land Army's Patron – a suggestion Her Majesty accepted at once.

Joining the WLA could be a daunting experience. Having never left home before, many of the girls were apprehensive about going on long journeys, especially as they had no control over where they would be sent: they might be suddenly dispatched to the far end of the country.

September 1939: a London bobby marshals children for evacuation from the capital. To prevent parents following, they were not told where their offspring were going.

A monkey, a teddy and a doll were the only consolation for children suddenly separated from home and family. Small wonder that they looked apprehensive.

Vigilance and quick reactions were the hallmarks of the Royal Observer Corps, here depicted manning a flimsy outpost in a watercolour by Eric Ravilious, one of the official war artists.

In voice and in person, Vera Lynn was the Forces'
Sweetheart. She received a thousand letters a
week begging her to sing 'We'll Meet Again',
'The White Cliffs of Dover' and other favourites.

A formidable organizer, Trudie,
Lady Denman, commanded the
Women's Land Army, establishing
its headquarters in her own house.
Girls flocked to join, and by 1943
the organization was 80,000 strong.

Land Girls learn the ins and outs of a tractor. Confounding sceptical farmers, many became not only good drivers but also expert mechanics, able to carry out their own maintenance.

Potato-picking was one of the dirtiest and least favourite jobs cheerfully tackled by the Land Girls. The spade lugs on the tractor's rear wheels gave it a grip in soft ground, but made it hellish to drive on hard surfaces.

All hands to the harvest: threshing, with the barn-worker in the foreground and the steam engine behind, was one of the great events of the farming year.

Lumber Jills – forestry equivalents of the Land Girls – did sterling work in woods and plantations, felling trees with axes and cross-cut saws, and cutting up slender poles for pit props.

In the great drive to increase vegetable production, pea-picking and shelling were tasks for the whole family, young or old.

For people in rural Britain, the arrival of black American GIs was a revelation.

Lord Woolton, the popular Minister of Food known as 'Uncle Fred', waged continuous propaganda campaigns urging people to be thrifty, to eat sensibly and to grow more vegetables.

Gert and Daisy – in real life Elsie and Doris Waters, shown here distributing cakes to bombed-out Londoners – were immensely popular radio and stage entertainers.

'Queue, queue, queue,' one woman remembered. 'What patience and stamina we must have had!' Housewives grew so addicted to queuing that they would join a line without knowing what lay at the end of it.

Sixteen-year-old Grace Wallace, from Blackpool, abruptly found herself at Aberystwyth, on the west coast of Wales. 'I looked all around,' she remembered, 'and all I could see were hills. I felt so trapped in.'

One volunteer from Derby, who weighed only eight stone, was greeted at her destination with a blast of sarcasm. 'What have they sent *you* for?' demanded the farmer. To which she retorted, 'There's many a big potato rotten' – and when she left he apologized, admitting that she and her colleagues had worked very well.

Recruiters naturally preferred farmers' daughters, or girls who had lived on the land and understood country matters; but nearly a third came from towns and cities. Their first hurdle was an interview, and nineteen-year-old Emily Braidwood was surprised to be summoned to an office in Oxford Street, in the West End of London, where she sat in front of a lady with what she called 'a five-pound-note voice' (perhaps it was Lady Denman herself, who also had a house in London):

> She wore a beautiful silk dress, a silk scarf, and she twirled a gold pencil continuously in her long fingers as she fired a barrage of questions at me. She wanted to know if I thought it was all feeding chickens, with lovely weather. I responded: 'I have been hop-picking, you know, since the age of three.' She jumped back as if I had fleas … I left the interview thinking 'That's that.' I felt elated when I received a letter to say I had been accepted.

After the interview and a medical examination Emily was issued with her uniform – fawn-coloured aertex shirt, stout corduroy breeches with a flap-down front, dark green pullover, knee-length woollen socks, overalls, an overcoat, an oilskin and a fawn felt hat embroidered with the WLA badge. Everyone hated the breeches, partly because they were so stiff that at first the wearer could hardly sit down, but – worse – because they increased the apparent size of one's behind.

Along with a dozen other girls from all parts of England, Emily took the train to Clacton-on-Sea, where the party was met by a lady with a clipboard from the Women's Institute and sent off to various billets. Emily found herself lodging with Mrs Wagstaff, a genteel widow with three sons, in a village called Little Clacton. Mrs Wagstaff was friendly enough, but 'there was a kind of hostility in the village. Servicemen were accepted – not the Land Girls', and the girls felt that their host was brave to take them in.

Next morning they went into action. Having broken the ice on their water jugs for a wash at 6.30, they were picked up by a lorry and driven out to a distant field, where the farm foreman held up two enormous sugar beets, one in each hand, demonstrating how to bang them together to knock off the half-frozen mud. Another task was to decapitate the beets with a billhook before throwing them onto a heap. After the first hour or so there was almost a mutiny – but the girls settled down and got on with it.

Sugar beet was their most hated crop – and the horror of dealing with it was vividly described by Mary Schofield, who abandoned office life in Leeds for a farm in the plain of York:

Row upon row of wet, muddy beet, half ploughed out but still needing a good tug to free them from the sticky earth. Working backwards up a field, and pulling two rows at a time, one with each hand. Every time I took a step backwards the leaves emptied half their rainwater down the tops of my boots, and every time I pulled a couple of beet they poured water over my hands and arms and dungarees. Banging them together to remove as much of the soil as possible, of course added mud to my dungarees too.

All over England recruiting went swiftly ahead. Muriel Berzins, who worked in a grocer's shop, became convinced that she would go mad if she 'became old counting food coupons'. So when a friend came home from the WLA looking tanned and fit, she too joined – even though, being less than five feet tall, she caused great hilarity when smothered by her new uniform. Young women from towns and cities adapted with extraordinary speed, happy to cut their nails short, abandon rings and other jewellery, and sleep in wooden bunks. For day after day they weeded rows of turnips or swedes, dug drains, cut back hedges, planted potatoes and cabbages, pruned fruit trees, helped with hay and harvest, killed rats, milked cows by hand, looked after calves. Some farmers admitted that they were better than men with livestock, and that animals responded well to their gentler care – but often they became exhausted. One girl who milked twice a day in Devon would fall asleep in a chair after tea with her hands still going up and down.

Weeding in summer was regarded as not too bad a job, as several girls usually worked together and could chat as they hoed – unless the farmer deliberately set them to start at opposite ends of the field to stop them gossiping. In winter, though, the combination of cold and wet made the task exhausting. Betty Olsen, who came from Leeds but was sent to North Creake, in Norfolk, remembered how 'Gus, our foreman, used to wrap sacks round our legs and bodies, tied with string. When you got to the end of a row, you just lay on the ground, with pebbles and stones sticking into your back, waiting for the other girls to catch up.' Another demoralizing task was potato-picking, which might last for three miserable months in autumn and winter. A tractor would go along the rows with a spinner, throwing out the spuds, and the girls had to collect them by hand and toss them into buckets, working furiously to clear the row before the tractor came along again and sprayed them with earth.

To work on the land in a bevy of girls was one thing: to strike out on your own demanded even higher resolution – and no one can have been bolder than Rachel Knappett, who bicycled up to Bath Farm, in south-west Lancashire, on April Fool's Day 1940, to be confronted by 'a rather formidable array of men: the boss, the two horsemen, Bill and Billy; Tommy, Billy's younger brother, pig man, pony man and hen man; Joe the tractor driver and Barney the Irishman'. As she wrote later, 'a land girl at Bath Farm was a thing unknown', and the men were 'rendered almost speechless' by their attempt to stop swearing in her presence. In particular they struggled to curtail their habitual and constant use of 'bugger'. Once they realized that it did not offend her, they relaxed, and instead of addressing her 'in a stiff and formal manner', they called her 'Owd yeller 'ead', 'Owd Knappoo', 'The bloody wench', 'Sparrer', 'the Poot' (pullet), 'Gaupie', 'Blondie', or 'Oo' (she).

Rachel won their hearts, and they won hers, so much so that she laboured on the farm for five years, doing every conceivable job, and came to love its setting, south of Preston, in 'the great plain stretching westwards to the sea', with the 'faint, blue shapes of the Cumberland mountains shadowy and magical in the distance'. In a beautifully written book, *A Pullet on the Midden*, crackling with jokes, she recounted her experiences, and concluded that 'End, in the language of a farm, is another word for beginning. Work without end. Amen.'

Land Girls exhibited no mean stoicism. By late autumn 1940 there were 200 of them working in Kent, and at the end of November six were ploughing in a particularly dangerous coastal area. Their tractor engines were so noisy that they were oblivious of their surroundings, and only when shrapnel started falling around them, or even *on* them, clattering on metal surfaces, did they realize that a dogfight was in progress overhead. Far from asking for a transfer to somewhere safer, they simply applied for steel helmets – which they got.

Volunteers could never tell what job they might be called upon to do. A girl on a Shropshire farm milked eighty cows in the afternoons, but she was also put to drive a milk van with faulty brakes. Early one morning, in the blackout, she and her companion 'got in the middle of a tank convoy – don't ask me how'. She remembered her friend 'holding her hands in prayer and saying to Himself and her husband (who was in the Army in the Middle East), "Don't let the tank stop suddenly on this hill, cos the guns are right on a level with my ear 'ole."'

Jean Redman joined the WLA at sixteen and first worked in a market garden at Colnbrook in Berkshire, living among gypsies, who invited her into their spotless and highly decorated caravans. Then she was put in sole charge of a poultry farm at Datchet. In summer the task was easy, as the 3000 chickens spent the day in an orchard, and she could gorge on fruit; less pleasant was learning to kill, pluck and draw the birds – and her first attempt was disastrous:

It took many tries to break the neck by screwing and pulling. When that didn't work, I tried a blow on the head, and was getting more and more desperate. Eventually I thought I had killed it, and put it down on the ground, but it got up and ran drunkenly around … I was horrified, because I knew the neck was broken … I discovered later that although the bird was dead, the nerves made it react in this way.

For parties working in the fields, lunch was a couple of sandwiches – usually fish paste or cheese – and maybe a bottle of cold tea (to buy a flask they had to go through the cumbersome process of obtaining an agricultural voucher). Mabel Thomas, who was posted from Barrow-in-Furness, on the edge of the Lake District, to Letterston in Pembrokeshire ('a very long way from home'), came to loathe the beetroot sandwiches given out by the housekeeper in her hostel.

A posse in Dorset acquired a big black kettle for making tea; they would go to a nearby cottage and ask for water, but the kettle was so heavy that it took two of them to carry it when full. 'Then,' remembered Irene Johnson, a twenty-one-year-old from Leeds, 'we built a bonfire out of branches and made gipsy tea. We would boil the kettle, put in the tea leaves, put the kettle back on the fire. The leaves settled on the bottom, and the tea poured clear. I've never had tea like it since.'

One summer night in her hostel Irene was woken by a strange whistling. The sound remained a mystery until the post boy told her it was the song of a nightingale, which came to a particular copse at that time of year. A recording of a nightingale was broadcast over the radio when programmes closed down at midnight; but, having heard the bird live, Irene knew it was nothing like the real thing.

Out in the country, of course, no lavatories were available, so when girls had to answer a call of nature, it meant crouching in a hedge or ditch or behind a tractor and hoping no men put in a sudden appearance. Grace Wallace had a particularly unsettling experience: during haymaking she once inadvertently squatted over a rabbit burrow, from which the startled occupant suddenly erupted at high speed. She too bolted, and in her fright she staggered down the field with her trousers round her ankles.

In the evening the girls would be ferried back to base and given a meal; working in the open air, they developed raging appetites, but also lost weight. Their only entertainment was the local cinema, an occasional dance in the village hall, or a visit to the pub, where, because they were so poor, one half-pint had to last out the evening. The WLA had a stock of bicycles which the girls could use. Sometimes they rode them into town for dances, and returned late at night without lights, risking collisions and a fine from some lurking policeman. More often, they had to ride to work: once, at threshing time near Colchester, Emily Braidwood pedalled sixteen miles in each direction.

They worked for fifty hours a week in summer, 7.30 a.m. to 5 p.m., and forty-eight in winter, from 8 a.m. to 4 p.m., with an hour off for lunch, for a wage of £2 2s a week, with half a day off every week and sometimes a long weekend. At harvest time, when dew lay heavy on the corn until midday, they might not get started until lunchtime, and did not finish work until nine or ten at night. Because machinery was so short, they were usually issued with basic equipment – hoes, spades, scythes, billhooks – and when it came to ploughing, most of them drove horses rather than tractors. But they soon proved that they could do almost anything that men could accomplish.

Their cheerful outlook was epitomized by Iris Newbold, a shop assistant from Hull, who particularly enjoyed scything thistles on a farm at Malton, in Yorkshire. There the girls worked three or four in a row, making their way across the pastures; Iris developed a 'powerful swing and a good rhythm', but her neighbours had to jump about 'to avoid losing a foot' because she was left-handed and swung in the direction opposite to everyone else. 'I was ridiculed as a cack-handed townie and sent to the back', but 'I loved standing at the edge of the field with the long, curved blade in the air as I sharpened it with the flint stone and a bit of spit'. In the evenings she danced at the Malton Rooms to 'wonderful music from the Coldstream Guards, as they played their delightful Military Two-Steps and rousing Quicksteps'.

Living conditions varied enormously. Some girls were billeted in comfortable farmsteads, and were well fed by farmers' wives. But seventeen-year-old Edna Dallas, who had dreamed of living in 'a lovely old farmhouse', found herself along with forty other girls in a prefabricated building in the middle of a field (one of hundreds hastily built to accommodate the new workforce). The inmates slept in cubicles with double bunks, and as there were only three bathrooms, 'we often ended up four to a bath. There was no privacy, and modesty soon vanished.' The whole colony of girls was employed by the local War Ag committee, and when farmers asked for so many of them for hoeing or ditching, lorries took them out to their places of work. Another hostel for forty girls, in Worcestershire, was nothing but a converted fowl house, and the inmates each had to pay the owner, Captain J. E. Bomford, £1 a week for food and shelter.

Hard toil and basic living quarters were not the only hazards. Renée Dorras joined the WLA at the start of the war and was sent to a farm near Ross-on-Wye, but became emotionally involved with a man who had separated from his wife. As the woman was seeking reasons for a divorce, Renée felt she must leave the farm; yet she had no choice about another appointment: 'I had to go to the Board and tell them I wanted to move, and go wherever I was sent.' After a spell in a munitions factory, she joined the army and became an ambulance driver – a job which proved alarming at night, when headlights were banned: 'You could only tell something was coming past when you felt the vibrations.'

Betty Merritt, sent to work in Sussex, specialized in tractors, and became not only a skilled driver but also a proficient mechanic, able to do her own maintenance – reset the spark plugs, clean out the carburettor, grease the nipples and change the engine oil. On winter mornings her Fordson was often so frozen that it 'took a lot of muscle to get it going'; because there was no anti-freeze, she would have drained the radiator the night before, so first she had to fill it with water. If she could not rouse the engine after a struggle with the crank handle, she would sometimes 'flop over it and cry'. The occasional loan of a Ferguson, which had a self-starter, was a rare treat.

One of her fellow labourers was not a Land Girl at all, but a small black man. When she met him, he was shifting piles of manure, but she was struck by how smart he looked in his blue and orange short-sleeved shirts and khaki shorts, and by the fact that he spoke English so well. Apparently he was a university lecturer, and had been forced to stay in England when war broke out. Only much later did she discover that in 1946 he returned to his native Kenya, leaving behind an English wife and son; that in 1953 he was given a seven-year prison sentence for his alleged involvement with Mau Mau terrorists, and that in 1964 he became President of his country. His name was Jomo Kenyatta.

Sometimes girls formed themselves into mobile squads for specialized activities. One was the outstanding four-girl vermin team who rode about North Wales on bicycles dealing death and destruction to pests of all kinds. In little over a year, from February 1941 to April 1942, they accounted for 7869 rats, 1668 foxes, 1901 moles and 35,545 rabbits. Their task was made easier by the fact that they were allowed to use Cymag gas and a variety of poisons: even so, it was no mean achievement.

In a Christmas message to the Women's Land Army, the Queen thanked and saluted the girls, telling them, 'By your skill and devotion you have released great battalions of men who now fight for the land which formerly they tilled.' Echoing that royal accolade, an agricultural expert on tour reported: 'To observe them in their green pullovers, open-neck shirts and corduroy breeches, cheerfully grappling with difficult farm work, and making light of the hardships involved in it, is to reassure one's faith in the invulnerability of Britain.'

Other people fancied them for different reasons. 'Then there are the Land Girls, an unfamiliar sight in the orchards and among the cows,' wrote Vita Sackville-West in the early days of the war:

> Picturesque in their brown dungarees, tossing their short curls
> back and laughing. I came across two of them picking plums;
> very young they were, and standing under the tree loaded with
> the blood-red drops, their arms lifted, the half-filled baskets on
> the ground beside them, they could scarcely have looked
> prettier in their lives than on that sunlit morning.

Harvest was always a time of intense activity, but one girl – Daphne Cross – lamented the arrival of a Lend-Lease combine in 1942. Until then she and a farmhand, Fred Banks, had worked with 'our dear old binder', and in the evenings soldiers had helped them stook up the sheaves. 'The general feeling of fun and banter between us was all so different from the solitary work of the combine, which gradually took over and required only two people.' Another volunteer, Jean Bradley, gave herself a nasty fright when, trying to load a sheaf onto a wagon, she gave a violent upward thrust with a pitchfork and speared the hand of the man on top. She never forgot how she 'learned a whole new vocabulary in the few minutes before he was carted off to hospital'.

Later in the war disillusion began to set in. Many members of the Land Army resented the fact that they were never awarded the privileges enjoyed by other women's services. They were not granted travel warrants. They were denied cheap railway fares, as they were not working in munitions, and were not classed as war workers. They were not allowed to use NAAFI canteens. As one remarked, 'We had discipline, rules and punishments, just the same as the ATS, the WAAF and the Wrens – but no one seemed to know what we were.'

Praise for their efforts came, strangely enough, in an advertisement by the British Omnibus Company: 'They've upset a lot of old notions, have the Women's Land Army, as many farmers will admit. There would have been more tightening of belts in Britain if they hadn't.'

Every Land Girl, when she left, received a certificate of thanks from the Queen; but almost more highly valued was the strong sense of comradeship which members of the force had established among themselves. 'Everyone was away from home, but we were working with a common purpose,' said one; and another, who had spent countless days perched with three colleagues on a tractor-towed potato planter, remembered simply, 'We sang the hours away.'

No Land Girl looked back on the war with greater warmth than Mary Schofield:

I loved working with the horses far more than I ever should
with a tractor ... I am glad that I had the chance to ride on a
swaying, horse-drawn load of hay ... glad to know that I could
feel at home there; that the ways of the city are only a thin
veneer, and that underneath I belong to the country – to the

land of green fields and brown earth, of smokeless skies and wide horizons.

I have learned to love the land, as well as the people. Now I look at them with eyes which see much more than they once did, because I understand what I see. I have a deeper respect for the people and the problems they have to face … However long I live, I shall always thrill at the sight of a line of stooks up the stubble, or new lines of corn up a dark brown field, or at the touch of the soft muzzle of a horse. In spite of the work, it was a wonderful life, and I would not have missed it for anything.

In their search for extra labour, the War Ags pressed everyone they could find into gangs – alien refugees, unemployed farm workers, prisoners of war and conscientious objectors, known to all as Conchies. These motley crews were housed in fleets of caravans, and the Conchies worked on the land in ever-increasing numbers.

Anyone who objected to taking part in the war effort had to give his or her reasons before a tribunal chaired by a lawyer, usually a judge. The panel had the authority to grant full exemption from military service, or from any kind of war work, or to dismiss the application. Of the 60,000 men who applied for Conscientious Objector status, 3000 were given unconditional exemption and 18,000 were dismissed, but as the war progressed the proportion of men unwilling to serve in the armed forces fell from sixteen per thousand in March 1940 to six in a thousand after the evacuation from Dunkirk.

Neville Chamberlain, who had served on a tribunal during the First World War, was sympathetic to objectors, but most of them found life uncomfortable. Their children were cold-shouldered at school. Landlords declined to repair their houses after bomb damage. Neighbours would not speak to them, except to make disagreeable remarks, calling them cowardly, selfish, irresponsible, pro-Nazi and a danger to society: 'If everyone was like you, Hitler'd be here.'

One of the most cheerful Conchies was the writer Edward Blishen, whose father had returned from the First World War wounded, shell-shocked and unable to talk about his experiences. Teddy declined to fight, but took a positive view of life, and left a lively account of his fellow objectors' antics in his autobiographical book *A Cackhanded War*.

Sent to a flat, wet, cold farm on the Essex coast, he found the hedges overgrown, the ditches filled in and the fields full of bramble bushes. On arrival he was put straight to work. His mentor Bert – 'the fattest foreman in the world … a great quantity of waistcoats, a small cloth cap above an immense face' – handed him a blunt sickle, known as a bagging hook, and left him with the sole instruction: 'Keep low on they bushes, won't 'ee.'

The landlady who accommodated Blishen's gang had 'come under sharp fire from some quarters in the village' for taking them in, and she got her own back on the Conchies by giving them little lunch packets containing 'two sandwiches of a vague sort of meat savaged by her home-made mustard pickle … covered by a mist of green corruption'. All too often there was 'a sad burying at mid-day'; but sometimes, having learned to make fires from tiny twigs and then bigger branches, they cooked their sandwiches round a brazier.

In Blishen's memory, their work was 'all thorns and icy water'. They cut hedges and dug ditches to drain the fields for ploughing, spurred on by occasional visits from the War Ag's labour officer, whose attitude was 'one of perpetual rage'. In spite of this aggravating superintendent, Blishen came to love the ditching, getting pleasure from carving out spadefuls of clay and relishing the moment when, with the last block removed, water began to flow along a new channel. If ever he and his mates were seen standing idle, Bert would mutter, 'T'nt a bloody circus.'

Presently he fell in love with Joan Boulting, a slim, dark Land Girl with a boyish figure and her hair in 'a little cupola of a bun'. She never wore the regulation breeches, which were 'all corduroy bum', but brown linen jeans. He thought her 'a neat, lively little parcel of a girl', and when he saw her driving one of the big tractors, he 'trembled to think that anything so powerful should be in the charge of anyone so slight ... It struck me from time to time that I was rather near to wishing myself a Fordson tractor.' In summer, when the girls went into shorts, he was 'sharply shaken by this view of Joan Boulting's lean brown limbs'. When another of the girls took off her sweater, a colleague, Ralph Tarbox, 'pawed the ground like a stallion and neighed brilliantly'. At harvest time, particularly, sexual tension simmered in the fields and rickyards, and the air was as thick with innuendo as it was with dust and flying chaff.

Apart from the Land Girls, nobody liked the Conchies much. As they moved from farm to farm, soldiers who confronted them called them 'fucking yellow-bellies', and demanded to know what they were frightened of. What was the matter with them? Why did they refuse to fight? One farm bailiff, who had 'a sort of lazy, loose viciousness towards Conchies', was scarcely less offensive. As they struggled to manoeuvre the trusser – part of the threshing equipment – he remarked, 'I'd like to put *you* through that, and then the prisoners of war.' Then to a Land Girl: 'Shouldn't bend over like that, love. Not with these Conchies around. But they wouldn't know what to do, love, would they?'

In spring the Conchies sowed the fields by hand, scattering the seed as they swung in arcs. In late summer, when they cut the corn on headlands with scythes, the 'inert weight and wilful sway of the long blade' grievously endangered their unprotected shins – 'They'll have all their damn legs off, the way they're going.' Experts kept coming to stare at them: equipment officers, authorities on drainage, specialists in ploughing, specialists in the maintenance of tractors, in the use of pesticides and fertilizer ... Bert would be summoned to what looked like a board meeting in the middle of a field, only to report, 'More bloody papers.'

Like many of the Land Girls, Blishen developed a particular hatred of sugar beet, whether he was hoeing it or harvesting it in the fields or taking it to a factory. 'The sun beat down and we knew a fresh dimension of boredom,' he remembered as they hacked away with their hoes, and a newcomer to the team observed gloomily, 'Goes bloody on and on.' Beet became 'like a delirium' in Blishen's mind, and he worried that someone would make him count the roots, 'millions upon millions of them heaped in lorries, in railway trucks, in great storage bays'. How he would have hated the beet singling competition organized by the British Sugar Corporation at Coupar Angus in Fife, for which there were fifty-four entrants, two of them women.

With constant exercise he grew so fit that he was able to handle two-hundredweight sacks of wheat without trouble. His first attempt simply felled him. 'There was a horrid sensation as of a sack having gone straight through me and out the front. Then I was a heap of bones and jelly on the ground.' But in time he got the knack of settling the sack at exactly the right spot high up on his back – and with that he could go on carrying all day.

Slowly the seasons moved on. He got a new mate called Bernard who believed that the war had been caused by 'the opposition of electrons'. Italian prisoners arrived wearing green caps, crying '*Carissima!*', chanting '*O sole mio*' and throwing billets-doux out of their lorries – a development not at all to the liking of the Land Girls, who set out both 'to sharpen and to thwart' the newcomers' interest in them: 'They would posture, stare, sing boldly. They would call out encouraging remarks, and then, among themselves, and loudly, discuss their contempt for the prisoners.' To Blishen it seemed that the girls had a huge hatred of strangers: their instinct was to close ranks, even against Americans, and at times he felt that the fields were 'full of harpies'.

When it came to German prisoners, you had to be careful: if they waved at you, and you waved back, the guards might threaten to arrest you for plotting an escape. One girl, Peggy Chapman, appealed so strongly to a German called Christoph whom she met at threshing time that he made her a handsome needlework box from salvaged wood – the lid from birch, the sides from sycamore and the base from pitch pine. A geometric inlay on the lid incorporated mahogany, walnut and sycamore veneer – altogether a rare labour of love.

Ten

In the Woods

What will the axemen do,

when they have cut their way from sea to sea?

James Fenimore Cooper

In 1939 the Forestry Commission, created by Government Act of 1919, and presented in 1923 with 120,000 acres of Crown woodlands, was already a large organization. But most of its equipment was still old-fashioned, and, as on farms, horses still played a large part in timber operations. The thirty-ninth edition of *Webster's Forester's Diary and Pocket Book*, which gave the names and addresses of more than 2000 foresters, recorded that 'five horses will haul on ordinary roads about 150 feet of timber at 3 mph. A tractor will haul anything up to 220 feet of timber at 6 to 10 mph and will cover forty miles per day … With a long haul in the woods, where a tractor cannot go, and a short haul on the road, horse transport would undoubtedly be cheaper.'

News of the urgent need for timber production soon crossed the Atlantic. In September 1939 the Newfoundland Government created the Newfoundland Overseas Forestry Unit, and during the next five years 3500 volunteers came to Britain to work as fellers and loggers. Crisp instructions from Captain Jack Turner, the officer in charge, sent them on their way:

When you get instructions, carry them out at once. When the man in charge of your group tells you to do something, do it – don't argue about it … When a lot of men have to be moved a long way in a hurry, there is no place for debating societies.

Food, transport and accommodation were free, but the men earned only $2 a day, or $12 a week, and had to provide their own clothes. Each had to sign an exacting Form of Engagement, of which the first clause promised:

I shall work faithfully, industriously and efficiently in any work that forms part of a logging or sawmill operation in the United Kingdom and obey the orders of foremen, superintendents and other persons in charge of operations and generally behave in an orderly and law-abiding manner.

The term of the engagement was 'for the duration of the present war'. The volunteers were not allowed to join 'any unit of H.M. Armed Forces', and if any man's conduct was less than satisfactory, he could be 'dismissed forthwith'. If incapacitated by illness or accident, he would be returned to his home in Newfoundland free of charge.

The first of the loggers arrived in the bitter cold of January 1940: tough guys, they went straight to work in Scottish mountain forests with their axes and cross-cut saws, building log huts to give themselves temporary shelter. In the woods at Ballater on either side of the River Dee they were soon felling 3000 trees a week and hauling the trunks out to a sawmill on sledges. They lived in camps – the first at Dalcross, in Inverness-shire – and over the next five years established seventy more camps and sawmills, closing old sites and opening new ones as areas of forest were cleared. A postcard sent home by one of them, Raymond Rogers, carried a photograph showing a cluster of single-storey huts and bore the official caption 'Ministry of Labour

Instructional Centre, Cairnbaan', on the Crinan Canal in Argyll; but the sender described it as 'one of our camps'. 'I am enjoying myself to the full,' he wrote, 'only where we are now is more or less an isolated spot. Very few people except four miles away there is a "bonnie wee" village as the Scotch people say, and there are only a few people living there.'

Help in the forests came also from Down Under. In response to a request from Whitehall, the New Zealand Government sent over three companies of men from the Corps of Engineers – 645 fine specimens, who had to be single, under thirty-five, physically Grade One and at least six feet tall. They brought with them techniques and equipment well ahead of those available in Britain, and, besides felling thousands of trees, built new mills all over the south – at Bowood and Grittleton in Wiltshire, Hungerford in Berkshire, Basing Park in Hampshire, Wickwar in Gloucestershire and many other places. Formidable workers themselves – they cut down 2000 beech trees in three months – they were not impressed by the equipment in British mills, or by the refusal of Forestry Commission officials to cool circular saws with water. One exasperated New Zealander was reported to have let fly at an opposite number:

> Now look here, mate. If you turn forty-eight-inch diameter
> circular saws at a thousand rpm spindle-speed, and feed them
> at two-and-a-half inches per revolution, and butt one flitch
> after another so that you are cutting timber all day instead of
> cutting wind, you are going to have bloody hot saws which will
> fly to bits unless you run a film of water on the cutting surfaces
> all the cutting day.

The New Zealanders had one special admirer in the form of Queen Mary, who several times visited them at work. She was fascinated by the accuracy with which they could fell large trees directly onto the mark they had set, and she was deeply interested in their names, telling them that Thomson, without a 'p', probably meant that a man's ancestors came from the Scottish Lowlands. After several visits to working sites, she invited officers and other ranks to tea at Badminton House, where she was living in Gloucestershire; but when she suggested that, in view of the heat, the men might like to take off their tunics, only half responded, because the rest were wearing nothing underneath.

British forestry organizations became alarmed by the inroads the war was making into the nation's timber stocks. During or just after the First World War some 450,000 acres of trees had been felled, and now woods were again being cleared at a drastic rate: by the spring of 1945 the Minister of Agriculture, Robert Hudson, estimated that no more than a million acres of woodland were left in England, most of it young or second-rate. Conifers planted in 1920 were far from mature, but big enough to make pit props – and both the Commission and private owners began to get an unexpectedly early return on capital. Landowners with little regard for the look of the country also took advantage of the demand, and felled hardwood trees growing in the middle of their fields or in the hedges.

Some of the work was done by schoolboys sent out to forestry camps: in 1941 900 boys of fifteen or over were paid to weed and clean young plantations, as well as to cut and peel pit props. Older boys were allowed to fell small trees and do snedding – the removal of low branches in plantations.

Toiling in parallel with men and boys were the Lumber Jills, who, as members of the Women's Forestry Service (a branch of the Women's Land Army), worked in woods and plantations with no less skill and energy than their equivalents on farms. They learned how to handle heavy axes, sliding the upper hand down the shaft to increase the momentum of each stroke, and to use long, cross-cut saws, with one girl pulling on either end as they felled trees and cut them up for pit props, railway sleepers or telegraph poles. Like farming, forestry always meant hard labour. Cross-cut sawing, exhausting even for men, demanded tremendous stamina from girls. In one yard, even though the circular saw was driven by a steam engine, water for the boiler had to be hauled by horse and cart from a standpipe three-quarters of a mile away.

The girls also managed horses for timber extraction, and turned their hands to charcoal-burning and other woodland tasks. At lunch-time in winter, when it was snowing, they built bonfires with small branches and baked potatoes in the embers as they sat round eating their sandwiches. Rosalind Elder, posted to Advie, a small village in Strathspey, learned all the skills and lived in wooden huts, lit by Tilley lamps and heated by wood-burning stoves. Several of the girls were injured, but she and her comrades became 'well-seasoned lumber jills', able to hold their own with 'any man in the woods'.

After a year in the WLA, seventeen-year-old Pamela Richards went to work in the Timber Corps at Oakhampton, in Devon, where she was billeted at a house out in the country and had to walk home at night past an American camp. Although small and slight, she soon became adept at felling trees with a 7-lb axe; but one day she got hers wedged in a trunk just as her neighbour yelled 'Tim-BER!' – too late. The neighbouring tree hit Pamela's, and nearly killed her.

Maggie Dixon, a Lumber Jill sent to Shropshire, found herself sawing pit props in a gang that included a Russian from London and a beautiful Lithuanian girl who won the Most Lovely Eyes contest at the local fête. When heavy rain turned the woodland floor into a bog, a railway track was laid, and a small engine appeared, together with some trucks. Her friend Marjorie volunteered to drive it, and Maggie became her mate. Then Americans arrived, 'preceded by horror stories from other parts of Shropshire, where many girls had had babies by these better dressed and richer men'. Here, however, they were very well behaved, 'especially the black ones who were good dancers and very pleasant'.

Another spirited and resourceful Yorkshire lass, Barbara Beddow, worked in many parts of the kingdom. In 1939 she married a boy she had known at school. When by cruel chance he was killed by a cross-Channel shell which landed in a barracks in Dover in September that year, she joined the Land Army – to her mother's horror – and was sent to the Forestry Training College in the Forest of Dean. At her first job at Fearby, in North Yorkshire, the village wives were 'very suspicious and not at all friendly', and locals regarded her and her fellow girls as 'beings from another planet'. In Markington she stayed with a family whose mum was having fun with army lads: someone wrote to her husband, who came home and chased her with Barbara's axe.

Next, on the Swinton estate, she did timber-measuring, and lodged for a while on the bank of the River Yore, in a beautiful house owned by a woman who suffered from sleeping sickness, but nevertheless was a man-eater. 'Her men ate all our rations,' Barbara remembered, 'but she had a boat on the river, and we had many midnight parties.' Promoted to forewoman-in-charge, she was sent to the New Forest to find and extract a shrub called alder buckthorn (*Rhamnus frangula*), which in peacetime was worked by gypsies. Having settled into digs in Carlton, she was given a hut as an office, and placed in charge of twelve girls sent straight from home, who worked in an open-fronted wooden shed, soaking the bark off buckthorn branches and drying it on sheets of corrugated iron heated over fires. Sacks of bark went off to be made into *Cascada segrada* (a natural laxative), and the wood was turned into best-quality charcoal for the manufacture of gunpowder, particularly for use in time fuses, because of its even burn rate. In their off-duty moments the girls watched herons fishing and went rabbiting with ferrets.

Married again, Barbara returned to Yorkshire, to work at Foggathorpe, in the East Riding, and again she was given an amazing amount of responsibility. She and her colleagues walked to work and clear-felled two twelve-acre woods – but, as she said, 'it was only small stuff, so the girls managed'. She had no supervision except a visit from a manager every three months, and although she had never been given any financial training or done office work, she had to manage her team's pay. When money came through the post office, she placed it in a bank account and handed it out as appropriate.

Some of her tree-fellers, who were on piece work, could not read or write, but they could always calculate their earnings to a penny. They also understood the use of pit props and larger timbers in the mines, and knew that straight softwood trees like larches, marked with a circle of white paint, were to become telegraph poles, thousands of which were needed to carry telephone lines to new military camps and airfields, or to obstruct farmland on which enemy gliders might try to land.

Looking back on her career in the forests, Barbara concluded that some older citizens saw the Lumber Jills as a threat, bringing a challenge to their own young people, and that younger people were jealous of the girls' itinerant autonomy: 'We were probably seen as a bit wild and a bit too free.' Whatever people thought of them, Land Girls and Lumber Jills emerged from the war not just physically robust, but mentally and emotionally strengthened as well. They had seen what they were capable of, and had gained a new outlook on life.

Women took on many other jobs which they would not have dreamed of tackling before the war. Those who became volunteer ambulance drivers as members of the ARP needed strong nerves, for they were required not only to drive with masked headlights during night raids, but also to clear up the remains of people caught in bomb blasts. After minimal training, which often concentrated on double-declutching (but no formal test), they went on duty in pairs: a driver and her attendant, another woman. Theoretically they worked in three shifts – eight hours on, eight hours on standby (reporting for duty if the sirens sounded) and eight hours off; but in practice air raids made mockery of their schedules and they were sometimes on the go for days and nights on end.

Their vehicles, kept under corrugated-iron shelters, often in school playgrounds, were large saloon cars with the rear bodywork cut off and replaced by a canvas hood which could be rolled back: they carried no medical equipment, and their sole function was to ferry injured people to the nearest casualty station or hospital. Whenever a major air raid began, each crew drove out of town to a prearranged rendezvous in the country, often a garage on a main road, to await orders. They were not supposed to pick up bodies, but if the mortuary ambulance was fully occupied, they often had to wrap corpses in their blankets and take them in – and then clean out their vehicle. Their work was particularly tough in winter, when snow was lying and they needed chains fitted round the rear tyres to negotiate hills: they were not allowed to drive with chains on tarmac, and one woman remembered having to fit them and take them off seventeen times in a week. Not all the hazards that beset them were natural: investigation of a boiling radiator once revealed that children had topped it up with sand.

Still more intrepid were the women who flew new aircraft from factories to RAF airfields all over the country. At first there was much disapproval, especially during the Phoney War, when regular RAF pilots were sitting around with nothing to do. The editor of *Aeroplane* magazine declared that women, many of whom were too stupid even to scrub a hospital floor properly, were a menace at the controls of a fighter or a bomber; and readers agreed that it was disgraceful to employ them in such a dangerous role. The pilots thought otherwise. They were exhilarated by flying, and by the knowledge that they were doing an essential job. They started on little Tiger Moths, dozens of which had to be flown to Scotland for storage – and every journey was a marathon, as Lettice Curtis remembered:

> It was a ghastly journey in winter in those little, light planes. It was about four hops up there. When you arrived, you got straight on a night train, and sometimes when you got back

there was another one waiting for you, and off you'd go again for a whole night and a day.

Lettice remained undaunted when the engine of her Typhoon cut out and she came down in a field at 100mph. 'The aircraft turned over and the tail broke off. I was lucky, but I was knocked about a bit on my face and leg.'

Later, when the factories were churning out huge numbers of new planes, and the RAF was desperately short of pilots, nobody minded *who* moved new aircraft, whether 'you were a man, woman or monkey', and the girls delivered Spitfires, Hurricanes and Oxfords – but navigation was by no means easy:

The main problems were weather and balloons. You could never fly straight from one place to another, because all the big towns had their balloon barrage. You had to find out where the balloons were in advance, but you weren't allowed to mark them on your map, so you had to remember. You studied the master map before you took off, and you did your best to memorize any special features such as roads or railways ... You had to keep below cloud, looking at the ground, and you jolly well had to know where you were ... [But] you did have some fabulous flights, taking a Spit up to Prestwick.

After the war Lettice realized, like the Land Girls, how much the experience had changed the flying women's existence and broadened their outlook. 'Girls where I came from, who would have just lived in one small village all their lives, were called up and went into the world to join the forces.'

* * *

Notwithstanding the Land Girls' contempt, the number of prisoners working on the land increased rapidly in 1943. At first most of the foreign labourers were Italians, captured in North Africa, but later, as the Allies drove deep into Europe, there came an ever-increasing flood of Germans, who were graded into four categories. Grade A were deemed anti-Nazi and graded White; Grade B (Grey) were thought tolerable, but less reliable; Grade C (Black) probably embraced Nazi ideals, and Grade C+ definitely did. The blacker they seemed, the further north they were sent. The last two categories were housed in secure camps in remote areas, but the others lived in camps insecurely surrounded by barbed wire, and quite a few escaped, only to be caught within a few days.

The biggest breakout, made through a tunnel, came early in the morning of 11 March 1945, when fifty-six officers got out of the Island Farm camp at Bridgend, in South Wales. All were recaptured: some had gone only a few miles, but others had managed to reach Southampton, having made their way through 150 miles of enemy territory. To frustrate rescue attempts, possibly by paratroopers, prisoners were not told where they were, and the names of camps were frequently changed.

Many of the young Grade A Germans came from farming families and were content to work on the land, greatly preferring a tough but safe life in the English countryside to one of constant danger on the continental battlefields. They went out into the country wearing brown uniforms, each with a big purple triangle dyed on the back of his tunic, allegedly to make a good aiming mark for the armed soldier in charge, should anyone try to run away; but country people often befriended them, if only through occasional meetings along the way.

Work on the land was relatively safe in the middle or west of the country; but in the south-east and east the hazards were greater. One day during the harvest of 1943 young Malcolm Rees was perched on the mudguard of a Fordson tractor, on the lookout for rabbits as it towed the binder round and round a field of corn. Suddenly he heard an earth-shaking *thud*, and smashing through the tops of a line of trees came a stricken four-engined American Liberator:

> The bomber flew right over us, casting us in its dark shadow as it soared only a few feet above our heads. Then it hit the ground and slid on the harvest field, its propellers bent back by the force of the crash landing. Suddenly it spun round, and this huge monster of aluminium and steel stood still. From its belly appeared men in khaki over-suits and fur-lined caps, and they raced off towards the ditch on the edge of a wood. Staying close to the wheel of the tractor, we prayed that the plane would not explode.

Running for home to spread the news, Malcolm met a huge American recovery truck whose black driver scooped him up into the cab as a guide, and they sped back to the wreck across country. It turned out that the mighty thump had been caused by the plane's undercarriage hitting a road: the impact had bounced it back into the air and sent it through the tree tops. The crew were unhurt – and the boy and his friends were rewarded by being allowed to play in the cockpit and the gun turrets.

Just as the Women's Land Army sprang from the initiative of Lady Denman, so another invaluable wartime body, the Women's Royal Voluntary Service, was the creation of another energetic woman, Stella, Marchioness of Reading, widow of the former Viceroy of India. Set up in 1938, the WVS was at first intended to be no more than a back-up to local authorities in time of war, but, thanks to the persuasive advocacy of its founder, by August 1939 more than 300,000 women had joined the new organization and a thousand WVS centres had been set up. Their original role – of helping other civilian services during air raids – quickly expanded in many directions: they set up canteens for firefighters and others, cooked in mobile wagons, provided hot baths for soldiers in camps, made camouflage nets, refashioned old clothes, brewed tea for grave-diggers, staffed makeshift hostels and sometimes even acted as marriage brokers – all without pay. Their relationship with the WI was uneasy, and there were frequent disagreements about what responsibilities each organization should take on. Yet the volunteers, in their bottle-green uniforms, lived up to their motto, 'The WVS never says no', and accomplished an amazing amount. Looking back after the war, Lady Reading reflected: 'We have done work we never thought to approach and have carried burdens heavier than we knew existed.'

Eleven

Laying Up Treasure

Bury them in the bowels of the earth,
but not one picture shall leave this island.
Winston Churchill, 1940

The threat and outbreak of war led to a prodigious amount of secret excavation, some small-scale, some immense. Government agencies, military units, individuals – all began digging frantically in attempts to commit their most valuable assets to the safety of the ground before they were destroyed by bombs or fell into the hands of an invading enemy. The burrows made in 1939 and 1940 by, or for, the men of Auxiliary Units, who would go to ground if the Germans came, were so well concealed that even people living close to them never knew of their existence. But those excavations were like mouse holes compared with the huge subterranean projects in train elsewhere.

In 1934 teams of Royal Engineer officers had been sent out to survey possible sites for the underground storage of ammunition, inspecting and assessing obsolete railway tunnels, limestone quarries, slate quarries, gypsum quarries and worked-out salt mines which seemed capable of adaptation. The most promising was the huge network of abandoned workings south-west of Corsham, in Wiltshire, which for seventy-five years had been yielding high-quality oolite limestone. There in the mid-1930s the War Office bought four quarries – Ridge,

Tunnel, Eastlays and Monkton Farleigh, covering 150 acres in all – which over the next few years were reconstituted as the Central Ammunition Depot.

The task of converting the old diggings was immense. Because the galleries were so cramped, it took 12,000 men working mostly by hand four years to clear two million tons of rubble out of the Tunnel Quarry alone – and the workings had to be strengthened with new support pillars and steel roof girders, before lifts, conveyor belts, narrow-gauge railways and ventilation systems could be introduced. From 1940 until the end of the war and beyond, vast quantities of munitions were stored beneath Wiltshire. Contemporary photographs show staff handling bombs, shells, mines and cases of ammunition without any protective clothing – not even gloves or overalls. In 1940 yet another use was found for part of the Corsham complex, when an underground operations centre was built for No. 10 Group of RAF Fighter Command in Brown's Quarry, north of the Tunnel and connected to it.

Elsewhere, new facilities were created by burying them, rather than by hollowing out existing cavities. In 1938, for instance, the Air Ministry bought a disused limestone quarry near the village of Harpur Hill, on the outskirts of Buxton in Derbyshire, and filled in the 100-foot-deep excavation with a single-storey structure of parallel arched tunnels cast from reinforced concrete, topped by a forty-foot layer of loose rock to protect it from bombs. Standard-gauge trains carrying ammunition could roll right into the depot and unload in safety.

At much the same time the Admiralty commissioned a new mine-storage depot at Trecwn, in a secluded valley three miles south of Fishguard, where two groups of tunnels were bored into the rock on opposing hillsides and lined with concrete. Fifty-eight cavernous chambers, each about 200 feet long, led off them, and to minimize manual handling (and so reduce the risk of accidents) munitions were distributed around the site on a specially designed narrow-gauge railway, with rails made of copper to reduce the risk of sparks; as a further safety precaution two reservoirs were built, one on either side of the valley, with the water supply connected to high-pressure hydrants in the storage chambers (all reservoirs were placed off limits for the duration of the war, to reduce the risk of sabotage). The construction of the site was such a huge undertaking, in a remote location, that the Ministry of Defence built three new housing estates for its workforce; but one of its advantages was that it lay only a short distance from the ports on the Welsh coast.

Any place in which large quantities of mines, bombs, explosives and small-arms ammunition were stored was obviously at risk, and although elaborate precautions were taken to forestall accidents, disasters did occur. At Llanberis, in Snowdonia, an RAF bomb depot was built in the bottom of an old slate quarry on the same principle as at Harpur Hill, except that it had two layers of arched concrete tunnels, one above the other, instead of one, with a forty-foot covering of loose slate rubble on top, for protection from air attack. A standard-gauge railway line ran into the depot, so that ammunition trains could pull in and be unloaded inside, and electric lifts raised bombs from the platform to the upper storey. Unfortunately, the structure proved disastrously weak. The depot was completed in January 1941, but on 25 January 1942 the ceiling of the lower tier collapsed, burying an entire train and trapping 14,000 tons of high-explosive bombs. There was no detonation, but it took more than a year to recover the ordnance.

At least that accident did not rearrange the local landscape – which is more than can be said of the disaster which overtook the Fauld gypsum mine at Tutbury, near Burton-on-Trent in Staffordshire. There the RAF had established its main storage depot in two areas of disused subterranean workings, either side of a central pillar of dark-red gypsum – a core of undisturbed rock, which had been left in place to support Castle Hayes farmhouse and buildings, on the surface ninety feet above. The depot contained thousands of tons of bombs, shells, cordite and dynamite, and 500 million rounds of small-arms ammunition, stored in bays and bunker passages twelve feet high and twenty feet wide – broad enough for trucks to drive along beside the piled stocks of ordnance.

At 11.11 on the morning of 27 November 1944 one mistake underground precipitated the largest non-nuclear detonation the world had ever known. Black smoke and flames shot thousands of feet into the air. Two million tons of rock, earth and exploding bombs were hurled skywards. Upper Castle Hayes Farm, directly above the seat of the blast, evaporated, along with its six human inhabitants, its animals and its wagons. At Hanbury Fields Farm, a short distance to the west, the house and buildings were shattered by falling debris, which included lumps of earth weighing a ton or more. There was widespread damage in surrounding villages. The Cock Inn in Hanbury, half a mile from the blast, had one wall blown out and was left a tottering wreck. The dam of a reservoir was obliterated, releasing six million gallons of water and a torrent of mud which swamped the local plaster factory, killing several of its workmen. Two church steeples were cracked, and one had to be dismantled. As the debris settled, it left a carpet of dust up to four inches thick, so that people walked in a deathly hush.

The explosion left a twelve-acre crater 300 yards long, 230 wide and 380 feet deep. Seventy people were killed, including civilians and Italian prisoners of war who had been working on the site, but eighteen of the dead were never recovered. The whole area was littered with the corpses of cattle and horses: some 200 cows were killed and many injured. One was found dead on its feet: air pressure had inflated it to dreadful dimensions, and when rescuers discovered it looking grotesquely swollen, they immediately shot it, only to find that it had already expired, and that all that had kept it standing were its rigid, pumped-up legs.

The cause of the blast was never precisely established, but it was thought that, in trying to remove a detonator from a 4000-lb bomb, an inexperienced airman had used a brass hammer instead of a wooden one, and that the impact on his chisel had caused a fatal spark. The only positive circumstance was that natural barriers of rock, still intact underground, had saved two-thirds of the munitions from exploding, and only one third of the stocks had gone up.

Plans to save the nation's art treasures had been laid well before the outbreak of war. In 1935 the Museums and Galleries Air Raids Precautions Committee had drawn up a list of large country houses, in areas thought to be beyond the range of German bombers, whose owners were willing to accommodate pictures and other artefacts if they had to be evacuated from the capital. Then, in 1938, Martin Davies, Assistant Keeper at the National Gallery, made a reconnaissance of possible repositories, keeping acerbic notes about the properties he visited. 'The owner is nice, ruled by his wife, a tartar, anxious to have N[ational] G[allery] pictures instead of refugees or worse … Owner seems obliging but in a haughty way.'

Some contents of the British Museum, it was decided, would go to the Duke of Buccleuch's palatial Boughton in Northamptonshire, some to Drayton House, the crenellated home of the Stopford-Sackville family in Northamptonshire, and some to the Clifford family's medieval Skipton Castle in Yorkshire. Pictures from the National Gallery would be sent to Penrhyn Castle, to Caernarvon Castle, and also to the Pritchard-Jones Hall in the University College of North Wales at Bangor; smaller pictures were destined for a tunnel repository near the National Library of Wales at Aberystwyth, which also accommodated some of the most valuable books from the Royal Horticultural Society's library at Wisley. Artefacts from the Victoria and Albert Museum were allocated to Montacute House, the Elizabethan mansion in south Somerset, one of the first properties acquired by the National Trust, which had plenty of space, as it was scarcely furnished. Pictures from the Tate Gallery were assigned to various destinations in Cumberland, Herefordshire and Worcestershire. The artworks would travel most of the way by train, and at night, before being transferred to container or flat-bed lorries for the last stages of their journeys.

In the evening of 29 September 1938, at the height of the Munich crisis, the first consignment – two containers of paintings – was taken from the National Gallery to Camden goods station and loaded onto a train equipped with a special coded array of lights on the front of the engine that would identify it to officials down the line. The train reached Bangor at nine o'clock next morning, but during the night Chamberlain had signed the Munich agreement with Hitler, and the danger of war seemed to have been averted – so back to London the pictures came, without ever being unloaded.

The major dispersal of treasures took place just before the human evacuation of cities, starting in the last week of August 1939 and ending on the day before war was declared. Some 6000 pictures were taken out of London, minus their frames, and for the time being pictures and artefacts were safely stored in new homes. When the immediate threat of bombing receded, many were returned to London. Those that remained in the country, however, began to cause problems, as stately home owners resented the expense incurred by acting as the nation's guardians: they found themselves having to provide extra heating to keep paintings at the right temperature, and – worse – to entertain, at their own expense, experts who came down from London to carry on their normal work of cataloguing and maintenance. In the words of the subterranean expert Neil McCamley,

> To their horror, the property owners found that the museum
> and gallery trustees expected these staff members to be treated
> as country house guests – as if on a weekend retreat – that free
> accommodation should be provided for them and that the
> family servants should wait upon them.

Of all the owners, the most tiresome was the fifth Baron Penrhyn. At his immense, neo-Norman castle in North Wales the largest pictures had been stored in the garages, which still had the big doors needed for horse-drawn carriages and could take in even the tallest – Van Dyck's portrait of Charles I on horseback, which is thirteen feet high – but some of the smaller canvases had been stacked on edge in the dining room and elsewhere. The castle was felt by many visitors to be pulsating with ghosts – sinister dark shapes flitting along corridors, sensations of icy cold in some rooms – and perhaps it was these that drove his lordship to the bottle. At any rate, the National Gallery staff found him insufferable – witness a letter from Martin Davies to Kenneth Clark, his Director in London, written in the spring of 1940:

> For your most secret ear: one of our troubles at Penrhyn Castle is that the owner is celebrating the war by being fairly constantly drunk. He stumbled with a dog into the Dining Room [where 200 pictures were stored] a few days ago; this will not happen again. Yesterday he smashed up his car, and, I believe, himself a little, so perhaps the problem has solved itself for the moment.

Friction with the owners was disagreeable, but infinitely more dangerous was the swift advance of Hitler's armies to the Channel coast in the summer of 1940. All at once German bombers, flying from captured airfields, became able to reach any part of the United Kingdom. Even North Wales might not be safe, for Liverpool and Manchester were high among the Luftwaffe's targets. A new plan was suggested: that the National Gallery's pictures should be evacuated to Canada – but Clark disliked the idea, because so many ships were being sunk by U-boats in the Atlantic; and when he put the proposal in a memorandum to the Prime Minister, it was roundly dismissed. Back came a note in red ink, the same day: 'Bury them in the bowels of the earth,' wrote Churchill, 'but not a picture shall leave this island. W.S.C.'

The only way to render works of art impervious to bombs was to store them underground, and a search for possible sites in tunnels, caves and mines brought up two leading contenders: Westwood, an immense, disused stone quarry south of Bath, and Manod, an old slate quarry far to the north in the wilds of Snowdonia.

Part of Westwood had already been cleared of rubble and used as a mushroom farm, but now a separate area of 25,000 square feet was developed to make a secure repository for objects from the British Museum and the V & A. The stone walls were treated with a sealing compound to repel damp, and air conditioning was installed to maintain the correct degree of humidity. Persistent stories claimed that the Crown Jewels were stored at Westwood, but the rumour has never been confirmed, and the jewels' wartime whereabouts have never been revealed. From the V & A came carpets, tapestries, furniture and a large collection of watercolours. The Elgin Marbles had already been consigned to the obsolete Aldwych tube tunnel in central London, but many of the British Museum's other priceless artefacts went to Westwood, including Greek and Roman statues; and at one point J. C. Gadd, Keeper of Egyptian and Assyrian antiquities, amused himself by inscribing on the wall of his office a memorial in cuneiform, which, being translated, read:

In the year of our Lord 1942
The Sixth year of George, King of all lands,
In that year everything precious,
The works of all the craftsmen
Which from palaces and temples
Were sent out, in order that by fire
Or attack by an evil enemy they might not be lost,
Into this cave under the earth
A place of security, an abode of peace,
We brought them down and set them.

Of all the sites chosen, the most impregnable was the Manod slate quarry in Snowdonia, with its entrance 1700 feet up on the slopes of Manod Mawr, approached by a narrow road that wound up for four miles through the mountain wilderness. Nearly a hundred years earlier, a horizontal level, or entrance tunnel, had been driven through layers of hard slate rock, and inside a series of huge caverns had been excavated, some of them 100 feet high, protected by a natural roof of rock nearly 300 feet thick. One of the chambers was so vast that it was nicknamed 'the Cathedral'.

An immense amount of work was needed to make the quarry suitable for its new role, the first task being to increase the size of the entrance from a six-foot square to an opening thirteen feet six inches high by ten feet wide. Inside, the floor was levelled by removing 5000 tons of slate rock, and the headroom of the entrance tunnel was increased to allow lorries to drive in for a quarter of a mile to a transit shed.

Outside the mine, one essential modification was made to a railway bridge near what Clark called 'the hellish town of Blaenau Ffestiniog', once the Slate Capital of Wales, where the surface of the road had to be lowered by two and a half feet so that lorries carrying the biggest pictures could pass beneath the arch. What looked at first like a simple task – the cutting away of some rock – turned out to be more complicated, as the pillars of the bridge were found to be resting on shale, and deep concrete footings were needed to support them.

After various delays, the refurbishment of the mine was not completed until the beginning of August 1941, and only then did the first pictures arrive, brought by lorry from their temporary resting places in Bangor, Caernarvon and Aberystwyth. Photographs show the immense triangular crate known as 'the Elephant Case', containing *Charles I on Horseback* and *The Raising of Lazarus*, poised precariously on the back of an ancient looking truck as it crawls through the stony wilderness. In spite of the alterations to the Ffestiniog railway bridge, the crate jammed on the underside of the arch, and the driver had to reverse and make another approach. Only when he let down all his tyres did the irreplaceable cargo squeeze past – as Clark himself described it, 'grinding under, scraping over, the huge packing case passed through'. On the final approach, up the narrow road, precise timing of journeys was needed, for there were no passing places, and if two heavily laden vehicles had met head-on, one of them might have had to back for miles.

Inside the mine, paintings were unloaded from lorries in the transit shed and moved to their assigned places along a narrow-gauge railway by men pushing and pulling high-sided wagons or a specially built bogie seventeen feet long. Because the mine was exceedingly damp, six separate brick buildings with concrete roofs had been constructed inside it to house the pictures, each with its own air conditioning to control temperature and humidity. The system was primitive: electric fans blew air over trays of dehydrated silica gel, which absorbs moisture, and when the trays became saturated, they were taken away and dried out in a row of domestic electric ovens. Laborious though it was, the process effectively prevented the growth of mould, and the inner buildings were maintained at sixty-five degrees Fahrenheit and 42 per cent humidity – an atmosphere which proved as good as that in the National Gallery itself. Since oil paint and tempera tend to degenerate if deprived of light, low-level illumination had to be maintained for twenty-four hours a day, and a powerful diesel generator proved a crucial back-up investment, as the mains electricity often failed in bad weather.

The main drawback of the air conditioning was that the reduction in humidity threatened to destabilize the roofs of the caverns, which were inspected frequently by safety men who went up long, extending ladders kept in position by other workers holding ropes, and tapped at the rock with hammers. The sound revealed the state of the roof at that point: if tapping produced a hollow sound, it meant that the area was unstable – in which case loose rock could be dislodged deliberately, or holes could be drilled and the dangerous area pinned to firmer rock above, with chains slung beneath suspect patches to give further protection.

In spite of constant vigilance, on 9 March 1943 a heavy fall smashed through the rear wall of Building No. 2 and damaged some of its contents. 'One Poussin torn but repairable stop,' Davies cabled London. 'One Ruisdael slightly damaged stop trivial scratches on three others stop building now being cleared of its contents stop.' The incident alarmed officials of the National Gallery so much that they prepared plans for removing the whole collection from the quarry; but they were reassured by positive reports from civil engineers. The pictures stayed put, and no more major rockfalls occurred.

Throughout the rest of the war the Gallery maintained a staff of fifteen men at Manod, and two picture restorers worked away, cleaning and repairing, in a daylight studio constructed near the entrance to the mine. But the hero of the mine was Martin Davies, who, Kenneth Clark remembered,

> had always been a solitary character, and was said by his contemporaries in Cambridge to have emerged from his rooms only after dark; so this sunless exile was not as painful to him as it would have been to a less unusual man. In the morning he would emerge, thin and colourless as a ghost, and would be driven up to the caves, carrying with him a strong torch and several magnifying glasses. With these he would examine every square millimetre of a few pictures.

The wisdom of moving the pictures to Wales was demonstrated again and again: between October 1940 and April 1941 the National Gallery was hit by bombs nine times, the worst attack coming on 12 October 1940, when high explosive destroyed the room in which paintings by Raphael had hung. In spite of the danger, the dauntless pianist Myra Hess gave lunchtime recitals which became immensely popular, creating an oasis of calm and beauty amid the horrors of war. One of her most enthusiastic supporters was Joyce Grenfell, who came to the Gallery again and again to make sandwiches for performers and audience alike.

While the nation's treasures went to ground in caves and cellars, many householders buried their own in garden, orchard or field. Like hundreds of others the Earl of Limerick (a veteran of Gallipoli and the Western Front in the First World War) became convinced that invasion was imminent and decided to safeguard some of the family's valuables. At home in Sussex he and his wife, who was Deputy Chairman of the British Red Cross, wrapped necklaces, bracelets and rings in oilcloth, packed them in a small brass box and buried it one evening in a woodland garden several hundred yards from the house. To define the position of the cache he composed a verse which he made his son Patrick (then nine) and daughter Anne (seven) learn by heart:

> Young, by a roundish pond, a cypress stood;
> North-east its stream, and in a little wood
> East of this pond a dyke's north end is seen –
> Eight yards north-east of this we all have been.
> A little bridge of sleepers lies across
> A winter runlet, twenty-four yards' course.
> Due west of this our cypress lies, and there,
> At three feet south its foot, the ground is fair.

Many months went by before the family returned in search of their jewels. In the summer of 1940 Patrick, Anne and their small brother Micky were packed off to stay with cousins in America, and they did not return to England until September 1943. The elder children remembered the poem, but it was only in the summer holidays of 1944, with all fear of invasion gone, that they returned to the hiding place. They were disconcerted to find that the young cypress had grown several feet in their absence, and that near it were signs of disturbance. But the digger turned out to have been only a rabbit, and they recovered their little hoard intact.

Twelve

White Elephants

The stately homes of England
How beautiful they stand,
To prove the upper classes
Have still the upper hand.
Noël Coward, 'The Stately Homes of England'

While bombs hurtled down on cities and industrial sites, and battle raged in the sky above southern England, another long-drawn-out struggle was in progress – on the land – to save country houses, long regarded as one of the nation's glories, which were in mortal danger.

In 1914–18, when the average survival time of a subaltern on the Western Front in France was three months, the fighting had claimed the heirs apparent of countless estates. After the Great War such premature losses were compounded by ever-rising death duties, which rose to 40 per cent on estates worth over £200,000 in 1919, to 60 per cent in 1939, and to 90 per cent in the 1940s. These swingeing increases put landed owners under such strain that in the years between the wars the countryside became a white elephants' graveyard, with houses being demolished or burnt down at a terrible rate. The Second World War inevitably accelerated the decline – and as Evelyn Waugh remarked in an introduction to *Brideshead Revisited*, 'It seemed then that the ancestral seats which were our chief national artistic achievement were doomed to decay and despoliation like the monasteries in the sixteenth century.'

Big country houses, isolated from unwelcome contact with outsiders by their parks and surrounding estates, made ideal centres for clandestine military activities. During the mid-1930s the Government had carried out a covert survey of buildings that might be taken over for national use in the event of war; owners were not warned that their properties had been earmarked, and now, in 1939, many were given only a week's notice to quit. Some, at their wits' end in the search for money or servants, were positively glad when the Government requisitioned their homes for occupation by the army, the RAF, a Government Ministry, a hospital or a school evacuated from a danger area.

'Even the most unmanageable white elephant of a mansion is now securely harnessed to the wartime machine,' reported *Country Life* at the end of September. 'Indeed, the more rooms and wings and outhouses a residence possesses, the more desirable it has seemed' – an observation which made no acknowledgement of the fact that military personnel were usually careless and philistine, and often riotous after dinner, with a propensity for smashing up, or even setting fire to, their gracious accommodation.

The most active predator was Special Operations Executive, known as SOE, the sabotage and guerrilla-warfare organization charged by Churchill with the task of 'setting Europe ablaze' by sending in men and women to train, arm and generally encourage resistance movements in occupied territories. For its own training establishments and experimental stations in Britain SOE took over so many country houses that its initials were soon said to stand for Stately 'Omes Executive.

Most of the bases were in the Home Counties, and arguably the grandest was Audley End House, palatial home of the Braybrooke family near Saffron Walden, south of Cambridge. Now much reduced in size, but still vast, it was once a royal palace, owned from 1668 until

1701 by King Charles II, who valued it for its proximity to the races at Newmarket. In 1940 the eighth Lord Braybrooke suggested that the military might take it over, but his offer was rejected – only for the Government to requisition the house in March 1941. After being put to various other uses, it became STS 43, training headquarters for the Polish branch of SOE – and it was lucky to survive, for the Poles laid explosive booby traps all round the grounds – even going so far as to pack an Adam bridge with explosives – in case the enemy should make a sudden appearance.

Nefarious activities flourished in and around numerous other large country properties. At Wanborough Manor, the Elizabethan country house on the Hog's Back in Surrey (Special Training School No. 5), SOE recruits received their initial instruction, not least in unarmed combat and silent killing. Brickendonbury Manor in Hertfordshire became STS 17, a school for saboteurs. The eighteenth-century, redbrick Chicheley Hall (STS 46) in Buckinghamshire housed Czech trainee parachutists. At Brockhall (STS 1) in Northamptonshire the celebrated Sergeant Harry Court taught recruits how to maim rather than kill Germans, his point being that crippled enemy took more looking after than dead ones. Arisaig House in Inverness-shire (STS 21) specialized in Commando techniques, and at Station XV, the Thatched Barn, a mock-Tudor roadhouse at Borehamwood in Hertfordshire, trainees were taught to make explosive devices such as bicycle pumps which blew up when used normally.

All these establishments contributed powerfully to the Allied cause. Yet there were two country properties which did more than all the others to turn the tide of war. One was Danesfield House, which looks out over the Thames from a plateau above the river between Marlow and Henley; and the other was Bletchley Park, in the gentle farming country of Buckinghamshire.

Danesfield, a huge wedding cake of a building, described by one inmate as 'a pretentious edifice of whitish-grey stone, with castellated towers and fancy brick chimneys', was of little interest to organizations like the National Trust or the Society for the Preservation of Ancient Buildings; for although its site had been inhabited since Neolithic times, the latest edifice was scarcely forty years old – a mock-Tudor mansion built at the turn of the century. But – after being briefly occupied by eighty boys evacuated from Colet Court school in London – in its role as the home of the RAF Intelligence Branch it played an absolutely vital part in the war.

As RAF Medmenham (named after the nearest village) it became the centre of photographic interpretation, analysing film taken by high-flying Spitfires, Mosquito fighter-bombers and other aircraft, and from this evidence divining enemy plans and intentions. Work at Danesfield began on 1 April 1941 with the creation of the Central Interpretation Unit, which brought together most of the RAF's aerial photo interpreters for the first time.

At the end of each photographic sortie a 'first phase' examination of the material was made at the airfield where the reconnaissance plane had landed, to pick out anything of immediate importance; negatives and prints were then taken to the CIU, where photographic interpreters known as PIs examined them minutely through 3D spectacles, comparing them with older pictures in search of anything that had changed. The stereo photographic techniques used, together with the PIs' own skilled observation, enabled them to glean an extraordinary amount of information from blurred images, many taken from 30,000 feet.

As the unit's role expanded in 1942 and 1943, wooden huts proliferated all over the Danesfield grounds: increasing numbers of the staff were American – some came from the Hollywood film studios – and on 1 May 1944 the establishment was renamed the Allied Central Interpretation Unit. Many of the newcomers were civilians – and many of the British girls were still in their teens or early twenties. Among the ablest was the journalist Constance Babington Smith, known to her colleagues as 'Babs', who before the war had written articles for

Aeroplane magazine. In 1939 she joined the WAAF and was seconded to the ACIU, where she played a key role in identifying the role of the V-1 flying bomb experimental station at Peenemünde, off the north German coast.

This was one of the unit's most crucial achievements – an extraordinary feat of interpretation, based on intensive study, in which the PIs went back over earlier photographs again and again, re-examining images to see what tiny details they could pick out. In her memoirs, *Evidence in Camera*, Babington Smith recalled how she detected structures that looked like launching ramps in woodland clearings at Peenemünde, and how, one morning in December 1943, scanning a newly taken photo, she made the crucial breakthrough:

> Even with the naked eye I could see that on the ramp was
> something that had not been there before. A tiny cruciform
> shape, set exactly on the lower end of the inclined rails – a
> midget aircraft actually in position for launching.

The Medmenham interpreters rapidly identified ninety-six installations in north-western France that looked like launch sites, some complete, others under construction. In all of them angled ramps were accompanied by long, narrow buildings the shape of giant skis laid on their sides. But until Babington Smith's discovery, the purpose of these 'ski sites' had remained obscure. Now suddenly it was obvious that the Germans were planning a mass attack on London with flying bombs. 'It seemed that the V-1 attacks, when they came, might be of an appalling magnitude,' she wrote.

> The ski buildings provided storage space for twenty flying
> bombs at each site, and as there were nearly 100 sites it seemed
> possible that the target for launchings was something like 2,000
> flying bombs in each twenty-four hours.

The threat was acute. If London were deluged with a devastating hail of V-weapons, the ensuing chaos – apart from killing thousands of people – would inevitably disrupt the planning of Operation Overlord and delay the liberation of Europe. The Allied response – Operation Crossbow – was swift and effective. The answer to the ski sites was bombs. By the end of December 1943 British and American bombers had destroyed all but four of the known ski sites, and, as Babington Smith wrote, 'The first round of the battle against the flying bomb was an overwhelming victory for the Allies.' The first V-1 did not reach England until 13 June 1944.

Hitler's other revenge weapon, the V-2 rocket, proved more elusive. On 5 May a Mosquito crew photographed a rocket with four fins at its base standing upright on the Nazi test site at Blizna, in south-east Poland. Similar rockets had been spotted at Peenemünde, and the PIs at Medmenham searched frantically for launch sites in Holland and France; but because the rockets were moved around on huge road trailers, which could be hidden under trees, and fired vertically from small asphalt pads, they were almost impossible to detect. As Babington Smith put it, 'General Dornberger's almost ridiculously simple conception of how the V-2s should be launched defeated Allied photographic reconnaissance.'

Another of the WAAF girls at Medmenham, working in the high tower, was Winston Churchill's rebellious daughter Sarah, who before the war had taken to the stage and (to her father's distress) married the Austrian comedian Vic Oliver. Babs described her as 'a quick and versatile interpreter', but she was luckier than most in that she was able to take two long, stimulating breaks accompanying her father to the Teheran Conference with Roosevelt in 1943 and the Yalta Conference with Roosevelt and Stalin in 1945.

At Medmenham, as at Bletchley Park, secrecy was all. Outside the station, nobody talked about their work. The amount of material handled grew to phenomenal proportions: in 1945 the daily intake averaged 25,000 negatives and 60,000 prints, and by the end of the war the ACIU had accumulated millions of aerial reconnaissance images, which had yielded intelligence vital to the planning of almost every major Allied operation. For the D-Day landings the staff at Medmenham produced more than 300 synthetic rubber models of the Normandy beaches, based on photographic data of gradients, and giving details of tides and currents.

Purely in terms of physical size, Bletchley Park was insignificant. Some fifty miles north-west of London, the house was of no great architectural merit, and certainly not famous before the war; but it had the advantage of being bang in the middle of England, with good road connections, close to teleprinter links, and within 300 yards of a mainline railway station.

The present building was bought in 1887 by Herbert Leon, a London financier who several times extended and embellished it in flamboyant Victorian style. Its south front became a blaze of orange-red brick and white stone or painted wood, with windows of different sizes and assorted shapes. A bell-shaped, copper-clad cupola lopsidedly crowned one wing. Inside were garishly coloured skylights, ceilings decorated with heavy plaster mouldings, dark panelling, a spacious ballroom and twenty-seven principal bedrooms (though only four bathrooms).

One wartime recruit, the American architect Landis Gores, called it 'a maudlin, monstrous pile probably unsurpassed, though not for lack of competition, in the architectural gaucherie of the mid-Victorian era … inchoate, unfocused and incomprehensible'. To someone else it was the embodiment of 'lavatory Gothic'. But the fact that the house struck many of its inhabitants as a monstrosity did not spoil the attraction of its surroundings: it sat in a park on a low hill, looking out over an ornamental lake, and all around were pleasure gardens, a ha-ha, a yew maze, grottoes, many fine trees and open farmland.

In 1938 the house was acquired by the much-loved Chief of the Secret Intelligence Service, Admiral Sir Hugh Sinclair – the 'C' of the day – who decided to move the Government Code and Cypher School (GC&CS) out of London to somewhere safer, and chose Bletchley as its new home, attracted by the proximity of the teleprinter repeater station at Fenny Stratford, immediately to the north, and by the house's position beside the railway, with the North Western line cutting through the estate, and branch lines leading off conveniently to east and west towards Cambridge and Oxford.

In May 1938 Sinclair bought the house and surrounding land for £6000, apparently on his own initiative and with his own money. Until his death from cancer in November 1939 the place nominally belonged to him; but in 1940 his sister Evelyn, to whom he had left it, transferred it to the SIS for the princely sum of 10s, and in due course it passed on to the Ministry of Works for the same amount – which suggests that the money for the original purchase had come out of SIS funds.

Sinclair sent the Code and Cypher School to Bletchley during the Munich crisis of August 1938; but when the alarm died down the codebreakers went back to London. Then in 1939, after telephone and teleprinter lines had been installed, they returned to Buckinghamshire, and the Park was given the code name 'Station X', it being the tenth site acquired by MI6 for its War Stations. The advance guard arrived under the guise of a shooting party led by Captain Ridley (a naval officer in MI6) and the other pioneers at the Park were Section IX, a new organization recently established by Sinclair to develop sabotage material, including incendiary devices and plastic explosive. They evidently had fertile imaginations, for one of their ideas was to place mustard gas in the seats of the Berlin opera house before a major Nazi rally took place there.

From that modest beginning Bletchley grew into what its own publicity leaflet later described as 'the centre of a great communications web, receiving intercepts from all directions and disseminating information [known as Ultra] to those who could put it to strategic use in the major theatres of the war, throughout the world'. The station's achievements included a decisive contribution towards the defeat of the U-boats in the Battle of the Atlantic (because the code-breakers, intercepting the captains' messages, could tell where the submarines were, and warn Allied ships to keep clear), and above all to the success of Operation Overlord, the invasion of Europe in June 1944. In the opinion of Sir Harry Hinsley, the official historian of British Intelligence during the war, Ultra shortened the conflict by between two and four years – and without it the outcome might have been quite different. One leading German historian speculated that the first atom bomb might have been dropped on Berlin rather than Hiroshima.

This priceless harvest resulted from the breaking of Enigma, the code used in communications between the Nazi armed forces and the German High Command. Because the portable Enigma encoding machines, like typewriters equipped with lights, generated hundreds of millions of different letter combinations, and the settings were changed every night, the Germans were confident that it was impossible for an enemy to penetrate the system's secrets.

They reckoned without the phenomenal intellectual power concentrated at Bletchley. Mathematicians, philosophers, classical scholars, chess players, writers, musicians – all contributed to the code-breaking. The irascible senior cryptographer, Dillwyn Knox – always known as 'Dilly', and described by one colleague as 'the mastermind behind the Enigma affair' – was a gangling figure in his fifties 'with a prominent forehead, unruly black hair, and his eyes, behind glasses, some miles away in thought'. His colleague Frank Birch, a theatre actor and director, had been a memorable Widow Twankey in a West End production of *Aladdin*. But if these two – and many others – were highly intelligent, one man stood out from the rest as a genius: a twenty-seven-year-old mathematician from King's College, Cambridge – Alan Turing, known as 'the Prof'. With his stammer, his high-pitched voice and irritating laugh, reinforced by his habit of wearing a gas mask while bicycling in summer, he soon established a reputation as an eccentric; but his manner concealed robust physical qualities, and he was a good enough runner to compete in marathons. Besides, he wore the mask for practical reasons, as he suffered from hay fever.

The first chink of light into Enigma was opened up by Polish experts in the summer of 1939; but by December that year, Turing, working on his own, had managed to break into some old Enigma material. He was also developing the first of the enormous proto-computers known as 'bombes' – electro-mechanical monsters six feet high, seven wide and two deep – which became instrumental in cracking the code. Mathematicians and engineers worked together to construct the war-winning machines.

Trade and personnel at Bletchley built up fast. At the beginning, the cryptographers could fit into the main house and the buildings in the stable yard – the tack room, feed room and so on; but new accommodation was soon needed. Elmers School – a nearby boys' school – was taken over, and the maze at Bletchley was cleared away to make room for the first long huts, made of timber and plasterboard insulated with asbestos. By early 1941 there were eleven huts, known by their numbers, which also referred to their inhabitants and the tasks done in them.

Working conditions were incredibly uncomfortable: the huts were divided into small rooms, and since almost everybody smoked continually, the air was permanently dense with tobacco fumes. In winter smoke from the coke-burning stoves was positively toxic, and in some of the huts the noise was barely tolerable. Facilities were basic, to say the least. Huts 3 and 6 were connected by a tunnel through which documents could be propelled on a tea tray pushed by a broom handle. Later many more substantial buildings of steel and concrete were added: teleprinter building, cafeteria, garages, dormitory blocks and lecture hall. An eight-foot, chain-link perimeter fence topped by barbed wire encircled the park, reminding some inmates of Whipsnade Zoo; during the invasion scare Lewis machine guns adapted for use on the ground were installed at the gates, and a dedicated unit of the Home Guard was on standby.

Staff were recruited largely by personal contact, and included many civilians, not least dons from Oxford and Cambridge. They worked in three shifts – from 8 a.m. to 4 p.m., 4 p.m. to midnight, midnight to 8 a.m. Such was the strain of concentrating for eight hours, with only one thirty-minute meal break in the middle of the shift, that many girls collapsed. Of the 12,000 people who worked at GC&CS at some point during the war, over 80 per cent were women. This was a classless society, quite different from the old-fashioned order still prevailing in the world outside. Here, class and gender were of no consequence: intelligence, hard work, enthusiasm and integrity were what counted, and men treated women as equals.

At first the staff lodged in hotels and pubs. Later they were found accommodation in surrounding towns and villages – in some discomfort, for the Buckinghamshire countryside was still rustic, and most of the local families who provided billets had no electricity or inside lavatory. From early 1942 the Admiralty began requisitioning big country houses to serve as quarters for the Wrens who managed the bombes. Some were lodged in style at Woburn Abbey, others at the Elizabethan Gayhurst Manor, where they slept in bunks in the ballroom and worked in one of the five local bombe outstations – a job that demanded intense concentration and often led to temporary breakdown. Girls who became ill irritated doctors by refusing (quite correctly) to divulge what work they did, and so contributing to their own problems. A further hazard of OSG – Outstation Gayhurst – was that the Wrens slept in the house but had to walk to work in a prefabricated building in the woods – a journey which spooked them at night, as there was talk of a resident ghost, and the path ran by the cemetery in which past manor pets were buried.

The transportation of such a large workforce, in and out of Bletchley Park, day and night, became a major undertaking. By 1942 111 shift buses were in use, and it was reckoned that the transport service made 28,351 journeys per year. Had a German spy been at large anywhere in the neighbourhood, he could hardly have failed to notice the extraordinary amount of traffic that the place generated: it was like a beehive, with the denizens constantly whizzing along the country lanes, in and out. Many of the Wrens bought bicycles or had their own sent from home; those billeted not too far away came and went by bike, and on days off the girls based at Gayhurst would ride out for a scrumptious tea in the WVS canteen at Olney, a village five miles to the north.

Feeding the staff at Bletchley was another enormous task: a new canteen was built in the summer of 1941, and by February 1943 almost 3000 meals were being provided every day. In the run-up to D-Day new restrictions were imposed: workers were forbidden to go more than twenty-five miles from base – but when a notice appeared on the girls' board saying 'All Wrens' clothing will be held up until the Navy's needs are satisfied', an officer, hearing raucous laughter, shot out of her room and tore it down.

Secrecy was paramount. All ranks were sworn to silence about their work, and a personal security form issued in May 1942 told people not to talk at meals, in the transport, while travelling, in billets, or even 'by your own fireside'. The form ended, 'Be careful even in your hut'. The buses which brought the workers in decanted them at the door of their hut, and they were forbidden to talk shop with other huts. No doubt the embargo was observed on the premises; but it is hard to believe that men and girls off duty, riding round the lanes or walking the footpaths through the fields, did not exchange some confidences. And what did they say about their work to their families when they went home on leave? To disguise the workers' whereabouts, all post destined for them had to be sent via a PO box in London.

It seems extraordinary that the whole installation survived with practically no damage from bombs. The network of railway lines converging on Bletchley from all points of the compass must have been a tempting target for any Luftwaffe crew wanting to shed the remains of their load before they headed home, even if they had no idea what lay beside the tracks, which shone in moonlight. The huts were as fragile as eggshells, and they housed human beings and machines of incalculable value to the war effort, besides irreplaceable stores of knowledge. Yet Dorothy Gait, who went to Bletchley as a clerk in June 1940, and worked in one of the upstairs bedrooms, remembered that when air-raid sirens wailed her instructions were to gather up as many heavy ledgers as she could carry and dash to what was optimistically known as the 'shelter', a slit trench halfway across an adjacent field.

On 21 November 1940 a single bomb did fall between the house and Hut 11, and it blew the hut four inches sideways – but the building was so insubstantial that it could simply be pushed back into position. On the same night another bomb landed in the stable yard, but failed to go off. One deliberate, well-aimed attack, one stick of high explosives or incendiaries into the centre of the complex, and the heart of the installation might have been destroyed, the course of the war irrevocably altered.

As it was, the stringent security rules observed by all who worked at Bletchley Park preserved its secrets throughout the war. The Germans may, towards the end, have begun to suspect that the British were breaking their Enigma transmissions; but they never got the slightest idea of where the detective work was taking place, and the most potent weapon of the war came through unscathed.

Thirteen

Rescue Operations

An Englishman's home is his castle

Traditional proverb

If a country house was not appropriated by the Government, its owners were left to fend for themselves; and as James Lees-Milne wrote about the owners of Lyme Park – the 'splendid Elizabethan and Georgian palace' approached by a mile-long drive through parkland on the outskirts of the industrial town of Stockport – 'their predicament was the sad but not singular one of deciding what to do with a vast ancestral white elephant'.

When Lees-Milne arrived there in November 1943, the place was in a poor state. Forty evacuated children had just left the building, and the park had been 'cut to pieces by thousands of RAF lorries'; but his task, as Country House Secretary of the National Trust, was to negotiate with the owners, Lord and Lady Newton, and arrange the handover of the property. It says much for his diplomacy that, after protracted disagreements, he eventually achieved the transfer in 1946.

Although founded in 1894, the Trust was still an embryonic organization, which had concentrated on the preservation of open countryside rather than of buildings. When Lees-Milne joined the Trust in 1936, at the age of twenty-nine, only three other male employees were working in a cramped office in Buckingham Palace Gardens. But he – a

highly intelligent and personable young man, with boundless enthusiasm for architecture, literature, art and music – launched out on what
he called the most enjoyable summer of his life, visiting a succession of
stately homes by train or bicycle or on foot, in the 'pioneer days of the
country house enterprise'.

Some of his encounters were humiliating. At Longleat, after a fruitless interview, Lord Bath rang a bell and ordered his visitor's non-existent car to be brought round. He then insisted on accompanying the
young man to the front door of the huge Elizabethan house, whose
steps were lined by footmen in livery. 'In place of my uniformed chauffeur,' Lees-Milne recorded, 'an extra footman wheeled my bicycle to the
front of the steps. I shook my host's hand, descended the perron and
mounted.'

He found more sympathy, but also greater urgency, at Stourhead in
Wiltshire. The owner, Sir Henry Hoare, wished to leave the whole property to the Trust: the eighteenth-century house, its glorious gardens
graced with lakes, temples, grottoes and follies, and 6000 acres of land,
which encompassed 2000 acres of forest, mainly exceptional soft-
woods. He also promised an endowment of £150,000.

Sir Henry, seventy-four when the war began, was an old-fashioned
sort. A 'bluff, bullish figure', he dressed in pepper-and-salt knicker-
bockers, winter and summer, and wore a fawn billycock hat, which he
kept on at meals. His wife Alda ('tall, upright and tightly corseted') had
an unfortunate way with servants, who found her 'impossibly exacting'.
An idea of her temperament can be gained from her habit of using a
pen with an extremely thick nib to annotate her novels in the margins
and endpapers with 'explosive interjections of indignation: "Pshaw! …
What rot! … What next? … Splendid … Genius … I agree"'.

In May 1939 Sir Henry was distressed by finding a man from the
Ministry of Aviation surveying the ground for an airfield less than half
a mile from his house. He implored the National Trust to stop the
scheme, and after protests it was withdrawn – only for the land to be

requisitioned for a military camp and a grass runway for training flights.

As the war went on, and discussions with the Trust stagnated, the Hoares' most pressing concern became the shortage of servants, who had been reduced from the pre-war total of ten to five. Rattling around in the huge house, quite unable to do things for themselves, the old people desperately needed help. 'We are in terrible difficulties in carrying on here,' wrote Sir Henry in 1942. 'We now want a cook *and* a butler. We have only got a boy of seventeen, and he will shortly be called up.' By then most of the house was shut up, or occupied by 'a squadron of the liaison regiment ... six or seven officers and about fifty men'. All the same, Sir Henry wrote piteously: 'We are up against it now, as our only housemaid is leaving. Only a char left.' Negotiations for the handover had begun in 1936, but there were so many points to be settled that agreement was not reached until 1947, when house and estate eventually passed to the Trust.

Absurd as it may now seem to make such a fuss when England was fighting for its life, there is no doubt that the old Hoares were genuinely distressed. Having never had to fend for themselves, they could not cook, clean, do the laundry, light a fire, change a fuse or mend anything else that got broken.

The realities of owning a white elephant were starkly described by the Dowager Countess of Radnor, whose home was Longford Castle, a palatial house overlooking the River Avon in Wiltshire:

> It must be remembered that old houses were once new houses
> and purpose-built for their times, so there are pastry-larders,
> game-larders, sculleries, lamp-rooms, brush-rooms, china-
> closets etc., all once necessary but now empty and useless, as
> useless as the kitchenmaids' bedrooms and the housemaids'
> sitting room, where old furnishings linger on, growing damp,
> dirty and decayed ... [In earlier days] not only were there

cooks and butlers, but strange grades that we have lost, like
stillroom maids, laundry maids, lamp-men.

Longford Castle survived the war, occupied by British and
American troops, and remained in the family; but the Countess also
lamented the decline of the garden – not just at her own home, but at
all the big houses whose staff were drastically thinned out by the war.

Jim Lees-Milne saw the problems at first hand when he travelled
about wartime Britain visiting houses that seemed most worthy of preservation. The biggest by far was Knole, home of the Sackville family at
Sevenoaks in Kent. Founded in the fifteenth century, with 365 rooms,
fifty-two staircases and seven courtyards, the house was so vast that it
looked like a whole village. The fourth Lord Sackville had approached
the Trust in 1935 to discuss Knole's future, but claimed that he had difficulty in finding enough money to endow the place with the funds
necessary for its maintenance, and, as at Stourhead, negotiations
dragged on for years.

In February 1944 minds were concentrated when a bomb fell in the
park close to the house's west front, spinning the stone heraldic beasts
on the gable finials round on their plinths and blowing much glass out
of the windows. Later that year, summoned to discuss numerous problems, Lees-Milne found his Lordship 'as exquisitely dressed as ever, in
a blue tweed suit and canary-coloured waistcoat which, when his delicate build and abrupt movements were taken into account, brought to
mind that domesticated bird'. Nearly two more years went by before in
July 1946 Mr Justice Vaisey at last made an order vesting Knole in the
Trust, subject to a lease in favour of Lord Sackville.

A still more captious customer was Colonel Sir Henry William
Cameron-Ramsay Fairfax-Lucy, owner of Charlecote Park, where
William Shakespeare stole deer in the sixteenth century – a crime for
which he was arraigned by the first Sir Thomas Lucy in the Great Hall
of the house. Charlecote, on the banks of the Avon, had been the home

of the Lucy family for 700 years, but now Sir Henry wanted to hand it to the Trust. Although a qualified barrister, he seemed to Lees-Milne to have developed 'a tortuous mentality which revelled in ambiguities, misinterpretations and confusions … He was pernickety, fussy, consequential, very pleased with himself and displeased with everyone else. He strutted like a bantam cock. He spoke with a peevish lisp.' Much as Lees-Milne disliked him, and gravely though he was exasperated by his 'preposterous self-importance', other members of the Trust found him still more difficult. 'He thinks he knows everything,' wrote Donald Matheson, the Trust's secretary, 'and is extremely difficult, tiresome and stupid.'

Blocked by his endless prevarication and changes of direction, negotiations (which had begun in 1937) meandered on for years, until just before Christmas in 1943 Lady Lucy died. On 5 August 1944 the Colonel suddenly married again, and two weeks later as suddenly expired. 'It is dreadful to say so,' Lees-Milne wrote, 'but nobody seemed to regret his demise very much.'

His sons brought up further problems; then abruptly in April 1945 they offered the house and certain chattels to the Trust as a gift, subject to an agreement that they might live in the Victorian wing. So ended one of Lees-Milne's most drawn-out battles.

No such aggravation awaited him at Gunby Hall, a relatively small but perfectly proportioned house of plum-red brick, built in 1700 on the edge of the Lincolnshire Wolds, surrounded by a 100-acre park full of magnificent trees. One day in 1941 Field Marshal Sir Archibald Armar Montgomery-Massingberd, husband of the owner, was walking in the garden when he met three men measuring the height of the trees with a theodolite. Without having consulted him, the Air Ministry was planning to build an airfield on land adjoining the estate – a scheme which would have entailed the felling of 800 trees and demolition of the house. Appalled by the prospect, the owners offered to hand the property to the National Trust, if that would avert disaster.

When Lees-Milne went to see them in November 1943, he instantly fell for the place and its inhabitants. The Field Marshal, whom he described as 'tall, very handsome, with a clear complexion and bright blue eyes', was then seventy-four, and he presided at dinner in a 'snow-white pleated shirt-front bulging from a black velvet coat, immaculate, impeccable'. Even in wartime a guest was expected to wear a dinner jacket. Wharton, the butler, was 'a sort of Lincolnshire Jeeves', as much a gentleman's gentleman as a butler, wearing black tail coat, starched collar and white tie. There was no wine at dinner, but the food was good and adequate, and beyond the green baize door, besides Wharton, were his wife (the cook), a pantry boy, two housemaids and a chauffeur. The Montgomery-Massingberds, Lees-Milne concluded, were still managing to lead 'a feudal life on a modest scale'.

Vigorous protests from the Trust brought the RAF officers to their senses: they modified their scheme so that the house could remain intact, and only a few trees would have to be topped. The Montgomery-Massingberds were so delighted that they decided to make the property over to the Trust there and then. Even so, a high, lattice-work tower topped by a revolving beacon went up in the middle of their tennis court, and for the rest of the war bombers roared overhead a few feet above the roof of the house. But, as Lees-Milne remarked, 'the transfer of a large estate to the Trust never happened more smoothly'; and, with tower and Nissen huts speedily cleared away, Gunby Hall opened to the public on May Day 1946.

By no means Lees-Milne's smallest success was to organize the takeover of Blickling Hall, in Norfolk, left to the Trust in his will by Lord Lothian. This prime mover of the Trust's shift towards country-house ownership had been appointed British Ambassador to Washington in 1939; but after eighteen months in office he died *en poste* from food poisoning aged only fifty-eight – a Christian Scientist who refused medical treatment.

It took lawyers many months to sort out the provisions of his will; and when Lees-Milne first went to Blickling in May 1942 he found the place in a sorry state. The park had been divided up by fences, and was growing corn and cabbages. The RAF had occupied the house and grounds. A sea of Nissen huts obscured the orangery; a brick NAAFI complex had been built opposite the front door.

The resident guardian was Lord Lothian's former secretary, Muriel O'Sullivan, and Lees-Milne reckoned that the lusty young pilots were more terrified of Miss O'Sullivan, whom they called 'the dragon', than they were of night flights over Germany. Miss O'Sullivan was a remarkable character. Although poor and delicate, she regarded Blickling as a sacred trust and 'cherished its every content, tradition and even superstition'. She also believed in the existence of a ghostly black dog which she claimed to have seen scampering down the long gallery and disappearing through the floorboards to an exit in the south-east turret. Yet there was nothing fey about her when she waded into the Wing Commander's office, 'abusing his subordinates as barbarians'.

No matter how much she scolded the junior officers for vandalizing the house, they smashed the old crown glass of the windows and broke open doors leading to the state rooms, in which the furniture was under dust sheets. When the war ended and the airmen left, there was an immense amount of restoration to be done.

Aristocrats and eccentrics were not the only people obliged to lower their standards. Even landowners not burdened with a white elephant found that the war was changing things. Some in the north of England had begun letting their vegetable ground to market gardeners, who, in return for loads of manure, would fettle up greenhouses in need of repair. Social life had diminished greatly. 'Dinner parties at castle, hall and manor have been few and far between during the winter of 1941–42,' observed *The Estate Magazine*, issued by the Country Gentlemen's Association. Never had there been 'so little intercourse among the

misconstrued her instructions and ate the offering himself – to the delight of the family.

Queen Mary was by no means au fait with country life: when, early in her stay, her niece pointed out a field of exceptionally good hay, she replied, 'So *that's* what hay looks like.' Nevertheless, she soon found an outlet for her energy in the form of attacks on ivy, towards which her enmity 'had long been proverbial at Sandringham'. Quite rightly, she believed that ivy destroyed stone walls, brickwork and trees, and at Badminton she had endless scope for assaults. Having drafted members of her staff into her Ivy Squad, she progressed to forming her four bodyguard dispatch riders into a Wooding Squad, which thinned plantations under her direction.

At her disposal she had a green Daimler, but to save petrol she usually went out to distant sites on a horse-drawn cart, she and her lady-in-waiting sitting in two basket chairs on its flat platform. 'Aunt May,' said her niece. 'You look as though you were in a tumbril!' To which she replied, 'Well, it may come to that yet – one never knows.' Another of her passions was searching the countryside for salvage: she scoured the hedges for scrap metal, bottles and even old bones, and occasionally, as her biographer remarked, 'her enthusiasm for salvaging scrap iron, combined with her ignorance of country habits', carried her away:

> Several times the green Daimler would return loaded with field harrows and other implements ... which Queen Mary espying had concluded to be discards ready for the scrap dump. In these cases the objects were quietly returned to their owners without the Queen's knowledge.

When she arrived in Gloucestershire, invasion scares were at their height. The villages of Badminton and Little Badminton, with about 100 houses and 400 inhabitants between them, lie in gently undulating land north-east of Bristol; and as there were several airfields in the neighbourhood, a Civil Defence pamphlet voiced fears that Germans might land there in preparation for an assault on the city:

> Germany might seek to secure as much of the Cotswold escarpment as possible, as part of a plan to capture the Bristol Channel ports … Badminton may be regarded as one of the key villages (a) for dealing with an enemy airborne attack, (b) for resisting the enemy's land advance.

The local Home Guard was strengthened by a detachment of the Royal Berkshire Regiment, whose task was to 'form an outer ring of defence, of which Badminton House forms the approximate centre'. Troops would be used 'to wipe out isolated enemy airborne landings within a limited distance', but the Home Guard remained responsible for ringing the church bells in the event of invasion.

Preparations in the villages were directed by the Local Defence Committee. A careful survey was taken of wells – sixteen in all: 'In Mr Hudson's kitchen garden, one well. Depth of well 45' 6". Depth of water 26' 6".'

All local telephone numbers were listed, including that of Major His Grace the Duke of Beaufort, whose number was 2. A stock of food was earmarked for distribution in case of invasion. Lists were drawn up of tools 'available for use': spades, felling axes, cross-cut saws and pickaxes owned by individuals. A decontamination station was established in the Estate Yard, with separate rooms for males and females. In the fields stout poles were set upright in five-foot-deep holes to deter enemy pilots from trying to land. Arrangements were made for the burial of the dead. As for emergency accommodation – the Memorial Hall would be the first line, backed up by the school, churches and private houses.

At the beginning of September the village had been deluged with refugee children from Birmingham – to the satisfaction of Queen Mary, who sent her niece to the school, suggesting that some of the older pupils might like to come and give her a hand with the gardening. They came, and evidently enjoyed themselves. When one, George Brown, had his head cut by a flying stone, the teacher's report diplomatically ascribed the accident to 'over-eagerness, as the boys were hurrying to complete their assignment of work [i.e., having an agreeable fight]'.

On 9 July 1940 the school had a narrow escape, when bombs – presumably jettisoned by a fleeing Luftwaffe pilot – fell in the lane during lessons without exploding. One landed within thirty yards of the building, and the crater was immediately put out of bounds. Then another was found near the first. All the children were marshalled in the hall, where they sang, played games and recited poetry before being shepherded out in the evening. A report described their behaviour as 'splendid throughout the day'. Much of the village was evacuated, but on the evening of the 11th the second bomb was removed, and people returned to their homes – only for two more unexploded bombs to be discovered, dug out and dealt with.

The Badminton Village Club did what it could to 'provide comfort, amusement and refreshment at the lowest possible cost', not only for local people, but also for soldiers stationed nearby. At the end of October 1939 the committee invited men from the detachment of Royal Gloucestershire Hussars at Hedington Camp to consider themselves temporary members, and in April 1940 extended the invitation to the 8th Gloucestershire Regiment, from which 120 men were guarding Queen Mary. The staff of the searchlight unit at Little Badminton were also invited – NCOs first, then privates – and finally membership was opened up to members of the Queen Mother's household, 'owing to their prolonged stay in Badminton'.

Queen Mary inevitably felt cut off from the rest of the royal family, and frustrated by her inability to help them with the war effort; but she was kept in touch by frequent letters from her daughter-in-law, the Queen, who, with her husband, King George, was showing remarkable courage and resilience in comforting victims of the Blitz.

Unlike Hitler, who refused to visit ruined cities in spite of the exhortations of his acolytes, the royal couple moved freely about the country, and an appearance by them always had a miraculously cheering effect on people who had been bombed out of their homes. Wherever the King and Queen went, picking their way among the rubble of shattered buildings, they lifted morale by the warmth of their response and their direct contact with working-class families. By no means all their excursions were in or near London: they also went far afield, to Plymouth, Sheffield and even to Scotland. They themselves lived partly in Windsor Castle, partly in Buckingham Palace, but travelled widely in the royal train, in which they sometimes spent the night out in the country, parked in a cutting or tunnel safe from air attack. They also tended to sleep in the relative safety of Windsor and return to London early in the morning, to give the impression that for most of the time they were in the capital.

After Christmas 1940 the royal family drove to Norfolk for a short holiday. At Sandringham the big house had been closed and surrounded by barbed wire, so they stayed at Appleton, a smaller house on the estate which was warmer and made more comfortable by the importation of carpets and furniture from Sandringham itself. Protected by an armoured-car unit and Bofors anti-aircraft guns, they were able to relax and enjoy themselves, and the King went shooting pheasants in the snowy woods.

Norfolk always attracted them. One January afternoon they drove out to visit the RAF's 167 Squadron at Ludham, on the airfield just north of the village, not knowing that a plane had just been scrambled to engage a marauding JU 88. Hardly had they arrived when Pilot Officer Code and Sergeant Nash landed, having shot the German down. Code was elated to have got his first victim – and the King was no less delighted.

In letters to her mother-in-law Queen Elizabeth lamented the barbarity of the Germans and the destruction they were causing; but she also comforted the old lady by sending news of her granddaughters' progress. The Princesses, Elizabeth and Margaret, were living at Windsor, where they were being taught mainly by their governess, Marion Crawford (always known as 'Crawfie'), who wrote often to report on the strides they were making, both with their lessons and with their general development. For history, Princess Elizabeth's tutor was the austere Henry Marten, then in his seventies, who had taught at Eton for more than forty years (and in 1945 became Provost of the College). He had been lecturing boys for so long that sometimes he would say loudly to the Princess, 'IS THAT QUITE CLEAR TO YOU, GENTLEMEN?' He thought his royal pupil showed exceptional promise, and compared her favourably with Etonians a year older. Such news must have been welcome to Queen Mary, but unfortunately any replies she sent appear to have been destroyed.

Around Badminton the old lady did much to raise morale by visiting local people, evacuees, army units, hospitals and industrial sites. The house and village survived the war largely unscathed, and the Queen Mother remained there throughout. No mention of her temporary home appeared in the press, but from occasional reports of her surfacing at events in Bath, Cheltenham, Dursley and Malmesbury, any intelligent person could have formed a good idea about where she was living. In August 1942 the Canadian Prime Minister Mackenzie King, visiting Balmoral, suggested that she might like to go and live in Canada until hostilities ceased; but, nervous though she was, she stayed put.

By the time she returned to London in June 1945 she had come to love Gloucestershire. She gave carefully chosen presents to each of the nine heads of departments on the Badminton estate, told one of them how happy she had been, and left with tears in her eyes. She magnanimously agreed that the Duke should inherit the Aga cooker which she had installed in the kitchen, and he reciprocated by writing off the wear and tear of carpets and furniture incurred during her occupation. Yet no one could account for two boxes which were missing after her departure. 'Stokes says the smaller toothpick box was locked up with the silver cups in the cupboard in the pantry,' Lord Claud Hamilton, Comptroller to Queen Mary, told the Duke in a letter of 20 June 1945. 'Of the larger racing-scene box, Copple says it was withdrawn early. Stokes does not remember seeing it.'

Another great house which survived with minimal damage was Chatsworth, the palatial home of the Devonshire family near Bakewell in Derbyshire. Its escape was partly due to the foresight of the tenth Duke, who knew that the Government would certainly requisition the immense building – with its 175 rooms, 17 staircases, 359 doors and 1,704,000 cubic feet of living space – unless he found other worthy occupants first. Reckoning that schoolgirls would make far gentler tenants than soldiers, he offered the place to Penrhos College, a Methodist boarding school on the seafront in Colwyn Bay, which was about to be requisitioned as a temporary refuge for the Ministry of Food.

When the headmistress, Miss E. L. Edman, went across to Chatsworth with a colleague to carry out a reconnaissance, they were both staggered by the splendour of the house and its surroundings. Set in a 3500-acre park laid out by Capability Brown, with the River Derwent winding lazily below, and the hills all round crowned by woods as far as eye could see, the huge building presided majestically on a gentle slope. But the visitors, though overwhelmed, were put at ease by the welcome they received from the Duke and Duchess, who seemed too human and sympathetic to be the real owners of such a place.

With agreement reached, frantic preparations went ahead at both ends. The Devonshires moved out to live at Churchdale Hall, another of their houses. At Chatsworth carpets were taken up from corridors, the Yellow Drawing Room was stripped of furniture; silk-covered and panelled walls were boarded over, and some of the most valuable paintings – the Rembrandts, Poussins, Van Dycks, Reynoldses, Halses – were stacked against bookcases. The main rooms were cleared in eleven days, as were the relics of a party held to celebrate the twenty-first birthday of the Marquess of Hartington (heir to the Dukedom).

In Colwyn Bay a mass of furniture had to be loaded into lorries: chairs, desks, beds, mattresses, to say nothing of twenty-six pianos. On 26 September 1939 some 250 girls aged eleven to eighteen, together with thirty-six staff, set off in buses for Derbyshire.

As another mistress, Nancie Park, remarked, 'Great Britain was never invaded during World War II, but Chatsworth House most certainly was.' The girls were temporarily dumbfounded by the first sight of their new home: one of them always remembered how fountains were playing, 'the stone was lit up with sunshine, and the house smiled a glorious welcome'.

Recovering the power of speech and movement, they swarmed into the building and soon occupied almost all of it except the Library. New arrangements fell quickly into place. Assembly, morning and evening chapel were held in the Painted Hall, which was also used as a cinema. Piano lessons took place in the Chapel. The Large Dining Room, State Drawing Room and State Bedroom all became dormitories; thirteen bathrooms, and a limited supply of hot water, enabled each of the new inmates to have two baths a week. 'The loos,' one girl recalled, 'were marvellous, like thrones.' Great care was taken to minimize damage: dustless chalk was used on blackboards; there were no inkwells, and only members of the VIth form were allowed fountain pens. Running indoors was a punishable sin.

In the bitterly cold winter of 1939–40 the lake froze, and on 20 January there were forty degrees of frost. At least the girls could skate and toboggan, but snow lay late into the spring, and – in spite of central heating and coal fires in some of the rooms – most of the house was icy. The roof leaked, and the electricity kept failing. When coal ran short, the staff were given permission to saw up fallen trees in the park and burn the wood on the fires. Black knitted tights, known as 'passion killers', became indispensable. It was hardly the girls' fault that, as twenty-one of them slept in the State Drawing Room, their breath produced so much condensation that fungus built up on the backs of pictures left hanging. Sometimes the cold drove the inmates to seek refuge in out-of-the-way places. One day later in the war, as the Dowager Duchess was showing some US servicemen round the house, she took them to see the four-poster in which King George II had died. The bed was covered with protective sheets, and when the Duchess drew them aside, she flushed out five girls snuggled underneath.

Food was meagre. One pupil remembered how, after school lunch, she and her friends were so hungry that they fried sausages over a fire, then cooked some tomatoes, then ate bread and fish paste. Another time a girl somehow acquired a can of baked beans, but, lacking a tin opener, in a fit of frustration threw her trophy into the fire, where it soon exploded, blasting super-heated tomato sauce over anybody in reach.

In summer things were easier. Peggy Bennett, games mistress, became an ace at handling the thirty-inch Ransome automatic mower, and so enabled the girls to play tennis on eight courts marked out on the South Lawn. Lacrosse and athletics took place on the cricket pitch, but if games were cancelled because of bad weather the girls were obliged, for exercise, to walk up to the Hunting Tower, a turreted folly 400 feet above the house, built on the escarpment in the sixteenth century for Bess of Hardwick so that she could watch hounds running in the park below. Working parties weeded turnips on neighbouring farms and helped Mr Link, the head gardener, thin the vegetables planted in the herbaceous border and walled garden. In return, he sold the girls potatoes, which they baked on their form-room fires.

Isolated though it was, the house did not escape the war entirely. Luftwaffe aircraft passed to the north on their way to bomb Sheffield, and to the south as they made for home. After a raid, fires burning in the city lit up the sky with a blaze of reddish gold, clearly visible from ten miles away. The arched beer cellar of the house made an excellent air-raid shelter, and while raids were in progress pupils and staff sat close together down there, eating cream crackers and Bovril.

One day in 1940, when invasion scares were at their height, the Dowager Duchess took the headmistress off to a remote valley, to inspect some caves in which she thought the whole school might hide if the Germans arrived. Luckily this last resort was never needed; but the war edged nearer on a lovely summer evening in 1942, when it seemed almost as if the Almighty had scored an own goal. At the close of prayers, just after Miss Edman had intoned the words 'The peace of God which passeth all understanding', there came a shattering crash as a bullet smashed through one of the windows. Luftwaffe aircraft had been trying to bomb the factory in Bakewell which produced batteries for submarines, and peppered the north front of the house with cannon fire as they made for home.

Later, in 1944, the moors above the park were taken over as training areas by troops, and one aggrieved local walker complained, 'The military, whoever they are, are using live ammunition … On Friday, August 4th, Chatsworth House, grounds and part of the park were sprinkled with machine-gun bullets by the American contingent.'

Many of the estate staff had disappeared into the armed forces, but the Duke agreed that if their service pay was less than they had been earning before call-up, the estate would make up the deficit. He also ordained that all their posts would be kept open for them, should they want to return when hostilities ceased. In the foresters' absence, the woods were plundered for pit props by contractors, and 500 acres of immature trees were cut down. 'I hear that the timber murderers have felled all we marked for them last Friday and want some more,' wrote a member of the office staff. Late in the war twenty-five German prisoners, under a British foreman, were brought in to burn up the tops left in the cleared areas.

During the war the Devonshire family suffered a major bereavement. There had been great rejoicing when Billy Hartington married Kathleen ('Kick') Kennedy, daughter of Joseph Kennedy, the American Ambassador to London, on 6 May 1944; but then, only four months later, he was killed on active service in Belgium, leaving his younger brother, Andrew, heir to the Dukedom.

When Churchill declared victory in Europe on 8 May 1945, the girls at Chatsworth were playing cricket on the lawn; but the moment they saw a double-bed white sheet hoisted on the roof, they abandoned the game and sprinted for the house. Eager though they were to return to their proper base in Colwyn Bay, they had to wait for most of a year before they left Derbyshire in May 1946. After their departure the house was uninhabited except by two housemaids, Emily and Annie, who, in the words of Deborah Duchess, 'perched in a distant room at the north end'.

Chatsworth remained empty for years. When the tenth Duke died suddenly in 1950, the family was faced with appalling death duties of £7 million (some £180 million in today's rates); but Penrhos's occupation had been such a success that in 1951, when the Cold War threatened to turn hot, the eleventh Duke suggested to the headmistress that the school might like to return. Nothing came of this overture, or of the idea that the Red Cross might take the house over; but in due course, with tremendous courage and resolution, the new Duke and his wife, Deborah, decided to live in the house themselves. By selling land and pictures, and giving the magnificent Elizabethan Hardwick Hall to the Treasury (who passed it on to the National Trust), they paid off the death duties, refurbished Chatsworth, and in 1959 moved into it with their family.

*   *   *

Vanbrugh's splendid baroque Castle Howard, near York, was not so fortunate. Part of the house was let to Queen Margaret's School for Girls, which had been evacuated from Scarborough, and early in the morning on 9 November 1940 a disastrous fire broke out, vividly described by Anne Hollis, a sixteen-year-old sixth-former. Woken at 5.15 a.m. by someone shaking her shoulder, she heard the matron telling her, 'in a high-pitched, unnatural voice', to get up and rouse the rest of the bedroom. Anne saw that, outside, the sky was a lurid crimson, and the woods were lit up by the same brilliant light. Then she saw flames billowing from the other side of the house.

The girls rapidly dressed as they did for air raids – sweaters, socks, shoes and cloaks over their pyjamas. Holding wet sponges clasped to their faces, they made their way through dense smoke down to the shelter in the Underworld, a long, broad cellar with stone floor and walls and a vaulted stone roof, equipped for air raids with mattresses and rugs. Anne had just reached it when one of the staff appeared and asked for four or five sixth-formers to go up again and try to save some of the pictures.

> We made our way up the stone steps into the corridor which runs straight down the central block, and here we saw the fire. The far end of the passage was ablaze from floor to ceiling, and dull red smoke poured down the corridor.
>
> In V a [form room], the Reynolds Room, we found three staff tugging at the pictures – immense portraits, one of which took up nearly a whole wall. There was no time to unscrew the rails on which they were hung, and the ladders we had were not nearly long enough for us to be able to reach their tops, so we just had to tug at them until the wires broke and they crashed on top of us. Many of the pictures broke out of their frames when they fell, and the bare canvases were taken to the Long Gallery. Someone suggested getting into the studio and

trying to rescue the priceless mirrors which hung there. On opening the door, however, we discovered that the fire had already claimed them, for the windows and mirrors were cracked and falling in, while flames licked up the wall …

Fifteen minutes later we were sent for again, as the priceless old books in the Tapestry Room and corridor had to be saved at all costs. By then the fire was well up to the Studio, and the whole lower end of the corridor was a blazing inferno. Red-hot timbers were crashing from the roof, and through the haze of smoke and flame we could see that the Studio, V b [form] room, the office, the headmistress's room and the dining room – which contained several mirrors each worth £2,000, priceless Canalettos and several family portraits – were nothing but a smouldering ruin.

The corridor was knee-deep in water, as the hoses bringing water from the lake had at least been persuaded to work (no fire engine arrived for two hours), so we used our cloaks for carrying the books in, and when we reached the Long Gallery we dragged them along the floor; my cloak was in ribbons by the end of it …

By then it was about 7 am, and the fire was at its height when an air-raid warning came through. It was the only time of day when the staff began to look desperate, for they suspected that, drawn by the glow (which must have been seen for miles and miles), enemy planes would be returning to bomb what they supposed they had set alight. Nothing happened, however. Then breakfast miraculously appeared, and plates of steaming porridge were passed down to everyone, for the kitchens were in a safe quarter of the castle.

I was sent with another girl to stand guard in a little corridor which led off the shelter into other parts of the building. Water was pouring on to us from the corridors above.

Then we went outside and saw the exterior of the building blazing.

Above us, 100 feet high, towered the dome, and already flames were licking through its windows … The garden was full of stuff which had been rescued from the house – bedding, clothes, carpets, books, pictures and crosses, vases and altar cloths from the chapel lay everywhere. All this had to be somehow moved again, for it was pouring with rain, and everything was getting ruined. Somehow or other it was got into the staff flats, whither we were all sent too, as the dome was falling in, and it was not safe to be anywhere near it. Molten lead splashed all round as it finally crashed, and the timbers which constituted its framework were left stark and glowing against the sky until they too fell in.

The cause of the fire was never precisely established, but the trouble seems to have started in one of the eighteenth-century flues which twist through the walls and had never been swept. Caked soot probably started to smoulder, and the heat burst through a wall immediately behind a cupboard full of paper, which ignited at once.

Miraculously, no one died in the blaze, but many of the girls and staff lost all their belongings. Besides the celebrated dome, some twenty of the house's rooms were destroyed, including the Garden Hall and the High Saloon, with their eighteenth-century interiors painted by Antonio Pellegrini. For the rest of the war the south-east wing and much of the central block were left open to the sky; but, after being granted an exceptionally long, nine-week Christmas holiday, the 100-odd girls of Queen Margaret's returned to the front of the building, where fourteen rooms were put at the school's disposal. The house was cold, and still damp after its sousing during the fire, and the girls had to eat their meals in the antiques corridor.

*   *   *

Stately homes were not the only rural casualties of the war. Many fine gardens also went to ruin. If a property was requisitioned, the military had neither the time nor the skill to maintain the house's immediate surroundings, and nature soon destroyed man's efforts, reducing lawns to hayfields, borders to riots of undergrowth, hedges to belts of tangled forest. Beyond the gardens, parks also fell into dereliction, or were ploughed for growing wheat.

One park which survived intact was at Chillingham Castle, in Northumberland, where a herd of unique wild white cattle had lived for centuries. Primeval creatures, they regulate their own existence without interference from humans; during the war they were never bombed, and although their number fell from forty to twenty-nine, it built up again soon afterwards.

The Tudor castle, in contrast, received some rough treatment. For six years it had stood empty, peopled (in the opinion of a later owner, Sir Humphry Wakefield) only by spirits. Yachts and aeroplanes, he reckoned, had called the previous owners, the Tankerville family, away, allowing the castle's world-famous ghosts to take over. In his view, it was the spirits who arranged for irresponsible Canadian troops to be billeted within the massive walls, and to start 'a controlled house fire' which destroyed the dark Victorian panelling and heavy plaster in the North Wing, leaving only the original stone, 'firm and sound'. Miraculously, the rooms were restored with national funds – only for the ghosts to provoke another blaze of destruction, this time in the East Wing, described in a letter to the owner, from a Canadian officer:

> Should I tell you this? But it remains a glorious memory of the perfect Christmas. Frost-cold was everywhere and the snow had drifted deep against the outer doors. Ice hung in frozen spirals from roofs, broken drains and gutters. We had a bonus delivery of Christmas liquor, returning our much-needed will to live. Ghosts, drink, happiness, all 'free spirits' for sure. An

open fire roasted a massive carcass. I hope it wasn't [one of] your rare cattle. The fire cracking and pungent smell is with me for all time. The fires blazed into the dawn morning as the troops stripped all-manner of wood from the walls of our great meeting hall.

The carcass on the spit may well have come from the park. But when rain fell on the remains of the Victorian plaster, and that too came off, in Sir Humphry's words 'the return to the medieval was complete, with the revelation of fine stone-work and well-crafted masonry'. The soldiers' philistine rapacity had laid bare many secrets:

We can now see a wall built out to twenty-feet-thick to repel cannon fire in the early 1500s. We can now see flagstones laid over cobbles for the royal visit [by King James I of Scotland] in 1603. We can see sets of spiral steps, that could help an invader, removed in the 1500s and changed to latrines.

What heritage or planning officer, what professional aesthete, would dare remove Georgian, let alone 1500s, plasterwork with the off-chance of exciting masonry below? Only the ghosts could achieve that, with their most carefully-controlled 'accident'.

Fourteen

Plane Fields

Up, up the long, delirious, burning blue
I've topped the windswept heights with easy grace
Where never lark or even eagle flew –
And, while with silent lifting mind I've trod
The high, untrespassed sanctity of space,
Put out my hand and touched the face of God.

From a poem by Pilot Officer John Gillespie Magee Jr,
an American serving with the Royal Canadian Air Force,
killed when his Spitfire collided in cloud with another plane
over Digby in Lincolnshire on 11 December 1941

At the start of the war there were only fifteen active military airfields in East Anglia, and only one of these had hard runways: the rest merely had marked grass tracks. Aircraft were taken into hangars for maintenance, but for most of the time they stood in the open, dispersed round the perimeter of the field, and they were usually neither protected nor concealed. Sometimes they were partially hidden under trees, and sometimes covered with camouflage netting; but this took so long to put on and remove that its use was soon discontinued. Air-traffic control was extremely primitive, as many aircraft had no radio, and pilots came in to land after a glance at the windsock. For night operations, landing strips were marked by oil-burning gooseneck flares.

During the Munich crisis in 1938 ground defences were set up on airfield perimeters, and searchlights were deployed in adjoining fields.

Come 1939, rapid change set in. All over the east of England sites for new airfields were found, and construction began – with brutal disregard for the old patterns of the landscape. Fences, hedges and gates were ripped out; ditches and ponds were filled in, farm buildings and cottages demolished. To the consternation of country folk, who were used to walking everywhere, traditional footpaths were suddenly severed by new fences, so that they had to make lengthy detours to reach their destinations. People travelling by bicycle also found this no small aggravation. Farmers were dismayed for a different reason: at a moment when the Government was urging them to grow more corn, they saw thousands of acres of good land being taken out of their hands – and they were understandably annoyed when military personnel stationed on outlying sites started blazing trails through cornfields to make short cuts to their headquarters.

The expansion was extraordinarily rapid. By the end of the war there were forty-seven airfields in Norfolk alone, and thirty-two in Suffolk, two-thirds of them built during the conflict. Some, like RAF Bassingbourn, south-west of Cambridge, had been laid out with grass runways before the war. The site had been chosen because the boggy ground, between tributaries of the River Cam, often produced mist, which was considered a good form of camouflage – but it also had the disadvantage of becoming so soft in wet weather that even light bombers such as Bristol Blenheims gouged channels out of the grass when taking off and landing. For the new base, three converging hard runways were set out in a triangular A pattern so that they could be used in any wind; at first they were surfaced with asphalt and painted in stripes, to camouflage them, but later they were replaced with concrete.

Another base bedevilled by soft ground (and frequent fog or low cloud) was Ludford Magna, at 430 feet above sea level the highest

airfield in Lincolnshire, yet known from the state of the ground as
Mudford Magna. The station's first commanding officer, Group Captain
Bobby Blucke, described the place as 'a joke in very bad taste played by
the Air Ministry at our expense'.

New airfields were greedy. For each take-off and landing strip a belt
of land 200 yards wide was cleared and graded. Centred along this
main strip was a concrete runway fifty yards wide and at least 2000
yards long (that alone took up twenty acres – the equivalent of eight
full-sized football pitches). Such was the stress exerted by heavy bombers that the concrete had to be six inches thick, laid on a base of hard
core and covered with asphalt.

The construction of one airfield could swallow 90,000 tons of
aggregate and 18,000 tons of dry cement, some of which was conveyed
to the site by steam-powered lorries. All round the new field, outside
the runways, ran a perimeter track fifty feet wide, with another thirty
feet of ground levelled and cleared on either side. Along the track were
concrete hard stands, set well apart so that in the event of an attack
aircraft parked on them would not all be destroyed in a single conflagration, and damage would be minimized if there was an accident
when bombing-up. Two, three or four hangars up to 300 feet long occupied even more space, as did rows of Nissen huts clad in sheets of
hooped steel, which soon became ubiquitous. Electricity was laid on to
all but the most remote stations, which relied on their own
generators.

Another change, necessitated by the new fields, was the provision
of piped water. Most farms and outlying cottages had no mains water,
but relied on springs, wells or underground tanks which collected the
run-off of rain from house and barn roofs. On the wartime bases, in
contrast, a regular supply was essential, for fire-fighting as well as for
drinking and washing. The result was that water-storage tanks – big,
square boxes on top of scaffolding towers – began to spike the low East
Anglian horizons. The new airfields were also more sharply defined: no

longer surrounded by friendly hedges, they were encircled by barbed wire for greater security.

One of the most destructive, in environmental terms, was RAF Great Dunmow, in Essex, where building began in 1942 on the ancient parkland of Easton Lodge, once the home of Daisy, Countess of Warwick, mistress of King Edward VII and celebrated for the extravagance of her parties. Unfortunately, the park was ideal for an airfield, as the land was almost completely flat, stretching across the top of a low hill, so that there were no obstructions around it. Ten thousand trees, including 200 mature oaks, were felled, and their stumps blown out, to make room for three concrete runways and an encircling perimeter track, and in 1943 the 386th Bombardment Group of the US Air Force moved in.

The new airfields brought thousands of contractors, servicemen and women into the East Anglian countryside. On the base at Ludford Magna there were nearly 3000 men and 300 women, most of them living in Nissen huts scattered about various farm fields on inconvenient sites north of the village.

In the midst of all the building and flying, indigenous inhabitants carried on as normally as possible. Early in the war at Bardney, in Lincolnshire, people thought the townie evacuees dumped on them 'rather odd' and nicknamed them 'Fish and Chips'. When trenches were dug across the green and covered with boards and sandbags, children were told that the work had been done so that they could play trains. Barter of eggs, butter, corn, pig meal and cigarettes was soon flourishing. Mrs Smithson, with her trap and pony, Dolly, organized street collections of salvage, and in the matter of amassing aluminium cooking vessels and iron railings, Bardney had the best response in the county – a triumph for which the locals were congratulated by a parade through the village, led by Billy Butlin, pioneer of holiday camps, riding in a large model ship.

Then, in 1942, two farmers received orders from the War Office, requisitioning some of their land, and the construction firm Moss moved in with a swarm of Irish labourers. At first people thought they were going to build a munitions factory, but the project turned out to be an airfield. As the foundations of three concrete runways were laid to the north-east of the village, one of the farmers, Mr Laughton at Thickthornes, was offered alternative land, but refused to move, so that the airfield had to be built round him. Soon 2500 service personnel arrived to swell the community, greatly increasing the level of social activity. Local people went up to the airfield for dances, and the airmen came to the village pubs, to the Methodist Hall, to the canteen of the garage at Alderlea, and to families' homes.

Besides its main bases, the RAF had nearly fifty Satellite Landing Grounds (SLGs) – fields used by maintenance units, and also for storage and as dispersal points, which reduced the number of aircraft that might be destroyed or damaged by Luftwaffe attacks on bomber or fighter airfields. The SLGs were designed to be as inconspicuous as possible, so that they blended into the countryside. Runways were grass, and buildings were camouflaged or sited among trees.

Such was the demand for more stations that the RAF considered resurrecting the First World War field on Salisbury Plain, on a 300-acre site a few hundred yards to the south-west of Stonehenge. Fortunately the plan was dropped: had it gone through, it would have furnished the Luftwaffe with another target and substantially increased the chances of England's most celebrated prehistoric monument being blown to bits. There is even a rumour that the airmen recommended demolition of the standing stones, on the grounds that they were a flight hazard.

Most of the new fields, with Nissen huts made of hooped steel, were a good deal less comfortable than the old, in which airmen had been housed in brick buildings. Also, for safety, new living quarters were often sited a long way from operational areas. One new base, Metheringham, built in the winter of 1942–3 on the flat fenland south-east of Lincoln, was so cold and damp that men slept in their greatcoats. Eric Brown, a flight engineer with 106 Squadron, had bitter memories of his time there:

> It was a terrible place, cold, bleak, isolated. We faced a two-mile walk to our huts, which were as bad as you would find anywhere in the RAF. They were draughty, ran with condensation, and we had so little fuel for the single stove that some of the Aussies on the squadron took to stealing other people's doors to burn. By the time I left there was hardly a lavatory door left.

Senior ranks were generally far more comfortable. At Woodhall Spa, also in Lincolnshire, which opened as a bomber base in 1940, the officers' mess was the Petwood Hotel, formerly Petwood Park, once the home of Grace Maple, of the furniture family. Built in the early years of the twentieth century, in heavy Tudor-Jacobean style, the house had been a fashionable Edwardian health resort, served by through trains from London; in the First World War it had become a convalescent home, and now it was taken over again by the military.

The need for modern bases was driven partly by the increase in size and weight of the RAF's bombers. The Hampdens, Whitneys and Wellingtons which began the offensive against Germany were too slow, too limited in bomb-carrying capacity and too poorly armed to be war winners. At least they had the merit of being able to land on grass. But it was in 1942, with the emergence of the four-engined Avro Lancaster, developed out of the underpowered Manchester, that concrete runways became essential.

'Indisputably the great heavy night-bomber of the Second World War,' wrote the historian Max Hastings, 'the Lancaster inspired affection unmatched by any other British heavy bomber ... Cruising at 216 mph, intensely durable and resistant to punishment ... beautiful to the eye and carrying the bomb-load of two Flying Fortresses at 20,000 feet,

[it] ranks with the Mosquito and the Mustang among the great design successes of the war.' A Lanc, powered by four Rolls-Royce Merlin engines, could carry 14,000 lb of bombs and had a range of 1660 miles. In its final form it could accommodate the monstrous Grand Slam bomb, at 22,000 lb the largest carried by any aircraft in the war.

Lancasters were still supplanting earlier types when Bomber Command launched its first mass attack, on 30 May 1942. Frank Mee, the boy with a passion for dancing who lived at Norton-on-Tees in Co. Durham, could identify all the planes that took part. He was already something of an aircraft expert, since he frequently rode shotgun when his father, a haulage contractor, delivered material for the construction of runways.

Now, on a lovely summer evening, Frank and some friends were sailing their boats on the duck pond at Norton Green as people strolled round the garden, or sat about chatting – an idyllic scene.

> Suddenly we all became aware of a steady humming sound which got louder until it was a roar. There above us were bomber planes, masses of them, flying in a wide arc. The roaring got louder as more groups of planes arrived in blocks, one above the other. They flew in wide circles, seeming to be centred on the Green.
>
> All playing had stopped, the boats forgotten, as we stared at such a magnitude of four-engined bombers, by now deafening in their noise … The sky was now black with bombers blotting out the last rays of the sun, and the noise overhead had reached a crescendo. Suddenly they started to straighten out and head for the coast. As the last engine sound died away, it was quiet and tranquil once more.

In the morning the boys learned that they had witnessed the start of Operation Millennium, the RAF's first 1000-bomber raid, dispatched by Air Marshal Sir Arthur (Bomber) Harris as a demonstration of strength soon after his own elevation to the summit of Bomber Command. The lads learned that forty-three of the aircraft they had seen did not return, and that a lot of the men were missing or dead; but for the time being they could have no conception of the devastation the raid had created.

The original target had been Hamburg, but because of bad weather at the last minute the assault was diverted to Cologne: 1455 tons of bombs were dropped, causing havoc in the city on the Rhine. More than 3000 houses were destroyed, another 9000 more or less severely damaged. Some 45,000 people were left homeless, and nearly 500 were killed. The glorious Gothic cathedral, with its towering twin spires, miraculously escaped destruction – as it did for the whole of the war.

RAF Bomber Command's core territory was Lincolnshire, which became 'to all intents and purposes, one enormous airfield, populated by around 300,000 civilians and 80,000 airmen and women'. At the peak of activity there were forty-six military airfields in the county, sixteen of them within a ten-mile radius of Lincoln itself, and the sky became so crowded that circuits overlapped. Besides the RAF stations, there were four bombing ranges on the coast, two on the Wash and two further north.

The most famous of Lincolnshire squadrons, 617, was formed in March 1943 with the express purpose of destroying the Möhne, Eder and Sorpe dams in the Ruhr. Only seven weeks after the unit's inception, on the night of 16–17 May, Wing Commander Guy Gibson took off from Scampton and led a force of nineteen Lancasters to their targets deep in the heart of Germany. By brilliant, courageous flying, the crews breached the first two dams with a raid that won the participants thirty-three awards for gallantry, including the Victoria Cross for their leader; but eight of the bombers were lost, fifty-three out of 133 air crew were killed and three captured.

Around the bomber bases in East Anglia, as well as in Lincolnshire and Yorkshire, villagers lived in close proximity to the airmen, sometimes right on the perimeter of the field. On summer afternoons, when they saw RAF crews stretched out on the grass beneath their machines, catching up on sleep before the next night's mission, the country folk sensed something of the courage, dedication and sheer endurance needed for every raid. Boys had special observation points from which they counted bombers taking off, and people of all ages waited anxiously for their return, knowing almost for sure that some would have been shot down. At Binbrook 460 Squadron of the Royal Australian Air Force established a particularly close bond with the people of the village – even though, when blond men with strange accents first appeared on the scene, one girl ran home and told her mother that the invasion had begun. Elsewhere farming families befriended WAAFs attached to the various stations and supplied them with fresh eggs.

Relations were not always so harmonious. According to Max Hastings,

> Holme-on-Spalding Moor was a bleak, unfriendly sort of place.
> It was widely felt by the aircrew that the village had turned its
> back on the war. The locals resented the RAF's domination of
> their bowling alley. Wives and girlfriends who lodged nearby
> were treated with ill-concealed disdain, scarlet women from
> the cities.

The war brought work and money to East Anglia. Large numbers of airmen were billeted in private houses; thousands of civilian workmen supported the air bases, and pubs found trade hugely increased by airmen in search not only of a drink but also of company and conversation. Yet the airfields also greatly increased the danger for everyone living near them. With huge numbers of aircraft constantly taking off, flying and landing, crashes were inevitable: during the war more than 1000 planes came down in Lincolnshire alone, one (a Hampden bomber) onto Lincoln Girls' High School, killing the four-man crew and the senior French mistress.

Further north, Yorkshire also became densely populated with bomber bases. Several new airfields had been laid out during the 1930s, but the war set off a rapid expansion, and by 1945 the county contained no fewer than forty, most of them in the flat land along the River Ouse. Like East Anglia, the county became a virtual aircraft carrier. Thousands of acres of farmland were taken for new bases, and thousands of servicemen and women moved into what had been empty countryside. Some of the airfields, like Church Fenton, between Selby and Tadcaster, were fighter stations, charged with the task of defending the east coast, and had grass runways; others – among them Leeming, south of Catterick – began as fighter bases but converted to bombers. Between 1940 and 1945 the RAF flew more than 100,000 sorties from Yorkshire fields and lost over 18,000 men.

Lying not far inland, the bases were vulnerable to sudden attacks, and the most destructive raid of all took place on 15 August 1940, when a force of about fifty Junkers JU 88s was picked up by radar as they came in over the North Sea from Aalborg in Denmark. Spitfires and Hurricanes intercepted them and shot down nine, but the rest pressed on to cross the coast south of Bridlington and put in a lethal attack on RAF Driffield, some ten miles inland. The airfield got no warning – except that a family dog in a house two miles away took cover a few seconds before the raiders arrived. Suddenly a swarm of them was dive-bombing and strafing the airfield with cannons and machine guns. To one survivor it seemed that the raiders were 'so low you could almost reach out and touch them'. Farm workers in the fields dived for cover into the stooks of corn as the Luftwaffe pilots opened up on them. In the words of the air historian Patrick Otter,

Within a few short minutes they devastated the airfield. Four of the five big brick-built hangars were badly damaged, many ancillary buildings were left on fire, twelve Whitleys [bombers] were destroyed, and thirteen people were killed and numerous others wounded.

Enemy attack was one hazard; but accidents also took a severe toll, often the result of training flights. Clarrie East, who grew up in the village of Tockwith, remembered a Halifax bomber from RAF Marston Moor taking the top off the vicarage before crashing on the airfield boundary. On the night of 22–23 November 1943 two Halifaxes collided soon after take-off for a raid on Berlin; both crashed into farmland at Barmby, and all fourteen men on board were killed. Later fourteen oak trees were planted on the site, each bearing the name of one of the dead. Jean Didlock, a WAAF ambulance driver, had an unnerving experience when she was asked to go and pick up a flying helmet which someone had spotted lying around after a crash. 'When I did,' she reported, 'I found a head inside it.' Young John Dawson, a school-boy, was almost killed when riding on a tractor. A crashing Halifax came down so close that he and the driver were both showered with blazing fuel and suffered severe burns, which put them in hospital for months.

In Yorkshire, as in all RAF bomber stations, WAAFs played a vital role, handling all the operational information which came down from headquarters, and also bolstering the air crews with emotional support. At Pocklington they would assemble on the roof of the watchtower as aircraft took off. 'We felt it helped the boys to know we were there,' said Edith Kup.

I have always felt one of our most important functions was to provide a shoulder to cry on and a sympathetic ear to any member of the air crew wanting to get something off his chest.

It was always highly confidential, and no one ever breathed a word to anyone else about it.

Carnaby, near Bridlington, became an emergency landing ground, with an immense runway, 3000 yards long and 250 wide – five times the normal width – extended by 500 yards of grass at either end. It was also equipped with the fog-dispersal system known as FIDO, in which pipes laid along either side of the runway were pumped full of petrol. The fuel was released through burners placed every few yards, and when lit formed parallel lines of fire, visible in low-lying fog. In the memory of Jack Bainbridge, a flight mechanic, it was 'an amazing sight … Many aircraft used this facility when they were unable to land at their own drome. It was an eye-opener to see just how many types of bomber were parked up when the fog had cleared.' During the war Carnaby recovered more than 1500 aircraft either suffering mechanical failure or shot up in battle.

With such intensive flying, civilian casualties were inevitable – as when another damaging raid hit Yorkshire in the last weeks of the war. On the night of 3 March 1945 a mass of German fighters attacked British bombers on their way home. About 100 JU 88s infiltrated the incoming bomber streams and shot down at least twenty-four of them. One Junkers pilot, Hauptmann Johann Dreher, brought down two Halifaxes of 158 Squadron returning to RAF Lissett, near Bridlington on the Yorkshire coast. Clearly fired up by his success, he pressed on inland to hit the airfield at Elvington, near York, strafing the road and a passing taxi; but then, curling round at very low level to make another attack, his aircraft clipped a tree and crashed into Dunnington Lodge farm, killing him and his three-man crew, as well as the wife and daughter-in-law of the farmer, Richard Moll. The farmer himself was severely burnt, and later died of his injuries.

Fifteen

American Invasion

Comin' in on a wing and a prayer,
Looky-look, there's our field over there.
Though we've one motor gone,
We can still carry on,
Comin' in on a wing and a prayer.

USAF bomber crews' song

When the Americans came, they came in thousands. Goaded into action against the Axis powers by the devastating Japanese attacks on the US fleet in Pearl Harbor on 7 December 1941, they hastened to Britain's aid. The first servicemen arrived in packed troopships on 26 January 1942 – the vanguard of a tremendous influx, which over the next three and a half years amounted to three million men and women, including those who passed through Britain to fight in continental Europe.

The American invasion wrought huge change in the countryside, as great stretches of farmland were taken for airfields, and one village after another was beefed up not just by hundreds of temporary inhabitants, but also by whole new camps. While concrete runways lanced across the fields, and control towers and hangars sprouted, around villages and towns barrack huts, canteens, hospitals and ammunition stores sprang up: parks were tarmacked or concreted for lorries and tracked vehicles, with a guardroom, barrier and sentry box at the entrance. Almost everything was new. Whenever a big country house was requisitioned for military use, not only was the main building taken over, but stables and cottages on outlying parts of the estate were also occupied. The main concentration was in East Anglia, which was so densely populated by US servicemen and vehicles that it became known as 'Little America'.

A BBC survey made in April 1942 suggested that most Britons held practically no opinions about America except what they had gleaned from Hollywood movies. The majority of people seemed never to have thought much about the Yanks – but now suddenly they were infiltrated by hordes of them.

'Over-sexed, over-paid, over-fed and over here' was *not* the verdict of most country folk. Some found the GIs brash and vulgar, with an inclination to boast, and some resented the fact that – through no fault of their own – the soldiers hung around with little to do as they waited to go into action; but on the whole the newcomers were received with good humour. They were friendly, high-spirited, generous and polite: officers billeted on private homes almost invariably addressed the lady of the house as 'Ma'am'. The servicemen were furnished with inexhaustible supplies of food, particularly chocolate and chewing gum – rare treats for the children. In no time five-year-olds were dancing round them pleading for handouts. All Yanks appeared to be loaded with money: their pay was five times higher than British equivalents, and, as they had no living expenses, they boosted many a local economy by spending freely in pubs.

Most of the GIs were conscripts, drafted into the army, and as hardly any of them had left America before, the United States War Department issued a seven-page pamphlet designed to introduce them to the peculiar habits of their British allies. But the booklet had another purpose as well: to refute Nazi propaganda, which claimed that Britain and America were not securely united.

'You are going to Great Britain as part of an Allied offensive – to meet Hitler and beat him on his own ground,' the pamphlet began.

For the time being you will be Britain's guest … America and Britain are allies. Hitler knows that they are both powerful countries, tough and resourceful. He knows that they, with the other United Nations, mean his crushing defeat in the end. So it is only common sense to understand that the first and major duty Hitler has given his propaganda chiefs is to separate Britain and America and spread distrust between them.

The advice given was sensible and down to earth. Remember that the British are 'more guarded in conduct' than us. Don't show off – the British dislike bragging. British taxicabs look antique because Britain makes tanks for herself and Russia, and hasn't time to make new cars. The British make much of Sunday, and all the shops are closed. 'The British don't know how to make a good cup of coffee. You don't know how to make a good cup of tea. It's an even swap.'

Many other subjects were covered in a light-hearted way – pubs, cricket, football, cinemas, driving on the left – but now and then the tone of the pamphlet hardened:

Don't be misled by the British tendency to be soft-spoken and polite. If they need to be, they can be plenty tough. The English language didn't spread across the oceans and over the mountains and jungles and swamps of the world because these people were panty-waists.

Sixty thousand British civilians – men, women and children – have died under bombs, and yet the morale of the British is unbreakable and high. A nation doesn't come through that if it doesn't have plain, common guts.

The British are tough, strong people and good allies. You won't be able to tell the British much about 'taking it'. They are not particularly interested in taking it any more. They are far more interested in getting together in solid friendship with us, so that we can all start dishing it out to Hitler.

Any GI who read the pamphlet soon saw that it was talking turkey, and many were shocked by the state to which bombing had reduced British towns. One man, docking at Avonmouth after twenty-eight days at sea, remembered 'all around the area, huge craters – *fresh!* The fear ran through the ship like a shot.'

Some incoming Americans went first to transit camps, like the one at Bettisfield Park, near Wrexham, before moving on to more permanent accommodation. Having arrived by sea, often at night, they spent two or three days under canvas before being transferred to their new destinations: thousands went by rail, but many travelled by road, and country lanes were constantly blocked by convoys of troop-carrying trucks.

The more permanent camps were generally on the edges of towns, or out in the country, but their inmates naturally gravitated into centres of civilization. Officers were often billeted in hotels, and the GIs came in for recreation. The genteel town of Cheltenham, for instance, was soon full of American troops walking the streets in their well-cut uniforms of smooth cloth (far more chic than rough, ill-fitting British battledress) or driving around in green Willys jeeps embellished with the emblem of a white star in a circle. Saturday-night dances at the Town Hall boiled with activity, as local girls, eager for the silk stockings and make-up which they knew they could wheedle out of their suitors, happily teamed up with new partners for the night. At weekends the pubs filled with GIs, who generally described British beer as 'warm and weak'. But any who over-indulged were liable to be grabbed by the US Military Police – martinets who patrolled the town in jeeps and threw drunks into the back of their vehicles like sacks of potatoes. Whenever air-raid sirens sounded, all loitering Americans would take off at such a speed for their camps that locals reckoned the danger from hurtling vehicles was greater than that from falling bombs.

Similar scenes were common in the West Country, where cider often proved a knockout. Pub landlords would limit GIs to two pints apiece. If they stuck to beer, they could manage, but if they drank locally made scrumpy, a couple of jars would put them under, and away they would be carted.

At Chipping Norton, in Oxfordshire, the Americans had a camp behind the brewery in Albion Street and kept their tanks parked in fields outside the town. On Saturday evenings trucks carried off loads of girls to dances on the base, and many an unofficial union took place in out-of-the-way corners. But there was one particular address which attracted off-duty American soldiers like a honey-pot. Richard Hunt, thirteen in 1944, never forgot how, at weekends, they booked them-selves into his mother's boarding house in the Market Place, ate spam and eggs with jam on them for breakfast, and spent every free moment playing poker or pontoon in the dining room. Smoking continuously, for hours on end, they hardly spoke, except to say 'Raise ya' or 'See ya', totally absorbed in a war of cards, with the real war far from their minds.

Some of the Yanks, away from home for the first time, found England depressing. 'The sun doesn't come out much,' wrote one private to a friend in Pennsylvania. 'I don't know why I ever thought I'd like to come here' – and of course waiting for action was unsettling: 'I sure wish they would get started here. It really gets on your nerves just to sit and think about it.' Most letters home, though, were more cheer-ful: 'You don't have to worry about being a bachelor ... The air-raid shelters sure come in handy when you are courting a girl.'

As always with soldiers away from the battlefield, awaiting action, sex was a problem: GIs became notorious for their predatory behav-iour, and any number of naïve English girls succumbed to their advances – so much so that a contemporary joke promoted an alleged new brand of knickers: 'One Yank and they're off'. With so many young British men away at the war, it was hardly surprising that visitors took advantage of the vacuum. As the American historian David Reynolds pointed out,

> The disruption of family life in Britain made a young male
> presence more desirable. The dark, pinched and anxious
> atmosphere of wartime encouraged escapism and the search
> for fun.

For most country folk, the arrival of black soldiers was a revelation – for the black population of the British Isles was still tiny (fewer than 10,000) and confined to ports like Cardiff, Liverpool, Newcastle and London, and people outside those places had hardly ever set eyes on a black person. Somebody put about a rumour that black American servicemen could not talk, but only bark, and this led to exchanges in several Cotswold towns, with black troops barking at local citizens, and locals barking back as part of the edgy joke.

Nobody was more delighted by the arrival of blacks than Ken Clark, a boy growing up in Monmouthshire:

> He leaned down from his jeep and scooped me up into the
> passenger seat, and I was dazzled. Gleaming white smile,
> flashing brown eyes, shining brown skin and a beautiful
> uniform … Homer was a black American soldier who arrived
> in Talywain in the autumn of 1943. He was awesomely
> attractive, a huge man, with a uniform that was well-tailored –
> all smooth cloth, colourful insignia and very smart …
>   Our black friends were friends despite swarms of children
> following them, tugging at their clothes and asking, 'Got any
> gum, chum?' They never lost their tempers, were always

smiling, and were extremely generous. We loved those first American soldiers, and did not even think about colour, except that they were black and we were white – a natural state of affairs.

Another boy had a similar experience when delivering bread to the cookhouse at Abbotsinch airport, which was manned by black personnel of the US Air Force. He was standing there, looking around, when suddenly he was lifted off his feet by a huge American sergeant.

I was so small, he simply lifted me and put me on a table like a doll. Then he shook my hand and gave me some chocolate with a big smile, and off he went. I was amazed at the size of him, so I asked some of the other airmen who he was. They looked at me as if I was mad. 'Sonny,' one of them said, 'don't you recognise him? He's the heavyweight champion of the world. That is the great Joe Louis himself, the Brown Bomber.'

In the American military, segregation was strictly enforced. Ditchingham Hall, in Norfolk, was requisitioned for use by the RAF, but handed over to the US Army for occupation by Company A of the 279th Quartermaster Service Battalion. Members of this all-black unit lived in tents on the estate, while an all-white Engineering Company occupied the Queen Anne manor house.

GIs from the southern states of America were reluctant to accept the fact that in England race relations were far more relaxed than those at home. The result was that open wars broke out, particularly in dance halls and other places of entertainment, when British whites would back up men of West Indian origin against black Americans. International relationships became strained when, to the chagrin of British Tommies, village girls seemed to prefer dashing black American soldiers to white English ones. The girls knew that the blacks were quartered in camps of their own, but they probably did not realize that the separation from whites reflected the strict segregation that still existed in the United States.

White Americans keenly resented the ease with which black GIs formed relationships, and irritation (or was it jealousy?) often simmered at a dangerous level. 'One thing I don't like is the fact that the English don't draw any color line,' wrote an Engineer corporal:

> I've seen nice-looking English girls out with American Negro soldiers as black as the ace of spades … I have not only seen the Negro boys dancing with the white girls, but we have actually seen them standing in doorways *kissing the girls goodnight* … [The situation] irks the boys no end, especially those of the outfit that come from the south. No doubt there will be bloodshed in the near future.

The corporal's prediction proved all too accurate. The first major altercation occurred in Antrim in October 1942, when a black GI was killed by white American troops because of interracial dating; and in Leicester in 1943 white paratroopers of the 82nd Airborne Division attacked black GIs escorting white women to pubs and dances.

It was not only American soldiers who got into trouble. On 7 October 1942 two Canadian marines were on exercise high on the heathery slopes of Hankley Common, near Godalming, in Surrey, when they came on a female arm sticking out of a mound of earth near the top of a ridge. Local police immediately set a guard on the site, pending the arrival of the Home Office pathologist Professor Keith Simpson, who came down from London with a colleague next day. Working carefully with shovels, the two specialists exhumed the sprawling, badly decomposed body of a girl, lying face-down, clad in a green and white summer dress. Her protruding fingers had been chewed by rats, and her remains were alive with maggots.

Detective work soon established her identity. She was Joan Pearl Wolfe – a girl of twenty-one who had run away from home and taken to living rough in a wigwam built from branches and twigs. The architect of that flimsy shelter was August Sangret, a twenty-eight-year-old French-Canadian private soldier of part Cree Indian birth, stationed at Jasper, a nearby Canadian Army camp. Searches of the area where the girl was found turned up various small belongings scattered about the hill, among them a letter she had written to Sangret, saying she was pregnant by him, and hoped he would marry her. Her simplicity was revealed by the fact that in the days before her death people had seen her knitting baby clothes.

Forensic analysis by Professor Simpson revealed that she had been stabbed in the back with a knife; that she had fallen on her face, knocking out three teeth; that while lying face-down she had been dealt a tremendously heavy blow on the back of her head which had fractured her skull, and that her assailant had then dragged her body 400 yards uphill to the spot where he half buried her, apparently re-enacting tribal ritual whereby a chief hauled the body of his victim to the highest point in the neighbourhood to advertise his victory.

Sangret at first denied having killed Joan, but the evidence against him was overwhelming, and during his trial Simpson created history by producing the dead girl's skull in court, so that the jury could appreciate the severity of the blow that killed her. They found the prisoner guilty, but, strangely enough, recommended mercy. When Sangret appealed, his plea was considered, but rejected, and he was executed at Wandsworth Prison on 29 April 1943. Even though it was one tiny incident in the turmoil of war, its gruesome details gripped the public imagination, for the case had been prominently reported in the newspapers.

The popularity of black soldiers among English girls posed a difficult problem for the US military authorities, who could not enforce the colour bar which operated at home. In September 1942 General Dwight D. Eisenhower (always known as 'Ike', and at that time Commander of

the European Theatre of Operations) acknowledged this in a letter to
Washington:

> To most English people, including the village girls – even those
> of perfectly fine character – the negro soldier is just another
> man, rather fascinating because he is unique in their
> experience, a jolly good fellow and with money to spend.

The build-up of black GIs in Britain increased rapidly. At the end of
1942 the total was just over 7000; a year later it had reached 65,000, and
by D-Day it was 130,000. The US military authorities could not prevent
casual sexual encounters between black Americans and white English
girls, many of which took place out of doors: in the summer of 1943
alfresco assignations became so frequent that Derbyshire police began
prosecuting couples because of the damage they were inflicting on
growing crops (echoes of Shakespeare's 'Between the acres of the rye/
These pretty country fools would lie').

One acute problem was that of VD, which was rife both in American
troops and in lower-class British women. In the autumn of 1942 the VD
rate among GIs in England hit a peak of fifty-eight cases per thousand
men (compared with thirty-nine at home), and the problem took on
political overtones when, in December, the House of Commons
rejected a motion for the compulsory notification of British VD
suspects. In 1943, however, Mass Observation recorded a change of attitude among working-class people in London, calling it 'a minor revolution', and this led to more active efforts, both military and civilian, to
control the spread of the disease. The US Army did all it could to
discourage its soldiers from marrying British girls, and the British
authorities took a similar line. But in 1944, before D-Day, there was an
immense upsurge in weddings as men and women became reckless,
driven on by the certainty that huge numbers of GIs would lose their
lives in the invasion of Europe.

In the United Kingdom rape was not a capital crime; but it was in much of the American South, and in the US Army. Thus in April 1944, when two black GIs were sentenced to death by a US Court-Martial for raping a sixteen-year-old girl at Bishop's Cleeve, near Bath, the British Government was powerless to intervene, as America had exclusive jurisdiction over its own troops, and in due course the men were hanged.

The case seemed to arouse little public interest; but another which followed immediately after it caused a storm in the press. At about midnight on 5 June 1944 – a few hours before the launch of the D-Day invasion – Leroy Henry, a black truck driver, allegedly raped a thirty-three-year-old woman in Combe Down, a village near Bath. A military court held in a camp near Warminster, before a jury of one black and seven white officers, unanimously found him guilty of rape and sentenced him to be hanged; but the outcry, led by the *Daily Mirror*, caused a furore: 33,000 citizens of Bath, including the Mayor, signed a petition to General Eisenhower, demanding clemency on the grounds that the woman was a prostitute and had a record of consorting with black GIs for money. It emerged that she had twice voluntarily had sex with Henry, for which he had paid her – and the judgement was quashed after a personal intervention by the General.

Another phenomenon associated with the military camps was the way they collected dogs. How the soldiers acquired them it was difficult to say, but packs of them assembled with remarkable speed, and often accompanied squads of men on route marches. Whenever a dog disappeared from a farm or a village, the owners usually blamed gypsies and accused them of transporting it to a different part of the country and selling it to the Americans there.

A month after the arrival of the US Army chiefs, the first American airmen flew in. On 23 February 1942 an advance party of the US Eighth Air Force Bomber Command arrived at RAF Daws Hill, near High

Wycombe, Buckinghamshire. Chief of the Eighth was Lieutenant General Ira C. Eaker, an articulate, softly spoken but ardent advocate of strategic bombing, and a natural partner for Air Marshal Sir Arthur (Bomber) Harris, who had just been appointed Commander-in-Chief of RAF Bomber Command.

Eaker wanted his base to be within five miles of the RAF headquarters so that officers from both commands could attend each other's briefings with the minimum of travel; and, having scouted the area within a five-mile circle, he decided that the only establishment with suitable buildings was Wycombe Abbey girls' school, set in a beautiful 160-acre park in the middle of High Wycombe.

When the Ministry of Aviation requisitioned the property, the school was given only sixteen days to find other accommodation. In the words of the official history, the headmistress's 'trust in the School's security of tenure had been cruelly betrayed', and after a frantic search for alternative premises had failed, the establishment was forced to close down for the remainder of the war. Not only Wycombe Abbey's own pupils, but also those of St Paul's Girls' School, who had joined them when evacuated from London, were cast upon the world, scattered among more than forty different schools – and the American airmen moved in to what they regarded as 'sumptuous premises'.

A few survivors remained *in situ*, including the headmistress, Miss W. M. Crosthwaite, described by an American officer as a 'true friend alike of the school and the Eighth'. But she would have been dreadfully shocked if she had known what happened on the first night the Americans occupied her buildings. The enlisted men were sent to sleep in the girls' dormitories, and soon officers were roused by bells ringing in the teachers' offices, where they themselves had bedded down. Investigation revealed that, up aloft, above the bell-pushes were signs, 'If mistress is desired, ring bell'.

Inevitably the peace of the Abbey's lovely grounds was torn apart. Subterranean bunkers were dug and lined with bomb-proof concrete, to become operations rooms. A city of tents and Nissen huts sprang up. Machine-gun emplacements sprouted. Bulldozers gouged new roads out of the turf. Tarmac coated a new parade ground. Jeeps scorched over open fields. Inside the Abbey, the school hall was divided into a dozen separate offices, and the various girls' houses were designated headquarters for Air Force Surgeon, Air Force Engineer, Public Relations Officer and so on.

After the war one US Air Force officer sought to justify such vandalism by quoting the results which it produced. 'It is worth recording the achievements of one year of operations conducted from the Abbey,' he wrote.

In 1944 the Eighth reached the peak of its offensive power. On December 24th it despatched in one day 2,034 heavy bombers and 936 fighters. Over 21,000 Americans flew in that armada over marshalling yards, communication centres and airfields behind the enemy lines. Many times that number worked on the ground to launch these planes and to direct their assault. During 1944 alone the Eighth hit the enemy with 43,000 tons of bombs ... More than 3,000,000 bombs and incendiaries were loaded on the planes, and 53,000,000 rounds of ammunition were hand-linked and loaded. At the Abbey headquarters the telephone exchanges handled as many as 14,000 telephone calls in a single day. Without the smooth operating brain of operations housed in the Abbey, these achievements would have been impossible.

RAF Bomber Command had begun the war by launching daylight offensives against German industrial installations and cities, but these had proved disastrously expensive, with flak and Luftwaffe fighters taking a heavy toll. By the time the USAF arrived, the RAF had switched to night bombing, leaving the Americans free to mount high-altitude daylight attacks on enemy targets. As always, the Yanks planned on an enormous scale: their aim was to build up a force of 3500 aircraft in the United Kingdom within a year, and they predicted that more than eighty new airfields would be needed, mainly in East Anglia, but some in Northern Ireland.

Soon American airmen were pouring into England. 'Rumour was part of everyday life in wartime English villages,' wrote the air historian Roger A. Freeman (who himself, as a boy, had been thrilled when the Americans slapped down a base on farmland near his home in Suffolk):

> So it was not surprising that when Americans were said to have been seen on the local airfield at Polebrook, Northamptonshire, speculation was rife. Rumours were soon given some substance in June when a troop train pulled into the little country station at nearby Oundle and disgorged several hundred men clad in olive drab, speaking English with accents that most of the locals associated with the cinema. On July 6th native curiosity was roused still further when large, four-engined aircraft marked with a white star on a blue disc background landed at Polebrook.

These were the first of the Flying Fortresses, the B-17s, which, for most British people, became the symbol of United States' airpower over the next three years, outshining in public imagination the other American heavy bomber, the Liberator. One factor for which the Americans had not bargained was the fickleness of British and continental weather, with its heavy cloud cover and frequent rainstorms. Used as they were to flying in clear skies, the pilots of Eighth found not only that precision bombing was difficult, but that even assembling a large force of heavy bombers at altitude posed serious problems. The first combat mission from Polebrook was ordered on the evening of 9 August 1942, but bad weather forced its postponement. On the 11th a B-17, caught in cloud, flew into a mountain in Wales, killing all on board. Next came another postponement, and the group did not take off until the 17th. Then a relatively small force of a dozen B-17s, escorted by RAF Spitfires, carried out a successful raid on railway marshalling yards at Rouen.

From that modest start the USAF's efforts expanded mightily until Essex, Suffolk and Norfolk were thickly peppered with American bases, all of them substantial installations. For instance, Ridgewell, in Essex, built for the RAF but taken over by the USAF in 1943 as a heavy-bomber station, needed – besides its runways and hangars – thirty miles of drains, 500 buildings and a sewage plant for almost 3000 people.

Country people living round the airfields – sometimes right up against them – were fascinated by the size and power of the aircraft, most of which were emblazoned beneath the cockpit windows with a saucy painting of a naked lady and her name – Iza Vailable, Any Time Annie, and so on. Many formations had their own decorators – for instance the 385th Bombardment Group's resident nose artist, Anne Heyward. Rejected for service in the British Red Cross because she had an Austrian mother, the former art student was taken on by the American Red Cross and became a permanent fixture at the Great Ashfield base near Bury St Edmunds, Suffolk, painting murals in mess halls and on individual flying jackets as well as on B-17s. Such was her reputation that one B-17 was named after her – Haybag Annie, which flew 105 combat missions.

Locals watched in awe as the bombers went lumbering off with a thunderous roar in the morning, and awaited their return in the evening with as much anxiety as the American ground crews:

Suddenly a shout goes up from an officer with binoculars on the control-tower roof. Following his outstretched arm, straining eyes locate the first tiny specks on the horizon. A fuselage glints in the sunlight. The counting begins ... The specks get nearer and the familiar outline of a Flying Fortress takes shape. The lead plane is clearly damaged. Its landing gear is still not down. The one behind fires a double red flare – casualties on board. The ambulances rev up. In the Forts come, just clearing the church and the big trees by the farm. Along the village street, women stop chatting and gaze upwards. Kids point at the smoke pouring from one of the planes.

Losses were appalling but there were also many lucky escapes. One day a B-17 put down in a barley field on Gypsy Farm, near Langley, Hertfordshire. The aircraft was not badly damaged, and was soon repaired. But how to get it airborne? Engineers solved the problem by laying down 450 feet of steel matting and attaching six rockets to either wing: with that terrific thrust, the bomber took off after a run of 370 feet, in only eight seconds.

Downed aircraft of any nationality were an irresistible attraction to boys. When a Flying Fortress pilot misjudged his approach to Woodbridge air base, beside the River Deben in Suffolk, the bomber came down in fields and skidded to a halt. The crew climbed out unhurt and asked a gang of boys where the nearest pub was. Off they went, telling the youngsters to keep away from the plane – but of course their orders were disobeyed. Ignoring the potential danger from live bombs or leaking fuel, the boys swarmed aboard, discovered the emergency rubber dinghy, made away with it and hid it in a wood. Once the aircraft had been recovered, they dragged it out, and for the rest of the war sailed it up and down the river.

The Americans, for their part, were fascinated by the rusticity of their olde worlde surroundings: decrepit farmhouses with outdoor privies, broken-down farmyard walls, thatched cottages leaning all ways, horses working in the fields, hardly a tractor in sight. Later in the war all this began to change as the agricultural revolution took hold; but in the early days the countryside was much as John Constable had known and painted it. One evening Roy Jonasson, an airman serving with the USAF 389th Bombardment Group at Hethel Airfield in Norfolk, cycled out six miles to the village of Hethersett, and afterwards wrote home:

> Coming round the bend in the road I could see the little
> English church sitting on the side of the hill. It was one of the
> most beautiful sights I have ever seen – the church on the hill
> and the sheep grazing in the green meadow.

In these Arcadian surroundings the Americans made their own entertainment, setting up 'hostesses' clubs', whose members were automatically invited to every party at every base, with free transport laid on. Land Girls were always welcome, provided they came nicely dressed ('Don't wear those goddam breeches, honey'), and they never forgot dancing on the concrete floors of hangars to the music of Glenn Miller. Visits by film stars always generated huge excitement.

'As an area of interest for any enthusiast, East Anglia was unbeatable,' wrote one historian. 'Operational aircraft passed that way in thousands, so that one acquired the feeling, "Oh no, not another 300 B-17," or "It's only a Lancaster."' Security was tight, but aficionados were constantly trying to spot rare visitors and identify the occupants of any new airfield.

By the summer of 1944 the inhabitants of East Anglia were well used to having their sleep broken by the sound of aircraft engines. As one enthusiast put it, 'the early-morning chorus of Cyclones and Twin-Wasps had grown in volume over past months until few places were free from the reverberating throb when ten million horsepower sought the thinner air'. If a thousand aircraft assembled in the sky over East Anglia, the bombers swarmed so thickly that on some days they seemed to be affecting the weather. Contrails of white vapour, created when hot exhaust loaded with particles blasted into the cold air of the troposphere, formed into clouds that blocked some of the sun's rays.

This happened on 11 May 1944 (three weeks before D-Day), a warm and cloudless morning, when 363 B-24 Flying Fortresses and 536 fighter escorts took off from airfields in the South East on a mission to attack marshalling yards in France where the Germans had concentrated troops. For hours the aircraft climbed, circled and eased into one vast formation, producing contrails when they reached 12,000–15,000 feet. Their exhausts, being white, reflected sunlight back into space, so that from 7 a.m. to 1 p.m. the area over which they flew remained distinctly cooler than the land outside their shadow.

Cooperation between the air forces, American and British, was excellent, as depicted in the film *The Way to the Stars*, released in 1945, based on a play by Terence Rattigan and starring John Mills and Michael Redgrave. In the United States the movie was renamed *Johnny in the Clouds*, a title taken from the moving poem which John Pudney wrote for the film, commemorating the death of a leading character, the American bomber pilot Captain Johnny Hollis.

> Do not despair for Johnny head-in-air,
> He sleeps as sound as Johnny underground.
> Fetch out no shroud for Johnny-in-the-cloud,
> And keep your tears for him in after years.
> Better by far for Johnny-the-bright-star
> To keep your head and see his children fed.

So East Anglia became the USAF's stronghold; but in June 1943 the Americans had also taken over Burtonwood Airfield, north of Warrington in Lancashire, which until then had been an RAF servicing and storage centre for the modification of British aircraft. In American hands it grew into the largest airfield in Europe, with huge statistics: twenty-eight miles of road, four miles of railway track, thirteen hangars, 1800 buildings, four million square feet of aircraft parking space, and sixteen miles of fence enclosing an area of nearly 1500 acres. Among the buildings demolished was the Limerick Pub on Cow Lane.

Burtonwood was used principally for building, servicing and repair rather than for the launch of operations: hundreds of aircraft were built, refurbished or scrapped there. Fighters like the P-47 Thunderbolts and P-38 Lightnings came to Liverpool by sea and were driven through the streets of the city on trailers for assembly on the base. More than 4000 B-17 bombers went through Burtonwood's hangars, 71,000 parachutes were repaired and packed and 38,000 machine guns were overhauled or modified. The roar of aero engines running on test beds continued day and night, audible for miles around. The Germans seem never to have realized the importance of the site: Luftwaffe reconnaissance planes made several flights over the airfield, but it was bombed only twice and little damage was inflicted.

At the end of the war there were 18,500 servicemen on the base: celebrated entertainers flew in to give concerts, among them Glenn Miller and his band, and the singer Bing Crosby. Relations with the town were excellent and many of the men sent their laundry out to local housewives. One woman pushed her old pram out to the nearest camp, to make collections and deliveries, earning enough money for her husband to keep his little Austin Seven going through the rest of the war. Children who ran errands could charge outrageous prices.

The dances Americans organized (often in the lunch hour) became highly popular, especially when they introduced the latest craze, the jitterbug. In three years 6500 marriages with British women took place, but many of the children sired by GIs never saw their fathers – either because they had been killed in action, or because they had been sent home before the child was born. In 1945 illegitimate births in England reached a peak of 65,000 – although how many of these involved American fathers it is impossible to say. In 1948 *Life* magazine estimated that in Britain 22,000 war babies were born out of wedlock to white US soldiers; but many children were also got by black GIs – and some liaisons left tragic consequences.

One day in 1943 or 1944, in a typical English village, a local girl gave birth to a child sired by a black American serviceman from one of the nearby bases. Let us call the baby Jessie. Such was the sense of shame among the family that the young mother was vilified – and her coffee-coloured daughter the same. Indoctrinated from her earliest years to believe that she was a disgrace to the community, unworthy of human attention, she grew up a recluse. For this, her father cannot be blamed, since he may not even have known of her existence; what condemned the girl to a life of misery was the rigid attitude of her mother.

Most of the houses in the village were owned by the lord of the manor; many still are, and in one of them Jessie has spent her entire life. Now in her seventies, she lives alone in a small, damp cottage and rarely ventures forth, except on twice weekly visits to the village store. Dressed in shabby but clean clothes, she walks a few hundred yards to the shop and hands the proprietor a short list; he makes out her order, for which she hands over money, and back she goes, carrying her purchases. She seems to exist mainly on tinned food. But her list is always the same – the same piece of paper – and local people believe she cannot read, having been hidden away at home as a girl and never gone to school. So repressed is she that she will hardly speak: if somebody meets her and tries to make conversation, she merely nods.

What does she do all the time? Nobody knows, because nobody can penetrate her reserve or her front door. She remains totally withdrawn. She never goes for a walk, never communicates with neighbours, never smiles. She has a radio, but no television. At one stage there was a move in the community to buy her a TV; but when a man who had made efforts to befriend her suggested that the church should give her a set, he was seen off by a male cousin, who growled in a menacing voice: '*Don't you interfere!*'

Successive parish priests have tried to make contact, only to be repulsed. The one occasion on which she opened up fractionally was at Christmas some years ago, when a church warden asked if she would like to see the tree and other decorations which he had just put up. To his surprise, she agreed, and walked with him to the church.

At the door he stood and watched her go up the aisle ahead of him, towards the altar. Then she turned left and disappeared into the vicar's vestry, without pausing to look at the splendid tree or anything else. After a while, when she did not reappear, he went up and found her gazing at a stained-glass window, the bottom panes of which showed a scene from the nativity.

Fascinated, he asked, 'Have you seen this before?' She replied, 'Yes' – and that was that. Next year he tried again, but she did not want to go.

Did her father ever know that Jessie existed? Seventy years on, the villagers remain distressed that she should live among them in such isolation, a pathetic victim of the war.

Sixteen

On the Wing

'Hope' is the thing with feathers
That perches in the soul,
And sings the tune without the words,
And never stops at all.

And sweetest in the Gale is heard;
And sore must be the storm
That could abash the little bird
That kept so many warm.

I've heard it in the chillest land
And on the strangest sea.
Yet never in Extremity
It asked a crumb of me.

Emily Dickinson, *'Hope' is the thing with feathers*

In war, even more than in peace, birds kept human spirits up. The sight of them flying free gave people hope that life would return to normal – and in the autumn of 1939, whenever country folk, hearing a far-flung clamour in the sky, looked up to see skeins of geese heading south on their annual migration, they trusted that the V-shaped formations were a sign of victory.

Nevertheless, the war was harsh on many species. Garden birds must have perished by the thousand in air raids on cities and towns. House sparrows were particularly vulnerable: before the war they had been in decline, and now they were being annihilated by the blast and fire of air raids – but they were still being persecuted by householders everywhere on Government orders.

The stresses of war put other birds in peril. A War Ag pamphlet declared that in Derbyshire the abolition of grassland had caused a decline in numbers of insects, and this in turn appeared to have led to 'a serious deterioration in the feeding habits of rooks'. It seemed that rooks had run short of wireworms and leatherjackets, which they normally ate in huge numbers, to the farmers' benefit. 'Large areas of winter wheat have been destroyed, and reluctantly we have to recognise the need for a reduction in the number of rooks in the province.'

Not mincing its words, the pamphlet recommended that 'the attack' be launched during the nesting period, in early summer, and followed up by the shooting of young rooks as they left the nest. Hollow-nosed bullets were the preferred ammunition, and it was suggested that the .22 rifles used for Home Guard practice 'could serve a good double purpose in this work'.

Most other birds in the country presumably carried on as usual; but rationing, and the shortage of food for humans, left some at greater risk than in peacetime. From a report in the *British Birds* magazine of 1942 it is clear that countless poachers, professional and amateur, were after them.

In Volume 36 the magazine departed from its usual observations – 'Aerial Evolutions and Soaring of Cormorants in the Lake District', 'Remarkable Behaviour of Green Sandpipers' – to report on the prices being charged by poulterers for birds on sale. The list would give latter-day conservationists cardiac arrest, but no hint of criticism or disapproval coloured the wartime report: it was merely a statement of what was available.

At 'one of the great London stores' the shelves 'were lined with coots and moorhens. Curlews were on sale at 3s 6d, lapwings at 2s 9d.' There were also rows of starlings at 9d each – though these were mendaciously described as 'Grey Log – not starlings, but very like them'. Cock capercaillie were available at 12s apiece, blackcock at 7s 6d, grouse at 6s and ptarmigan at 3s 6d, besides common or garden pheasants at 9s and partridges at 5s. At various times of the year one of the magazine's correspondents had seen two dozen land rails (or corncrakes) on offer. There were also many types of wild duck 'which are not normally welcome as table birds', including goosanders and red-breasted mergansers.

It is hard to imagine anyone who ate a coot or a merganser deriving much nourishment or pleasure from the experience. Nor can starlings have been very appetizing – for when they go to roost, doing their synchronized diving in huge, swirling swarms, they give off a nauseating smell; but the only species listed as 'unmarketable' was the heron. Two parrots stolen from Bristol Zoo by boys in 1944 were probably taken for pets rather than for consumption; but the variety of birds on offer seems less surprising in view of the fact that many species were then regarded as inimical: one old river-keeper was offering a bounty of £1 for every heron killed on his beat, and 2s 6d for a kingfisher.

In spring boys living in hill country could make extra pocket money by climbing down cliffs or wading out to the nests of black-backed gulls in marshes or lakes and collecting the mottled eggs, which were (and are) highly prized by connoisseurs. Fishmongers would pay 2s 6d a dozen. That was legal. Not so the robbing of plovers (lapwings or peewits), which lay their eggs on bare fields, but betray the position of their nest by agitated aerial manoeuvring and screaming designed to decoy marauders away from the vulnerable area. Although protected by the Lapwings Act of 1928, which forbade the sale of birds or eggs between 1 March and 31 August, their eggs, also, sometimes appeared in butchers' shops.

Country dwellers found that birds became accustomed to the noise of war with remarkable speed. When bombs landed in fields or woods, the craters would soon be visited by robins and finches in search of insects or seeds. Watchers noticed that at the beginning of the conflict duck took off from rivers or reservoirs if a single aircraft passed over, but later they became so inured to noise that they stayed put even if several planes roared low across the sky. Owls, which hunt by sound as much as by sight, pinpointing the tiniest squeak of a mouse, must have been seriously inconvenienced by night flying, especially in areas like East Anglia and Lincolnshire, where bombers were taking off and landing in such numbers at all hours of the day and night that the sky shook with thunder.

Luckily for owls, ideas about them were gradually changing. Gamekeepers had always regarded them as a menace because they killed young pheasants and partridges. Now people started to point out that they were splendid catchers of vermin, and therefore allies in the campaign against rats. In 1942 one observer watched a pair of nesting barn owls bring in twenty-seven mice, four rats and an assortment of voles during a single night, and the Ministry of Agriculture spoke up for the birds in a press release:

> Every farmer should make it his business to encourage a bird
> that is working so diligently on his behalf ... There is no bird
> that is more worthy of protection, and none that will more
> quickly pay for its keep.

On land used for military training, birds fared badly. Caerlaverock – a huge expanse of mudflats and salt marsh on the Solway Firth, where at low tide channels of water wind through banks of glistening brown and grey mud – was already a gathering point for Barnacle geese, which collected there in vast numbers for the winter. But when riflemen from military camps began to use the roosting birds for target practice, many were killed and the rest driven away.

Seabirds also suffered. In 1943 the American Air Command applied to use Grassholm Island, off the west coast of Pembrokeshire, as a bombing target; but since the island was inhabited by thousands of gannets – the only gannetry in Britain – the Royal Society for the Protection of Birds objected strongly, and the Air Ministry refused the Americans' request. Two years later, when a party of distinguished ornithologists, including Dr Julian Huxley and Ronald Lockley, visited the island, they were dismayed to find much of it pitted by craters, with bomb cases scattered everywhere, and some of the nests occupied by dead birds. Yet, to their surprise, the number of live gannets, far from diminishing, seemed to have increased from the pre-war figure of 6000 pairs; even so, the RSPB remonstrated with the Air Ministry in the strongest possible terms.

For British homing pigeons, the war brought a complete change of life. When hostilities broke out, racing stopped, and 1400 fanciers seconded their birds to the National Pigeon Service, a newly formed voluntary organization which took them over as couriers for military use. Skilled fanciers who had joined the army or the RAF needed only a few days to train a pigeon to recognize a new base, from which it could be sent on missions; but did the birds notice any difference in the landscape over which they travelled? Like humans, they can see in colour; and even if they navigate by sensing the earth's magnetic field (as is generally believed), and even if they have a sense of smell, as well as an ability to detect low-frequency sounds at huge distances, these stalwart fliers are thought also to use roads and other landmarks for direction finding. As they sped on their journeys in the autumn of 1939, more and more of the familiar smooth green spaces below them were turning brown and furrowed as ploughs cut through the turf, and then gradually going green again as the new-sown corn germinated and began to sprout.

Over the next five years the military birds carried out an astonishing number of missions, sometimes as passengers in outgoing aircraft, sometimes on their own, each carrying a small pouch slung over its back, or in a tiny canister tied to a leg, in which a message could be stowed. During the war nearly 250,000 birds were used by the army, the RAF, MI5 and civilian defence services, including the police, the fire service and Bletchley Park. A great many died on duty, and no doubt quite a few were eaten: it is thought that at least 20,000 lost their lives, and that a bird's chances of survival were less than one in eight. But their skills were highly valued, not least because they travelled fast and were extremely difficult to intercept. In the words of the Home Guard's official training manual, 'Pigeons cannot talk, and, if captured, will not give away their origin or destination.' Along the south coast predators such as sparrowhawks and peregrines were culled to give carriers free passage on their way back across the Channel – but the Germans were also using falcons in attempts to capture British pigeons and gain access to their messages.

In Germany strict rules governed the Fancy – officially the German Pigeon Federation – which was enormous, with 57,000 members. The organization came under the control of the SS, whose head, Heinrich Himmler, was himself a lifelong fancier – so, of course, Jews were banned. In 1937 the Federation had arranged a race in which 1400 German birds were brought to England and released over Lympne, in Kent, to fly home. MI5 suspected that the event had been organized as a covert training exercise, to familiarize the pigeons with routes back to their bases, and that this was only the precursor of a systematic attempt to infiltrate British lofts.

In MI5, in the Pigeon Service Special Section, B3C, the Pigeon King was Flight Lieutenant Richard Melville Walker, a fanatical fancier, devoted to the birds, who at the start of the war convinced himself that the Germans were trying to flood Britain with pigeons, bringing them by parachute and sea, to provide Nazi agents with an undetectable method of sending messages to Europe. His theory seemed more plausible when, early in 1940, a small metal container was picked up in

north London containing a message in German giving accurate information about British warships; and he became still more suspicious
when a storm blew two German birds across the Channel, even though
it turned out that they were carrying nothing but training messages.
'Both birds are now prisoners of war,' he reported, 'working hard breeding British pigeons.' Later in the war he arranged for a falconry unit to
be set up on the Isles of Scilly, tasked with the interception of enemy
messengers. Under his auspices, a young man was sent to Wales, where
he took half a dozen young peregrines from their eyries, brought them
to England, reared them and hacked (trained) them. Three of them did
in the end account for a dozen pigeons in the Scillies and along the
south coast, but all were British – blue-on-blue casualties.

From 1940 large numbers of British pigeons were dropped into
occupied Europe in the hope that Allied sympathizers would send
information about enemy troop dispositions back to the United
Kingdom. An agent parachuting in could carry six birds in a container
strapped to his chest. Otherwise, they made solo descents. Loaded into
a single-bird box, with food for ten days, each messenger was lowered
through a hatch in the belly of an aircraft, protected from the slip-
stream by a canvas sack, which was then opened by a jerk on a long
string, so that the bird was released and parachuted into enemy territory. The hope was that Resistance workers would continue to send
messages if their radio was captured or went down, or their situation
became too dangerous for them to transmit.

'*Vive la patrie!*' began a sheet of instructions for French recipients.
'*A bas les Boches!* … Help us chase the enemy out of your country …
Send us information about the Germans. You can collect important
information. This pigeon will transmit it to us.' During the invasion
scare of 1940 the message asked specific questions: 'What preparations
are in train? Are there important concentrations of troops or ships in
your area?' There followed instructions for dealing with the bird:

As soon as you arrive home, give the pigeon some water and food. Give it enough space to relax until its departure. Look after it well, if necessary for several days ... Don't sign any message with your own name ... To despatch the pigeon, launch it gently in a safe place. If at night, put it on a roof, at an open window, on a wall or in a tree. It will take off at day-break.

Most of these birds were lost: of 16,544 parachuted in, only 1,842 returned. A special effort was made in August 1943, when, at the instigation of the ever-optimistic Flight Lieutenant Walker, 1000 pigeons were dropped over Calais and the west coast of Brittany. Every bird carried a questionnaire about local beaches, defences and so on, suggesting that the Allies were eager to acquire information which would help them plan an invasion of that area, and so decoy German forces away from Normandy, which had already been chosen as the real point of attack. The huge release of feathered spies produced no discernible result, but Walker was not dismayed.

In due course all RAF bombers and reconnaissance aircraft carried pigeons housed in watertight baskets and containers, so that if the aircraft went down on land or in the sea, a bird could be released and sent back to its loft in England with a message bearing the coordinates of the site or the last-known grid reference, and a rescue could be mounted. One of the most celebrated recoveries took place in October 1943, when a Catalina flying boat stricken by engine failure ditched in a rough sea in the Hebrides at 08.20 one morning. Foul weather frustrated attempts at rescue by sea, and an air search was rendered impossible by mist so thick that no aircraft could take off; but at 17.00 that afternoon a pigeon called White Vision arrived at its loft bearing a message which gave the position of the downed aircraft. The sea search was resumed, and although the aircraft sank, the crew were rescued. The pigeon had flown sixty miles over a heavy sea, against a twenty-five-mile-an-hour headwind, in visibility of only 100 yards at the crash site and 300 yards when it came home. For this feat of endurance and navigation it was awarded the Dickin Medal, the animal equivalent of the Victoria Cross.

Another hero and medallist was Royal Blue, who, a fortnight earlier, flew 120 miles in four hours ten minutes to report a ditching in Holland; and a third was Paddy, the Irish pigeon which outpaced all rivals when bringing news of the successful D-Day landings in June 1944. Hundreds of birds were dispatched, but Paddy beat them all home, flying 230 miles in four hours and fifty minutes. Another star was William of Orange, who flew the 250 miles from the battle of Arnhem in only five hours.

Messages could go astray even in England. One fancier lived in Barrow-on-Furness with his Italian mother, and when his brother visited he persuaded him to take home a promising young pigeon and release it, to see how it performed before he handed it over to the National Pigeon Service. This the brother did – but the bird never returned to base. Three months later two men in suits appeared at the fancier's house – and only after they had asked many awkward questions was the matter cleared up.

It turned out that the brother, before setting the pigeon off on its return flight to Barrow, had attached to it a message for his mother, written in Italian because her English was poor: 'The weather here today is sunny. Hope you're feeling better and the wireless is repaired.' A farmer had shot the pigeon, and, as he was about to pluck it, had found the message, which he handed in to the police. For weeks members of the family had been followed by agents of MI5: their letters had been opened, their telephone tapped. Eventually it became evident that the message was entirely innocent, and that they were not Fifth Columnists – but they were severely reprimanded.

* * *

One ornithological activity which continued throughout the war, improbably enough, was the ancient practice of swan-upping – a ritual carried out on the Thames and other rivers for at least 900 years, in which mute swans are herded together, caught, marked and released. In earlier days roast swan was a delicacy and frequently appeared at banquets, royal or otherwise – and no doubt during the war many birds found their way onto the tables of hungry citizens along the river. The House of Commons did not set a good example. When *cygnet à l'orange* appeared on the menu, one member pronounced it 'delicious', another 'awful'.

Traditionally the ownership of all unmarked mute swans in open water resides with the Monarch, but in practice the Queen claims ownership only of those on some stretches of the Thames and its tributaries. In an archaic form of census, held over five days in the third week of July, the Queen's swan-uppers (in scarlet shirts), led by the Queen's Swan Marker, and their opposite numbers from the Worshipful Company of Vintners (in white) and the Worshipful Company of Dyers (in blue), row up the river in six wooden skiffs from Sunbury to Abingdon. When a family is sighted, the uppers give the cry 'All Up!' and converge on the swans until they can corral them with the boats. They then lift each one out of the water to weigh, measure and ring it before returning it to the river.

During the Blitz of 1940 some seventy swans were killed by enemy action on the Thames in London, either burnt by incendiary bombs or so badly contaminated with oil that they had to be destroyed. By the end of the conflict there were few left in the capital, partly because of disturbance, partly because so many stretches of the river banks had been concreted over, leaving the birds nowhere to graze. But they were flourishing further upstream. In the annual census of 1941 559 swans were upped on the Thames, compared with annual totals of about 450 half a century earlier.

Seventeen

Fun and Games

But his captain's hand on his shoulder smote –
'Play up! Play up! And play the game!'
Henry Newbolt, *Vitaï Lampada*

With the outbreak of war the Government imposed an immediate ban on the assembly of crowds at sports events, for fear that a single German bomb might cause unprecedented slaughter in a crowded stadium, and within three days the Football League cancelled its League competition. Soon, however, the rules were relaxed, and it was announced that friendly games would be allowed, provided police approval had been obtained – but in the interests of public safety the numbers of spectators were limited. The blackout naturally put paid to any matches that depended on artificial lighting.

The first-class cricket season stuttered to a close. On 26 August 1939 the West Indies touring team cancelled the remaining games of their tour and set off for home, sailing out of Glasgow aboard the *Montreal*. The Marylebone Cricket Club called off its projected tour of India. After 1 September no further first-class fixtures took place until 1946 – the longest gap since such matches had started a hundred years earlier. The shutdown brought a premature end to the careers of many celebrated players, not least Hedley Verity, Yorkshire's classic slow left-arm spinner, who, in the county's last game against Sussex, took seven wickets for nine runs. During that season he took 191 wickets at an average of just over thirteen runs each; he was only thirty-four, and had already played for England forty times. Always an optimist, while training Green Howards recruits at Richmond, in Yorkshire, he told readers of *The Cricketer* that Hitler's invasion of Holland was merely an early season setback. But he never played first-class cricket again, for he died of wounds as a prisoner of war in Italy in 1943.

Another outstanding player whose career was interrupted – but by no means concluded – by the war was the Middlesex batsman Denis Compton. In 1938, aged nineteen, he had made his first Test century against Don Bradman's Australian team, and in the 1939 season he scored 2468 runs. Then, however, he was posted to India in the army for the whole of the war, before returning to the English team for the 1946–7 Ashes series in Australia, where he scored a century in each innings of the Adelaide Test. His flamboyant batting delighted fans, who speculated endlessly about how many more runs he might have scored had Hitler not denied him five seasons at the height of his youthful exuberance.

In the autumn of 1939 at Lord's – headquarters of the game – members of the staff removed the famous little urn containing the 1883 Ashes and hid it in some secret redoubt. The bust of W. G. Grace was also taken from the Long Room for safekeeping.

Lord's, in the heart of London, was obviously vulnerable to air attack. Already in October 1938 the Practice Ground, behind the stands at the eastern end of the main field, had been occupied by an anti-aircraft detachment; from April 1939 a barrage balloon was anchored on the field, and in August a searchlight detachment joined the other military installations. Members of the armed forces quartered in various parts of the site were given facilities for cricket and football, which, MCC's annual report recorded, were 'greatly appreciated by all ranks'. Windows in the pavilion were blacked out, seats were removed from the stands, and air-raid shelters built.

Throughout the glorious summer of 1940 the game went on all over the country. On 1 June, in the words of the social historian Eric Midwinter, trains crammed with exhausted survivors of the Dunkirk evacuation 'wound their way past cricket match after cricket match on rural meadows, and people remarked on that strange contradiction'. On the same day, before a crowd of 42,000, West Ham beat Blackburn Rovers 1–0 in the Wartime Cup Final at Wembley.

On 9 July German radio reported that 'a revolt against plutocratic cricketers' had swept through the country, and that 'the people tried to destroy the playing grounds at night' – an attempt which 'led to a state of war between the population and the English sports clubs'. Ignoring this phantom insurrection, the Government decreed that all cricket fields must be rendered useless for enemy aircraft landings, and Lord's, like many other grounds, was obstructed by obstacles set out whenever no game was in progress. Yet matches continued, not only at cricket's headquarters, but all over the kingdom.

On 7 September, the day the Blitz on London began, a match was in progress between a Middlesex XI and a Lord's XI when the sirens sounded: the players ran for shelter and a long delay ensued. But a recent edict from Lord's had laid down that games must be finished, if at all possible, and this one eventually ended in victory for Middlesex as dusk was settling on the ground. Twenty-six matches, including several between schools, were played at Lord's that summer, and most of them drew large crowds.

During the Blitz between thirty and forty incendiary bombs fell on the Match and Practice Grounds, and one 1000-lb high-explosive bomb left a large crater, blowing out the windows of the Committee Room. The resident barrage balloon proved frisky, twice breaking loose: once it merely damaged some roofs, but the second time its dangling cable wrapped itself round the iconic figure of Old Father Time, with his long, pointed beard and his scythe over his shoulder, and dragged the weather vane down from the roof of the Grand Stand

– after which mishap it was consigned to the Committee Room for the time being. A famous hit was made on 29 July 1944 when the Army were batting against the RAF and a doodlebug was heard approaching. As the engine cut out, the players flung themselves face-down on the turf, certain that the V-1 was about to crash on the Nursery Ground: in fact it fell in Albert Road, and when the game resumed, the batsman, J. D. Robertson, hooked the first ball derisively for six.

The Oval, in south London, fared worse than Lord's, being taken over by the Government and converted into a cage for a prisoner-of-war holding point. In the event no prisoners ever went there, but the field was much damaged by having lines of twelve-foot wooden posts, set in lumps of concrete, erected to support walls of rolled barbed wire. The ground also housed an anti-aircraft site, a searchlight battery and an assault course. To restore the playing area after the war, Bert Lock, the groundsman, had to import 45,000 rolls of turf from Hoo marshes in Kent, and he himself spent innumerable hours repairing the practice nets, which had been put into storage and chewed by rats.

Another casualty was the Lancashire county ground Old Trafford, in Manchester, which was first taken over by the military and then heavily bombed, with the result that the Lancashire Cricket Club closed for business and diverted members' subscriptions into a war fund. Grounds in Kent, Sussex and Essex which lay within 'defence areas' could not be used for the duration, but at others the game carried on, even after the field had been pock-marked with craters. 'Local cricketers are as pleased as you,' said a sign outside one club on the south coast. 'Each peardrop which falls on this ground saves life and property. We shall carry on. Nothing which falls from the skies will deter us, except RAIN!' In many people's minds the continuation of cricket became an emblem of the nation's defiance.

Village cricketers kept going as best they could, hampered though they were by a shortage of players. With husky young batsmen and bowlers gone away to fight, teams tended to consist of veterans and schoolboys, although servicemen posted nearby could sometimes be drafted in to stiffen the ranks, and the Home Guard might furnish opposition. Lack of transport put a constraint on inter-village matches, and often a horse-drawn wagon was the only means of travelling to away fixtures. Scarcity of fuel also meant that outfields became more like hayfields, unless a horse-powered gang mower could be dragged out of retirement. Many grounds, rented from farmers, were not improved when the owners turned sheep or cattle onto them – and cowpats seemed to attract the ball like magnets. Players had some lucky escapes. At Bettisfield, a village in North Wales, a gang of boys had just drawn stumps after a game and gone to a nearby farmhouse for refreshments when a Spitfire *in extremis* came past at ground level, hit a bank and crash-landed in flames, killing the pilot instantly, on the field on which they had been playing.

For all their difficulties, players remained cheerful – like the farmer in Kent who, when his barn was destroyed by a doodlebug, remarked, 'Thank God it wasn't the square!' But some clubs, like that of Penn Street in Buckinghamshire and Gotham in the Midlands, had to close down for the duration because their fields had been requisitioned, the first for an army camp, the second for growing corn; and at Goldhanger, on the Blackwater Estuary in Essex, a searchlight unit took up residence on the square itself: its brilliant blue-white beams were so powerful that when they came on, it was possible to read newspapers anywhere in the village. Desecration of the pitch was bad enough; but a far longer-lasting loss was inflicted on the community when the fine old elms in The Avenue were felled to produce timber for the war effort.

Golf also carried on – but games could be hazardous, as Luftwaffe pilots amused themselves by spraying courses with machine-gun bullets on their way home: on 15 September 1940 a Dornier 17 was shot down by a Spitfire onto the course at Barnehurst, in Kent.

Taking place in the open, golf was a relatively safe occupation, as players could scatter in all directions and take cover in bunkers if an air attack threatened – and at least one Luftwaffe pilot made a positive contribution to a club's facilities. On a clear evening in the autumn of 1940 a formation of German aircraft jettisoned ninety incendiary and high-explosive bombs on and around the Berkshire village of Sunningdale. One of these blew a large crater beside the eighteenth green of the Old Course, damaging the clubhouse and almost putting paid to James Sheridan, the fearless caddie-master, who had dived for shelter into a bunker nearby. Rather than fill the hole in, someone had the idea of shaping it into two new bunkers, and so made the approach to the green far more challenging. Throughout the war the Old Course was maintained as far as limited manpower and resources would allow, but military training on the New Course caused serious damage, and so much restoration work was needed when peace returned that no formal reopening could take place until 1950.

Few clubs can have been as unlucky as the one at Newark, in Nottinghamshire. In 1939 the committee let the first nine holes of its course to a neighbouring farmer for grazing – a move which annoyed members so much that thirty-one of them (a sixth of the total) resigned. Then in January 1943 the local War Ag ordered the club to plough up the land – about seventy acres – for corn production. Members of the committee and a few co-opted members did what they could to maintain the remaining half of the course, mowing the greens themselves, and in the clubhouse the stewardess, Miss Robb, was instructed to conserve stocks by restricting sales of gin and whisky to half a bottle of each per week. All members were shocked when a Stirling bomber crashed onto the course on the night of 14 January 1945, killing five of the seven-man crew; but somehow the club struggled through and survived the war.

Other celebrated clubs fared even less well. At St Andrews in Fife, where golf had been played for over 500 years (except when banned in 1457 by King James II, who thought that young men were giving too much time to the game, and not enough to archery practice), the Open Championship was abandoned between 1940 and 1945 because the fairways of the Old Course were being used as runways by the RAF. At Worcester Golf Club, in contrast, a fine crop of peas was grown on the fairway.

One activity which achieved huge new popularity during the war was bicycle racing. Until then the sport in Britain had been crippled by the reactionary attitude of the National Cyclists' Union, which had refused to allow races on roads until 1921, and even after that banned mass starts. When war broke out, and petrol rationing cleared the highways of most motor traffic, Percy Stallard, who had ridden for England in international events and was known as 'the father of cycling', strongly advocated that racing should be allowed on public roads. Getting no satisfaction, he took matters into his own hands and in July 1942 organized a mass-start race of fifty-nine miles from Llangollen (in North Wales) to his home town of Wolverhampton.

He was acting in defiance of the rules, but secured the permission of every Chief Constable through whose territory the race would pass, arguing that, with scarcely any cars on the road, this was an ideal time for such an event. The NCU attempted to strike back by suspending him in advance, but he carried on regardless. The race went off without incident; forty riders started, fifteen completed the course and more than a thousand people watched the finish, at which the crowd was kept back by a cordon consisting of the Chief Constable of Wolverhampton, an inspector, a sergeant and fifteen uniformed policemen. The event raised £105 for the Forces' Comfort Fund. Reacting furiously once again, the NCU banned not only the organizer but also his assistants and the riders who had taken part.

A prickly character, and never one to admit defeat, Stallard responded by helping to create a new group, the British League of Racing Cyclists, whose first stage race was held over three days in Kent in 1944, on circuits round Tonbridge, and was interrupted by a spectacular interlude:

During a 'red alert' warning all the spectators disappeared and the villages were absolutely deserted. The field of twenty-four riders were hammering along when two of our planes came in sight in hot pursuit of a doodle-bug. They flew parallel with the riders before banging away at the flying bomb and shooting it down into some woods. The next time the riders came through the village, the main street was again packed with cheering crowds, for the all-clear had been sounded.

Another athlete whose career (and life) were cut short by the war was Prince Alexander Obolensky, a meteor among rugby players, whose parents had fled from Russia during the Bolshevik revolution of 1917. After school in Derbyshire he went to Brasenose College, Oxford, where he read PPE, and his exceptional pace gained him a place in the University XV as a wing three-quarter. His exotic background, good looks and attractive personality earned him a reputation for extravagance – he was said to breakfast on oysters and champagne.

On his first appearance for England at the age of nineteen, at Twickenham on 4 January 1936, when the home team won their first-ever victory over the All Blacks, he scored two tries, the second after an astonishing, diagonal, right-to-left run three-quarters of the length of the field, with one devastating change of direction, described by a sports writer as 'a stupendous exhibition of the hypotenuse in rugby'. 'Obolensky's try' became the most famous in the game's history. Later that year he won three more caps for England, toured with the British Lions in Argentina, and from 1937 to 1939 played for the Barbarians. In 1939 he joined the Auxiliary Air Force, and on the outbreak of war went into the RAF as a pilot officer and was posted to 504 Squadron; but on 29 March 1940 – the day after he had been recalled by England for the match against Wales – he was killed when his Hurricane crashed as it tipped into a hollow while landing at Martlesham Heath in Suffolk.

* * *

After a brief interval caused by the ban on public gatherings, horse racing started again with a meeting at Newmarket in October; but the resumption was not universally popular. In June 1940 uncharitable questions were asked in the House of Commons. Did not racing take up much-needed transport? Spectators heading for meetings burnt up scarce petrol or occupied seats on packed trains. Was racing not a vast waste of money? Was it not tarnished by its seediness and its aristocratic overtones?

Like many other racecourses, Epsom was requisitioned by the military, so on 12 June 1940 the Derby was held at Newmarket – and in the words of the racing historian Roger Mortimer, 'The most extraordinary thing about the 1940 Derby was that it took place at all, coinciding as it did with the disintegration of the French resistance and the evacuation … of the British Expeditionary Force from Dunkirk.' The fact that the race was run, he concluded, was either 'a tribute to national imperturbability' or 'a deplorable example of sheer lack of imagination combined with a refusal to face unpleasant facts'. What he did not mention was that the event had been preceded by a fierce debate among Ministers, four of whom spoke strongly in favour of ordering the Jockey Club stewards to cancel the race. It was saved by the intervention of Tom Williams, then Joint Parliamentary Secretary in the Ministry of Agriculture, who argued that cancellation would be a grave psychological error, in that it would disappoint many thousands of racegoers.

For the rest of the war the Derby was held at Newmarket, with part of the course unfenced, and the horses running across the open heath. The 1941 race had a stormy passage. The original plan was to run it at Epsom, but in March it was announced that the event would be held at Newbury. There, however, the Town Council and Chief Constable objected to the plan, and the race was moved to Newmarket, where it was run at 2 p.m. on 14 June, a fine, hot day. Petrol rationing notwithstanding, the crowd was enormous; there were traffic jams on the road from London, and some of the punters, frustrated by delay at the turn-stiles, stormed one of the gates.

Afterwards more complaints were made in Parliament and in the newspapers about the waste of fuel, manpower and time – but, as Roger Mortimer pointed out, 'Racing … in the minds of the more spiteful critics, was the sport of the rich, and therefore a suitable target', whereas 'the dogs' and football were 'the pastimes of "the people" and therefore immune from attack'. The fact that William Nevett, the jockey who rode Owen Tudor to victory in the Derby, was serving as a private in the Royal Army Ordnance Corps went some way towards stifling complaints – but it did nothing to appease George Orwell, who wrote in his diary on 25 April 1941:

> There are said to be still 2,000 racehorses in England, each of which will be eating 10–15 lbs of grain a day. *i.e.* these brutes are devouring every day the equivalent of the bread ration of a division of troops.

Disappointment, rather than a riot, was the distinguishing feature of the 1942 Derby, again run at Newmarket. Thousands of supporters hoped that the outstanding colt Big Game, leased to the King by the National Stud, would be the winner. The King – who recognized the importance of maintaining bloodstock lines, and knew how much racing meant to the public – had been having a miraculous season. Big Game had won the 2,000 Guineas, and next day the King's filly Sun Chariot (the favourite) had carried off the 1,000 Guineas. Then, on 12 June, his staff having skilfully arranged an agricultural tour of Cambridgeshire to mask his travel costs, he was able to watch Sun Chariot win the Oaks at 4-1, and, after a night spent aboard the royal train in a convenient tunnel, to be present for the Derby, wearing Field Marshal's uniform and accompanied by the Queen. Alas, royal hopes were dashed: Big Game started favourite at 6-4 on, but faded badly and came sixth.

Many other meetings were abandoned, as racecourses were requisitioned for military purposes or ploughed up for agriculture. Among those taken over by the Government was Newbury, which had been used as a prisoner-of-war camp in 1914–18, and now became a US Army supply depot.

The 1940 Grand National was held at Aintree, as usual; but Flight Sergeant Mervyn Jones, who rode the winner, Bogskar, had been given special leave to take part, and many of the crowd were in uniform. In 1941 Aintree became an American military base, and no further races took place there until 1946.

In 1940 the National Hunt meeting at Cheltenham was restricted to two days, and part of the course had been ploughed. The Gold Cup was won by Roman Hackle, owned by one of racing's most recognizable characters, Miss Dorothy Paget. Described by Roger Mortimer as 'a unique and remarkable personality', the second daughter of Lord Queensborough was then in her thirties, and owned Golden Miller, the only horse to have won both the Gold Cup and the Grand National. 'Her appearance was distinctive,' wrote Mortimer, 'and no one could ever have accused her of being a slave to fashion.'

> Stout and ungainly, she invariably wore a blue felt hat and a
> long blue coat that eventually terminated within easy reach of
> her ankles. Her face, large, round and pallid, was framed in
> hair that was dark and austerely straight. She had a
> disconcertingly retentive memory, a sound knowledge of
> bloodstock breeding, and she habitually betted in very large
> sums indeed.

Miss Paget lived a reclusive existence at her home in Chalfont St Giles, Buckinghamshire, where she kept unconventional hours and ate prodigiously, and she was prone to explosive outbursts of temper. But she poured huge amounts of money into National Hunt racing, and gave the sport a much-needed shot in the arm.

The Gold Cup took place again at Cheltenham in 1941 and 1942, but in 1942 there was an extraordinary finish. At the last open ditch the two leading horses both fell, and Red Rower, who was lying third, almost toppled over them. He recovered, but was overtaken by Medoc II, who won by eight lengths.

In September that year the Government declined to sanction National Hunt racing during the next season, and steeplechasing did not start again until January 1945. Then, with war news better, the Gold Cup, run at a one-day meeting on 17 March, attracted an immense crowd, in spite of petrol shortages and the general difficulty of travel. The race was won by Red Rower, who had clearly forgotten his earlier setback. By then only three other courses – Windsor, Wetherby and Catterick – were in use, and of the seventy-nine courses licensed by the National Hunt Committee, only forty-seven remained. Some were resuscitated, but sixteen, including those at Aldershot, Derby, Totnes and Gatwick, never opened again.

Greyhound racing also came under attack from politicians. On 13 June 1940 the persistent critic Glenvil Hall, MP for Colne Valley, asked Sir John Anderson, Secretary of State for Home Affairs: 'Is the Right Hon. Gentleman aware that this afternoon 30,000 or 40,000 people are attending dog race meetings, at a time when Paris is fighting for its very life?' Another MP, Mrs Tate, echoed him: 'In Oxford Street yesterday there were boards chalked with details of Derby betting, and alongside of them another saying, "Paris a besieged city". Does not that offend against public decency?' Anderson said he recognized the strength of feeling on the matter, but added: 'It is necessary to give consideration to the forms of relaxation available to the workers.'

For most people, fancying horses and dogs did *not* offend against public decency. The Government maintained, and most people felt, that a certain amount of frivolity must be allowed to ease the stress of war, and that racing was therefore not only acceptable, but positively beneficial. Yet Hall persisted. In another question he asked:

> Is the Hon. Gentleman aware that many of these racing greyhounds are fed upon brown bread, whole meal, eggs, fresh meat, brandy and many other things, amounting to many hundreds of tons per year, and does he not think it is grossly unfair that foodstuffs should be wasted in that way while poultry keepers, for example in my own division, cannot get supplies?

Hall's vapourings were in vain, for greyhound racing was immensely popular: Mass Observation calculated that during 1939 twenty-two million people passed through the turnstiles at dog tracks, and enthusiasm continued unabated throughout the war, especially among night workers, who, having slept when they came off shift in the morning, could relax at meetings in the afternoon.

Football also flourished throughout the war. Millions of punters filled in their Unity football coupons every week, hoping to win the maximum prize of £11,000 for an investment of one penny, and big matches attracted enormous crowds – 85,000 for the League South Cup Final at Wembley in 1944, and full houses of more than 140,000 for Scotland v. England games at Hampden Park, Glasgow. The great Stanley Matthews was a magnetic attraction wherever he appeared, whether for the RAF (which he joined in 1940 as a physical training instructor), the England wartime team, or his own club, Stoke City. Young Tom Finney – for many fans the most magical dribbler of all time – was called up into the Royal Armoured Corps and fought in Egypt and Italy before returning to make his debut for Preston in 1946. Matt Busby, who played for Liverpool, took charge of a British Army team sent out to raise the morale of troops in Italy.

One admirable feature of wartime sport and games was that they raised large amounts of money for charities. In 1943 the Duke of Gloucester, President of the joint Red Cross and St John fund, announced that since the inception of the fund in 1939 sport had already generated the splendid sum of £1,000,000 (£50,000,000 in today's values). Indoor activities were by far the biggest moneymakers. A combination of whist, bridge and dancing contributed £365,000; next came billiards, with £80,000, then darts and bowls (£72,000). Outdoors, football produced £70,000, golf £67,000, greyhound racing £50,000, and cricket £22,000.

No one reacted more vigorously to the vexations of war than Richmond Golf Club, which produced a new set of temporary rules:

1. Players are asked to collect Bomb and Shrapnel splinters to save these causing damage to the Mowing Machines.
2. In Competitions, during gunfire, or while bombs are falling, players may take cover without penalty for ceasing play.
3. The positions of known delayed-action bombs are marked by red and white flags, at reasonably, but not guaranteed, safe distance therefrom.
4. Shrapnel and/or bomb splinters on the Fairways, or in Bunkers within a club's length of the ball, may be moved without penalty. On the fairways of the ball, they may be moved without penalty, and no penalty shall be incurred if a ball is thereby caused to move accidentally.
5. A ball moved by enemy action may be replaced, or if lost or destroyed, a ball may be dropped not nearer the hole without penalty.
6. A ball lying in a crater may be lifted and dropped not nearer the hole, preserving the line to the hole, without penalty.

7. A player whose stroke is affected by the simultaneous
    explosion of a bomb may play another ball from the same
    place. Penalty one stroke.

Somehow this new disposition came to the notice of Hitler's club-
footed propaganda chief, Josef Goebbels, who reacted with a characteristic combination of mendacity, irritation, ignorance and
sense-of-humour failure:

By means of these ridiculous reforms, the English snobs try to
impress the people with a kind of pretended heroism. They can
do that without danger because, as everyone knows, the
German Air Force devotes itself only to the destruction of
military targets and objectives of importance to the war effort.

Eighteen

Field Sports

'Unting is the sport of kings, the image of war without
its guilt, and only five and twenty percent of its danger!

R. S. Surtees, *Jorrocks*

In the autumn of 1939 hunting men were determined to carry on with
their sport, come what might. The Masters of Foxhounds Association
sent out a circular pointing out 'how prejudicial it would be to the
country in general' if hunting were to lapse altogether. The Association
claimed that hunts were keeping fox numbers down, even though they
were going out two days a week instead of their normal four. A ministe-
rial report noted: 'The Hunts are treating hunting as a necessary business rather than as a sport.' The MFHA recommended that the sport
should continue, 'as local conditions permit, in order to kill foxes and
keep the packs going', and predicted that 'many a "woman" huntsman
will now cheer hounds into covert'. Difficulties abounded. Shortage of
girl grooms meant that horses were left unclipped or turned out wearing all-weather New Zealand rugs. Oats were scarce, as they were
controlled by orders from the Ministry. Flake maize (for the hounds)
was difficult to obtain – but on the other hand horseflesh (for feeding
hounds) was plentiful, as many animals were being put down.

Hunting people, though determined, were not happy. New airfields,
they claimed, were taking away much of their best country, and so

many aircraft were flying noisily around that during a run it was often difficult to hear what hounds were doing, or even to tell where they were. In wild areas huge tracts of land were being set aside for military training: when the War Office announced that it was about to acquire 40,000 acres on Eppynt Mountain, in Breconshire, the Welsh Department of the Ministry of Agriculture feared that 'this area was likely to assume a Whipsnade for foxes, without the possibility of control by hunts or anyone in particular'.

People recalled how hounds had been exported to the United States during the First World War in order to safeguard bloodlines if England were invaded; now some packs were thinned out, and some closed down for the duration, but most kept going with skeleton staff and small fields. Some had lucky escapes. When a bomb fell on the kennels of the East Kent Hunt, thirty hounds were blown in every direction, but all were recovered uninjured over the next two days.

Few men kept going more doggedly than Charles, third Earl of Leconfield, the choleric squire of Petworth Park in Sussex, once described as 'the most blimpish peer imaginable'. He continued to hunt with his own hounds throughout the war, and his nephew John Wyndham left a memorable description of a visit to Petworth in the winter of 1940. 'Dinner was, of course, more austere than usual,' he recalled. 'Uncle Charles nevertheless drank a bottle of champagne himself and pressed me to do likewise. We then had some port, after which we had some brandy.' Next day they went hunting:

> We found a fox and lost it, and while Uncle Charles's huntsman was casting for it we heard a tremendous hullaballoo about two miles away. Uncle Charles abused the huntsman and shouted at him, 'Can't you hear a holler?' and bade him 'Get going thither.' So we galloped in the direction of the noise, only to find that it had nothing to do with fox-hunting: it was a village football match. The hounds, the huntsman, the whipper-in, Uncle

Charles and I all slithered to a stop. The footballers and the
bystanders who had been making the noise all stopped too.
There was silence, then Uncle Charles, who had turned red in
the face, stood up in his stirrups and shouted: 'Haven't you
people got anything better to do in wartime than play *football*?'
We then went on hunting.

Another incorrigible chaser of foxes was Henry, tenth Duke of
Beaufort, always known as 'Master'. The name derived from his child-
hood, when, at the age of eight, he had been given his own pack of
hounds – and hunting had been his passion ever since. Many people
thought him intolerably rude and arrogant, especially when he roared
abuse at anybody who got in the way of horse or hound; but others,
who stood up to him when he tried to bully them, found him friendly
enough underneath his difficult exterior. One such was the sporting
artist Raoul Millais, who hunted with the Beaufort in the 1920s and
1930s, and after an exchange of insults, which he won, decided that
Master was 'really a very nice man, but perhaps rather far down the list
for Brain of Britain'.

Whatever his intellect, Master was obsessed with the pursuit of
foxes – to which, when not pursuing titled ladies, he devoted a great
deal of his time. With his own pack of hounds, and the freedom of a
vast country, he carried on hunting through the war with astonishing
single-mindedness, as if nothing more important were happening. No
mention of global conflict intruded when, on 8 December 1941 – the
day after the Japanese attack on the United States' fleet at Pearl Harbor
– he sat down to record his ideas on the subject. Writing in his big, bold
hand, he covered sheet after sheet with reminiscences, heading the
document *Thoughts on Hunting by the Duke of Beaufort* and addressing
it to 'My Dear T'.

'I have been reading through my hunting diaries,' he began, 'and I
need a large piece of paper to write down my thoughts and the few

conclusions that I have reached.' He then divided his recollections into three periods. 'A' covered 1920–28, 'B' 1928–35, and 'C' 1935–40.

> In all three periods we hunted six days a week … In 'A' we killed on average slightly over 100 brace of foxes per season. Great was the excitement when we first killed 100 brace, and at the time we agreed we would not approach my father's record of 153½ brace. There were several good points and good hound hunts, but the average of sport was not on a high level. Foxes, however, did conform to the Rules.

By 'the Rules' Master meant that foxes should run for miles and not go to ground in small earths, from which they could easily be dug out. Period 'B' (1931–2) included the 'best season and the best scenting season' he had ever known, during which the hunt killed the 'stupendous total' of 193½ brace. But doubts were creeping in: 'I first began to think that foxes were easier to kill and therefore must be getting soft. But still they conformed to the Rules.'

Not for much longer. In 1938–9 the record was broken again with a cull of 226½ brace, and in the first year of the war the hunt accounted for 204 brace, 'largely by foul means'. Master claimed that the fox population had 'increased tremendously during the past twenty years', and that digging out had become essential to reduce numbers. He had also noticed that foxes did not run downwind as much as they used to, and he complained that his woods were more disturbed than heretofore by 'a large increase of cur-dogs'.

In spite of wartime privations, children's meets were popular in many parts of the country. The Herefordshire farmer Gwen McBryde recorded how one mother, whose daughter aged five and son aged four were mounted on small ponies, once ran and walked with them for two and a half hours. Every time she drew breath there were shouts of 'Run, mummy, run!' The ponies 'never batted an eyelash', even when they got

With supplies from abroad threatened by U-boats, Government posters urged gardeners and farmers to grow all possible food at home.

Paintings from the National Gallery were manhandled into the former slate mine at Manod, in Snowdonia, in purpose-built wagons.

Inside the cavernous mine the paintings were stored in six specially-built brick buildings, with air-conditioning to control temperature and humidity.

On 27 November 1944 an accident in the bomb-storage area of the former gypsum mine at Faulds, in Staffordshire, caused the largest non-nuclear explosion the world had ever known, hurling two million tons of rock and earth into the sky.

As the war went on, more and more downed German aircraft littered the fields – but the presence of swastika-clad wrecks was of no consequence to sheep.

Passion-killer black tights were essential in the bitter winter of 1939–40 for the girls of Penrhos College, evacuated from Bangor to Chatsworth in Derbyshire, when skating on the lake in front of the great house.

RAF Medmenham, based in Danesfield House near Marlow, became the vital centre of Allied photographic interpretation, analysing films taken by aircraft flying high over occupied Europe.

Winston Churchill, here with his wife Clemmie, enjoyed visiting the London Zoo. He was positively enchanted by Ming the panda, who began the war at Whipsnade but was then moved back to Regent's Park. The animal, he said, 'has exceeded all my expectations, and they were *very* high.'

In 1940, when Hitler was threatening invasion, farmers' problems were increased by lines of obsolescent cars parked across fields to prevent glider landings.

Juan Pujol García, nicknamed Garbo, was the mastermind behind the D-Day deception plan in 1944. The Germans believed he had 24 agents in England, when in fact he had none.

At Sidcup in Kent, after Doug Holland's forge had been shattered by a bomb, he promptly set about rebuilding it.

The country was safer than towns during the Blitz, but even so many farms were hit. Here, Land Girls help clear up after a strike.

Italian prisoners went out to the fields singing '*O sole mio*' and ogling girls, but farmers found that they did far less work than Germans.

Rubber tanks, which could be inflated with a stirrup pump in three and a half minutes, were an essential element in the Fortitude deception scheme before D-Day.

mixed up with an army convoy of tanks and lorries. As Gwen remarked, it was 'a high test to have an armoured car cutting in under your tail and a Waltzing Matilda tank under your nose. Any hunter would have gone over the hedge into the nearest field.'

A reader of *Country Life* noticed what a powerfully tonic effect hunting had on refugee children – better than any amount of cod liver oil, Minadex or rose-hip syrup. Usually, he wrote, they look miserable.

> But when hounds meet, what a difference! A hundred and twenty London schoolchildren … give tongue as hounds move off. It is strange music, and the face of the Master colours; the grim huntsman is a philosopher, but it is a trying moment. The children reach the covert a little before the puzzled hounds, and vanish into it with Bedlam noises. Three hours later they drag back from points four or five miles away, thoroughly tired, covered with mud, and gloriously happy … Good luck to the little horrors, for hunting is one of the few subjects that tiresome pedagogues have not lectured them upon.

Unlike members of the hunting fraternity, shooting men were much agitated by the question of whether or not they should take up their main winter pastime as usual. The more sensitive among them felt that downing partridges and pheasants might not seem particularly lauda- ble when the nation's more important targets were German soldiers, sailors and airmen. Besides, war broke out most inconveniently just after the start of the 1939 season: partridges were normally fair game in September, pheasants in October.

Various factors suggested that shooting should be abandoned. Thousands of birds had been bred for the sport, but food for them was short. Many of the men who would normally have taken part – keepers, beaters, dog-handlers – had disappeared into the services. The scarcity of petrol made it difficult for participants to reach any rendezvous that had been set. Nevertheless, some landowners insisted on carrying on as if nothing had changed, and at the beginning of 1940 the Government extended the pheasant season from 31 January to the end of February, on the grounds that the abnormal number of birds still alive would seriously damage growing crops. Shooting men defended their sport on the rather specious grounds that their bags produced much-needed food, augmenting ordinary rations.

Surprisingly enough, Bendor, the second Duke of Westminster, was not for carrying on as usual. Owner of the vast Eaton Hall estate in Cheshire, and of many other rural properties, he was normally a glutton for shooting and had always presided over huge massacres of pheasants. In the summer of 1939 the twenty gamekeepers at Eaton had reared thousands. According to Norman Mursell, Head Keeper on the estate for the past ten years, the woods were crawling with birds, and the first major shoot was planned for the beginning of November. Then along came Major Basil Kerr, the Estate Agent, on one of his routine visits, but this time with orders from His Grace that the shoot was to be brought forward into October. So it was – and it was not very successful, no doubt because the leaf was still on the trees and the birds, still young, did not fly well.

At the end of the day the Duke turned to Sandy Myles, another of the estate staff, and said, 'No more shooting this season. Catch them all, and make it as soon as possible.' So the keepers went out and killed all the birds which they had spent the summer rearing, driving them into coops and knocking them on the head. Why the Duke ordered this slaughter it is impossible to say – unless it was because he feared that the feeding of wheat to game birds might be prohibited in the near future, and that the pheasants would starve.

For Norman Mursell and his assistants, it was a savage blow: all their efforts during the build-up to the season had gone for nothing. So had the tips which they would have got on shooting days. But later in the war Mursell himself had one outstanding success against bigger game.

Having joined the armed forces, he was posted to a light anti-aircraft regiment, and one dull, misty day in November he was manning a Lewis gun – a machine gun of American design, capable of firing 500 rounds a minute – on the roof of Leyland Motors' factory, when he spotted a low-flying aircraft. As all British aircraft were obliged to keep flashing a sequence of lights which changed from one day to the next, and this plane was showing no lights at all, he knew it was an intruder and brought his Lewis gun to bear onto it:

> Swinging the gun right round and giving the target a good lead (like a high flying pheasant), I pulled the trigger and emptied the 'pan' at it. The magazine was loaded with every fifth cartridge a tracer, so I could see where I was shooting, and the plane was catching some of the bullets. As it disappeared into low cloud I could see flames and smoke coming from one engine.

Mursell later heard that the plane, a Heinkel, had crashed in the Pennines, away to the east – and surely he must have congratulated himself on the shot of a lifetime. But later, when he went back to Eaton on leave, he found the keepers reduced to 'a skeleton staff of older men', one of whom had a strange new task. The gardens of the big house had been made proof against rabbits, either with wire netting or by a water-filled ditch; but one ancient retainer had been told to catch some rabbits alive, as the Duke wanted a few for his new sport of coursing them inside the gardens with his pack of dachshunds.

The outbreak of war cast gloom over the angling fraternity. On the Wye at Hay (*The Fishing Gazette* reported on 9 September) 'owing to the depressing times hardly any fishing has been done'. The Tavy and

Walkham rivers on Dartmoor were 'almost deserted, because with the Navy and Army mobilised and many residents actively employed in ARP and in other ways, there are few people left to fish'.

A week later the National Federation of Anglers took what it called 'drastic decisions', among them to cancel the annual English Championship, in which teams were to have competed on the Trent in Nottinghamshire. This caused huge disappointment to the 700 contestants already selected, 'several of whom have already paid visits to the Trent at Newark in order to get some knowledge of what tactics to employ'.

Occasional items of good news brightened the piscatorial scene: on 23 October the record salmon for 1939 – a fifty-four-pounder – was caught on the River Don in Aberdeenshire; and sea anglers were apparently unmoved by the outbreak of another world war. Early in October 122 of them fished off Hastings Pier; at Dartmouth, also, there were no restrictions, and *The Fishing Gazette* predicted that it was going to be 'a first-rate season for flatfish'.

Petrol rationing, and the lack of country buses, made access to rivers difficult; but on some beats the few remaining regular anglers were joined by evacuee boys, often wielding good-quality rods – no doubt the fruit of an appeal to owners to hand in their equipment for use by amateurs. Around Oxford, *The Fishing Gazette* reported, 'the fishing fraternity have been disturbed from their haunts by the children with nets and jam-jars; in fact, the banks of the river are literally "swamped" with boys and girls trying their luck'.

During the Blitz thousands of fish, killed by bombs, could be seen drifting down the Thames in and below London. Elsewhere there was much anxiety that sewage effluent from the new military camps being constructed all over the country would pollute rivers; and the number of freshwater fish licences taken out by members of the public fell sharply from 74,000 in 1939 to 55,000 in 1940. A large number of professional river bailiffs were called up into the armed forces, but their places were taken by volunteers, and occasional prosecutions for poaching show that the amateurs were fairly vigilant. In November 1941 the Lune Fishery Board in Lancashire fined Joseph Parks £2 10s for being in possession of a gaff at night, and the same for possession of a lamp, with £2 1s 9d costs; and in January 1942 Ernest Brockbank was fined £5 for using a snatch for the purpose of taking salmon from Borrowdale Beck in Cumbria.

The demand for fish was much strengthened by the rationing of most other kinds of food, and when two enormous cod, together weighing 'three stones and three quarters' (about 53 lb), were landed at Hartlepool in February 1941, they were snapped up for £2 11s by a local fish fryer, who said that he must have raw material 'to maintain his connection' with customers. Attempts were made to persuade people to eat coarse fish: in twelve days of May 1942 250,000 perch were caught in Lake Windermere for an experiment with tinning, and the President of the National Fishing Association pronounced their flavour excellent. Would he have said the same of the six-foot-six-inch sturgeon, weighing 81 lb, which was caught off Ulster and sent to Belfast to be divided among the inmates of the Royal Victoria and Mater hospitals?

Numerous pundits extolled the therapeutic value of fishing, especially in times of high stress, and when the King invited troops to try their luck in the waters of the Great Park at Windsor, so many other proprietors followed suit that soon fifty rivers were available to service personnel, and the demand for borrowed rods far exceeded the supply – even though, in 1940 alone, more than 1000 had been collected and distributed.

Terence Horsley, an RAF delivery pilot, wrote lyrically of the release from stress that fishing gave him. Whenever he had to test an aircraft, or take it from one end of the country to the other, he would have his rod on board, so that after landing he could make straight for the nearest chalk stream or Highland loch. To him a river was 'a place of escape, without harsh sounds or bustle'.

In time of war, when good men can feel fear and still be good men, a night's fishing can bring everything again into true perspective. I have stood by the river in the gathering darkness, and as though I was passing through a door, have been taken into the night so that I became part of it as much as the shadows. Out there, where the water is flowing, there is no end and no beginning, but something which goes its way for ever in peace.

Game birds had to take their chance. The rearing of pheasants was prohibited by an Order dated 29 June 1940, mainly to save wheat, and some landowners, among them Lord Derby, reported that they had given orders for all eggs found on their land to be destroyed. Other estates carried on rearing pheasants more or less surreptitiously, under the pretence that they were breeding the birds for food rather than for shooting. One syndicate shoot in Lancashire was rumbled by an amateur investigator who reported that two young men were secretly rearing 2000 birds, and that in the woods he had discovered huts 'carefully locked up and screened, absolutely FULL OF GRAIN'.

On 31 July 1940 the Defence (Game) Regulations advanced the start of the grouse season from the traditional 12 August to 5 August, and pheasant shooting from 1 October to 1 September. As many gamekeepers had departed on military service, wild birds were less effectively protected from predators than in peacetime; on the other hand, far fewer were shot than in pre-war days. Landowners snatching a few days' leave in winter organized a day's shooting whenever they could reach home, but had to be content with much smaller bags than before the war.

Manufacturers of sporting weapons looked elsewhere for work. Holland & Holland, the leading London gunmakers, turned to the production of No. 4 (T) sniper rifles for the Government, and during the war converted 23,000 weapons. The company also managed to retain its most valuable asset – the grounds of its shooting school at

Northwood, on the western outskirts of London, where it had bought sixty acres of farmland in 1932.

Farmers under pressure to produce more food accused shooting men of letting their pheasants eat vast amounts of corn, and complaints set off absurd chain reactions among the pen-pushers. In March 1942 Captain Aldred of Beesthorpe Hall, near Newark, applied for a licence to shoot out-of-season pheasants, which he claimed were damaging his crops. His letter went on a fine bureaucratic journey. Passed to the Rodent Control Section of the Ministry of Agriculture and Fisheries in the Imperial Hotel at Colwyn Bay, in North Wales, it was forwarded by the Pest Officer there to the War Ag committee, suggesting that the matter be discussed with the Ministry's Land Commissioner. At the end of May the Ministry at last issued an ad hoc Order, 'The Killing of Pheasants Lincoln (Parts of Kesteven)', which gave Aldred the permission he had been seeking – far too late to be of any use.

Meanwhile another countryman, seeing an old cock pheasant pecking away on a field of wheat which was just sprouting, shot it and sent it for scientific examination. The report revealed that its crop contained 554 wireworms and other harmful insects, but not a grain of corn.

As for grouse moors – some survived astonishingly well, even though predator control and systematic burning (to renew the heather, on which the birds feed) were much reduced through absence of manpower. Shortage of ammunition also contributed to the difficulties: in May 1940 the police called for 12-bore cartridges to be handed in to equip the newly founded Local Defence Volunteers – although it was acknowledged that enough must be retained by the estates for the keepers' use. The general lack of maintenance during the war had a damaging long-term effect on many moors, in that bracken encroached round the edges, reducing the area of heather and harbouring ticks, which infest and infect grouse chicks.

One of the most successful estates was the Duke of Devonshire's Bolton Abbey, in North Yorkshire, which maintained an astonishing record – 3500 brace of grouse shot in 1941, 4500 brace in 1942 and 3500 brace in 1943, before a crash in 1944 was brought on by disease. How enough guns, cartridges and beaters were assembled, history does not relate; but much of the credit must have been due to the head keeper, James Stitt, who had been appointed in 1925 (and did not retire until 1959, when his son William took over). He must have had the support of several under-keepers – three or four, probably – for in the winter of 1939–40 they managed to burn a thousand acres of heather in strips and patches.

Another Yorkshire estate, Allenheads, also did well. Between 15 and 24 August 1939 seven driven days yielded 1400 brace; but then a note in the game book recorded: 'Owing to the international situation, all guns left on 25 October.' Next year, after a bitter winter, May and June turned out hot and dry, enabling broods of grouse to grow well. Shortage of petrol made the assembly of guns and beaters difficult, but 'a few evacuees' were press-ganged as beaters, and shooting continued until the end of November. Whether these recruits were girls or boys, and what they made of their days in the heather, the record does not relate.

Three moors in Westmorland belonging to the Lowther family – Crosby, Shap and Bretherdale – went steeply downhill. In the early 1930s Crosby had yielded 3000 brace a year, and Shap about 1000; but with the keepers reduced from fourteen to four there was little or no shooting during the war; the butts fell into disrepair, and the general deterioration increased when more sheep were put onto the hill as part of the effort to grow food.

Elsewhere, bags fluctuated wildly. At Abbeystead, in Lancashire, which then belonged to the Sefton family, more than 1000 brace were shot in the autumn of 1938, but in 1939, over the outbreak of war, the bag amounted to only eighteen birds. The seasons of 1940–43 proved more prolific, with the Littledale moor consistently producing days of 200 brace; then in August 1944 only one shoot was held, and that yielded a mere seventeen grouse.

On Egton High Moor near Whitby no driving took place, but energetic members of the Foster family, reinforced by the occasional friend on leave, managed to walk-up on an amazing number of days: twenty-nine in 1941 and twenty-three in 1942. The largest turnout of guns was five, the smallest two, and bags were modest – about ten brace a day.

A different pattern developed on Midhope Moor, also in Yorkshire. In the 1930s it had been producing 1000 brace a year; driving continued in 1940, but the season's bag was down to 500 brace, and in 1941 it again fell 50 per cent, to 250. No more shooting took place during the war, for the moor was used as a tank range by US forces, and at one point the peat was deliberately set alight on the higher parts of the ground to create a decoy to divert Luftwaffe bombers away from Sheffield and its industrial areas.

Between Upper and Lower Midhope lies Langsett Reservoir, and there (as on the Derwent Reservoir in Derbyshire) trials took place of the bouncing bombs developed for the RAF's Dam Busters' raid. After 617 Squadron had managed to breach the Möhne and Eder dams on the night of 16–17 May 1943, it was feared that the Luftwaffe might retaliate by trying to destroy the Langsett Reservoir, which provided the essential water supply for the Sheffield steel works. As a precaution, gun emplacements were built at the ends of the dam; wires with chains dangling from them were slung across the water between steel towers and a system for generating an instant smokescreen was installed; but although Sheffield was heavily bombed, the reservoir was never attacked.

No moor can have had rougher handling than Westerdale, in North Yorkshire, which was used as a gunnery range by both army and navy. Repeated shelling from land and sea burnt off most of the heather, and no game shooting was possible during the war. The result was that vermin from nearby forestry plantations ran riot: when keepers returned to manage the ground again in 1946, they killed 300 foxes in the first season, and, as one remembered, 'carrion crows were going about not in gangs of a dozen, but in hundreds'.

As for deer – the continental practice of culling with rifles was not yet established in England, mainly because before the war there were few wild deer at large in the countryside. In contrast, many of the parks surrounding country houses held substantial herds, which for centuries had been a prized feature of the landscape; fallow deer of the Menil strain, strongly spotted with white, were considered the most pictur-esque species. But now winter weather began to break down the walls, fences and palisades enclosing the sanctuaries; rain and frost cracked the stone and trees fell through the fences. With most of the estate staff gone to the war, there was no one to repair the damage, and deer broke out through the gaps. One typical casualty was Stonor Park, in the Chilterns, where fallow deer had been kept since time immemorial. With the park's boundaries breached, some of the herd escaped into the surrounding woods, where they began to breed, laying the foundations of a problem which has grown more and more serious ever since. Other parks, like Surrenden near Maidstone, whose owner had evacuated his school to the West Country, were taken over by the military and wrecked.

Wandering deer irritated farmers, who killed some in shotgun drives, but many went away wounded because the weapons and ammu-nition being used against them were not powerful enough. In May 1940 a letter from the Ministry of Agriculture acknowledged that deer escap-ing from a park in Cheshire were doing a good deal of damage, but also revealed the writer's total ignorance of the subject:

> I gather that farmers do their best to destroy them, but that they have difficulty in getting near, as they are rather wild. I do not see how this can be dealt with under an Order except by entering on the park and destroying the whole of the stock, which seems rather drastic.

Landowners were divided on the question of whether or not it would be a good idea for the Government to authorize the killing of deer; but in June 1940 the Ministry gave in to pressure and issued the Deer Order, which gave the War Ags the power to initiate culling.

In the Scottish Highlands things were different. For 100 years stalking the red deer had been an established sport, and a deep reservoir of skill had built up among the hill men – the stalkers, or gamekeepers, and the ghillies, their assistants – who escorted riflemen to shoot stags in the autumn, and then in the winter themselves culled the hinds. When war broke out, many of these professionals enlisted in Scottish regiments, particularly those specializing in sniper or Commando work, for which their ability to stalk, to move across difficult country and to observe with telescopes ideally suited them.

Stalkers too old for active service remained in place and carried on the annual cull; but their efforts were hugely augmented when the army decided to set up paramilitary training in the mountains. The hills came alive with Commando-type soldiers of many nationalities making forced marches, firing live ammunition and setting off explosives. Local stalkers were called in by the military to help with instruction in mountain skills – and students were all too keen to try their hand at stalking, with whatever weapons were to hand.

The result was that the number of deer reported culled in Scotland rose sharply from 7130 stags and 10,971 hinds in 1939–40 to 9890 stags and 12,844 hinds in 1940–41; but these figures took no account of the animals being shot by poachers or soldiers out on their own, and the total cull was certainly a good deal higher. Inevitably, the cull became indiscriminate: a Commando with deer in the sights of his rifle or Bren gun was not likely to distinguish between male and female, young and old.

Because venison was not rationed, it was in strong demand, particularly before Christmas, when people who could not find a turkey bought a joint instead. Game dealers raised the prices paid for carcasses from 9d to 1s 3d per pound, and butchers lost no time in passing on the increase to customers. Frank Wallace, an expert appointed official Deer Controller by the Government, was not worried by the upward trend, as he believed that the deer population was far too high; but then the exceptionally hard winter of 1940–41 changed his calculations, as nature killed perhaps 20,000 animals through starvation and disease.

Nineteen

Animals Under Fire

Sporting the lion ramped, and in his paw
Dandled the kid; bears, tigers, ounces, pards
Gamboll'd before them; th' unwieldy elephant
To make them mirth, us'd all his might, and wreathed
His lithe proboscis.

Milton, *Paradise Lost, Book iv*

The war caused severe problems for circuses and zoos. Apart from the risk that enclosures might be bombed, and that valuable or dangerous animals might escape or be killed, feeding them adequately became more and more difficult. Humans could be rationed, and have the need for restrictions explained to them; animals could not.

Like many others, the Chipperfields, who had built up their family circus throughout the 1920s and 1930s, saw no option but to close their travelling show. Chamberlain's broadcast of 3 September 1939 caught them on tour in Norfolk, and they decided to head straight for home in Hampshire. For those with mechanical transport, the journey was simple; but Dick Chipperfield, who ran the show with his brother Jimmy, had to take thirty horses on foot, slanting down across England from north-east to south-west, and in three days he rode 165 miles. The family kept their lions for as long as they could, but in the end they could not get enough meat to feed them, and had to shoot them. As

Jimmy said, it was a heart-breaking business, for they had invested countless hours in training the big cats, and they had become part of the Chipperfields' lives.

The third of September 1939 was a blank day for outdoor entertainment all over the country, as the Government Order prohibiting the assembly of crowds forced circuses and zoos to close. In London Zoo – which normally never shut except on Christmas Day – the keepers noticed that after a day or two the absence of visitors seemed to depress the inmates, especially the apes, who missed the usual milling crowds. To cheer them up, the Zoo got permission from the War Office for some soldiers billeted on the edge of Regent's Park to come in and walk around – a substitution which seemed to have a good effect. After ten days the prohibition on gatherings was rescinded, and visitors returned to the Zoo, but the fear of bombardment was so acute that the poisonous reptiles – cobras, kraits, puff adders and rattlesnakes – were put down, along with the venomous spiders, and attendance in September was reduced by 90 per cent from the total the year before. Aquaria were emptied, the fish either killed or released. In the Kursaal Zoo at Southend the carnivores were shot by an RSPCA inspector, and the poisonous snakes in Edinburgh were put down. (Painful as these losses were to owners and operators, they did not rival those of the Tiergarten, Germany's oldest zoo, in the centre of Berlin, most of which was bombed into rubble, and where, out of 3700 animals, only ninety survived the war, including one elephant, one chimpanzee and three lions.)

In England big carnivores were obviously a liability wherever they were – and alarming to members of the public when they were on the move. One night in the winter of 1940 a family in the Cumbrian town of Dalton-on-Furness were woken by angry roars: when they looked out, they found a circus wagon full of lions lying on its side in the street right outside the house, with the inmates giving vent to their displeasure.

Luckily for the London Zoological Society, it had a priceless asset thirty miles to the north-west of the capital, in the form of Whipsnade, where, in December 1926, it had bought a rundown, 600-acre farm on the windswept crest of the Dunstable Downs. On a site fifteen times larger than its home in Regent's Park, it had laid out an animal park with large, fenced paddocks, mainly on the gently undulating land on top of the hill, but partly on the slopes of the Downs, one of which was embellished with the figure of a huge white lion carved in the chalk. When the new zoo opened on a fine Whit Sunday, 23 May 1931, there was such intense interest, and such a press of cars and charabancs, that many prospective fanciers never reached their target.

When war broke out, the largest of London Zoo's animals – the elephants and rhinos – were already at Whipsnade, having been sent to the country because new quarters were being built for them in Regent's Park; and when the threat of bombing became acute, the Zoo's star attractions – the giant pandas Ming and Tang – were taken to the country as a precaution; but Tang died on 13 April 1940, and two factors prompted Ming's return to the capital. One was petrol rationing and the lack of buses, which drastically cut the number of people able to visit the park out in the wilds; and the other was the disappointment of the metropolitan public, who were saddened by the panda's absence from Regent's Park and clamoured for her to come back. One of her keenest admirers was Winston Churchill, who, when taken to see her, gazed at the animal for a long time before saying, 'It has exceeded all my expectations ... and they were *very* high.'

A few bombs fell harmlessly on Whipsnade during the war, and some of the craters they made were put to good use, being fashioned into ponds. A former circus elephant delighted keepers and visitors alike with her prowess at ploughing up grassland for the planting of wheat. But London Zoo was more heavily bombarded. The keepers were issued with rifles, in case any dangerous animal escaped, and although there was only one major fatality – a giraffe which was so frightened by an explosion that it died of a heart attack – many of the enclosures were badly damaged.

Among the casualties of a night raid was the zebra house, which was totally destroyed. One of its inmates, a zebra called Johnson, cantered off through the tunnel onto the Outer Circle road, heading for Camden Town. In pursuit went Julian Huxley, the Zoo's Secretary, who, with help from the air-raid squad, managed to round the stallion up and drive him towards home. Every time the anti-aircraft guns opened up on Primrose Hill, the zebra backed violently towards the little cordon behind him, and Huxley was convinced he was about to be disembowelled by an almighty kick in the stomach; but by 4 a.m. the runaway was safely back in an empty shed, and when next day Huxley confessed his fear, the zebra's keeper said, 'Cor bless you, Sir. You needn't have been frightened. 'E's a biter, not a kicker.'

Bristol Zoo remained open throughout the war, even though there was a constant risk that bombs might set dangerous animals loose – a possibility vivid in the minds of residents of Clifton, who would not have enjoyed having a tiger at large in the blacked-out streets. The Zoo never suffered a direct hit, but the polar bears were put down, and some of the lions and tigers were sent elsewhere.

Elephants had always been one of Bristol's most popular attractions, in spite of their propensity for the removal and consumption of hats, particularly those made of straw. One, Celeste (named after the Queen in the Babar stories), was sent off to Dudley Zoo, but Rosie, who had been sold to Bristol by the Chipperfields, remained *in situ* throughout the war. As a member of the travelling family circus, she had once distinguished herself by bolting down Monmouth High Street and becoming jammed in the outdoor lavatory of a pub. She had also smashed up a lot of church furniture stored in a barn, and eaten a pair of Jimmy Chipperfield's trousers. But by 1939 she had become more sedate, and throughout the war she delighted scores of children by giving them rides.

The Zoo was obliged to accommodate some outsiders: the army annexed the tea rooms, and the Bristol Aeroplane Company, bombed out of its works at Filton, took over the Pavilion at twenty-four hours' notice. Damage, however, was surprisingly small. One high-explosive bomb did fall in the gardens, badly injuring a keeper and wrecking the gatehouse, but the animals seemed little worried by the frequent air raids on the city and the docks, and they appeared to regard the noise as nothing more tiresome than a prolonged series of thunderstorms. As the Zoo's historian related,

> One golden opportunity for escape was missed by some
> baboons when a great hole was torn in their roof; but they took
> no notice of it, and were found quietly seated in their quarters
> when their keeper arrived to survey the damage.

Star of the show was Elizabeth the lioness, who in 1943 gave birth to five cubs, raising her total since 1932 to twenty-six. 'It reads strangely today,' wrote the historian twenty years later, 'but is nevertheless a fact, that two Russian bears acquired in 1944 were named Stalin and Stalina in compliment to "our gallant ally".'

Feeding the animals was a problem, but the difficulties were eased by digging up flower beds and planting them with vegetables. Financial help came from an adoption scheme, similar to one in London, whereby Friends of the Zoo contributed to the upkeep of their chosen animals. This proved extremely successful, but in 1942 it was discontinued because, after a sharp fall in the two preceding years, the gate money had risen spectacularly, as people stayed at home for their holidays and had little else on which to spend their cash. Funds were further increased by the Government, which paid a substantial rent for the use of the tea rooms. From 1942, when Clifton College became the head-quarters of the US V Corps and then of the First Army under General Omar Bradley, native visitors were augmented by American soldiers,

many of whom came in the hope of spotting that well-known rarity and
aficionado of the Zoo, Queen Mary, a sighting of whom ranked alongside one of a panda.

Before the war Chessington Zoo, in south-west London, had
become immensely popular. It was founded by Reginald Goddard, who
began work in a pet shop but did so well that he was able to buy Burnt
Stub, a Victorian Gothic house in Kingston-upon-Thames, on a site
that had been a Royalist stronghold in the Civil War, and set up a
private menagerie in the grounds. He several times travelled to West
Africa collecting exotic animals, and he bred lions with particular
success. In 1931 he opened his estate to the public and quickly drew
large crowds; but his master stroke was to persuade the Southern
Railway to build a special station only a mile from the Zoo's gates, and
to run coaches to and fro. This stratagem raised attendance to record
levels, the peak figure being 38,000 in a day.

By the end of the 1930s his show had become part circus, enlivened
by animal acts – a monkey which walked the tightrope, bears' tea
parties, dog football and so on. Then came the war, and the
Government's ban on the assembly of large crowds. Chessington Zoo
was in a particularly dangerous place, on the fringe of London, and
Goddard had no option but to close it. Undeterred, he hired a train
and set off westwards with all his evacuees, animal and human, to join
forces with Herbert Whitley, who had founded another private
collection at his home, Primley, on the outskirts of Paignton in
Devon, and opened it as a zoo in 1923. In 1940 Whitley was about to
close his establishment, but the arrival of Goddard revitalized him,
and together the two ran the joint venture as the Devon Zoo and
Circus successfully throughout the war, sustained in part by the
patronage of evacuees who had landed in the town. As at Bristol, in
the weeks before D-Day Paignton was invaded by American troops,
who camped in the embryo nature reserve in Clennon Gorge, used
enclosures intended for bear dens as cookhouses, and thinned out the

flock of resident peacocks before departing for the Normandy beaches.

Many other zoos survived the war, among them Chester, which had been opened in the early 1930s, in the face of determined local opposition, by yet another collector, George Mottershead. He came from a family of market gardeners and in 1930 bought Oakfield Manor, a large house and nine acres of land, in Upton, a suburb of Chester. His first animals, including a tapir, a polar bear and a chimpanzee, arrived in 1932. In the early days the Zoo was run largely by members of his family, and supported by generous local benefactors.

One of his pioneering ideas was to establish an outdoor lion enclosure, surrounded by fourteen-foot wire mesh fences; but the Zoo council voted this too dangerous, and nearly half its members resigned. During the war – in spite of its proximity to Liverpool, and the risk of being bombed – Chester Zoo took in refugees from Bristol, Paignton and other collections: so popular was it that by 1941 its lion population had reached fourteen.

Many travelling circuses were forced to close down during the war, depriving country children of one of their favourite summer or autumn delights. But some shows kept going, and when Frances Partridge went to one at Hungerford in the autumn of 1942 ('too good a treat to miss'), she noticed a sharp division in the audience:

> At one end, on seats draped with red plush, sat the children of
> the upper classes, with their mummies and nannies. The
> children were clean and brushed, white as worms, and their
> clothes spotless and well ironed; their little legs hung down
> limply in clean white socks … The mummies and nannies
> pursed their lips at the clown's obscene antics. The side benches
> were filled with the children of the proletariat, strong, active,
> brown and uproarious. It was the class war in concrete form,
> and I saw it with proletarian eyes. The war has greatly

emphasised this war between the classes, while paradoxically enough reducing the difference between them ... Of course this only applies to the quiet domestic scene; danger and fear break the barriers instantly.

Of the shows which closed down, the largest was Bertram Mills, which for almost twenty years had travelled the country in summer and held its winter season at Olympia, in west London, with many star performers, not least Koringa, 'the only female fakir in the world', who mesmerized crocodiles into immobility, had a granite paving stone broken over her chest with 14-lb hammers and rolled with a naked back over freshly smashed glass.

After the death of Bertram Mills, the founder, in 1938, his sons Cyril and Bernard had taken over, and they made valiant efforts to carry on after war had been declared. With their depot at Ascot suddenly requisitioned and turned into a prisoner-of-war cage, they had to scatter their animals to various stables and hide their vehicles and trailers in the woods at Pollards Wood, their home in Buckinghamshire. It was out of the question to keep using Olympia, so during the winter of 1939 they put on shows in big variety theatres, having made sure the stages would stand the weight of elephants. Setbacks did not deter them. During the blackout in Nottingham a horse went through a plate-glass window, and when the circus train was derailed on the outskirts of Liverpool, the lions in their travelling dens had to be carried 200 yards through eighteen inches of snow and dragged through a hedge before they could be loaded onto a lorry.

In the spring of 1940 the Mills brothers were determined to restart their travelling show, but they had hardly opened in Worcester before France fell, and, as Cyril put it, 'we knew we were beaten at last ... Britain's biggest-ever circus had been destroyed overnight'. Another blow fell when their elephant trainer, John Gindl, was interned on the grounds that, being Austrian, he might have Nazi sympathies. It took the brothers five days of negotiation to secure his release, and during that time his wife Gertie never left the pachyderms, as she was the person whom they knew next best. A few weeks later a bomb fell within forty yards of where they were stabled in Buckinghamshire: terrified, and trumpeting so loudly that they were heard half a mile away, they tried to break out; but when John ran out of his house and called, the sound of his voice immediately calmed them.

For the rest of the war the Mills brothers had to be content with running the Royal Opera House in Covent Garden (on which they had a lease) as a dance hall, and hiring out animals to other circus men who were putting on stage shows. While their six elephants got through £11,000 worth of food, Bernard went into the RAF, and Cyril became one of the MI5 case officers who ran the Double Cross agents. For a few weeks in April and May 1942 he looked after the master spy Juan Pujol García, known as Garbo (see page 367).

Twenty

Slate Country

Tramp up Snowdon with our woad on;
Never mind if we get rained or snowed on.
Never want a button sewed on.
Go it, Ancient B's.

W. Hope-Jones, *National Anthem of the Ancient Britons*

The war brought an astonishing variety of people and activities to North Wales. Normally that harsh, rock-bound environment, drenched by the highest rainfall in the British Isles, was inhabited mainly by slate miners and sheep farmers; but for five years it became a hub of the diamond-cutting world, the guardian of priceless works of art, the site of colossal bomb stores, the location of a huge factory making aircraft parts, and the home of the army's top-secret school for snipers.

On top of all that, in October 1940 a coded signal about a camel falling ill in London Zoo sent the Light Entertainment Department of the BBC scurrying northwards from Bristol to Bangor, on the coast. From there the quickfire Liverpudlian Tommy Handley broadcast the radio comedy programme, *ITMA – It's That Man Again* – throughout the war, giving an immense weekly lift to the nation's morale and causing people to go about loosing off the show's catchphrases at each other – 'This is Funf speaking' (Jack Train impersonating a German spy); 'I don't mind if I do' (Colonel Humphrey Chinstrap's answer to any question that might get him a drink), and Mrs Mopp the office charlady's 'Can I do you now, Sir?'

'Who in Bangor prior to the war would have dared predict that the city would have become a centre of the important diamond-cutting industry?' asked the *North Wales Chronicle* on 21 March 1941. In fact a Dutch firm had set up shop in the High Street with a staff of sixty, among whom were spoken Dutch, English, Flemish, French and Welsh, the last by five local lads who were learning the trade. The company came from Brighton, where, after the First World War, the Government had started a scheme to teach disabled servicemen the art of cutting and polishing precious stones. In 1941, when the south coast became too dangerous, a Hatton Garden trader called Albert Monnickendam took several experienced diamond cutters with him and moved north. A similar enterprise was established at the seaside resort of Colwyn Bay by Gerrit Wins, a dealer from Antwerp.

Diamond-cutting employed relatively few people – as did the storage of pictures in the Manod mine. In contrast, the factory established in enormously long sheds in the Dinorwic slate quarry, near Llanberis, needed huge numbers of workers. The quarry was the second biggest in the world, covering 700 acres, and the wartime factory set up within it, which made wings and other parts of aircraft, eventually employed 3000 people, many of them mothers and housewives. As the author Reg Chambers Jones remarked, 'the role of the Unemployment Office was changed from finding work for people to that of finding people for work'.

The factory lay in a dramatic setting, with ledges of bare rock – the result of quarrying slate – rising steeply in squared-off steps above it. Remote though they were, the sheds were guarded by machine-gun posts manned day and night, and employees were forbidden to speak to outsiders about their jobs. They worked in two twelve-hour shifts, with overcrowded buses ferrying men and women to and fro around the countryside. Until war came, most of the women had never had the chance to do anything except look after their homes and families, but after training they soon became expert at assembling aircraft components. Many local women worked in a subterranean explosives factory at Marchwiel, near Wrexham, manufacturing gun cotton by saturating cotton wool with nitroglycerine – a dangerous and unpleasant process, from which the fumes could turn skin and hair yellow.

The Germans seem never to have realized that Llanberis was such a hive of production – and certainly they never attacked it. But the attention of Luftwaffe pilots might well have been attracted by the enormous Queen Mary articulated lorries which carried the aircraft parts to factories far afield. These leviathans, with their four-wheeled cabs and flat trailers sixty feet long, would leave Llanberis at 4 p.m. and grind southwards through the night, each piloted by two drivers, not reaching Weybridge in Surrey (for instance) until 10 a.m., so that much of their journey was in daylight, especially in summer. On the return trip they would pick up essential raw materials, but also, if they passed through the Vale of Evesham in season, baskets of fruit, which were eagerly bought by the workers in Snowdonia at 1s 6d a shot.

With its wild, rocky mountains and scarcity of inhabitants, North Wales presented ideal terrain for military training: live ammunition could be fired with abandon, and the rough going, exacerbated by extravagant rainfall, was a challenge for the hardiest of soldiers. Units of the regular army were based at strategic points, because it seemed possible that the Germans might try to invade Britain from the west, using Eire as a springboard. Early in 1940, for instance, the 46th (Liverpool Welsh) Tank Regiment was stationed at Llandwrog, south of Caernarvon, charged with the task of guarding the southern entrance to the Menai Strait.

Yet it was in Snowdonia that trainees really met their match. Among them were officer cadets from Sandhurst, who came by rail to Betws-y-Coed, were driven to Capel Curig and then pitched into a series of ferocious exercises, some of which lasted for days and nights on end and included a realistic ambush, rock-climbing and assault marches. Similar activities went on at the Command Assault School.

Another lethal skill taught at Llanberis was that of sniping. 'The sniper is the big game hunter of the battlefield,' wrote Captain the Hon. Tony Wills in a substantial, sixty-five-page training manual which he composed for the War Office. He defined the sniper as 'a soldier who is trained to locate an enemy, however well hidden … He must combine the art of the hunter, the wiles of a poacher and the skill of a target shot, with the determination to seek out his enemy.'

Wills certainly knew his subject, for before the war he had devoted much time to shooting and stalking. At Eton he had been captain of the Shooting VIII for two years, and he had stalked deer in numerous Highland forests, making himself as proficient as any professional stalker/gamekeeper, not only in his experience of fieldcraft and firing a rifle, but also in the specialist skill of spying with a telescope. The close correlation between spying, stalking and shooting was recognized by the military authorities, and in 1942, at the age of twenty-seven, Wills was appointed Commandant and Chief Instructor of the Army School of Fieldcraft, Observation and Sniping at Llanberis.

There were no deer in those wild and rain-sodden mountains – only sheep, which were supposed to be sacrosanct – but there was any amount of open space in which to manoeuvre and fire live ammunition. When ricochets whined away off rocks, there was no danger of anyone being hit, and Wills devised numerous routines to test his recruits. On the first day of a course he had twelve instructors go out and conceal themselves at various points in the training area, their hands and faces darkened with green and brown camouflage cream, their helmets garnished with grass and tufts of hessian. Also set out were twelve fence posts, each with an empty whisky bottle on top.

Having explained that twelve men were hidden in the rock-studded landscape, Wills would challenge his recruits to spot them. Then he would blow his whistle. After a pause, with nothing seen, he blew the whistle again, whereupon rifle shots cracked out and all twelve bottles exploded in fragments. The instructor then suggested that the recruits search the ground in front of them more carefully, as in future their lives might depend on careful reconnaissance – and at a third blast of the whistle the instructors rose into view.

Wills's manual was extremely thorough, and emphasized throughout that the aim was to kill enemy. It taught men how to walk silently, how to crawl belly-to-the-ground, how to use natural cover, how best to carry out observation. A sniper's objective, it said, is to kill with one round: he must be able to hit a man's head regularly at up to 200 yards' range, and a man's trunk up to 400. A natural aptitude for fieldcraft is essential. 'Stalking is the application of fieldcraft in its widest sense, to bring the sniper within range of his quarry.' As for night work: 'Man is not a nocturnal animal ... Sight is largely replaced by hearing, so that silence is of prime importance.'

Among the skills which the courses taught, they emphasized the advantages of using telescopes, which Axis snipers did not possess. A four-draw stalking telescope, with a magnification of twenty-five, was more powerful than any but the largest naval binoculars; in clear weather experienced users could see troop movements ten miles away, and at shorter ranges their ability to pick out fine detail was invaluable. Good observation, Wills wrote, was 'the first step towards offensive sniping'.

The shikaris of India, the trappers of Canada, the hunters of the European forests, deer-stalkers and poachers and all who have to pit themselves against wild animals, have retained the quick and perceptive eyesight that becomes of great value in war. But the townsman whose eyes need seldom exert themselves for day-to-day existence can only develop a keenness of vision with much training and practice.

The reputation of the school spread quickly, and in an attempt to advertise the usefulness of snipers attached to any infantry unit, two-day courses were started for battalion commanders. As one expert recalled, 'they came prepared to scoff, but stayed to applaud ... When they left they were as excited as children who had discovered a new game ... Their eyes were opened completely to the possibilities of this great sport of sniping.' Enthusiasm for sniping permeated even the Home Guard in the far south, where one veteran claimed that in the First World War he personally had had 'a bag of something like fifty Huns'.

Among the men trained at Llanberis were members of the Lovat Scouts, the Highland regiment first raised by Simon, the sixteenth Lord Lovat, to fight in the Boer War. In civilian life many of the men were deerstalkers, and when it came to targets for snipers, as the founder of the regiment pointed out, there wasn't much difference between a deer and a German, except that you could eat the deer.

Purely in terms of personnel, the largest establishment in North Wales was the naval training camp HMS *Glendower* at Penychain, outside Pwllheli, which housed 100 officers, 5000 ratings and (well segregated) 500 Wrens. It was sited and built by the redoubtable Billy Butlin, who had opened his first holiday camps at Skegness in 1936 and Clacton in 1938, and quickly established a new form of resort, in which brash popular entertainments, led by the Redcoats, persuaded people not to lurk in their chalets, and created a festive atmosphere, even in the most miserable British summer weather. In 1939 Butlin's two existing camps were requisitioned for military use, and he built the new one in Wales (and another at Ayr) on the understanding that after the war he would be able to buy them for his own use.

With its standard layout of one double bed, one single bed and a cupboard in each chalet, Pwllheli was by no means suitable for occupation by naval ratings, and to prevent a breach of King's Regulations the double beds had to be fitted with dividing boards. As the camps were designed for summer only, there was no heating, and at night the ratings huddled in their overcoats – until the Admiralty relented and put electric heaters in the chalets and blowers in the dining halls.

Twenty-One

Evictions

·

Sweet smiling village, loveliest of thy lawn,
Thy sports are fled, and all thy charms withdrawn.
Amidst thy bowers the tyrant's hand is seen,
And desolation saddens all thy green ...
Sunk are thy bowers, in shapeless ruin all,
And the long grass o'ertops the crumbling wall.

Oliver Goldsmith, *The Deserted Village*

As preparations for the invasion of Europe built up, so too did the number of Allied troops in Britain. At the beginning of 1943 Operation Torch – the series of battles which drove the Axis forces out of North Africa – had temporarily drained off thousands of American soldiers, and the total of US ground forces on UK soil fell below 20,000. But in the autumn and the spring of 1944 new drafts, and men returning from Africa, sent the total rocketing, and by May it was 620,000. There were also 170,000 Canadian troops in the UK, to say nothing of the British forces waiting to go into action.

Increasingly in 1943 and 1944, with farmers under pressure to produce more food, landowners complained vigorously about the havoc wrought by military units invading their territory. In designated training areas damage was acceptable, and property inevitably suffered – as on the South Downs of the Arundel estate in Sussex, where the

Duke of Norfolk's turf was ripped up by the tracks of tanks, exposing the underlying chalk and allowing erosion to set in. But farmers were incensed if unauthorized slit trenches were dug in their fields and left unfilled when the troops went away. Wire fences were cut, gates were smashed or left open so that cattle escaped, crops were trampled, chickens and ducks purloined, rabbits and hares shot (with weapons far more lethal than shotguns) as troops went on the rampage. After one exercise in which a Canadian unit carried out a mock attack on Horsham, a soldier wrote home: 'What with going through people's fields and hedges and cutting down big trees – the engineers actually blew up a farmer's bridge – and tearing across country the way we did, you can bet we enjoyed ourselves.'

The need to give all these men realistic training, which included the detonation of explosives and the firing of live ammunition with small arms and artillery, presented the War Office with an acute problem. Unlike America, Britain had not – and has not – vast, uninhabited spaces in which troops can fight mock battles without disturbing farmers or the civilian population; and by the middle of the war competition for the use of land had become intense. On the one hand farmers, goaded by the War Ags, were fiercely defending their acres on the grounds that they had been ordered by the Government to grow as much food as possible. On the other hand, senior American commanders were claiming that it was ridiculous for the Government to deny them adequate facilities for the sake of a few cows or sacks of wheat. The only way the War Department could find the space it needed was by clearing the inhabitants from whole swathes of country – a procedure which naturally caused anguish among families forced to leave home.

Anyone looking at a map of East Anglia will notice a large, clear space immediately north of Thetford. Everywhere else on the borders of Suffolk and Norfolk small roads wind about in all directions; but this one stretch of country is blank: no roads, no towns, no villages. The reason is simple: in 1942 it became the Stanford Training Area, and the exclusive preserve of the armed forces. The military takeover of the strange, sandy, gorse-covered landscape known as the Breckland, marked out by lines of Scots pines, destroyed three villages – Stanford, Tottington and West Tofts – as well as parts of ten surrounding parishes, and sent 1600 people into exile. Most of them were tenants of the main landowner, the eighth Lord Walsingham, an army officer who had had an outstanding record in the First World War, being wounded three times, mentioned in dispatches five times and winning a DSO. Having retired in 1923 at the age of thirty-nine, he had re-enlisted in 1939 and commanded a battalion of the Royal Norfolk Regiment. It was he, in the end, who lost most from the evacuation, for the Army took 17,000 of his acres and paid scant compensation.

The military started training on the Breckland well before the formal takeover, and they allowed people to remain in their homes while bullets cracked past them and armoured vehicles roared over the heath. One farmer of abrasive character, Lucille Reeve – an accomplished dowser and an avowed Fascist – distinguished herself by advancing furiously on some tanks which had invaded her land, and, with the assistance of her two dogs on leads, driving them off. By her own account, she was 'very tough' (she reminds one of Boadicea, Queen of the Iceni, who is said to have lived at what is now Thetford).

In a small book published after the war, *Farming on a Battleground*, she gave a graphic account of her battles, first with the all-devouring rabbits, then with disobliging neighbours, then with the military. Because she attended a Rogation service in the fields, people accused her of witchcraft and advised her sarcastically that for growing good crops in that sandy soil manure was more effective than prayer. When she fell over in the kitchen and bruised her face, they claimed she had been beaten up by soldiers for being a Fascist. 'Truly my enemies were more numerous than my friends,' she wrote, 'and annoyed, no doubt, that I had not been interned with other people who support Sir Oswald Mosley in his plans for Britain for the British.'

For a couple of years she struggled on, showing no mean courage as war training intensified all round her: she had a practice bombing range on one side of her house and a dummy aerodrome on the other. For one whole day her farm was surrounded by military police – to her 'the British Gestapo'. 'Of course,' she wrote sarcastically, 'I was planting the clover leas for Hitler to land his planes on.' Then on 13 June 1941 she was told that all her land was needed by the army. Soldiers pulled up her anti-rabbit fences of wire netting. Tanks drove over an avenue of young trees which she had just planted. 'How I hated the war, and more specially the tanks,' she wrote.

Other locals survived near misses – until one day in May 1942 another farmer, Chester Riches, was accidentally shot dead as he was driving his cattle near Orford, and the authorities decided that the whole battle area must be cleared. Provoked into drastic action, the War Office organized two public meetings, one in Tottington and the other under the beech trees in the school yard in West Tofts. General Kenneth Anderson, GOC Eastern Command, assured the assembled villagers that the army would not smash up their homes, but Vera Tolman, headmistress of the school, never forgot how he gave them 'the fatal news'.

> He didn't have to ask for silence. We all stood there stunned – even the babies and the children were hushed. I don't think we even discussed it with one another. We just went home too unhappy to speak. The war had taken our husbands, and now our homes and way of life were to go.

The General's colleague, the Earl of Cranbrook, Deputy Regional Commissioner of the Eastern Region, explained how accommodation would be found for displaced persons. He assured the people that their houses would not be used as targets, and that no street fighting would take place. If an accident occurred – if a burst of machine-gun fire or a shell splinter went through a roof – it would be immediately repaired in order to prevent damage from wind and weather. Both meetings were chaired by Walsingham, who was sympathetic to the villagers, regarding them almost as members of his own family; nevertheless, he urged them to go without making a fuss, saying that the training to be carried out on the Breckland would, in the long run, save a great many casualties among their relations and friends.

Cranbrook later remarked in the House of Lords that the people 'were much more shaken by the shock of eviction than would have been a more sophisticated and urban population, less tied by tradition to their homes and to the countryside on which they worked'. He also recalled, in the same debate, the 'quite unequivocal' promises that they would be able to return when the war was over.

Complaints proved futile. An appeal to the King evoked a bland answer supporting the War Office's decision. The clear-out went ahead at bewildering speed. Not only had furniture and belongings to be removed from the houses: live and dead stock also had to go, and new homes had to be found for animals as well as for humans. The squire was scarcely better off than his former tenants, as his family house, Merton Hall, had already been commandeered, and for the time being he had to live in a prefabricated bungalow. Lucille Reeve found temporary refuge in a wooden hut, but eight years later she hanged herself in an outhouse.

The War Ag committee, harvesting prematurely and using unskilled labour, managed to salvage £40,000 worth of grain and seed, but hundreds of acres of sugar beet were lost. Full-scale military activities began as soon as – or even before – the evacuation was complete. Vera Tolman was allowed back into West Tofts to collect some coal. She rode in on her bicycle and met the coalman, who loaded up his lorry. Then she locked the school door for the last time, and as she turned round she found herself face-to-face with a huge, antlered red deer, which must have come out of Thetford Forest. For a few moments she and the stag stared at each other; then both turned away, and she left the village for ever.

One site of international importance narrowly escaped destruction: Sutton Hoo, where a cluster of low, grassy mounds lie in flat ground beside the estuary of the River Debden, some seven miles from the sea in Suffolk. Excavations begun there in 1938, and continued in the spring and summer of 1939, caused huge excitement among archaeologists, for they revealed the miraculously complete remains of a seventh-century Anglo-Saxon burial, and the skeleton of an oak ship nearly 100 feet long. The body of the buried man – possibly a king – had been dissolved by the acid sand, and most of the artefacts had been crushed by the tremendous weight of earth above them; but the fragments were meticulously collected and given by Mrs Pretty, owner of the land, to the British Museum.

When war broke out the site was lying open, covered only by a blanket of protective bracken, and it was direly threatened by anti-invasion measures, when trenches to frustrate glider landings were gouged out of the heathland right to the edge of the mounds. In 1942 the burial ground became part of the Breckland training area; infantry and tanks began swarming all over it, until stopped by the initiative of Lieutenant Ted White, an archaeologist who later became a trustee of the National Maritime Museum. So, by a whisker, was saved one of the richest sites ever discovered in Britain.

On 1 November 1943 the people of Imber, a village in the middle of Salisbury Plain, were similarly driven out. Called to a meeting in the school, they were given forty-seven days' notice to leave their homes, making the deadline for their departure 17 December. The 150 inhabitants were appalled, but not entirely surprised, because the War Office had been buying up land on the Plain and using it for manoeuvres for more than fifty years, and indeed the ground on which their houses stood already belonged to the Government, which had acquired it from them between 1928 and 1932, so that they were tenants of the State. They were told that compensation would be paid, and most people offered no resistance when evicted. Only the family in one farm had to be forcibly turned out by the army; but Albert Nash, for forty-four years the village blacksmith, collapsed on his anvil and died a few weeks later – according to his doctor, of a broken heart.

Apart from immediate human problems, the sheer antiquity of Imber made its abandonment seem tragic. An ancient settlement, the village had existed in some form during the Iron Age, between 800 BC and AD 100, on a junction of track-ways crossing the plain. It was listed in the Domesday Book of 1086, and in 1850 it had housed about 450 people, mainly in the single street along the stream known as the Imber Dock. The thirteenth-century Church of St Giles, with its fine, square tower, contained rare wall paintings; there was a Manor House – Imber Court – a post office, a forge, a carpenter's shop, two stores and a pub, the Bell. The people were mainly engaged in farming, but many of them had special skills, and in summer four men travelled the country practising the ancient art of making dew ponds.

This humble community was evicted allegedly so that US troops could practise street fighting among the buildings; but in the event no such urban battle training took place during the war, and the only reason for the evacuation seemed to be the fact that the village would be in danger from the impact of artillery shells. Vague assurances were given that everyone would be able to return after the war – and some people were so sure of going back that they left their possessions behind. But no one ever returned to live in Imber.

A similar fate overwhelmed the people of Tyneham, a village tucked away in a valley between the Purbeck Hills and the sea on the Jurassic Coast of Dorset. In the middle of November 1943 the inhabitants were shocked by the arrival of a letter which brought echoes of the notorious

Highland Clearances of the eighteenth and nineteenth centuries, when families were thrown out of their homes to make way for sheep. The communication from the War Office was brutally direct:

> In order to give our troops the fullest opportunity to perfect their training in the use of modern weapons of war, the Army must have an area of land particularly suited to their special needs and in which they can use live shells. For this reason you will realise the chosen area must be cleared of all civilians ...

At the bottom of the sheet was a handwritten note: '*Including your properties – see overleaf.*' And then on the back:

> It is regretted that, in the National Interest, it is necessary to move you from your homes, and everything possible will be done to help you, both by payment of compensation, and by finding other accommodation for you if you are unable to do so yourself.
>
> The date on which the military will take over this area is the 19th December next, and all civilians must be out of the area by that date ... The Government appreciate that this is no small sacrifice which you are asked to make, but they are sure that you will give this further help towards winning the war with a good heart.
>
> C. H. MILLER
> Major-General I/C Administration
> Southern Command

At least the houses in Tyneham were not set on fire by vindictive factors, as they were in Sutherland and elsewhere; and at least the people were promised that they would be able to return when the war was over. But there was no appeal against the eviction order, and all 225 inhabitants had to leave the single street of scattered grey cottages. The last to go, Bessie Taylor, seamstress at the Manor, posted a notice on the door of St Mary's Church:

> Please treat the church and houses with care; we have given up our homes where many of us have lived for generations to help win the war to keep men free. We shall return one day, and thank you for treating the village kindly.

Most of the inhabitants walked out, up the long haul onto the ridge above the valley, driving their animals before them; and no doubt when they reached the top they paused to look down on the little village where they and their families had lived for so long. Not only their homes, but also their livelihood, had been seized from them. As they had no other land on which to keep their animals, their stock was sold off: 313 dairy cows and bulls, seventy-one sheep, thirty-three pigs and 167 fowls were auctioned by Henry Duke & Son. The people dispersed, some to their families, some to new houses in Wareham, others to whatever shelter they could find.

No one was more distressed than Lilian Bond, whose family had owned the Elizabethan Manor House. From the age of eleven she had grown up there, and she had lived there for fifteen years until she married in 1914. A talented amateur actress and artist, she took a keen interest in local history, and in a memoir published in 1956 she wrote lyrically of the valley's remoteness, its deep serenity, cut off as it was from the rest of the world by the unbroken line of the hills. She remembered especially how 'the clean salt breath of the sea and the Tyneham valley, healing, reviving and exhilarating, met and refreshed the traveller' as he came over the ridge. She recalled the mighty hauls of mackerel made by the fishermen down in Worbarrow Bay, and boasted mildly about how, as a girl, she had become a skilled mouse-catcher. Her record bag was seven in an evening, and although she never achieved her ambition of making a pair of mouse-skin gloves, she did make a 'satisfying mouse-skin table mat', which she treasured for years.

One suspects that she was looking back through rose-tinted spectacles, for in fact Tyneham had been in decline for years before the war. The isolation of the people from other communities was reflected in their quaint expressions: ants were *emmuts*, cows *bleared* instead of lowing, a mess or muddle was a *caddle*, and when you were out of breath you *panked* rather than panted. The inhabitants had become inbred, and since the 1920s the population had been falling as families drifted away. The school had closed in 1932. Nevertheless, the eviction came as a profound shock, and Lilian, for one, never went back. Having steadfastly refused to revisit her old haunts, she died in 1980, aged ninety-three.

One training exercise had already been carried out at Slapton, on the Devon coast, in August 1943, when ships of the Royal Navy put American troops ashore. It was a cheerful occasion: the landings went well in fine weather, and the Americans made many friends in the village pubs. But then in November something much more sinister began.

The inhabitants of Slapton and the surrounding villages received letters from the Admiralty telling them that in six weeks' time they would have to give up their homes and take their belongings with them: not only furniture, but farm animals and pets as well. No reason was given, and people could only suppose that a major exercise was about to take place on the shore. In this they were right – but what they could not know (because of the tight security cloaking the event) was that Slapton Sands, in Start Bay, had been chosen for its resemblance to Utah Beach, code name for the westernmost of the beaches identified for the invasion of Normandy – the one which would be on the right flank of the Allied attack. Slapton Sands – in spite of its name, a curving, two-mile stretch of fine pebbles, with a road on a narrow strip of land behind it, and a few yards behind that again, a shallow freshwater lagoon – closely resembled Utah, and was therefore ideal for a practice assault landing.

As in the other areas cleared for battle training, the people of south Devon were unsophisticated, and few of them had travelled far from home. Most of their houses had no electricity or running water. Now suddenly 3000 of them – 750 families from 180 farms and hamlets – were ordered out of an area covering nine parishes, and extending to 30,000 acres, most of it rich, red land. There were two reasons for clearing such a large space. One was the danger that civilians might be killed or injured by the firing of live ammunition; and the other, the risk that local people might witness what was happening and become privy to the secrets of Operation Overlord.

At first many of them thought the rumours about eviction were a joke; but at meetings in village halls they found that the stories were all too true. When vans began to load up their possessions for removal to the homes of friends or family beyond the exclusion zone, children were delighted, for they thought they were going on holiday; but for their parents the evacuation was a nightmare. Everything had to go: farm animals, chickens, dogs, cats. Even the corn ricks had to be taken apart, sheaf by sheaf, and transported to new sites. With orders to be out of their houses by 20 December, people were given the impression that they would be back in six weeks – but it was the old folk who suffered most, as many of them had never left home before.

Reg Hannaford, then a schoolboy, lived with his family in the coastal village of Torcross, four miles south of Slapton, and he was among the last to leave on 20 December. His father (a butcher) and mother had gone the day before, taking all the butchery equipment in a van, and his elder brother John rode his bike to Stokenham, where he had to hand in the key of the house. That left young Reg with two men whose lorry was full of the family's hen houses, coops and poultry. As there was no room for him inside the vehicle, he had to sit on a bag of coke on the tailboard, with his head between the rungs of a ladder tied to the roof for the short journey to his uncle and aunt's farmhouse at Chivelstone, another hamlet four miles to the south-west.

At the end of January one of the fields there was taken over, and a large camp was built by black soldiers – the first black people Devon had ever seen. By March the whole area was awash with Americans. Military vehicles growled along the road from Plymouth to Start Bay, and GIs came marching in single file on either side of the road through the village of Aveton Gifford, some ten miles inland from Slapton, as they massed for Operation Tiger. Oddly enough, although they had food galore, they craved fresh bread, and paid for it at five or six times the going rate.

Eisenhower, by then Supreme Allied Commander, considered it essential to accustom men to the noise and fury of battle by using live ammunition in training; and the central objective of the exercise was that LSTs – Landing Ship Tanks, flat-bottomed assault vessels of 4500 tons, carrying several hundred men as well as trucks and tanks – would come ashore at Slapton under a realistic naval bombardment.

The first flotilla of slow-moving LSTs set out from Plymouth during the night of 26 April, and the first landing was scheduled to begin at 7.30 a.m. on the 27th, but right at the start things went seriously wrong. The British heavy cruiser HMS *Hawkins* had been detailed to bombard Slapton beach with live rounds from H-hour minus sixty minutes to H-hour minus thirty, and at the same time troops on land were to fire live rounds over the heads of the men coming in on the LSTs, to accustom them to the noise of battle. But because several of the LSTs were delayed in transit, the officer in charge ordered the whole exercise put back by an hour. His message was received by *Hawkins*, but not by some of the LSTs, with the result that men began going ashore while the bombardment was still in progress, and some of them were killed by friendly fire.

That was a bad start, but far worse followed a day later. Another group of landing craft, which left from Plymouth at 9.45 on the night of the 27th, should have been escorted by two destroyers, but one was damaged in a collision and the other was left behind, apparently as the result of an error in communication, leaving the LSTs lightly protected.

German E-boats – fast-moving craft which could achieve nearly forty knots and were armed with torpedoes – were regularly patrolling the Channel on reconnaissance missions, and that night they set out from their base at Cherbourg soon after 10 p.m. Sometime later they spotted the eight LSTs – sitting ducks as they proceeded at five knots in line astern, 400 yards apart, with only a single corvette as escort – and moved in to the attack. Just after 2 a.m. LST 507 was hit by a torpedo which knocked out her electric power, and the ship burst into flames. Shortly afterwards two torpedoes struck LST 531, which rolled over and sank in six minutes. Then LST 289 was also hit.

LST 507, crippled by lack of electricity to power her firefighting equipment, had to be abandoned. LST 289 managed to reach Dartmouth harbour, but with many dead and wounded on board. Altogether, the number of casualties was horrifying: during the night 749 American soldiers and sailors died, most of them drowned because they had mistakenly fastened their life jackets round their waists, rather than under their arms, with the result that they turned turtle in the cold water, weighed down by their equipment. Altogether the exercise cost the lives of 946 US servicemen.

Their commanders were appalled by the fiasco and by the loss of life; but their greatest anxiety was that they had lost ten senior officers who were cleared to the highest security level, knew the plans for the invasion, and might, if captured, give them away. Until the men were found, Overlord was in doubt. Should it be altered or postponed? Miraculously, all ten bodies were recovered, and the Germans did not discover the significance of the exercise they had so successfully disrupted. Survivors of the landings were sworn to secrecy, and on land in Devon all news of the disaster was suppressed for the time being –

but the people outside the exclusion zone could hear the live firing which continued for several days and nights. Rumours spread that most of the dead were buried in a mass grave on a farm at Blackawton, five miles inland from Slapton, but casualty figures for Tiger were not released until the autumn.

In August, four months after the disaster, and nine months after the evacuation, the War Office allowed journalists to visit Slapton. They found 1000 black American troops helping to clear the ground of shells, shell cases and barbed wire; they also learned that the American authorities had allocated £6000 to a Slapton hardship fund. No doubt the newsmen's reports were carefully censored. One of them took an optimistic line, admitting that 'the houses in some cases were not what they were', but not saying that there were shot holes clean through the walls. He claimed that 'the [number] destroyed could be reckoned on the fingers, and those severely damaged were practically non-existent, except at Slapton and Strete'. Among the casualties was the hotel on the front at Slapton, which had been used as a target for naval gunfire. In the surrounding farmland gates had disappeared, and many field boundaries had been destroyed.

That same month – August 1944 – Reg Hannaford and his brother John, together with two friends, went to see for themselves. They walked five miles across country, sneaked into the evacuated area, and as they came over the hill into Torcross they were surprised to find most of the village intact; but the farm buildings at the back of their house had been demolished, and the trees in the orchard had vanished – apparently flattened to make a tank park. Reg thought the place 'quite ghostly – no birds, only rats and rabbits everywhere', and the garden was waist-high in weeds. But they discovered a great dump of food that the Americans had left behind, including plenty of tins, with labels missing; they swagged away what they could carry and had fun opening them, as they couldn't tell whether they were going to find bully beef, hash, cake or peaches.

There and elsewhere in the area, rats also had a bonanza. They drew into the food dumps in hundreds, and when they had eaten everything accessible, they moved into farm buildings, only to find that, because no harvesting had been done that summer, the barns contained no corn. Thwarted, they climbed trees to eat the unripe apples, and devoured the fresh putty recently put in place when broken windows were being replaced.

When official permission came for humans to return, on 8 November, the Hannafords were the first family back in Torcross, but it was ten days before the electricity was restored. Soon farmers were again at work in the fields, which were still littered with mortar bombs and shells, and the bomb-disposal squad went into action almost every day. As Reg remarked, 'It remained a miracle to us that no one was killed by what had been left behind.' Some people were less enthusiastic about returning: having experienced the joys of electric light, water laid on and good sanitation, they did not want to go back.

Twenty-Two

Far North

Lo! For there, among the flowers and grasses,
Only the mightier movement sounds and passes;
Only winds and rivers,
Life and death.

Robert Louis Stevenson, *In the Highlands*

Many specialist training schools were established in other parts of
Britain, but the area chosen for paramilitary instruction was
Lochaber, the wild country in the north-west Highlands, which
includes Moidart, Morar and the Rough Bounds of Knoydart. Lochaber
had unparalleled advantages for bringing men to the peak of physical
fitness and endurance, and teaching them irregular fighting techniques.
The environment was exceedingly challenging: precipitous bare hills,
outcrops of rock, cliffs, ravines, bogs, fast-flowing burns, patches of
thick forest, the sea coast close by – all offered scope for violently energetic exercises, live firing and demolition work. There were few inhabitants, but several large, isolated houses were big enough to accommodate
headquarter staff; there was good access by rail, for the importation of
trainees and supplies, and – a vital consideration – the region could
easily be sealed off from the outside world.

Early in 1940, to keep out unwanted observers, the whole of north-
ernmost Scotland, above a line from Loch Linnhe in the south-west

corner, up the Caledonian Canal to Inverness and beyond, was declared No. 1 Protected Area. Control points manned by the army were established on roads that crossed the line, and people living inside it had to obtain permits which allowed them to pass through, or to travel on the railway from Mallaig down to Fort William. Outsiders wanting to enter the exclusion zone were required to furnish some adequate reason for needing special passes, which were coloured, and changed at short notice. All civilian mail posted in the Protected Area was routed through a censor in Glasgow, and letters written by trainees were censored on the spot before being dispatched under special cover to Scottish Command, so that they carried an Edinburgh postmark and their place of origin was concealed. Telephone calls emanating from the Protected Area were also censored. On all military sites security was rigorously enforced. The big houses were designated Protected Places, and entry to their grounds could be gained only with a special permit issued by the officer commanding each establishment: a general permit for the Protected Area was not enough. Photography was forbidden, except by official cameramen.

Such was the haste with which the army moved in that eighty-one-year-old Christian Cameron-Head, owner of Inverailort Castle, suddenly found herself without a home. She had travelled down to London to visit her son Francis in hospital – only to receive a registered letter which told her that her house had been requisitioned by the War Office. Hastening back north by train, she found the place being stripped, and her furniture, pictures and china being carted away in army lorries. From the Lochailort Inn, where she took refuge a few hundred yards from home, she wrote in distress to her friend Sir Donald Cameron of Lochiel:

> When I arrived at Lochailort station there were only two officers who said the Castle was half-emptied and that they had no accommodation for me and I could not go to it. They have

taken my three garages and planted tents everywhere, even in the middle of the farmyard without any permission from me or anyone representing me.

To her solicitor in Edinburgh she wrote:

I have been refused every room except my bedroom in which I am allowed to store some things, but I am not allowed to sleep there or go near the house after the troops have moved in ... Please advise me if I have any redress or if the military have the right to turn me out in this way without a roof over my head.

She had no redress, and Inverailort – the first of the properties seized for military occupation – became the Special Training Centre. Soon other big houses were taken over for similar purposes: Glencripesdale on the Morvern Peninsula, on the south side of Loch Sunart; Dorlin on the north shore of Loch Moidart; Arisaig House, Traigh House and Camusdarach Lodge, the last three on the Road to the Isles. Remotest of all were Inverie and Glaschoille, both on the shore of Loch Nevis. There was (and is) no road to either, the only access being by sea or on foot through the rock-bound passes of Glendessary. Both houses belonged to the Brocket family, notorious for their Nazi sympathies, and in 1938, when their friend Neville Chamberlain came to stay, they had arranged for a telephone line to be laid ten miles across the bed of the sea loch from Mallaig, so that the Prime Minister could be in touch with Westminster if a fresh political crisis blew up.

In the words of Maurice Buckmaster, head of SOE's French Section from 1941 to 1945, men went to the Scottish toughening schools to train their bodies to withstand fatigue:

They walked, they ran, they swam, they bicycled … they learned to avoid skylines, to move silently through undergrowth, to use the natural background of rough country to get, unobserved, from one point to another. They scaled crags and cliffs, they stalked game, they practised rifle, Sten-gun and Bren-gun firing, they blew things up, they ambushed other parties … Undoubtedly this course of intense physical training saved lives, when lives depended upon the physical ability to walk thirty or forty miles a day up and down steep hills.

Although styled a castle, Inverailort was more a several times extended country dwelling, largely Victorian and bristling with sharply pointed roofs, set gloomily against the foot of a towering mountain, An Stac. For headquarter staff not the least of the building's attractions was the staircase rising out of the central hall; training officers could demonstrate their technique for falling by hurling themselves down the bare wooden steps, rolled up like hedgehogs and springing up unhurt in combat attitude when they reached the bottom. The hardwood banister rail was also excellent for sliding down after dinner. On the flat ground in front of the house a forest of tents and huts sprang up, and, inside, so sure were the military of their tenancy that instead of merely putting up notices to indicate the use of individual rooms, they had signs neatly painted on the wooden doors: INSTRUCTOR, SECRETARY and so on. Alas for the owner! The despoliation was more than Christian Cameron-Head could bear. She died (people said) of a broken heart at her sister's home, Dunain House in Inverness, on Easter Day 1941, and came back to Inverailort in her coffin, to be buried in the family vault.

'Intense' was the word for the training. Mornings at Inverailort began with a run to the top of An Stac – a climb of 2,500 feet – and students (as they were called) found themselves constantly swept into other strenuous activities designed to push them to their limits: night treks to distant rendezvous in the hills, competitive runs over assault courses, map-reading, fieldcraft, guerrilla raids, demolitions, river crossings, opposed landings on the coast, silent killing, and – the speciality of an instructor known as the Shanghai Buster – rolling off the footboard of a fast-moving train. To make things as realistic as possible, live ammunition and explosives were used freely, and, inevitably, a few men died of wounds, drowning or exposure, their deaths being recorded as 'On Active Service'.

It was not only the instructors' goading that kept students under pressure: the weather also played a part in the toughening process. On breezy summer days the Highlands were pleasant enough, but whenever the wind dropped, midges swarmed out of the heather and peat in millions and became an insufferable irritation, especially to men whose role (for instance in an ambush) required them to keep still for long periods. Repellent cream proved ineffective against the menace, and, minute though the aggressors were, people suffered torments. Again, in winter, when snow lay on the tops, cloaking the hills down to 1000 feet or lower, and torrential rain came blasting through the glens, prolonged exposure to the elements tested even the most resolute recruit. Gales sometimes blew so viciously that it was impossible to stand up, let alone make any progress against the wind.

One of SOE's precepts was that different nationalities must be kept apart, and at various times Czechoslovak and Polish students took over Traigh House – a white, solid looking building comfortably tucked in against a wooded bank and looking out over a beach to the sea, with the Sgurr of Eigg rising into the sky in a dramatic hook of rock on the horizon. One of the trainees, Antonin Petràk (later a general), never forgot the demanding PT sessions on the lawn in front of the house, or how he learned silent killing on the field behind.

The instructors in the various schools included many eccentrics, among them Gavin Maxwell, who later became fascinated by otters and enthralled thousands of readers with his autobiographical *Ring of*

Bright Water. Arriving at Arisaig in 1942, he soon gained an enviable reputation. 'His knowledge of fieldcraft and minor tactics is an eye-opener,' said one report. 'His knowledge of weapons is first class.' His lectures and demonstrations on the nature of night vision and hearing, the use of broken ground, approaching the enemy out of a low sun, and reading different footprints, were a revelation. He taught his pupils how to live off the land – for instance, by eating raw mussels and limpets; he could also behave explosively, and would 'interrupt students' ping-pong matches by bursting into the games room and blasting the ball in midair with a Colt .45'. According to Matthew Hodgart, another of the instructors, there was never any shortage of whisky in the training establishments:

> We used to drink like fish in the evenings after the day's work and talk about everything under the sun. Looking back, that's what it was all about – being young and alive in the most beautiful place in the world.

The difficulties for civilians living in the Protected Area were well illustrated by the diary of Rosemary Bowman (later Rosemary Law), whose family home was Camusdarach Lodge, close to Traigh, on the coast between Arisaig and Mallaig. At New Year 1941 a telephone call came from the War Office saying that the house was being requisitioned immediately, along with the walled garden, a quarter of a mile away. The family moved out and squeezed into a cottage on the shore, where they spent much of the next three and a half years. They were allowed to visit the farmhouse and collect belongings from the garage, but barred from the lodge and its immediate environs. As they had no car, Rosemary's father would walk into Mallaig and back, and once, in that round trip of eleven miles, he saw only three vehicles.

Civilian and military lives were curiously mixed. The Bowmans' farming tenant, Simon McLennan, continued to work the land, and delivered milk from his dairy herd to Mallaig every morning; but it was a fifteen-hundredweight army truck that collected the family's laundry in a hamper and took it to Morar station, whence it went down by rail to Glasgow, to be washed by nuns. One day in the autumn of 1941 when the Bowmans went to sea for a picnic tea, a party of Czech students floated past chanting 'The Song of the Volga Boatmen'.

Next year martial activity increased. Rosemary remembered how 'little parties of Poles or Czechs came tramping to and fro from Camusdarach across our shore at the cottage for their daily firing exercises on our bays'. Whenever the students fired out to sea, fishing expeditions became hazardous. One day Polish soldiers clustered on the rocks above the family's harbour, throwing home-made bombs into the water. 'Each explosion sent water about thirty feet into the air, and we thought that we should pick up dead fish, but when we went to collect them later, there were only shell-shocked eels floating on the water.' Rumours sped up and down Lochaber – among them, one that a German, probably an escaped prisoner, was living in a cave near Arisaig and being secretly fed by sympathizers.

The estate that suffered most was Achnacarry Castle, ancestral home of the Camerons of Lochiel, which early in 1942 became the centre for Commando training. There the regime was even more rigorous than at Inverailort. The tone was set the moment recruits came off the train at Spean Bridge and were launched on a forced, eight-mile march to the castle. Soon the environs of the castle were overrun by the army. The house itself became the Commando training headquarters, the officers' mess and staff accommodation – and the four-storey building's height offered scope for abseiling down the outside walls. The grounds sprouted Nissen huts and tents. Close by were small-arms and grenade ranges, and wooden building façades for instruction in street fighting. Obstacle courses added to the clutter, and climbing ropes dangled from trees, especially along the River Arkaig, which men crossed swinging Tarzan-style.

In the owners' absence, and without their knowledge, the main rooms of the house were decorated with wall paintings several feet wide. Although not perhaps what the Camerons would have chosen for themselves, the pictures were attractively done in watercolour, straight onto the plaster surfaces, and ranged widely in theme, from mermaids and old-fashioned sailing ships at sea to the Rock of Gibraltar and modern military subjects featuring aeroplanes and landing craft.

Already, in 1746, after the battle of Culloden, British troops had once burnt the castle to the ground; and now the fine, castellated house, built of grey stone, which had replaced the original early in the nineteenth century, was again set on fire by troops in the middle of the night – but by accident, rather than intention. Although the blaze was put out, part of the roof was destroyed.

Far more damaging was another conflagration, which started at lunchtime on 27 April 1942, high on the hill opposite the house, at a spot where students had been rock-climbing. Fanned by a strong east wind, the blaze spread through the old, woody heather and ignited the fir, spruce and Caledonian pine, with disastrous results. It also got into the peat, which kept it going, and along Loch Arkaig alone more than 3000 acres of woodland were destroyed.

Two days later Lochiel's secretary sent an urgent letter to the Command Land Agent in Edinburgh:

> I have to inform you that the whole of Lochiel's Old Forest, consisting of very valuable Pine Trees, has been completely destroyed, from Achnacarry to the head of Glen Maillie – a distance of nine miles. In addition, the fire spread across the River Maillie and continued along nearly the whole of Loch Arkaigside. There have also, I fear, been a number of sheep burned in the fire. The fire is still burning, in spite of all the efforts that have been made and the number of people that have been collected.

There was no proof that soldiers had started the blaze; but common sense made it clear that they were to blame, as no one else had been in the area at the time. The cause was probably just a cigarette butt carelessly thrown away. When Lochiel put in a claim for £100,000, the War Department offered him £20,000, and after numerous exchanges some intermediate figure was decided upon; but it took many years for the forest to recover, and charred skeletons of trees stand on the horizon to this day.

Another letter from Lochiel, written in February 1945, showed how uncomfortable life on the estate had become. Having given a list of civilians living in various cottages and estate houses (about a dozen in all), he estimated that at any one time there were between 600 and 1000 soldiers in the camp.

> Nobody goes off-road on account of danger from bullets, bombs, grenades and other explosives. No one knows when these practices take place, and they are practically daily. No one uses the private road except the military, their families and persons enumerated above ... The private road joins the public road at the east end of Loch Arkaig, but no one can go up the loch without a permit.

Thus, in the short term, military occupation brought widespread changes to the Highlands. For nearly five years the silence which normally reigned in the hills was punctuated by the clatter of small-arms fire and the boom of grenades or demolition charges. Rocks were rearranged by explosions, new pools were created on rivers, and mountainsides came alive with small groups of men scrambling across country or attacking each other on live-firing exercises. Not a few salmon were taken with the help of explosives, and the number of deer shot was far higher than usual, many of them mown down indiscriminately with automatic weapons.

In the long term – apart from the burnt forest at Achnacharry – not much in the countryside was altered by military activity. The Commandos were tough, but the Highlands were even tougher. Even the deer soon recovered. Lochiel, back from service with the Lovat Scouts in Italy, wrote in his game book:

> In the war years the deer on the estate were shot very hard …
> under the direction of the Deer Controller for Scotland. The
> Commandos also gained in skill on the hills and in
> marksmanship by constant practice with all kinds of weapons
> in the deer forest. As a result of such indiscriminate shooting,
> the deer forest had to be carefully nursed afterwards, to allow
> numbers to get up and the stock to improve. This was achieved
> remarkably quickly, and by 1953 there appeared to be as many
> stags and hinds as ever on the South Forest.

It was in the big houses that the damage was done. Inverailort Castle was left empty and scarred – an abandoned barracks. Most of the destruction had been caused by the cadet ratings of HMS *Lochailort*, the Royal Naval training school, who succeeded the army as tenants. The Cameron-Head family returned to find the walls of outbuildings riddled with bullet holes; the policies, bristling with barbed wire, were pitted with slit trenches and bomb craters. Yet the worst barbarity had been silently committed indoors. In 1940, as the military were taking over, a porch attached to the old library had been boarded up and sealed, for it contained irreplaceable family heirlooms: bits of Charles Edward Stewart's kilts and plaids, swords and dirks that had been carried at Culloden, gold rings and so on. When the family reopened the room, they found to their dismay that everything had gone: someone had cut his way in and stolen the lot. The CID were called in but nothing was recovered.

Glencripesdale House had also suffered. Most of the contents had been locked away for the duration in two of the largest rooms, but when the Newton family returned they found that many of their possessions had disappeared, and the house needed extensive renovation. Outside, much damage had been done, and the lovely fishing lodge at Duncan's Loch had been burnt to the ground.

Upsetting as such losses were for the owners, they seem trivial when set against the accomplishments of the Special Forces who went through their training in the Highlands. To put this into perspective, of all Commando exploits during the war, the most celebrated and perhaps the most valuable was the sabotage raid on the heavy water plant at Vemork in Norway, carried out on the night of 27–28 February 1943 by a Norwegian team code-named Gunnerside. Having dropped by parachute, they approached the site on skis, avoided a suspension bridge which they knew was guarded, scrambled down into a gorge, scaled a 600-foot rock face, cut their way through a security fence, entered the heavy water building through a service tunnel and laid explosives with thirty-second fuses. The charges went off while they were still within the site, but the German guards were slow to react, and the raiders escaped – having destroyed the entire stock of heavy water, and substantially set back the Nazis' efforts to develop a nuclear weapon.

Today the Commandos are immortalized by a splendid memorial, set high on a knoll in the rough, broken landscape near Spean Bridge, a few miles south of Achnacarry. Three bronze figures, eight feet tall, stand shoulder-to-shoulder on a pedestal, fully equipped for an operation, with their rifles, belt pouches and cap-comforters cast in realistic detail. The statue has a fittingly heroic air: the men gaze into the wide-open spaces of the Highlands, ready to take on all comers in the setting they knew so well.

As the Special Forces tramped the hills around the Road to the Isles, even more hazardous training was in progress at HMS *Varbel*, the headquarters of the Royal Navy's 12th Submarine Flotilla on the Isle of

Bute, some forty miles west of Glasgow. Although nominally a ship, HMS *Varbel* was located in the requisitioned Kyles Hydro Hotel, over-looking Port Bannatyne – the only British base for midget submarines and human torpedoes. The three- or four-man Xcraft – fifty feet long and five feet in diameter – were developed specifically to attack German warships sheltering in the Norwegian fjords; the first trials were held in March 1942, and crews trained in the bay below the headquarters, and in Loch Striven, immediately to the north. Another vital base was the shore establishment known as Port HHZ in Loch Cairnbawn, a sea inlet north of Ullapool. There capital ships of the Home Fleet acted as targets, surrounded by anti-submarine defences, to give the Xcraft crews practice at cutting their way through nets, booms and other obstructions.

Operation Source – an incredibly dangerous undertaking – was launched in September 1943. Six Xcraft, manned by passage crews, were towed across the North Sea by conventional submarines, but two were lost en route and a third returned to base without having engaged a target. This left three – X5, X6 and X7 – to attack the 43,000-ton *Tirpitz* (known as 'the beast'), which was moored in Kåfjord, at the head of Altafjord in the far north. X5 and her crew disappeared without trace, presumed sunk by a shell from one of the battleship's four-inch guns, but the crews of X6 and X7 cut their way through anti-submarine nets and managed to drop their 1½-ton Amatex charges underneath the ship. Trying to slip away, they were detected and attacked: both subma-rines had to be abandoned, and six of the eight crew survived in captiv-ity. Their explosives did not sink the *Tirpitz*, but they lifted the battleship seven feet out of the water and damaged her so badly that she was out of action for more than six months and never returned to active service. The commanders of X6 and X7, Lieutenant Donald Cameron and Lieutenant Basil Place, were both awarded the Victoria Cross.

* * *

While the Xcraft submariners risked their lives in the water, a hazard-ous trial of an entirely different sort was taking place on land. Gruinard Island – lozenge-shaped, a mile long and half a mile wide – lies aligned north and south a few hundred yards offshore in Gruinard Bay, on the coast of Wester Ross. From the beaches on its eastern (inner) side ragged fields of grass and heather climb gently towards a rocky spine; in the middle of the old pastures, surrounded by broken-down stone walls, stand the ruins of a few small houses, long abandoned. The west-ern edge of the land falls steeply to the sea, in cliffs alive with seabirds. Local memory recalls that seven families once lived on the island, but for at least forty years before the beginning of the war it had been unin-habited, except by sheep in summer, and by rabbits, many of which had gradually turned black, as they do with inbreeding in other isolated West Coast communities.

In 1942 this beautiful, lonely place was requisitioned by the Government from its owners, the Dunphie family, for a secret experi-ment – to test the potency of anthrax spores, which are lethal if inhaled by animals or humans. At the time the Government was considering the possibility of a biological attack on Germany, and assessing the damage that a similar attack on England might entail. The immediate aim was to discover whether it was possible to disperse anthrax germs in the air, and so make a useable weapon. Because the release of spores would cause immediate and long-lasting contamination of the surroundings, any experimental area had to be well isolated from humans and animals. Hence the choice of Gruinard.

The strain of anthrax used, Vollum 14578, was a highly virulent one, named after the man who supplied it, Professor R. L. Vollum, Professor of Bacteriology at Oxford University. Glass containers of anthrax culture looking like thick, liquid gruel were prepared at the Government's Microbiological Research Centre at Porton Down, on Salisbury Plain, and driven to Scotland embedded in crates of fuller's earth by a young Sapper officer, Lieutenant Tony Younger. In Gruinard

Bay he was joined by Dr Paul Fildes, the head of the Porton Down establishment, and sundry assistants.

The plan was to test the effect of the anthrax spores on sheep – and because corpses would be highly infectious, arrangements had to be made in advance to bury them. Younger therefore reconnoitred the seaward cliffs and found a place where bodies could conveniently be thrown over; he then cut a trench and buried 1000 lb of ammonal explosive in the top of the cliff, so that, when he set it off, hundreds of tons of rock would break away, crash down and entomb the victims.

The experiment was short and sharp. Sixty Blackface sheep were tethered at intervals along a rope, and a small bomb containing spores was detonated on top of a pole, held upright by cords, some 100 yards upwind. A brownish aerosol cloud drifted towards the animals, and within three days they began to die. Soon all were dead. Their bodies were duly buried beneath an engineered rockfall, but contamination of the heather and soil was so severe that only technicians wearing protective suits could venture onto the island. In a similar experiment a couple of months later a small bomb was dropped from an aircraft. The results were the same, and the sheep were buried by the same method; but the island was closed to the public indefinitely.

That winter – 1942–3 – there was a sudden scare when anthrax was discovered in sheep grazing on the mainland, opposite the test site. Returning to make a check, Fildes and Younger decided that spores might have survived in the island vegetation, and then been blown across the bay by the wind. They therefore set fire to the heather on the island and watched the blaze sweep across the low hills – after which there was no more trouble. In 1946 the Crown agreed to buy the island for £500 and take on the responsibility for it.

The experiments proved that anthrax spores could survive an explosion; they also convinced scientists that a large airborne release of spores over Germany would kill thousands of people and pollute cities so effectively that they would remain uninhabitable for generations. Drastic as the idea was, enthusiasm for biological attack persisted. In 1944 five million linseed cakes impregnated with anthrax spores were prepared and stored at Porton Down for Operation Vegetarian, an attack on German livestock by the RAF. Had they been dropped on farmland and eaten by cattle, they would have killed thousands of animals, and possibly thousands of humans who ate contaminated meat. At the least, they would have caused a crippling food shortage. The cakes, however, were never used, and were incinerated in 1945.

Just as in England large areas of country were cleared of their inhabitants to make way for military training, so in Scotland entire communities were suddenly obliged to leave home. Three of them were the hamlets of Inver, Tarbat and Fearn, way out on Tarbat Peninsula just south of the Dornoch Firth, some forty miles north of Inverness. On 11 November 1943 an order to evacuate gave the 800 inhabitants a month to leave their homes, and forty farms had the same amount of time to move or sell their livestock and crops. Most of the people from Inver sought refuge with families in Tain, a few miles inland – but they could not take their chickens with them and were forced to kill the birds. As Marion Fleming remembered of Inver, 'everybody, but everybody, was living on chicken soup, but we got so sick of it that for weeks and months afterwards I don't think there was one person who could look at another plate of it, however good it was'.

Nobody told the evacuees the reason for the upheaval – that the Admiralty wanted the 3rd Infantry Division to train for the D-Day landings on the Dornoch beaches. An area of about fifteen square miles was requisitioned; mock-ups of German defences were built on the shore, and the peninsula became a live firing range, shelled from the sea by support ships. Throughout a bitter winter the men of Assault Force 'S', the combined army and navy force destined to land on Sword Beach in Normandy, crawled and ran all over it.

The troops went south in April 1944, and within a month the people were back in their homes; but to this day stories of the evacuation persist, not least that of the collie which found its way home from Tain and lived alone in Inver, befriended and fed by the soldiers, until its master returned.

The war was only six weeks old when it reached the northern extremities of Britain. During the night of 13–14 October 1939 a German U-boat penetrated the anti-submarine defences of the anchorage at Scapa Flow, in Orkney. The eastern approaches to the natural harbour had been blocked by sunken ships, booms and underwater cables, but at high tide Günther Prien, commander of *U-47*, managed to manoeuvre over the obstructions and past three block-ships in Kirk Sound, between the mainland and Lamb Holm island, travelling on the surface. With three salvoes of torpedoes he sank the veteran battleship HMS *Royal Oak* before escaping eastwards. Five of his torpedoes missed, but two struck. Although 401 of the battleship's complement were rescued, 833 men and boys lost their lives. In Germany Prien became a hero and was awarded the Knight's Cross of the Iron Cross, the first submarine officer to receive the decoration. He was nicknamed *der Stier* [the Bull] *von Scapa Flow* – and a snorting bull was painted on his conning tower.

The disaster gave the Royal Navy a severe shock, for Scapa Flow had been considered an impregnable anchorage. To prevent further attacks, Churchill (then First Lord of the Admiralty) ordered the immediate construction of solid barriers linking Lamb Holm, Glimps Holm, Burray and South Ronaldsay to the mainland. Work on them began in May 1940. For their bases, 250,000 tons of rock were quarried, transported by a small-gauge railway and sunk in gabions, or wire cages. These were then topped with 66,000 concrete blocks of five or ten tons. The smaller ones were laid on the rock base, and the ten-tonners rested on the sides to act as wave-breakers.

The large labour force needed for the project was augmented by successive contingents of Italian prisoners captured in North Africa, who began arriving in Orkney early in 1942, and by 1943 numbered 550, out of a total workforce of over 2000. Because the Geneva Convention prohibited the use of prisoners of war on military projects, the barriers were described as 'improvements in communications', linking the islands for the benefit of the local community. After fighting in the desert, the newcomers must have thought the treeless, windswept northern islands the abomination of desolation, particularly in winter, when daylight lasted barely four hours a day, and especially as they could not get the ingredients for making pasta. At first the Italians sought to assert themselves by refusing to work on a project which they claimed was 'warlike'. Put on a punishment diet of bread and water for three days, with normal meals on the fourth, they held out until the arrival of Major T. P. Buckland, who spoke Italian and told them that they were there to build a road linking the islands, for benefit of local people. Whether or not they believed this evasion, they accepted it and got on with constructing the causeways.

Two hundred of them were quartered in Camp 60, on the otherwise uninhabited Lamb Holm, where they lived in huts and built a theatre, in which they put on plays and opera. One commodity they had in abundance was concrete left over from the barrier-building, and with it, late in 1943, they fashioned a chapel on the bare north side of the island. The skeleton of the building was two Nissen huts joined end to end, but the builders masked the corrugated iron with a coat of concrete, and created a charming little shrine.

The altar was made from concrete and decorated with painted glass; the ceiling, lined with plasterboard, was elaborately painted and a mosaic pavement covered the floor. A metalworker called Palumbo made candelabra, a rood screen and gates. At the entrance end, an Italianate façade, with a pillared porch flanked by slender windows and topped by a little campanile, concealed the hooped shape of the huts and gave the church a striking presence.

All this was achieved under the direction of a mastercraftsman from the Dolomites, Domenico Chiocchetti, who painted the frescoes and, behind the altar, a strikingly beautiful picture of the Madonna and child, garlanded with the legend *Regina Pacis, Ora pro Nobis* – Queen of Peace, Pray for Us. He also created a statue of St George slaying the dragon from concrete moulded on a barbed-wire skeleton.

Meanwhile, a colony of Wrens had been established at HMS *Tern*, the airfield at Twatt, in the north-west corner of mainland Orkney. Muriel Bacon, an air-mechanic electrician, remembered how they would supplement their meagre rations by buying eggs from the local women around Kirkwall and Stromness – a 'hardy bunch' who gave them tots of their home-brew. In their camp the Wrens held classical record concerts on Sundays – and great was the excitement when one of the officers brought a friend, the violinist Yehudi Menuhin, to play for them.

The Italian prisoners left Orkney in 1945, but Chiocchetti stayed on for a while to finish his work, before giving the chapel to the islanders. He returned twice, in 1960 and 1964, to supervise restoration, and after his death in 1999 a Requiem Mass was held for him on Orkney. For seventy years the chapel has been kept in good repair: it remains a remarkable tribute to the Italians' religious devotion, and to their determination to construct a comforting reminder of home in a foreign land.

Twenty-Three

On the Springboard

Say not the struggle naught availeth,
The labour and the wounds are vain,
The enemy faints not nor faileth,
And as things have been, they remain.

If hopes were dupes, fears may be liars;
It may be in yon smoke conceal'd,
Your comrades chase e'en now the fliers,
And, but for you, possess the field ...

And not by eastern windows only,
When daylight comes, comes in the light;
In front the sun climbs slow, how slowly!
But westward, look, the land is bright!

Arthur Hugh Clough (1819–61), *Say not the struggle naught availeth*

B y the beginning of 1944 many thousands of people in England were working on secret preparations for Operation Overlord, the Allied invasion of northern Europe. To divert German attention from the principal target area – the Normandy beaches – and to pin their forces down in Norway, Denmark, Bulgaria and the north of Italy, a grand deception was put in hand. Under the general title Operation

Bodyguard, two concurrent deception schemes were devised for Britain: Fortitude North and Fortitude South. The northern scheme created a phantom British Fourth Army in Scotland, supposedly gearing up for an invasion of Norway, where the Germans had 250,000 troops; while Fortitude South invented another non-existent force, FUSAG – the First United States Army Group, consisting of eleven notional divisions, based in Kent and Sussex.

The purpose of both schemes was to anchor German armies in places where they could do least to disrupt Overlord; but Fortitude South was by far the more important of the two, since it was designed to convince enemy commanders that the Allied invasion would be launched from the south-east corner of England, across the narrowest stretch of the Channel, rather than from ports a hundred miles to the west. By this means, it was hoped, the Germans would be persuaded to maintain their formidable forces entrenched in the Pas de Calais area, rather than move them down the coast to reinforce the defences in Normandy.

Fortitude North consisted largely of wireless traffic between the elements of the imaginary British Fourth Army, supported by equally non-existent American rangers coming from Iceland. Dummy aircraft were deployed at Peterhead and Fraserburgh to give an illusion of increased activity on the north-east coast of Scotland. Whether or not the scheme had any effect, it was hard for the Allies to determine; but the German forces in Norway stayed put.

Fortitude South was on a much larger scale, and was planned in six separate but closely coordinated phases. *Quicksilver 1* was the creation of FUSAG, the fictitious First United States Army Group. *Quicksilver 2* set up the radio network over which the fake units communicated. *Quicksilver 3* was the launch of dummy landing craft in south coast ports and south-eastern estuaries. *Quicksilver 4* was a series of bombing raids on the Pas de Calais, to suggest that this would be the target of the Allied invasion (for every bomb dropped on Normandy, five times as many were dropped on the Pas de Calais). *Quicksilver 5* was an increase in military activity in and around Dover. *Quicksilver 6* was the activation of diversionary lighting schemes.

Part of FUSAG *was* real: the First Canadian Army, whose signallers ran the radio deception. But the imaginary army as a whole was supposed to consist of a million men, and the main physical evidence supporting its existence was deployed just inland from the Kent and Essex coasts, where field after field was filled with inflatable tanks, trucks and twenty-five-pounder guns, some made of rubber, some of impregnated cloth, but all realistic enough to fool airborne observers. One lorry could carry about thirty Sherman tank kits, and a team could inflate one tank with a stirrup pump in only three and a half minutes before four men lifted it into a realistic position. Alex Lyons, a Royal Engineer during the war, remembered how the crews preferred to set out their 'deceptions' in the evenings or at night so that nobody saw them making encampments of twenty or thirty tanks deployed in realistic formations. He particularly liked working on wet ground, as the lorries left tracks which they would otherwise have had to create artificially, to make the picture look authentic.

> The actual erection of the devices was only a minor part of the operation, as the men would have to live on the site to give it life, build fires, walk in the open and, where necessary, wear the appropriate headgear and badges. We would need to put up latrines and make sure that there were tracks to them. Everything had to look just as if it was a real tank group or whatever we were imitating.

Besides the tanks, guns and lorries, hundreds of tents, sheds and bigger buildings sprouted from the fields. Dummy aircraft resembling Hurricanes and Spitfires but made of wood and canvas were set out on small airfields. They too could easily be moved about, and sometimes they *were* shifted by cattle trying to eat them.

To carry through the deception, dummy landing craft were needed to transport the imaginary troops and their heavy equipment across the Channel. The first of these – the LCA, or Landing Craft Assault, known as a 'Wetbob' – was a failure. An inflatable boat, ten feet wide and thirty feet long, it proved quite uncontrollable: it bounced about on waves in giveaway fashion, and was soon discarded. Far more effective as decoys were the LCTs (Landing Craft Tanks, known as 'Bigbobs'), which were much larger and heavier. Made of steel tubes, wire, plywood and fabric, these were 175 feet long and 31 feet wide, with walls of heavy canvas, and floated on forty-gallon metal drums. In spite of their size, the component parts of each one could be transported in a three-ton lorry, and assembled in eight hours – fast enough for the task to be completed in the protective darkness of a single night.

After elaborate trial exercises along the south coast, some prototypes were taken apart and stored, but in the spring of 1944 construction began in earnest near Ipswich, and by April 700 men were working all out (though again, for security, only at night) to put the huge kits together. The main launch points were the Waldringfield base on the River Deben and HMS *Wolverstone* on the Orwell, both in Suffolk; but by May Bigbobs were being assembled also on the beach at Folkestone and on the waterfront at Dover, where they were floated out into the harbour. Near Dover a whole dummy oil terminal, built from board, was visited by the King. Altogether some 270 Bigbobs were constructed, and all who saw them, even at close quarters, were amazed at how realistic they looked:

> The craft were crewed by the construction teams. Oil burners were fitted inside the funnels to produce the odd plumes of smoke, washing was hung out on deck, crews fished over the side, cradles were hung over the side to 'paint ship', coils of rope and all the deck furniture of a real ship were replicated, and … the White Ensign was flown during the hours of daylight.

Deceptive lighting also played a part in the preparations. Along the south and south-east coasts QL sites – displays of lights and basket fires – were set up, either to decoy enemy aircraft away from vulnerable points, or (in the east) to suggest unusual activity, as if a major force was assembling for departure.

All this would – it was hoped – be spotted by Luftwaffe photo-reconnaissance pilots making high-altitude passes. But the apparent reality of the objects set out on the fields, or floating in the estuaries and harbours, was reinforced by a blizzard of wireless traffic which suggested that huge forces were massing in the South East.

The main orchestrator of the deception was the XX or Double-Cross Committee, chaired by the Oxford don J. C. Masterman, and its team of twenty-four (mostly non-existent) double agents, led by the very real master spy Juan Pujol García, known as Agent Garbo.

In 1941 Pujol, a diminutive Catalan chicken farmer, had been living in Portugal. Aged twenty-nine and already balding, he loathed the Nazis and offered his services as a secret agent to the British in both Lisbon and Madrid. Spurned by the embassies, he approached the Germans, with the aim of doing them damage by feeding them false information, and in due course he was taken on by the Abwehr, who gave him codes, invisible ink and the cover name Arabel and sent him to England. Or, rather, they thought they had. In fact for the time being he stayed in Portugal, from which, with astonishing ingenuity and imagination, he sent fictitious reports of events and conditions in England, relying on a pre-war travel guide for many of his facts.

When Bletchley Park began intercepting his messages, the British were alarmed by the fact that a German agent seemed to be at large in the United Kingdom. But when they realized where he was (still in Portugal) and who he was, they recruited him, smuggled him to England, renamed him Agent Garbo and installed him in a house at 15 Crespigny Road in Hendon, where he was soon joined by his wife

Aracelli and their young son. To work with him, MI5 appointed a talented case officer, Tomás Harris. A half-Spanish, half-English artist, Tommy (as he was always known) made an ideal partner: under the direction of the XX Committee the pair created a fantastic array of non-existent agents and sent immense numbers of misleading messages to Germany.

Between them they put more than half a million words on paper – 315 handwritten letters, averaging 2000 words apiece, with their ostensibly important secret information concealed in invisible ink beneath banal covering texts. Furnished with a radio, they transmitted more than 1200 messages. Throughout the war the Abwehr supposed that the stream of information coming from Garbo was genuine. So skilful was he that the Germans came to believe that he was running a network of two dozen agents, when in fact none of them existed.

As Masterman later wrote, 'Garbo himself turned out to be something of a genius … The one-man band of Lisbon developed into an orchestra, and an orchestra which played a more and more ambitious programme.' The leader of the band was extraordinarily industrious. Day in, day out, year in, year out he took the Underground to an office in St James's and worked up to eight hours a day, drafting letters, enciphering messages and composing cover texts. His notional organization grew until it covered the whole country; by the spring of 1944 his twenty-four 'assistants', described as 'agents' or 'contacts', all imaginary, were scattered about from Glasgow to Harwich, to Exeter and Swansea.

As D-Day approached, through Garbo these alleged assistants reported American formations heading for the south-east corner of England. They transmitted details of tell-tale insignia glimpsed on passing vehicles, and sightings of shoulder badges representing previously unseen units. Some of the reports contained kernels of truth, but almost all were false. At the same time, notional agents in the south and west of England reported fewer troop movements than usual, as if units had been withdrawn from there and transferred to the east. But the web of deception stretched far wider than the Home Counties:

> British diplomats dropped misleading hints at cocktail parties to be overheard by eavesdroppers and channelled back to Germany. Conspicuously large orders were made for Michelin Map 51, a map of the Pas de Calais area. The French resistance, SOE agents, Jedburgh saboteur and guerrilla teams, MI6, the code-breakers at Bletchley, secret scientists and camouflage engineers would each play a part in this great, sprawling, multifaceted deception campaign.

By then Garbo and Tomás Harris had dreamed up some amazing inventions, not least the Brothers in the Aryan World Order, a group of twelve 'fiercely anti-semitic Welshmen dedicated to bringing National Socialism to the valleys and toppling the British Government by a campaign of assassination'. If the Germans believed in these Celtic Fascists – which they did – they would believe in anything that Garbo told them – as when he made an alleged visit to the coast between Southampton and Weymouth, where huge numbers of troops were already assembling, and reported, 'There is no concentration at special points.'

Towards the end of May his agents stepped up their flow of misinformation. One reported that the 4th US Armored Division was in Bury St Edmunds, another that the 6th Armored Division had been seen in Kent. The imaginary Wulf Schmidt, Agent Tate, was notionally sent from a farm in Hertfordshire to another in Kent, so that he could watch the build-up of FUSAG at first hand. 'Have found first-class lodgings with elderly couple in Wye,' he told his German handler. 'So far as I can see, ideal for radio purposes.' Through a non-existent friend – allegedly a clerk at Ashford railway station – he obtained and transmitted details of the plan for FUSAG's embarkation. Garbo himself reported troops of the 83rd Division forming up in a Dover car park, and then had the nerve to claim that he had got a job in the Ministry of Information, which meant that he 'now had access to propaganda documents intended to "hide the facts in order to trick us"'.

Further evidence of the existence of FUSAG was provided by the antics of its (all too real) commander, the rip-roaring, foul-mouthed American General George S. Patton. Earlier in the year he had created a scandal by slapping the face of a man in hospital, telling him there was no such thing as shell shock, and that it was an invention of the Jews. Forced by Eisenhower to apologize, he lost his chance of commanding the ground forces in the Overlord invasion. Instead, he was assigned the command of FUSAG.

Crashing about England, making appearances here and there, he dropped loud and apparently careless remarks in public – 'See ya in the Pas de Calais' – and distinguished himself particularly in April by appearing at the official opening of a Welcome Club for US servicemen at Knutsford, in Cheshire. He was under orders to make no public speeches, but because he had been told that reporters and photographers were banned from the meeting, he went ahead and spoke, apparently insulting the Russians when he failed to mention them as one of the nations, alongside Britain and America, destined to rule the world. Inevitably, his remarks appeared in the press, and Eisenhower sent him a furious letter of reprimand, whereupon he complained that he had been set up. In fact he had – by British intelligence officers, who wanted to make sure the enemy knew he was in England. The Germans regarded Patton as one of the ablest Allied officers, and his command of FUSAG confirmed their estimate of the formation's crucial importance.

As the phantom army was created in April and May, the prime growing season, it caused farmers no small aggravation to find that during the night their crops of hay and corn had been flattened by the arrival and installation of bogus military equipment. Then, in the final days before Overlord, they were still more circumscribed, when movement into and out of coastal areas was restricted. Travel to and from the Republic of Ireland was banned, and a news blackout put members of the public on edge: people knew that an immense event was imminent but they could not discover details. All they saw was interminable convoys of military vehicles streaming southwards.

Unknown to the Double Cross Committee – unknown even to the ubiquitous and apparently omniscient Garbo – in London and Windsor, at the highest level, there was in progress another tense struggle whose outcome might have altered the whole balance of the war. Churchill, the indispensable Prime Minister, had proposed that he should sail towards Normandy on the cruiser HMS *Belfast*, flagship of the invasion fleet, and he had persuaded King George to accompany him.

The King's Private Secretary, Tommy Lascelles, was appalled: as he recorded in his diary, he thought the idea was madness, and set out to stifle it by confronting the monarch directly. 'I think I shook the King,' he wrote, 'by asking him whether … he was prepared to face the possibility of having to advise Princess Elizabeth [then eighteen] on the choice of her first Prime Minister, in the event of her father and Winston being sent to the bottom of the English Channel.'

On Wednesday 31 May he persuaded the King 'without much difficulty', that it would be 'wrong, from many points of view, for either him or Winston to carry out their proposed *Overlord* jaunt'. Next day he took a handwritten letter from the King to Downing Street and gave it to John Martin, Churchill's parliamentary private secretary. He found that Winston, 'who is just like a naughty child when he starts planning an escapade', had said nothing about his plan to Martin, 'who was much relieved that the King was trying to deter him'.

After lunch on 1 June, Lascelles went with the King to the map room in the Downing Street Annexe in Storey's Gate. There Admiral Sir Bertram Ramsay, Naval Commander-in-Chief of the Expeditionary force, expounded to the visitors exactly what would be involved in Winston's scheme. It was soon obvious to Lascelles that any passenger on the cruiser would run serious risks from mines, torpedoes, bombs and shellfire, 'and would see devilish little', as the ship would at no time be closer to the French coast than 14,000 yards.

When Ramsay was told that Operation WC (as he called it) might include his Sovereign as well as the Prime Minister, 'the unfortunate man, naturally enough, reacted violently'. The King soon accepted 'with good grace' that he should not go; but Churchill was still determined to take part. Lascelles was worried: he thought that if the Prime Minister were killed in the early stages of Overlord, 'the news of his death might easily have such an effect on the troops as to turn victory into defeat'. He also saw that Churchill's presence on board *Belfast* would inevitably 'cramp the style of those engaged in fighting her'.

On 2 June, with three days to go, the King again wrote to Churchill, saying that it would be most unfair of him to embark, after he himself had advised his monarch not to, and that it was quite unnecessary for him to risk his life on a wild goose chase which could have no military value whatever. The letter went by courier from Windsor Castle to Downing Street, but Churchill had departed to spend the night in his special train, which was parked somewhere in Hampshire, and did not reply until next day. Only then, on 3 June, did he agree to abandon his idea, and Lascelles concluded triumphantly: 'We [I and the King] have bested him, which not many people have succeeded in doing in the past four years.'

Deceptive hints of many kinds were being dropped, some small, others heavy. Every morning *The Times* published a short weather report covering the Straits of Dover. RAIN CLOUDS was the headline on 5 June:

After a day of cloud and sunshine, with a gusty, south-westerly wind, it was cool in the Straits of Dover last night. The wind had moderated a little, but there were still white-capped breakers in the straits ... Rain clouds were gathering at nightfall after a further drop in the barometer.

What was the point of printing that – when wireless forecasts were banned – except to suggest that the weather off Dover was of prime importance? As for heavyweight emphasis of the deception: on the night of 2–3 June a force of nearly a thousand American bombers, escorted by 500 fighters, attacked the Wehrmacht's military installations in the Pas de Calais. To the Germans, a raid of this magnitude could mean only that the Allies were trying to soften up the defences in advance of their invasion.

In the run-up to D-Day – set for Monday, 5 June 1944 – the paramount need was to keep both the date and the destination of Operation Overlord secret. The Germans knew that an invasion of the Continent was imminent, but they did not know where or when the Allies would strike; every precaution was therefore taken to prevent information leaking out. Much of southern England was brought almost to a standstill by the tremendous build-up of troops as they moved down from concentration areas to marshalling areas, and by the security measures designed to prevent any escape of intelligence. Units briefed for action were confined to barracks or camps by barbed-wire barriers and extra guards; telephone lines were disconnected and letter boxes sealed.

Stan Blacker, of 606 Royal Marine Flotilla, remembered how 'the whole of Hampshire was becoming a vast arsenal, every roadside jammed with vehicles, every grass verge loaded with ammunition'. The Hamble river, leading to the Solent, was packed with landing craft, whose crews were marshalled and housed in the wooden huts of HMS *Cricket*, the Combined Operations base hidden away in woodland.

Canvas villages sprang up in adjacent fields and woods, temporarily housing another 4000 men. Footpaths were closed, and the public were excluded from the area.

Veronica Phipps, whose husband Alan had been killed fighting in Greece, had gone to stay with friends at their home near the coast in Hampshire. She found she had to drive down lanes and byways because the main and secondary highways were choked with convoys of military lorries, trucks, personnel carriers, jeeps, tanks – 'all the frightening might of a great army on the move', heading for their designated marshalling areas. The Winchester bypass, completed just before the war, was closed to civilian traffic and jammed with parked armoured vehicles of every description.

It was the same all over the south of England. On roads leading to the Channel coast it became impossible for civilian traffic to move, as vast military convoys were driving for five minutes and then stopping, so that the main roads were continuously blocked. As women came out offering cups of tea and sandwiches, GIs tossed pennies, threepenny bits and sixpences to children, convinced that they would never need them again.

On the Thursday before D-Day, as the Marines at HMS *Cricket* paraded on a road, RAF pilots flew captured German aircraft over them, so that they would recognize different types. Then, on D-Day minus one, at another parade on the main road, a local priest stood on a box and said prayers – 'God, teach us not to show cowardice … God, give us strength to face the enemy', ending with the Lord's Prayer.

D-Day had been set for Monday, 5 June 1944, with H-hour (the beginning of the assault) at 6 a.m. But on Friday the 2nd the Meteorological Office warned Eisenhower that a violent storm was approaching over the Atlantic: sure enough, a gale whipped up waves in the Channel to a dangerous level, and early on the 4th the Supreme Commander ordered a twenty-four-hour postponement. Hope rose again when the Met Office predicted a lull between that depression and the next: a thirty-six-hour window of opportunity, from the afternoon of Monday, 5 June until late on Sunday the 6th. Backed by his senior commanders, Eisenhower took the momentous decision at 5 a.m. on the 5th: 'OK – we'll go.'

On the 6th, the fateful day, people all over England were roused by the noise. The inhabitants of Lincoln were woken only half an hour after midnight by the roar of engines warming up on the airfields that ringed the city. At 5.45 Tommy Lascelles, in Buckingham Palace, became aware of an endless stream of aircraft passing overhead. Molly Lefebure, secretary to the Home Office forensic pathologist Professor Keith Simpson, woke 'dazedly in a green and silver dawn which shook with the noise of the outgoing planes streaming across the sky', and she hurried off to work 'in a state of tremendous excitement and apprehension'.

> This was the day we had all been waiting for, and working for, and praying for, during the past four long years, and we all both delighted in it and dreaded it. Everybody held their breaths, waiting for news of what was happening on the landing beaches. The entire British nation had its fingers crossed.

On her first call of the day, at Wanstead mortuary, a depressing surprise awaited her. On the slate post-mortem table lay the body of a soldier in battledress. The man had been found dead in his berth on one of the ships about to sail for Normandy. When the pathologist opened his body, it released a strong smell of bitter almonds – the unmistakable call sign of cyanide. Clearly, he had lost his nerve. 'That was our first p.m. on D-Day,' wrote Molly sadly. 'The young soldier who was cut up in Wanstead mortuary while his erstwhile comrades were landing in Normandy.'

Agent Garbo and his orchestra continued their bravura performance right to the wire. At 3 a.m. on 6 June he and four colleagues assembled in the upstairs bedroom at his home, and Charles Haines, his dedicated wireless operator, started trying to pass a message to the regular Abwehr operator in Madrid.

The content of the transmission – initiated by the Double Cross team and sanctioned by Eisenhower – seemed an explosive betrayal of secrets: it said, in a roundabout way, that the invasion had started. But the British knew that even if the message went straight through, it could not reach Berlin before 6 a.m., because the delay in transmission between Madrid and Berlin was three hours – so that by the time German High Command received the news, Allied troops would already be going ashore under heavy fire on the Normandy beaches.

As it happened, the Spanish operator in Madrid was either asleep or away from his post, and did not come on the air until 8 a.m. – by which time it was far too late for the information to give the Germans any advantage. Garbo sent angry messages complaining that the idle Spaniard had ruined his efforts to be helpful – and the episode merely strengthened his credibility still further in Nazi minds, leading them to believe him when he continued to tell them that the Normandy landings were only a feint, and that the real invasion was going to be aimed at the Pas de Calais.

German intelligence reports, captured later, estimated that on 6 June there were at least forty-two Allied divisions and 500 large landing craft assembled in the south-east corner of England, poised to swarm across the Channel. In fact there were fifteen divisions, held in reserve, and no real landing craft at all. Hypnotized by the XX Committee's masterly deception, German High Command kept the Panzer divisions of the Fourteenth and Fifteenth German armies on station in the Pas de Calais until it was too late for them to move down the coast and repel the assault on the Normandy beaches.

Garbo's work was by no means finished. On 9 June he sent the Abwehr a long message, re-emphasizing that the landings in Normandy were only a diversionary manoeuvre, and that the main Allied attack would probably take place in the Pas de Calais area. 'The whole of the present attack,' he said, 'is set as a trap for the enemy to make us move all our reserves in a hurried strategical disposition which we would later regret.' His message went all the way up to Hitler, and the resulting intelligence assessment showed that German High Command had swallowed the bait. A week after D-Day, only one German division had been moved from the Pas de Calais to Normandy, and both Eisenhower and Montgomery later agreed that the strategic deception had been an immeasurable help in allowing the Allies to establish a bridgehead on the Continent.

The Germans' faith in Garbo, and their gratitude to him, remained indestructible. On 29 July, six months after the British had thanked him for his services by making him a Member of the Most Excellent Order of the British Empire, he received a wireless message informing him that the Führer had awarded him the Iron Cross for his 'extraordinary merits'.

Twenty-Four

Flying Bombs

Hurled headlong flaming from th' ethereal sky
With hideous ruin and combustion down
To bottomless perdition ...

John Milton, *Paradise Lost*

Within a week of Overlord's launch Hitler retaliated with a vicious new device, the *Verwaltungswaffe Nummer Eins* – Revenge Weapon No. 1 – or V-1 – the flying bomb soon known as the doodlebug. Inspired detective work by the staff of the Allied Central Interpretation Unit at RAF Medmenham, and the consequent bombing of launch sites, had set back the start of his campaign by several months; but the first doodlebug was sighted coming in over the Kent coast at 00.40 on the morning of Tuesday, 13 June 1944. Observers in Folkestone thought the town was being heavily shelled; but then it was reported that an aeroplane flying fast, and in flames, was heading for London. In fact it crashed at Swanscombe, and within four minutes it was accurately reported as a pilotless aircraft.

So began a nightmare that lasted for the next six months. The first doodlebug to hit London landed in the East End early that same morning – 13 June – shaking people by the suddenness of its arrival and the size of the explosion it caused. A pilotless missile looking like a small, slender aircraft, twenty-seven feet long, with stubby, square-ended wings, a pointed nose and the pulse-jet engine belching flame from its raised position above the tail, a V-1 carried a warhead containing nearly 2000 lb of explosive. It flew at 350 mph and at a height of between 2000 and 3000 feet. Within a day people in Kent and Sussex, and also in London, were all too familiar with the noise of its engine – a rough, harsh roar like that of a badly tuned motorbike. As long as that sound continued, you were reasonably safe; but the moment it cut out – take cover! – for the sudden silence meant that the bomb had run out of fuel and gone into its terminal dive, about forty-five seconds from impact.

Weapons of mass destruction, the flying bombs were aimed at central London, but once they were airborne the length and direction of their flight could not be further refined, so that the Germans had no means of knowing exactly where they would strike. There could be no pretence that these devices were aimed at military or industrial targets: indiscriminate murder was the means by which Hitler hoped to pound the British into submission – and no doubt he was gratified when he learned that on Sunday, 18 June, a doodlebug scored a direct hit on the Guards' Chapel in Wellington Barracks during morning service, killing 121 members of the packed congregation.

Every possible effort was made to prevent the weapons reaching their destination: the facility at Peenemünde had been heavily bombed, and as Churchill revealed to the House of Commons on 6 July, more than a hundred launch sites along the French coast had been destroyed by Allied bombers. In England, barrage balloons were moderately effective, but on the leading edges of their wings the V-1s had cable-cutters which could sever tethering wires. At first the only British fighter fast enough to overhaul them at low level was the Hawker Tempest, recently brought into service; but if a Mosquito, Spitfire or Mustang dived on one from above, it had a chance of making a kill. Skilled pilots perfected a technique of flipping a doodlebug over by flying alongside, wing tip to wing tip, then pulling slightly ahead, so that the fighter's airflow unbalanced it and sent it into an uncontrolled dive. Of 1846 flying bombs destroyed by aircraft, Tempest pilots claimed 638, Mosquitos 428 and Spitfires 303.

The main defence against the intruders was the deployment of anti-aircraft guns in ever-increasing numbers, ranged in lines from the North Downs to the south coast, across the Thames Estuary, and in other lines up the coasts of East Anglia, Lincolnshire and Yorkshire. Because of their speed, doodlebugs were difficult targets, but successive technical refinements in fire-control systems and the introduction of radar sights quickly improved the gunners' kill rate: from 17 per cent of incoming bombs shot down in the first week of their deployment, the rate rose to 74 per cent in the last week of August, during which eighty-two were downed in a single day.

Tommy Lascelles witnessed the early difficulties. Out and about with the King and Queen in Surrey on the morning of 12 July, he escorted them first to East Grinstead, where he found 'a very nasty mess in the main street of the town', on which a doodlebug had landed at breakfast time. 'There were only three casualties,' he reported, 'but the devastation was considerable.'

> The appearance, as from the skies, of the King and Queen naturally had an immense effect [on morale]; they spent some time, every minute of which, from every point of view, was worth its weight in gold, talking to all and sundry.

Then, as the royal party visited an anti-aircraft battery at Lingfield, they had a fine view of a doodlebug heading for London.

> The klaxon sounded the alarm, and in a few seconds every gun in the battery had opened up at a target about 7,000 yards' distance. Soon we could see the flying bomb approaching, at fantastic speed – the experts said not less than 450 mph – and it passed almost over our heads at an altitude of, I suppose,

about 2,000 feet, looking incredibly sinister, like a cur-dog with its ears back and teeth showing.

The guns made beautiful and concentrated patterns of shell-bursts right in its path, but always just fifty yards behind its tail. It went on to London unscathed, flying with uncanny accuracy through the intervals between the balloons echeloned some three miles behind us. This happened four or five times during the afternoon … It gave one a feeling of physical sickness to see the devilish things flashing over the English countryside, to plunge into the bowels of poor, defenceless London.

The General conducting the royal party was disappointed with the performance of the battery, which had shot down three out of five birds the previous day; and he suspected that the ATS girls operating the target-tracking radar were overexcited by the presence of Their Majesties; but Lascelles saw how difficult it was to set the correct lead, and reflected that it had taken him many years to 'achieve much the same art of adjustment when confronted with driven partridges'.

Hitler's target was London; but Kent, which lay beneath the flight path from launch ramps to the capital, came under such pressure that it was soon known as 'Doodlebug Alley'. After the first bewildering surprise – what *were* these things? Planes with their tails on fire? Where were they coming from?' – people became inured to continual bombardment. On 22 June they saw the intruders plainly as they came in ones and twos, with the flames from their exhausts showing brightly against a backcloth of cloud. On 24 June a V-1, shot up by a fighter, crashed on Bartley Farm near Sneddon, killing six people. Soon a local log, kept at Edenbridge in the heart of the Eden Valley, reported: 'Too many coming over to keep count of, some high, some low.' Three days later the engine on one of the bombs cut out over the town, but it glided clear, went into a spin and crashed in a nearby wood.

Dora Basset, teaching at Frant primary school, was terrified when she heard a tell-tale engine go silent overhead. She told the children to get under their tables and crouched under her own desk. 'I peered at all the little white faces,' she remembered, 'and said a prayer: "Dear God, if this is the end of us all, please let the parents know I did my best to save their children."' No explosion came: the bomb made a harmless landing in allotments outside Tunbridge Wells. Guildford had a lucky escape on 28 June, when a V-1 fell and exploded in the middle of Stoke recreation ground: a short distance either side, and it would have killed dozens of people in the busy streets.

The night of 18 July was particularly bad. There were fourteen alerts in Kent, as more and more V-1s roared over. A few hit the cables of barrage balloons and exploded; others were attacked and downed by fighters, but most got through. On 28 July new tactics were tried: the balloons were hauled down, and rockets were fired into the doodle-bugs' path – but nothing, it seemed, could stop them. By the end of July they were appearing over Kent in waves, three or four abreast, and the daily average was ninety-five. The deafening noise of anti-aircraft guns intensified people's fear. On the night of Sunday, 6 August the bombs came six at a time, every half-hour, but then the rate slackened slightly, and the total for a week was only 450.

Luck played a huge part. One morning an eleven-year-old boy was walking his dog near Farnham when he saw a doodlebug coming straight at him:

Then it stopped and dived into a farmyard half a mile in front. I ran there, the dog ran in front. The farmer had just brought the cattle to the yard, and it landed in the middle. It flattened everything, sheds, haystacks, walls, house. I walked through a mountain of chopped-up cattle and debris. The family was underneath but I didn't know. I walked away again before anyone came.

In contrast, another doodlebug landed on a school in Godalming at 8 a.m., when only the caretaker was present. He was slightly injured – but if the bomb had crashed an hour later, when the children were present, there would have been a massacre. Occasionally a misguided V-1 did more good than harm – for instance by exploding in a stream near Maidstone and blasting out a perfect duck pond. Boys scavenging for metal, which they were encouraged to collect for the munitions industry, found that the remains of a bomb rusted very quickly, as if it had been made of inferior materials.

Morale in the South East was further depressed by the weather. The storms which had caused the postponement of Overlord continued through most of June, and the summer turned out to be one of the dullest and coldest that farmers had ever known. The hay crop was disastrous, and in some places the hours of sunshine during the month were the fewest since records began. 'At dawn on midsummer day,' *The Farmers' Weekly* reported, 'central and southern England were in the grip of a frost keen enough to ruin tomato crops.'

A map of V-1 landings in Kent looked much the same as the chart of conventional bombs: dots recorded a dense scatter of impacts everywhere – but they showed an intense concentration just off the coast opposite Folkestone, Hythe, Dymchurch and New Romney. There the strengthened anti-aircraft batteries did their job and shot down a thousand into the sea. Of the 8000 V-1s launched at England, 2400 came down in Kent, killing 152 people and injuring 1761; Sussex was not far behind; but those that reached the capital killed more than 5000 people and injured nearly 18,000.

Debate raged about whether or not the Government was right to order the doodlebugs to be shot down beyond the boundaries of London, thereby increasing the risk for civilians outside the metropolis; but for the majority of people, the answer was 'Yes'. It was the only sensible way to reduce the carnage caused by Hitler's foul weapon. The slaughter died down only when Allied bombers managed to knock out the launch sites.

The horror of strikes was graphically described by Molly Lefebure, who saw any number of mangled corpses working throughout the war as secretary to the Home Office pathologist Professor Keith Simpson. She had to admit that bombs – the 'devilish things' – were rather graceful. One that she saw was 'a delicate shade of bluey-green, with a beautiful long plume of vivid scarlet and orange flame spurting out behind it', and she herself once seemed to be pursued by a doodlebug, which went round in three complete circuits before crashing. Soon she developed a savage contempt for this 'form of death ... completely lacking the human touch, deriving from those master-minds that invented mobile gas-chambers for killing Jewish children, and human soap-factories ... A rather ridiculous little airplane, buzzing across the sky, drooling and lurching like a besotted bumble bee, finally to cut off into silence and plunge in a top-heavy, helpless dive on to streets and houses and people, sending everything and everybody up in fragments, with a bang!'

Few sights can have been more harrowing than one she saw: the body of a lorry driver killed by a flying bomb that landed close in front of his vehicle. The windscreen had been shattered in his face, 'and his throat was cut from ear to ear, as decisively as if he had been a fanatical suicide'. During another attack, in the middle of conducting a post-mortem Simpson took cover under the slab on which the body was lying, and as Molly remarked, 'the sight of one who hoped to live crouching under a corpse was rather striking'.

London was always most at risk, but hundreds of the flying bombs went astray and landed harmlessly in fields or woods – like one which shaved a bus going over the top of Nashleigh Hill, outside Chesham, some thirty miles beyond its target. The driver saw it coming at him and zigzagged wildly about the road in desperate attempts to escape from its path: the weapon skimmed over his roof and plunged into soft ground on the far side of a field, causing little damage. People waiting for the bus at the bottom of the hill congratulated the passengers on their good fortune. Another V-1 came down in the park of West Wycombe House, thirty-five miles west of London, shaking the house, blowing out two windows of the west drawing room and causing part of the decorated ceiling to collapse.

When the German launch crews were driven further up the coast of France, the approach tracks changed, and even the countryside of Hertfordshire, well north of London, was not immune. In the summer of 1944 the Basham family, who had been bombed out of their home in Hackney three years earlier, were living in a caravan and a tent about twenty yards from an old keeper's cottage near Brickendon. Around the site a few oak trees had been left as a screen when the rest of the wood was felled. Staying with the Bashams were two young cousins, a girl of eight and a boy of four, brought down from London to give them a respite from the flying bombs.

One summer afternoon fifteen-year-old Ben Basham went outside to watch doodlebugs crossing the wooded valley to the south on their way to London. With flames spurting from their tails, they made a stir-ring sight – but suddenly he realized that one of them had deviated from its course and was heading directly for him. When the engine cut, the bomb dived straight towards the cottage. Ben yelled a warning. His mother ran out of the caravan with the children and threw herself down on them beside Ben and his sister. His father was standing near the house, too shocked to move.

At the last moment a wing of the V-1 caught one of the oaks, and the contact tipped it down into the space between cottage and caravan. Both were completely wrecked by the explosion. Ben, his mother, his sister and two cousins, although only fifteen yards from the edge of the crater, were miraculously unharmed; but Ben, lurching to his feet in a cloud of dust and falling leaves, at first thought he was dead and in some afterlife – until out of the swirling mist came his dog, Pablo, and then his father, who had been blown into a ditch but was intact.

The family in the cottage were not so lucky. Mrs Dench, the mother, was killed and her daughter was badly injured. A baby, in a pram, protected by the chimney breast, was unhurt, but Grandfather Dench suffered a broken leg.

The Bashams were given shelter by a friendly farming family called Pateman, who built them a makeshift house made of straw bales and tarpaulins, and they lived in it for weeks, cooking and eating in a barn. Rats and mice rustled between the bales as they slept, and bats flitted above them as they ate; but they were so grateful for the kindness they received that afterwards Ben looked back on those troubled times 'almost with affection'.

Fighter aircraft, barrage balloons and anti-aircraft batteries offered partial defence against V-1s, but there was a more subtle weapon which also had some effect, and that was deception.

The aim was to deflect the flying bombs by transmitting false information about where they were landing. Because Garbo had told the Germans he was based in London, he could not fail to report the strikes – but what he could do was falsify the points of impact. If he slightly exaggerated the number of hits in the north and west of the capital, and said less about those in the south and east, he might encourage the Germans to believe that they were overshooting (which they already were), and lead them to shorten their range, so that the bombs would come down in less crowded areas.

The idea was accepted by the Chiefs of Staff, but initially rejected by the Cabinet, who believed it would be immoral to deflect the V-1s into other areas and onto other people. In August, however, the Chiefs won the argument, and Garbo was authorized to go ahead.

Soon he was forced to expand his coverage to include reports on Hitler's second revenge weapon, the V-2 – the world's first ballistic missile. On 8 September 1944 a thunderous explosion in Chiswick killed only three people but destroyed several houses in Staveley Road.

The detonation caused panic, because at first no one knew what had caused it. The V-2 had travelled through the stratosphere at 3000 mph, reached a height of fifty miles above the earth, and arrived without warning. Only after its warhead had detonated did the roar of its rocket engine catch up with it, and the double crack of it breaking the sound barrier was heard all over London.

Of more than 1300 strikes over the next few months, the worst was on the Woolworth's store in New Cross Road, Deptford, in the middle of the afternoon on 25 November 1944, which killed 168 people and put another 120 in hospital. Altogether some 2700 civilians were killed by V-2s in London, and 6500 were injured. The Germans' other main target was Antwerp, where 1700 Belgian civilians lost their lives in rocket explosions.

Since there was no possibility of intercepting the missiles in the air, and since the Germans were firing them from mobile launchers, which they kept moving, the only defence against them was disinformation. Proceeding with the utmost caution, Garbo and his notional sub-agents gradually managed to shift the mean point of impact (MPI) away from Charing Cross, where the Germans believed it was. As Masterman reported, 'Over a period of some months we contrived to encourage the enemy steadily to diminish his range: thus in the four weeks from 20 January to 17 February 1945 the real MPI moved eastwards about two miles a week and ended well beyond the boundary of the London region.' The last two rockets to reach England fell on 27 March 1945, one of them killing a woman in her house at Orpington, in Kent, twelve miles south-east of Charing Cross.

Twenty-Five

Unfinished Business

For we that fight till the world is free,
We are not easy in victory.
We have known each other too long, my brother,
And fought each other, the world and we.

G. K. Chesterton, *A Song of Defeat*

All through the summer of 1944 the sky over the south of England seemed to be permanently full of aircraft, as British and American bomber squadrons pressed home their raids on Germany, night and day. The poet, editor and publisher John Lehmann, staying at his mother's house in Buckinghamshire (part of which had been turned into a Red Cross hospital), described how

as sunset darkened into twilight on cloudless nights, slowly great armadas of bombers rose over the horizon and the tops of the chestnut trees, and their clustering formations, heading for the Continent, filled the sky for hours on end with their steady whine and roar … It was an awe-inspiring spectacle, this gigantic concentration of death-dealing power moving off to the kill.

Away from the eastern side of the country, in contrast, the land had suddenly emptied. Many thousands of soldiers had disappeared to fight on Overlord, taking their tanks, Bren-gun carriers, field guns, landing craft, lorries, jeeps, ammunition, explosives and other impedimenta with them. At the end of May there had been 640,000 American field force personnel in England. By the end of September the number had fallen to 33,000. Former GI camps stood empty and abandoned: no longer could children cadge gum and chocolate, or hitch rides in passing vehicles. What they could do, though, was to forage profitably on the huge dumps of canned food that the Americans had left behind. Also abandoned were hundreds of dogs, which the soldiers had somehow appropriated but could not take to war.

Over the next months the total of service personnel in England fluctuated sharply as wounded GIs came back from the battlefields – 65,000 of them in June and July alone – and reinforcements from America poured into ports on the south coast, to spend a few days or weeks in transit before moving on to the battlefields in France. Camps and depots had to be reopened, and training areas repossessed. This time, the main concentration of US forces was in Wiltshire and Hampshire; but most of the newly arrived units stayed only a short time before pushing on to join the fight for Europe.

Away from all the military installations, the landscape had altered greatly during the war. One man with a clear view of the changes was the itinerant Professor Gangulee, who described the campaign for growing wheat as 'a phenomenal success', and noted that by the close of 1942 six million new acres had been 'brought under the plough'. Nineteen forty-three was another record year: the Government set a target of 960,000 extra acres to be ploughed, but in the event farmers managed 1,376,000. Of the huge new area now under corn, nearly half had been derelict before the war, and, overall, better management had led to heavier yields per acre: both 1942 and 1943 yielded bumper harvests.

In his survey the professor found that, in spite of all the ploughing, the number of small dairy herds had hardly declined, partly because farmers were working their land better and alternating leys (new-sown grass fields) with crops of corn – a system which improved the quality of the pasture. As cheese was rationed, dairy farmers tended to keep back some of their milk so that they could make cheese for themselves or to sell locally. The number of sheep – some twenty-seven million in 1938 – had been reduced, but was still substantial. Herds of beef cattle had been considerably cut down, mainly because of the shortage of feedstuff.

For particular praise Gangulee singled out the Sandringham estate, where all suitable grassland in the park had been ploughed, and the golf course was growing oats and rye; six acres of lawn right up to the house were down to rye, and beds in the ornamental flower garden were full of beetroots and parsnips. Admirable though they were, such achievements were partly the result of benevolent man-management rather than agricultural acumen. The King took a strong interest in the welfare of his farm workers and arranged for a mobile canteen to ferry them out a midday meal. A van provided by the Ford Emergency Food Vans Trust distributed hot, two-course meals on four days of the week. Seventy-seven meals were cooked on each of the four days, and workers assembled at points nearest their jobs to await the arrival of the van. The cost to each of them was 6d a week.

On another royal estate – the King's farm at Windsor – the changes had been equally striking. Three Land Girls were employed; the horses which normally pulled gleaming carriages on ceremonial state occasions had been harnessed to mowers for cutting the hay, and 300 acres had been ploughed for corn – three times as much as in 1938. In the Great Park, which stretches away to the south-west in front of the castle, a mile-square block had been ploughed for the first time in centuries and planted with corn, constituting what the Commissioners of Crown Land claimed to be the biggest wheat field in Britain. The red deer herd, famous for the excellence of its stags, had been reduced from 1000 head to a breeding nucleus of under a hundred, and the animals had been fenced in, instead of being allowed to wander about the park freely.

In general, Gangulee considered that 'the remaking of rural Britain' was having a strongly beneficial effect on the population as a whole, and that among urban people there was now 'a keen interest' in agricultural and rural life. He discerned a distinct improvement in the relationship between farmers and farm workers, and forecast that if the wartime expansion of agriculture became permanent, the workers' status would certainly improve, and that the entire tempo of rural life would be altered, 'from which the nation as a whole will derive benefit'.

He was also a strong supporter of the Land Girls, whose training and experience (he thought) would help to 're-establish the dignity of agricultural labour and occupation. Some of these women will take up farming, and others will return to their pre-war professions with an intimate knowledge of rural life and environment.' In short, war had 'united the nation as never before'.

In 1944 the area of land under cultivation increased by another 700,000 acres; but in the autumn disaster threatened when the number of volunteers needed to bring in the vital potato crop during November and December fell far short of what was needed. The President of the National Farmers' Union, J. K. Knowles, sounded the alarm when fewer than a third of the 70,000 helpers he wanted had come forward; but the crisis was eased by the recruitment of children in Nottinghamshire, Leicestershire and Lincolnshire, who were granted extra leave from school.

Already the NFU was lobbying the Government for the increased use of prisoners of war, of whom at least 100,000 had become available. After the surrender of Italy in September 1943, and its withdrawal from the war, thousands of Italian prisoners had already been repatriated;

but since NFU officials reckoned that one German was worth a dozen Italians, their departure did not seriously weaken the labour force. Prisoners were allowed to work a maximum of forty-eight hours a week, all in daylight: for their labour farmers paid 1s per hour, of which the prisoners received 4d, the rest going to the provision of armed guards.

Besides initiating far-reaching social change, the drive to increase food production had led to one astonishing discovery. On a bitterly cold day in January 1942 a contract farm worker, Gordon Butcher, was sent by his employer, the agricultural engineer Sydney Ford, to plough part of an enormous field called Thistley Green near the village of West Row, in Suffolk. Butcher was thirty-eight, a fairly simple fellow, with a wife and three children, sticking-out ears and a habit of talking aloud to himself. He had a tractor of his own, and worked for farmers round about. Ford was a good deal older – fiftyish, with a bald head and a foxy look. He did not own the patch which he sent Butcher to plough: that belonged to a man called Rolfe. But Ford worked for several farmers around the area, and had a bit of a reputation as a collector: people took him small finds like arrowheads which had been dug up in the fields.

In a vicious north-east wind whistling over the Fens, Butcher worked away, up and down the field of barley stubble. Before the war his ploughshare would have been set at a depth of five or six inches; ploughing to eight inches 'had never before been dreamt of' in the stiff East Anglian clays. But now, because the next crop was to be sugar beet, to help ease the sugar shortage, Butcher had set his share at twelve inches.

In the afternoon the steel tip suddenly hit something hard, getting such a jolt that it broke the wooden pin linking plough to tractor (the pin was a safety device). Butcher got down, and when he started scrabbling with his hands to discover what he had struck, he saw the rim of a huge metal plate about two feet in diameter, encrusted with green corrosion.

For some reason he felt frightened. Instinct told him to get away from whatever it was he had found. He was also extremely cold. He turned his back and walked off to seek the help of Ford, who came out with a spade. A snowstorm swept over the two men as they dug away black earth, but they persevered, with growing excitement, until they had recovered thirty-four objects – plates, bowls, huge salvers ... Ford saw at once that they had hit on something immensely valuable, but he told the ploughman that it was useless old stuff, and Butcher did not object when he took the whole lot home in a sack.

Rather than declare the find, which he realized was a priceless hoard of silver, Ford kept it hidden for four years, and he seems to have spent much of the war cleaning it. Only at Easter 1946 was his secret laid bare. When Dr Hugh Fawcett, a well-known collector of antiquities, came to visit Ford, as he often had in the past, he noticed two spoons on the mantelpiece which he at once saw were Roman. Ford said they came from a find which he had reported to the police at Mildenhall, but that the coppers had promptly come along and 'pinched the lot'.

He then retracted this claim and showed Fawcett some of the plates, insisting they were pewter. Fawcett, seeing they were silver, had them turned over to the police, who started an investigation. Fawcett reported to Christopher Hawkes of the British Museum, who sent him back to Mildenhall, to make Ford declare the find. Ford refused. After an inquest held that summer, on 1 July 1946 the find was officially declared treasure trove. The highly decorated Roman silver, dating from the fourth century AD, included two enormous platters and several smaller dishes and bowls, as well as ladles and spoons. By the law of treasure trove, it should have been Butcher, the finder, who got a reward. But he did not know this, and Butcher and Ford were declared joint-finders, each receiving £1000 compensation. Had Butcher been ploughing at normal peacetime depth, one of the most magnificent hoards ever found in Britain might still be buried beneath the black earth of Suffolk.

In the second half of 1944, as the Allied forces drove deep into Europe from north and south, life in rural Britain grew more settled. With air raids less and less of a threat, the future of farming after the war became the subject of animated debate. To what extent should wartime control and crop-planning be continued? How should land be distributed between agriculture, forestry, industry, housing and sport or amenity? The immediate nationalization of land – 'Nationalism in our Time' – had been one of the key elements in the Labour Party's manifesto, but now the idea was dropped from the Five-Year Plan for Socialism. The Ministry of Agriculture proposed a scheme for training ex-servicemen and women who wanted to go on the land – but only those who were prepared to undertake a year's 'actual hard work' on a farm would be accepted. As some wise guy pointed out, 'The emotional appeal of life on the land is strongest with those who know least about it.'

In a speech to the Farmers' Club on 5 June 1944 the politician Sir John Barlow spoke up for the country, lamenting the fact that, with the growth of the industrial population in the nineteenth century, the physique of the nation had 'materially diminished', and that 'with every yard of cloth exported from this country, a particle of health of the individual went with it'. Surely it would be better, he suggested, 'even at some cost, to have a large and prosperous rural population than to adopt the negative policy of spending untold millions on social services in urban areas trying to regain what had been lost'.

By the autumn of 1944 the absence of gamekeepers and foresters had had a marked effect on wilder areas of land. For five years there had been no preservation of game; farmers had cut no bracken for bedding, and no thinning had been done in the coverts. In Montgomeryshire Captain Bennett Evans was alarmed by the increase in numbers of foxes, whose depredations were undermining the farmers' efforts – in response to Government appeals – to increase their output of sheep. 'It may even become necessary in North Wales,' he wrote, 'soon to decide whether it is going to be foxes or trees.'

In Scotland and the north of England many grouse moors lay derelict, blasted by bombs and shells, lacerated by tank tracks and raked by small-arms fire. The fire which was deliberately lit on Midhope Moor, to decoy enemy bombers away from Sheffield, took such a hold that it burnt down to the bedrock, which remains bare to this day, as do some of the targets, which were hammered by 75mm solid-shot rounds from Sherman tanks. The hard tracks made on the lower part of the moor are also visible, and in most years an army bomb-disposal unit is called out to deal with the live munitions still being found, including mortar bombs, American pineapple grenades and small-arms ammunition.

In his diary for August, George Muller noted how the balance of nature had changed:

> The fellside, long a sanctuary for feathered and ground vermin, has gone wilder even than during the last war. Magpies, jays, carrion crows, rooks and buzzards have taken complete possession of this foothill, with its peeps through the trees of the far-off mountain ranges. Foxes abound – the huntsman says there are enough here to keep a pack going the whole of a season; badgers from a nearby colony have set up new quarters among the gorse and broom; stoat and weasel overrun the ground. The ground vermin are seldom seen – the bracken conceals their movements – but there is much evidence of the ill they do … Small birds are nearly all gone. Sparrowhawk and kestrel drive away whinchat, thrush, blackbird and robin.

Early in 1945, on the human front, things were looking up all round. As hopes of peace increased, the property market began to move: prices were low, but numerous white elephants came up for sale, along with many more modest dwellings. In January 1945 a 'replica Tudor house' in Essex with five bedrooms and ninety acres was going at £7500. Among its advertised attractions was 'Telephone'.

Even with old houses available, there was a pressing need for new homes in the country. A survey carried out by the British Federation of Women's Institutes produced a damning indictment of water and sewage systems in the countryside. Research workers reported 'horrors undreamt of by the more fortunate village residents', and revealed that out of 3500 villages, a thousand had no piped water: even in places on the mains, the supply often went not to homes but to standpipes, which were liable to freeze in winter. In less favoured hamlets people still had to rely on wells or springs, many of which were contaminated, or even on water carts. More than half the houses surveyed had earth, bucket or chemical closets: in east Suffolk alone twenty-two villages had over a hundred earth closets apiece.

In December 1944 the Government announced that 50,000 'permanent houses' would be built in rural areas and let at 7s 6d or 8s a week 'in the first two years after Germany has been beaten'. Altogether the Ministry of Health had plans for 800,000 new homes in the countryside, with rural projects given higher priority than urban. At the same time an expert pointed out that growing crops of bungalows instead of crops of wheat had taken up much good land, and had 'prejudiced other farming land by the creation of ubiquitous ribbons of bungaloid growth'.

Some new homes had already been built, but in September 1944 they had received a scathing review in *The Farmers' Weekly*, when, 'after several months of closest secrecy, during which nobody has been allowed near the buildings', the Government's thirteen 'new type houses' were put on view at Northolt, in Middlesex, but turned out to be 'singularly uninteresting'. Built of brick, with three bedrooms and a bathroom but no central heating, they had a grim appearance and several major failings, among them the fact that there was no access to the coal store from outside, so that sacks of fuel had to be carried indoors and unloaded.

In contrast with that disappointment, a farm show held in Birmingham turned out to be an immense success. Staged by the National Farmers' Union in a blitz-cleared space in the city centre, it was supposed to last for a week, but proved so popular that its run was extended to a fortnight: 10,000 people crowded in every day, fascinated by the demonstration of how Warwickshire farms grew all the potatoes for the city's 1,000,000 inhabitants, as well as producing their milk and the flour for their bread and biscuits.

The show perhaps disguised the fact that prospects for that year's vital potato harvest were dismal. At the beginning of September the Ministry of Agriculture had put out a special call for volunteers, but few had come forward, and an official in Newcastle reckoned that 'people seem to think that the war is over, and that they needn't bother'. Such hopes were fostered by a report that the Royal Show – suspended since 1939 – would be held next year if the war ended in the autumn.

Country people grounded by scarcity of petrol were scenting the chances of greater mobility. As no new cars were being built, high prices were offered to owners of vehicles long laid up. 'Old cars will never fetch a better price than at present,' said one advertisement; if an old banger was too decrepit to take the road, farmers were advised to cannibalize it: use the wheels for carts, the chassis for the basis of a trailer, the body for a hen house. Motor manufacturers had begun to drop tempting hints about better times ahead. The Ford company promised that 'those Saturday afternoons at Brooklands [racing circuit] are not far off'. Bentley assured customers that 'The manufacture of Bentley cars will be resumed immediately conditions permit', and advertisements by the Park Ward company, showing a sleek Rolls-Royce, declared:

One by one the pleasures of those pre-war years will return. Among them, at perhaps no long distance date, will be the unsurpassed grace and dignity of Park Ward coachwork.

For the time being, the daily grind continued. January 1945 brought blizzards and the worst frosts for years. Many country roads were blocked by snow, and one night at Dalwhinnie in the Scottish Highlands the temperature fell to minus four Fahrenheit – thirty-six degrees below freezing. In Ross-shire marooned cattle were saved by air drops of hay, but hundreds of sheep perished in snowdrifts, and others fell victim to foxes driven down from the moors by the cold. In the Cheviots the barking of a collie led rescuers to four US airmen whose Flying Fortress had crashed in the hills. On the Solway salmon choked by snow and ice were sold by fishmongers for 4s 9d a pound. It became impossible to move threshing machinery from one farm to another, and potato and root crops could not be lifted from the ice-bound soil, even by Russian prisoners of war, liberated from their former existence as slaves in Germany, who were working on the land in Yorkshire and Lincolnshire.

In spite of many difficulties, the farming community was buoyed up by the record of its performance. In 1939 Britain had had thirteen million acres of arable land and 18.75 million of permanent grass. By 1944 the figures had been reversed, to 19.25 million of arable and 11.75 of grass. The average yield of wheat had gone up from eighteen to twenty hundredweight per acre, even though some of the corn had been grown on poor land. Yields of barley had also increased, from sixteen to eighteen hundredweight. The area down to potatoes had more than doubled, and the flax crop had expanded by a factor of seven. 'The battle of the land will go down as one of the great victories of the war,' declared W. McN. Snadden, MP for Kinross and West Perthshire. As *The Farmers' Weekly* remarked,

The face of Britain has been changed almost beyond
recognition during the past six years … but it has been
essential to her very survival. By comparison, the small
blemishes inflicted by enemy action or necessitated by military
operations are insignificant. The additional ploughing of nearly
seven million acres, all the dredging, ditching, draining and
bush-clearing, if continued and properly cared-for, should
leave the farm lands of Britain in radiant health when the scars
of war are effaced and forgotten.

Scars there were aplenty. Thousands of farm buildings were derelict.
Concrete pillboxes, gun and searchlight emplacements and Nissen huts
stood abandoned in fields or gardens, and no compensation was offered
to owners of the land to meet the heavy cost of their removal. Hundreds
of fields were pitted with bomb craters. 'The strange thing about them
is that there is never nearly enough subsoil surrounding them to refill
them,' wrote one farmer. 'Some must have been blown in small lumps
over a wide area, while the blast must have compressed the subsoil in
all directions and so left a hole bigger than can be accounted for by the
amount blown out.' Someone suggested that big craters should be left
empty and surrounded by trees, to make attractive dells. Robert
Hudson, the Minister of Agriculture, estimated that £5 million worth
of new farm buildings would be needed after the war, and warned that
the structures would not all 'be thatched and picturesque, and it would
not be possible to prohibit the use of concrete and modern materials'.

Was it the hope of peace that brought out new ideas for increasing
efficiency on farms? The rear wheels of tractors were still fitted with
spade-lugs for ploughing – even on brand-new models; but now someone had the notion of filling the hollows in the wheels with cement, to
increase the weight and grip. In 1939 there had been 50,000 tractors in
Britain. Now there were 150,000. Also announced – an amazing invention – was an all-weather tractor cab made of wood and canvas 'with

steel reinforcements'. At last, year-round protection for the driver! In Wiltshire a demonstration was held to determine the limit of a tractor's power. Can a Fordson pull seven furrows on ploughland? was the question asked; and the answer was, 'It can.' Local demonstrations by War Ag committees drew gatherings of a hundred or more. Almost every week ingenious American machines were advertised in the farming press. A delegation of British experts returned from New York with news of 'locker plants' – freezing stations to which farmers could deliver produce.

In spite of all this innovation, on upland farms oats were being cut with scythes, and horses were still used for farm work all over the country. At Evesham turnips were being washed by hand in the River Avon. Ploughing competitions flourished, with both tractors and horses taking part, and at the Percheron Horse Society's stallion spring show, held at Histon in Cambridgeshire on 9 March 1945, Canewdon Unique, 'a horse of much character, conformation and type', was sold for 1000 guineas.

With rationing still in force, there was such a sharp increase in the number of people creeping onto allotments to steal vegetables that the law was changed to make trespass an offence, liable to a fine not exceeding £50. When two boys claimed in court that they had raided an allotment in search of conkers, the magistrates refused to accept this as a reasonable excuse – but the case was dismissed under the Probation Act. 'The general public must realise,' the *Country Gentleman's Estate Magazine* had thundered, 'that allotments are in effect the absolute property of the allotment holders for the time being, and no unauthorised person has any right whatever to wander about them.' Another annoyance was that of military personnel 'blazing a trail' through fields as they took a short cut to headquarters.

*   *   *

With victory almost in sight, the Women's Land Army began to melt away as more and more of its girls drifted off, discouraged by the knowledge that they would not get the post-war benefits or privileges promised to the other women's services. In the last four months of 1944 their numbers fell from 68,000 to 63,000. Yet their efforts were still badly needed, as the Government was calling for at least 400 new recruits a week. When the national minimum farm wage for a man was raised by 5s to 70s a week, with one penny an hour more for overtime, no increase was given to the women on the land. This, said *The Farmers' Weekly*, was an unexpected disappointment, 'after six years in which their help has been praised about six times a week and twice on Sundays'.

By the beginning of 1945 the Land Girls' champion, Lady Denman, had become exasperated by the War Cabinet's refusal to grant her recruits any financial reward; and in February an announcement that the Government would pay Resettlement Grants of £150 to Civil Defence and other auxiliary workers, but not to members of the Women's Land Army, pushed her over the edge. Worn down by her exertions, and by poor health, she resigned from her position of Honorary Director, thereby provoking a surge of support from newspapers and from the Land Girls themselves. In due course this shamed the Government into making some concessions – for instance, that members of the Land Army would get state help in training for agricultural work – but many people felt that the rewards offered were inadequate. It was left to the Queen, in a valedictory message to Trudie, to point out that the organization would live on 'in the shape of thousands who have settled down in the countryside as the wives of farmers and farm workers, or who are themselves continuing to work in agriculture … in field and forest, garden, orchard and dairy'.

The Farmers' Weekly thought that the war had done a lot to change young women's outlook. An intelligent girl, said a leading article, 'will want to feel she is doing a job worthy of her highest ability', and not just be 'a domestic in the pre-war sense of a general-maid-of-all-work-and-no-initiative'.

Among the farmers' most enthusiastic supporters was Churchill, who praised their achievement at the Conservative Party's annual conference in London on 5 March 1945:

> The war has taught us that we have long neglected the treasure house of the British soil. Twice in a generation we have called upon the farming community, in spite of that neglect, to keep the wolf from our doors. They have not failed us. It would be madness, indeed, to cast away the increased food production which has been achieved in the war ... Agriculture, therefore, assumes a place in the forefront of our post-war policy.

Perhaps Churchill hoped that his support would win votes in the country – but he made no impression on one disgruntled farmer's wife:

> Reading, movies, politics ... The last I can soon dismiss ... no interest at all. At one time I regarded anyone who was not a Conservative as being from another and inferior plane; but after seeing two major wars, all I can say is, if this is the best they can do, then let socialist, communist or any other animal do their worst. I care not. There are none of them worth voting for. It is of more moment to me when the swallows arrive than when any politician departs.

Victory in Europe, proclaimed by Churchill on 8 May, left many country folk unmoved. John Alsop, who farmed at Morely Hill, near Newcastle, ploughed doggedly on through 1944 and 1945 with daily entries in his diary, and did not falter when the great news came through. 'Cleaning up stackyard,' he wrote on Monday, 7 May. 'Top dressing behind stackyard. Threshing wheat from below the railway in afternoon. Rowed up stackyard fields.' Then, as an afterthought (perhaps when he had heard a BBC news flash announcing victory at 7.45 p.m.), came 'Armistice'. His entry for 8 May read: 'War officially ends at 3 o'clock. Hubert and I took load for G. Moore to Limpetlaw. Heavy rain in afternoon.'

In London things were more lively. Thousands of people surged into Trafalgar Square and down Whitehall, hoping to catch a glimpse of Churchill. Aircraft kept coming over, dropping coloured smoke flares. Bands played and impromptu processions of students marched about. When the royal family made repeated appearances on the balcony of Buckingham Palace, a vast crowd estimated at 60,000 greeted them ecstatically. In Trafalgar Square searchlights and flood-lights turned night to day as 100,000 revellers, many dressed in red, white and blue, burnt effigies of Hitler on bonfires and let off thunder-flashes and rockets. Nelson was floodlit in green, the lions in mauve. When the band of the Grenadier Guards struck up with 'Land of Hope and Glory', the whole crowd joined in. The biggest blaze of all flared up after midnight on Hampstead Heath, where a dummy village of wooden bungalows, built in 1941 as a decoy for Luftwaffe bombers, and contain-ing many thousand tons of timber, burst into flames.

Similar exultation exploded in towns and villages: blackout curtains were torn down, pub doors thrown open, trestle tables brought into the open for street parties; people strolled arm-in-arm, singing; they danced in the streets and fields; bonfires blazed, and the night sky was lit up by fireworks, which had been confiscated and kept in police stations ever since the outbreak of war.

It took villages a few days to organize full-scale Peace and Victory Celebrations, like those held on the sports ground at Leverstock Green in Hertfordshire on 25 May. An elaborate printed programme announced: 'We, Britain's Old and Young, are celebrating today the *Liberation of Mankind* from Fascist Tyranny by the *United People's Victory* in the World War, 1939–45', and the festivities included a fancy-dress parade, races for ladies, gents, girls and boys, slow bicycling, a children's tea party, an adults' tea, a 'Non-stop Variety Show, dancing to the Valetoes (crooner Miss Iris Evans)' and a fireworks display.

But it was Sunday, 13 May that evoked the greatest expression of relief. All over the country churches were crowded as the bells rang out, and in London thousands of people congregated for open-air services. Emotion ran high in Coventry, where 20,000 people assembled for a service in the Memorial Park, mourning not only the death of relations and friends, but also the destruction of their cathedral, of which the spire was almost the only part left standing.

A leading article in *The Farmers' Weekly* hit an unusually lyrical note:

We have suffered, and worked, and waited a long time for our village bells to ring out their message of victory in the West. At last we hear the jubilant clamour from steeples that have celebrated many triumphs, but never one more hardly earned. Nor is the silence of ruined belfries less eloquent. Every shattered tower, every farm field in which bleak patches mark bomb craters, every torn roof and ravished woodland and scarred building is a muted string in our great symphony of relief and thankfulness.

The Lady, a magazine not normally given to analysis of social trends, pointed out what a powerful influence war work such as civil defence had played in uniting rural communities, 'where the Big House and the Vicarage have alike gone, and where nothing had arisen until the war came to bring the many newcomers into any communal effort'. But for all the privations and tensions of the conflict (the article continued),

Mrs B would never have discovered that Lady A was not an idle slob, or Mrs C found how capable and well-meaning the haughty girl in the post office could be, or how well-read the draper, how good a botanist the butcher's son, or how much feeling there was about the village school or the medical service.

As she accompanied the pathologist Professor Keith Simpson on his rounds, Molly Lefebure searched for the key agent which contributed most to the defeat of Hitler. She decided it was the fact that the British *enjoyed* the war, and found it immensely satisfying:

> It gave them the chance to do all the daring things they have excelled at throughout their long history, and a lot of new, twentieth-century daring things into the bargain … For six glorious years they were able to be soldiers, sailors, airmen, guerrillas, frogmen, spies, bomb experts, nurses, rescue workers, ambulance drivers, explorers, plotters, schemers, saboteurs. As a race they have thrived on adventure, and this war brought them adventures galore. It gave them a feeling of great purpose, for it united them in a just cause, and as a people they love just causes. It gave them a chance to be great, and they have a marvellous capacity for greatness.

Perhaps she was right; but the end of the war in Europe left country people exhausted rather than exultant, worn down by six years of all-out effort and sacrifice. They realized that they were infinitely better off than their counterparts on the Continent, whose lives and property had suffered far worse damage; but their hopes that things would improve quickly – for instance that rationing would cease – were soon dashed. Far from coming to a speedy end, food restrictions became even more stringent. Late in May 1945 the Government announced not just that the cheese ration was to be maintained, but that the weekly allocation of cooking fat was being reduced from two ounces to one, and bacon from four ounces to three. As for rice – there was no prospect of any more being released for civilian consumption. The worst blow of all fell a year later, in the summer of 1946, when bread, flour and oatmeal were rationed for the first time.

Country people were shocked when Churchill was defeated in the General Election of 5 July 1945, and the Labour Party won a landslide victory under its leader Clement Attlee (who reminded George Orwell 'of nothing so much as a recently dead fish, before it has had time to stiffen'). A key element in the Left's campaign had been the Beveridge Report of 1942, which had urged the creation of the National Health Service and the Welfare State; and Churchill made the mistake of suggesting that its recommendations were so dangerous that some form of Gestapo would be needed to control developments set in motion by them. Exaggeration suddenly helped land the great war hero in the wilderness.

It seemed that the change of government would make little immediate difference to farming. Public ownership of all land remained the Left's ultimate aim; but at Labour's Blackpool conference in May a spokesman had announced that the party, if it came to power, would not nationalize the land, at least during the next five years. In the election campaign the agricultural policies of all the main parties had been much alike, and, as someone remarked, 'The country still needs food, whatever political party may organise its resources.'

In the summer of 1945 there was a severe shortage of men to work on the land. Requests by leaders of the agricultural community that farm workers should be given priority release from the services went unheeded, and when the Government appealed for 200,000 volunteers, only 50,000 came forward. The War Office announced that 90,000 German prisoners were available, but there were arguments about how long they should be made to labour, and whether or not they should be paid the same as natives, who got 1s per hour. With the harvest approaching, it was agreed that prisoners could be worked for as long as a farmer needed them, provided they were released in time to return to their compounds before dark. Germans were certainly not shirkers: on the bank of the River Trent in Nottinghamshire a gang 635-strong cleared 144 acres of flax in three days, pulling the crop by hand. Some of them, besides being strong, were skilled distillers, and eased their homesickness by concocting a gin-like spirit from potatoes.

The presence of prisoners in the harvest field certainly made life more interesting for the boys and girls from holiday camps:

> Although some boys considered working with prisoners to be *infra dig*, Marjorie Rolfe and Eileen Terry from Birmingham got on well with both German and Italian captives, the Italians in particular refusing to believe that the girls had chosen to work on the land and had not been coerced. Again, Manchester girls working in the Ormskirk area found the Italians 'very glamorous, with their dark eyes and incomprehensible accents,' and very few thought of them as being 'the enemy'.

As the author remarked, in those days 'hard physical labour on the farm or elsewhere was something to be taken in one's stride and enjoyed'.

On VJ Day – 15 August – the Japanese surrender was greeted by the announcement of a two-day holiday. But because the news came through at midnight, many farmhands went out to work without hearing it, and they were offered overtime rates to carry on. But when one farmer took beer out to the harvest field and told his men they could stop for the day, they had no qualms about accepting his offer. 'Well, Bill,' he said to one of them, 'is it too early for beer?' 'Nearly, sir,' came the answer – whereupon twenty men drank ten gallons in three-quarters of an hour, and before ten o'clock were singing merrily.

Two weeks later there came an unpleasant shock, when the new President of the United States, Harry Truman, abruptly announced the termination of Lend-Lease, the programme of aid which had helped sustain Britain over the past four years. In 1944 alone America had sent Britain (besides a huge quantity of munitions) £40 million worth of meat, £44 million of butter, cheese, eggs and dried milk, and £5 million of grain. With these supplies cut off, further belt-tightening was in prospect.

Gradually the countryside was returning to normal. Weather forecasts were resuscitated for the first time since 1939, the great majority of them, unfortunately, wrong. Wartime airfields, some of which had taken up 500 acres, were abandoned by the dozen, allowing the land to revert to agriculture. To bring disused bases back into production, crawler tractors began ripping out the wire mesh and coarse string matting which had given strength to grass runways. New grass was sown at the rate of 200 lb to the acre; huts were demolished, ditches cut to reconnect disrupted drainage systems, and old boundary lines between farms re-established. Once all that was done, silence enveloped the land. For ten years after the war the concrete runways at Bardney were lined with every kind of surplus military vehicles, most of which were eventually sold at auction. 'The quietness of a forsaken airfield was quite eerie,' one man remembered. 'Silent roads where once military vehicles abounded were equally strange.'

Stranger still were the paranormal manifestations which seemed to haunt the abandoned fields, especially in Lincolnshire. At some stations people heard the noise of wartime engines – generally Merlins – both on the runways and overhead. At RAF Bardney people walking towards the old control tower felt the presence of an oppressive character, and at RAF Digby lights appeared in the tower long after power had been disconnected. On several airfields phantom airmen in full flying kit were seen walking, riding bicycles or trying to hitch lifts, and at the entrance to RAF Hemswell visitors several times saw two men who disappeared when approached. In the hangars at RAF Coningsby some invisible force was reported to have touched people and pushed them around. Inside the deserted officers' mess at RAF Manby unexplained footsteps were heard in the corridors; doors opened and closed by themselves, and voices emanated from the old kitchen. In 1962 at Lindholme, as two men walked past a hangar on the deserted airfield, they were suddenly surrounded by sounds of activity – hangar doors screeching open, aircraft engines starting up, and the patter of many feet running past them.

As farm boundaries were renewed, and tracks made up with rubble from London bomb sites, people suggested that disused hangars could be used for keeping pigs or large-scale poultry farming. Prison camps were handed over to the War Ags, who ran them as hostels for farm workers, many of them former inmates who had opted to stay in Britain rather than go home.

One species which had positively benefited from Hitler's madness was the grey squirrel. The six-year shortage of manpower and cartridges precipitated a population explosion. Breeding freely during the war, the squirrels began to inflict serious damage on young hardwoods, beech and sycamore especially. Their habit of chewing off patches of bark in early summer maimed or killed so many thousands of trees that in 1944 the Ministry of Agriculture responded by issuing free cartridges to grey squirrel shooting clubs.

By the end of 1947 members of the clubs had killed 100,000 greys; but stronger incentives were needed, and in March 1953 the Ministry launched the shilling-a-tail campaign, paying 1s (5p, but £2.50 in today's values), later increased to 2s, for every tail handed in. This spurred immense culls – 361,636 in 1953–4, 391,891 in 1954–5 – achieved mainly by poking out dreys with specially designed telescopic aluminium poles and shooting the squirrels as they emerged. But it was too late. After five years, and a million tails, the campaign proved ineffective, for whenever a wood was cleared it was quickly recolonized by immigrants from other stands of timber.

This was particularly galling for landowners who were trying to replace trees felled during the war. Foresters favoured the creation of mixed plantations, with three rows of conifers to one of beech, oak or sycamore. Their hope was that fast-growing larch or spruce would nurse the beech in its early years, and when the softwood was harvested, the beech would grow on to maturity. Squirrels soon put paid to that plan: as soon as the hardwoods reached the age of ten or twelve, with a trunk diameter of about three inches, they ruined them by chewing off the bark, usually just above the ground.

The greys' grip on British woodlands also accelerated the decline of native red squirrels, which are smaller and less aggressive, partly because greys compete for food and sometimes kill reds, and partly because reds are susceptible to the squirrel pox virus, which greys carry, but which does not affect them.

Rabbits continued to plague farmers until 1953, when the viral disease myxomatosis, which had already run riot in Australia and France, was illegally imported into Sussex. It was then deliberately spread by people translocating sick animals, and in two years, to the immense relief of most farmers, but also to the disgust of some, it killed 95 per cent of the rabbits in Britain. Survivors gained some immunity, but fresh outbreaks of the disease kept occurring, generally in late summer, and the population has never returned to anything like its pre-war level.

As for the big country houses, although some went under during the war, many survived more or less intact. But when peace returned a stealthy and poisonous agent, as deadly as dry rot or lack of money, was brewing: the class-hatred simmering among Socialist politicians. Less than a year after Labour came to power, Emanuel Shinwell, Minister of

Fuel and Power, sent heavy mining machinery into the garden of Wentworth Woodhouse, the largest country house in England (larger even than Knole), to dig for coal in the Barnsley seam only 100 feet beneath the ground.

In due course almost 100 acres of formal gardens and woodland were destroyed by open-cast mining, and numerous specimen trees were lost. Coal was certainly needed, particularly for the railways, and Shinwell insisted that the seam was of exceptional quality; but this claim was refuted in a survey carried out by Sheffield University, which said in effect that the coal was rubbish – and many people saw Shinwell's manoeuvres as a spiteful attack on the aristocratic owners of the property, the Fitzwilliam family. Although crippled by the nationalization of coal mines in July 1946, and by two sets of death duties, they managed to keep the house and eventually to restore its surroundings.

It was Britain's farmland that the war changed most. As early as 1940 Vita Sackville-West had sensed the shape of things to come. Although renowned as a denizen of the Bloomsbury literary jungle, she was brought up and lived in Kent, always at heart a countrywoman – as evidenced by her sprawling, prize-winning epic poem *The Land*, published in 1926, which celebrated the seasons and activities of the countryside. Soon after the start of the war, in one of her weekly essays for the *New Statesman and Nation*, she had written of her love of the traditional landscape and of the yeoman farmer, but she had also looked ahead with apprehension:

> It would break my heart to see the familiar aspect of England altered from our toy-like fields into wide stretches of undivided land where the gyro-tiller could churn the soil for two or three miles on end without coming to a turn. I should hate to see the yeomen swept away and replaced by so inhuman a thing as the communal overseer and the mechanised farm. Even so, I have always had a distressing suspicion that this is what we ought to

do, if the agricultural possibilities of our land were to be properly exploited.

Five years after she had written that, the scenario she dreaded was already taking shape. Accelerated by the necessities of war, drastic change had set in. Horses were fast giving way to tractors. The steam engines which had dominated threshing yards for half a century were hissing into retirement. Machines even more powerful than gyrotillers were tearing out hedges, copses and awkward bits of woodland to make room for six-furrow ploughs and giant combines – the process which eventually devastated much of East Anglia and turned it into prairies. Ancient barns, too small to be useful any longer, were being demolished or left to rot. Outlying wells were neglected and beginning to silt up. Age-old facilities no longer sufficed for workers on the land: new houses, piped water and electrification were on their way.

All this signified the start of a new era in British agriculture. Hitler's attempt to starve Britain had forced farmers to become more skilled and more competitive; although many grumbled, most realized how beneficial the changes had been, and would be, and there was no looking back. The land of my boyhood was disappearing: the old ways of the countryside were dying, and could never return.

Acknowledgements

I should particularly like to thank the following for allowing me to consult their archives:

The Duke of Beaufort (Badminton)
Donald Cameron of Lochiel (Achnacarry)
The Duke of Devonshire (Chatsworth)
The Hon. Simon Howard (Castle Howard)

I am most grateful to Lord Dulverton for the loan of his father's rare wartime sniping manual, and to Iain Thornber, for sharing his wide knowledge of Highland history; also for permission to quote from his privately printed memoir *The Cameron Collection*.

I am indebted to Xandra Bingley for permission to include a passage from *Bertie, May and Mrs Fish*; to Lord Egremont, for permission to publish a passage from *Wyndham and Children First*; to John Reymond for permission to quote passages from *Fortitude South*; to Professor David Reynolds for permission to include short extracts from *Rich Relations*, and in particular the passage on pages 261–2; to Nova Robinson for permission to publish extracts from James Lees-Milne's diaries; to Paul Varney, for welcoming a researcher to the Flyfishers' Club; and to Jo Warin, for permission to quote her mother Anne Hollis's account of the fire at Castle Howard.

The BBC People's War series of interviews has been a most useful source. Because the reminiscences are already in the public domain on the Internet, the Corporation cannot give permission to quote from them; but because it would now be exceedingly difficult to trace individual contributors, I hope those who are still alive will forgive me for including parts of their stories without their leave.

Others who have given generous help include:

Elizabeth Allen (RSPB), Lord Allendale, David Barber (Royal Swans), Janet Barber, Lord Barber, Sir Benjamin Bathurst, Cynthia Batten (Queen Margaret's School), David Beazley, Robert Benson (Moorland Association), John Berkeley, Bob Browning, Richard Bullen, David Burnett, Reg Chambers-Jones, Jane Cheape, Rollo Clifford, Mark Cunliffe-Lister, Susannah Davis, Peter du Feu, Brigadier Christopher Dunphie, the Earl of Eglinton and Winton, Francis Evans, Jane Fawcett, Jane Fearnley-Whittingstall, Elizabeth Fleming, Robin Fleming, Simon Foster (Egton estate), Gillian Gooderham, Roger Griffith, Stephen J. G. Hall, Ben Heyes (Bolton Abbey estate), Jane Higgs (the Eden Valley Museum Trust), Henry Hoare, Susie Keown, Jean Lindsay, John Luke (Wycombe Abbey), David Lyon, Barbara Mackintosh, Sarah-Joy Maddeaux (Bristol Zoo), Louise Martin (Grosvenor estate), Elaine Milsom (Badminton estate), the Hon. Lady Morrison, Mark Norris, Chris Perrins, Michael Palmer, Sandra Pallister, Lorna Parker (Archivist, Royal Agricultural College), Roger Patterson, Christopher Perrins (swans), the Hon. Michael Pery, James Pilkington, Christopher Ridgway (Castle Howard), Sir Christopher Royden, Richard Sidgwick, Dr Cathryn Spence, Michael Stone, the Hon. Mrs Peter Thorne, Erika Tobiassen, James Towe (Chatsworth archive), Hilary Wainwright, Sir Humphry Wakefield, George Winn-Darley, Jeff Woods.

The staff of the Library at the Museum of English Rural Life in Reading have been exceptionally helpful, none more so than Caroline Benson.

As always, the London Library has been a godsend to a country author.

Finally, I should like to thank my editor, Arabella Pike, for shaping the book most skilfully, and my copy editor, Richard Collins, for eliminating errors with lethal precision.

Duff Hart-Davis
Uley
Gloucestershire
September 2014

Sources

Sources consulted include (those more frequently used are abbreviated in the notes as indicated):

The National Archives, Kew – NA
Mass Observation records
Museum of English Rural Life
BBC WW2 People's War records – BBC PW
The Cameron-Head Archive
The Eden Valley Museum archive

Magazines
British Beekeepers' Association Journal
Country Life – CL
The Country Gentleman's Magazine
The Farmer & Stockbreeder
The Farmers' Weekly – FW
The Field
The Flyfishers' Gazette – FG
Illustrated London News

Books consulted include

Anon, *Instructions for American Servicemen in Britain, 1942*. Bodleian Library, 1994.

Arnold, Ralph, *A Very Quiet War*. Rupert Hart-Davis, 1962.

Babington Smith, Constance, *Evidence in Camera*. Chatto & Windus, 1958.

Baker, J., *Chimps, Champ and Elephants*. S. J. H. Publications, Paignton, 1988.

Bates, H. E., *In the Heart of the Country*. Robinson Publishing, 1985.

Bingley, Xandra, *Bertie, May and Mrs Fish*. Harper Perennial, 2006.

Blishen, Edward, *A Cackhanded War*. Thames & Hudson, 1972.

Blythe, Ronald, *Akenfield*. Penguin, 1969.

Bond, Lilian, *Tyneham: A Lost Heritage*. The Dovecote Press, 1956.

Botting, Douglas, *Gavin Maxwell: A Life*. HarperCollins, 1993.

Brooks, Linda, *Flights of Memory*. Scottish Homing Union, 2007.

Brown, Tim, Ashby, Alan and Schwitzer, Christoph, *An Illustrated History of Bristol Zoo Gardens*.

Butler, Simon, *Goodbye Old Friend*. Halsgrove, 2012.

Calvert, Michael, *Fighting Mad*. Airlife, 1996.

Campbell, Clare, *Bonzo's War*. Constable & Robinson, 2013.

Chambers Jones, Reg, *Anglesey and Gwynedd: The War Years*. Bridge Books, Wrexham, 2008.

Clark, Kenneth, *The Other Half: A Self-Portrait*. John Murray, 1977.

Croall, Jonathan, *Don't You Know There's a War On?* Hutchinson, 1988.

de la Billière, General Sir Peter, *Looking for Trouble*. HarperCollins, 1994.

Devonshire, Duchess of, *The House: A Portrait of Chatsworth*. Macmillan, 1982.

Devonshire, Duchess of, *The Estate: A View from Chatsworth*. Macmillan, 1990.

Elliott, Geoff, *Colyton at War*. Colyton Parish History Society, 2007.

Fearnley-Whittingstall, Jane, *The Ministry of Food*. Hodder & Stoughton, 2010.

Flint, Lorna, *Wycombe Abbey School, 1896–1986*. Privately printed, 1989.

Freeman, Roger A., *The Mighty Eighth*. Arms & Armour Press, 1989.

Gardiner, Juliet, *Wartime Britain, 1939–1945*. Headline, 2004.

Gough, Alison J., *Messing Up Another Country's Customs*.

Green, Brigadier-General A. F. U., *The Home Guard Pocket-Book*. Conway, 2009.

Green-Armytage, A. H. N., *Bristol Zoo, 1835–1965*. J. W. Arrowsmith, Bristol, 1964.

Grenfell, Joyce, *Darling Ma*. Hodder & Stoughton, 1988.

Hammond, R. J., *Food and Agriculture in Britain, 1939–45*. Stanford University Press, California, 1954.

Harrison, David M. (Compiler), *Special Operations Executive: Paramilitary Training in Scotland during World War 2*. West Word, 2001.

Hart-Davis, Duff, *Peter Fleming*. Jonathan Cape, 1974.

Hart-Davis, Duff, *Raoul Millais*. Swan Hill, 1998.

Horsley, Terence, *Fishing and Flying*. Eyre & Spottiswoode, 1947.

Howkins, Alun, *The Death of Rural England*. Routledge, 2003.

Huxley, Gervas, *Lady Denman, GBE*. Chatto & Windus, 1961.

Huxley, Julian, *Memories*. Allen & Unwin, 1970.

Jackson, Sophie, *Churchill's Unexpected Guests*. The History Press, 2010.

Knappett, Rachel, *A Pullet on the Midden*. Isis Publishing, 1997.

Leakey, J. H., *School Errant*. Dulwich College Preparatory School, 1951.

Lefebure, Molly, *Evidence for the Crown*. Heinemann, 1955.

Lehmann, John, *I Am My Brother*. Longmans, 1960.

Leslie Melville, Michael, *The Story of the Lovat Scouts, 1900–1980*. Librario Publishing, 2004.

Lynn, Dame Vera, *Some Sunny Day*. HarperCollins, 2009.

McCamley, N. J., *Saving Britain's Art Treasures*. Leo Cooper, 2003.

McCamley, Nick, *Subterranean Britain: Second World War Secret Bunkers*. Folly Books, 2010.

McKay, Sinclair, *The Secret Life of Bletchley Park*. Aurum Press, 2011.

McKenzie, Roderick, *Ghost Fields of Suffolk*. The Larks Press, 2012.

Maclean, Veronica, *Past Forgetting*. Headline, 2002.

Mauduit, Vicomte Georges de, *They Can't Ration These*. Michael Joseph, 1940.

Maund, V. A., *The Diary of a Bristol Woman, 1938–45*. Arthur H. Stockwell, Ilfracombe, 1946.

Middleton, C. H., *Digging for Victory*. Allen & Unwin, 1942.

Mills, Cyril, *Bertram Mills Circus*. Hutchinson & Co., 1987.

Mortimer, John, *The History of the Derby Stakes*. Cassell, 1962.

Mursell, Norman, *Come Dawn, Come Dusk*. Allen & Unwin, 1981.

Nudds, Angus, *The Woods Belong to Me*. Blandford Press, 1985.

Orwell, George, *Diaries*. Harvill Secker, 2009.

Otter, Patrick, *Lincolnshire Airfields in the Second World War*. Countryside Books, Newbury, 1996.

Park, Nancie, *School Days at Chatsworth*. Harwich Printing Company, 1996.

Partridge, Frances, *Diaries 1939–72*. Weidenfeld & Nicolson, 2000.

Pope-Hennessy, James, *Queen Mary, 1867–1953*. Allen & Unwin, 1959.

Priestley, J. B., *All England Listened*. Chilmark Press, New York, 1967.

Reeve, Lucille Maud, *Farming on a Battlefield by a Norfolk Woman*. Geo. R. Reeve, Wymondham, 1949.

Reymond, John, *Fortitude South*. KCC Arts & Libraries Publications, 1994.

Reynolds, David, *Rich Relations*. HarperCollins, 1995.

Robinson, John Martin, *Felling the Ancient Oaks*. Aurum Press, 2011.

Rose, Kenneth, *King George V*. Weidenfeld & Nicolson, 1983.

Sackville-West, Victoria, *Country Notes in Wartime*. Hogarth Press, 1940.

Schofield, O. M., *Down to Earth on the Farm*. Kindle edition, 2011.

Seth-Smith, Michael, Willett, Peter, Mortimer, Roger and Lawrence, John, *The History of Steeplechasing*. Michael Joseph, 1966.

Shawcross, William, *Queen Elizabeth the Queen Mother*. Macmillan, 2009.

Sheean, Vincent, *Between the Thunder and the Sun*. Macmillan, 1943.

Shore, Captain Clifford, *With British Snipers to the Reich*. Greenhill Books, London, 1997.

Stoate, Chris, *Exploring a Productive Landscape*. Game & Wildlife Conservation Trust, 2010.

Strong, Roy, Binney, Marcus and Harris, John, *The Destruction of the Country House, 1875–1975*. Thames & Hudson, 1974.

Thornber, Iain, *The Cameron Collection: Moidart and Arisaig in the 19th Century*. Privately published, 2007.

Vickers, Hugo, *Elizabeth: The Queen Mother*. Hutchinson, 2005.

Wainwright, Martin (ed.), *A Gleaming Landscape*. Aurum Press, 2006.

Wainwright, Martin (ed.), *All Hands to the Harvest*. Guardian Books, 2009.

Ward, Sadie, *War in the Countryside, 1939–45*. Cameron Books, 1988.

Wheeler, Rob (ed.), *German Invasion Plans for the British Isles, 1940*. Bodleian Library, 2007.

Wicks, Ben, *No Time to Say Goodbye*. Bloomsbury Paperback, 2009.

Williams of Barnburgh, Lord, *Digging for Britain*. Hutchinson, 1965.

Wills, Captain Anthony, *Sniping. Small Arms Training*, Vol. 1, *Pamphlet No. 28*. The War Office, 1946.

Woolton, Lord, *Memoirs*. Cassell, 1959.

Younger, Major-General Tony, *Blowing Our Bridges*. Pen & Sword Military, 2004.

Notes

One: The Old Ways

11s a week: In order to gain an idea of wartime values, one has to multiply by at least forty: £1 in 1940 would have been the equivalent of over £40 today.

when war broke out on August 4th: Akenfield, p. 41.

you could see the horses listening: Ibid., pp. 61–2.

leaving me to carry on: Private reminiscence.

only means of stopping anyway!: Darling Ma, p. 154.

is the ideal continuous: FW, 7 July 1944.

eight hours a day: The Woods Belong to Me, pp. 45–6.

fields of time: The Worm Forgives the Plough, p. 162.

Two: All Hands to the Plough

will be less efficient: FW, 15 September 1939.

training and experience: Food and Agriculture in Britain, p. 32.

friend as well: FW, 1 September 1939.

given to Jolly Beeston to farm: Akenfield, p. 250.

the farmer was shot dead: War in the Countryside, p. 24.

out of their despair: Private conversation.

as "Barber's folly": Ibid.

almost a vice: CL, 10 February 1940.

the rules of good husbandry: Hansard, 4 June 1940.

fifty years later: Private conversation.

money does not enter into it: FW, 28 February 1941.

lined by tall trees: Hansard, 4 July 1940.

to many at the time: Agricultural History Review quoted in www.bahs.org.uk/AGHR/ARTICLES/54n2a8.pdf

40 lb when full: Ibid.

spoke no English: Kids in the Corn, by R. J. Moore-Colyer www.bahs.org.uk/AGHR/ARTICLES/52n2a4.pdf

Three: Exodus

would immediately appear: Rememberingscotlandatwar.org.uk/Accessible/Exhibition/140Declaration

with a .22 rifle: Anglesey and Gwynedd: the War Years, p. 17.

a high-explosive bomb: The shelters' name came from Sir John Anderson, who, as Lord Privy Seal in Chamberlain's pre-war government, took charge of air-raid precautions.

let them both in: Private source.

due to the boss's cream: Glasgow West War Story. www. rememberingscotlandatwar.org.uk

they tasted delicious: BBC PW A3239930.

the younger ones: Orwell Past and Present website.

the seventy-two children present: Badminton archive.

his eyes peeping out: www. writingwomenshistory.blogspot. co.uk

fearsome terrors: CL, 23 September 1939.

while we were walking: Private source.

how potatoes grew: In the Heart of the Country, p. 59.

'Never on Your Life': The Oaken Heart, p. 49. In her book, written at high speed during the early stages of the war, Margery Allingham concealed the real identity of her village by calling it Auburn.

solved the immediate crisis: Ibid., pp. 91–2.

into that for the night: Daily Telegraph, 7 September 1939.

differing number of children: No Time to Wave Goodbye, pp. 29–30.

no longer his castle: CL, 9 September 1939.

the ones they liked: WW2 Talk.

under a table wetting herself: BBC PW A2007307.

the boss of the lot: No Time to Wave Goodbye, pp. 95–6.

corkscrew motion: All Hands to the Harvest, p. 122.

edge of the Cotswolds: Private source.

rewards at school: A woman in Folkestone saw an enormous swarm of cabbage whites flying into England from across the Channel, apparently to escape the clouds of black smoke cloaking the French coast.

'astonishingly exciting': Colyton at War, p. 9.

a long illness or something: BBC PW ID1130653.

his son in Northamptonshire: Wartime Britain, 1939–1945, p. 43.

they escaped unhurt: Private source.

they didn't like it: BBC PW A3202039.

not expressible in words: Country Notes in Wartime, pp. 15–16.

their way in the dark: CL, 9 September 1939.

leering from the darkness: Wartime Diaries, p. 122.

to interrogate the priest: No Time to Wave Goodbye, p. 86.

somehow help the enemy: They did not return until April 1945.

came within range?: Private source.

Canadian red cedar: The camp at Sayers Croft, at Ewhurst in Surrey, is now a Field Centre, and has been preserved partly as a memorial to Tait's work. The dining room's walls are decorated with murals depicting the life of the evacuees.

sparks into the sky: Looking for Trouble, p. 17.

this fresh blood: All Hands to the Harvest, p. 195.

between town and country: CL, 23 November 1940.

seemed far-fetched: The RSPCA estimated that in 1939 the animal population of the capital consisted of 40,000 horses, 6000 head of cattle, 9000 sheep, 18,000 pigs, 400,000 dogs and 1,500,000 cats.

the private aerodrome: The Duchess's son Douglas Douglas-Hamilton, who succeeded to the Dukedom on the death of his father in 1940, was a keen amateur aviator, and had created newspaper headlines by flying over Everest in 1933.

'that lady of the dogs': Bonzo's War, p. 52.

Four: Braced for Invasion

to occupy it completely: German Invasion Plans for the British Isles, p. 7.

a minimum of delay: The Last Ditch, p. 13.

condemned to death inexorably: Ibid., p. 15.

a bit of trouble: Between the Thunder and the Sun, p. 141.

reaching to toes and fingers: Diaries 1939–72, p. 18.

be near the sea!: Western Daily News, 17 June 1940.

and 'hubbies': Diaries 1939–72, pp. 35–6.

into thin air: All England Listened, p. 46.

syrup for vitamin C: www.thurgartonhistory.co.uk/

foxed the Canadians: Invasion 1940, pp. 101–2.

innocent nun: I Am My Brother, p. 70.

or even tomorrow: Hansard, 4 June 1940.

favourite programmes: The immensely popular television sitcom ran for eighty episodes spread over nine years, from 1968 to 1977, and at its peak gained audiences of eighteen

million. It is still repeated all over the world.

I salute him: The British Home Guard Pocket-Book, pp. 20–21.

so I shot him: Apley Hall, p. 112.

If so, what result?: North Highland Archives.

for 2d each: BBC PW A3516022.

on the offensive: The Defenders, p. 196.

shooting for the first time: With British Snipers to the Reich, p. 238.

into the dustbin: Orwell, Diaries, p. 274.

fields and homesteads: Postscript broadcast, 16 June 1940. Printed in All England Listened, pp. 14–16. These seven-minute talks attracted an audience of more than 30 per cent of the adult population.

they buggers at Axmouth, do us?: Colyton at War, p. 16.

two or three rows deep: A survey carried out sixty years later identified the remains of 20,000 structures.

over the whole island: Between the Thunder and the Sun, p. 140.

Skelton-on-Ure in North Yorkshire: Hindlip Hall, four miles north of Worcester, was requisitioned by the Ministry of Housing as a refuge for the War Cabinet and Ministers.

German agents in the Argentine: Invasion 1940, pp. 118–19.

hatred of Jews: The Times, 28 February 2014.

a long time to recover: Invasion 1940, p. 96.

and pails of water: Private source.

Five: Going to Ground

Calvert, a Royal Engineer: his nickname, 'Mad Mike', derived from the ferocity with which he attacked the Japanese while fighting with the Chindits in Burma.

got that far: *Fighting Mad*, p. 49.

and Eastbourne: At Folkestone, as a precaution, one of the celebrated water-powered lifts was hauled to the top of the cliff, but the cable on the second broke and it crashed to the bottom, never to be resuscitated.

fields and woods: In 1952 the house caught fire during renovations, and the blaze was so furious that it was visible from twenty miles away. The building was so badly damaged that the remains had to be demolished. The site now belongs to the National Trust.

tackled with enthusiasm: Peter Fleming, p. 235.

simply loved it: *A Very Quiet War*, p. 53.

what it was for: BBC PW A2685837.

messenger service: BBC PW 235141.

discreet munching: Peter Fleming, p. 236.

a cave existence: Ibid., p. 237.

enemy soldier to enter: *Fighting Mad*, p. 52.

middle of the 1950s: After stand-down Reg Sennet, Commanding Officer of the Dengie Group of Auxiliary Units, had 14,738 rounds of ammunition and 1205 lb of explosives left behind in his milking shed. In spite of his repeated requests to have the ordnance removed, it was twenty years before the army took the stuff away.

Six: Adapting to War

a working-class girl: *Daily Telegraph*: Britain at War: Readers' Memories.

Western civilisation: FW, 15 March 1940.

grease gun and nipples: FW, 4 July 1941.

independent of good weather: Ibid., 28 February 1941.

saving time and fuel: Private source.

moving of an evening: *Apley Hall*, p. 77.

their cargo had disappeared: BBC PW A4520765.

known as sticky boards: NA MAF 44/6.

into the woods to roost: CL, 30 December 1939.

any the worse: FW, 15 March 1940.

live off his flesh for a week: *Bertie, May and Mrs Fish*, pp. 101–2.

after each broadcast: In September 1939 the regional and national services of the BBC were merged into the National Programme, which later became the Home Service.

their original owners: FW, 22 September 1944.

fish and chips: BBC PW A2553761.

worrying about the war: Ibid., A5937203.

collected in Yorkshire: FW, 26 September 1941.

Seven: Rain of Death

also heavily bombed: Dorset became a highly dangerous area: during the war as a whole, 4300 high-explosive bombs and 37,000 incendiaries fell on the county. Fifty-four British aircraft were shot down above it, eight of them crashing into the sea. German losses in the same sector amounted to ninety aircraft, thirty-five of which ditched in the Channel.

stick at nothing: All Hands to the
    Harvest, p. 117.
the width of the bole: Ibid., p. 121.
'Lovely to watch': Country Notes in
    Wartime, p. 79.
with the RAF: BBC PW AD2743607.
by comparison very playful: In the
    Heart of the Country, p. 57.
No one in the houses was hurt: The
    Oaken Heart, p. 227.
beyond hope of recovery: FW, 26
    September 1941.
a few scraps of skin: Private source.
back over the Channel: Colyton at War,
    pp. 22–3.
west of Birmingham: The unpublished
    diary is in the archive at Newquay
    Zoo.
injured in the air raids: In the autumn
    of 1941 Doreen found work as a
    secretary in an engineering firm
    evacuated to Tenbury Wells from
    Birmingham. After the war she
    moved to Essex and became a
    teacher, finishing her career as
    Deputy Head at Prince Avenue
    Primary School in Westcliff-on-Sea.
    In her forties she met and married a
    serving police officer, Norman
    Lonergan; but they had no children,
    and Doreen lavished her affection
    on pet dogs. She and her husband
    left a legacy to the Blue Cross, the
    animal charity,
a taste to a stew?: Diaries 1939–72,
    p. 56.
for a cup of tea: FW, 13 October 1944.
and quickly absented himself: Private
    information.
their trust is never misplaced: All Hands
    to the Harvest, p. 137.

Eight: Food from Everywhere

measure of control essential: By
    January 1941 the normal supply of
    food from overseas had been cut by
    half.
intricate network: Food and Agriculture
    in Britain, 1939–45, p. 66.
in a British Restaurant: London at War,
    p. 253.
to do a little turn: Memoirs, p. 251.
my horse and cart?: A Very Quiet War,
    p. 122.
in the black market: Memoirs, p. 230.
war makes us do that: Wireless
    broadcast.
chased by my kettle: All Hands to the
    Harvest, p. 169.
a radio broadcast: The Times, 4
    October 1939.
are [sic] immeasurable: National
    Allotments Society Annual Report
    for year ending 31 May 1939, p. 4.
contribution to the war effort: The
    Battle of the Land, p. 57.
demonstrations and meetings:
    Akenfield, p. 174.
tasters at the Ministry of Food: The
    Kitchen Front, 2 February 1942.
cabbages have vanished: Mass
    Observation diarist 5098.
mustard and cress: War in the
    Countryside, p. 13.
pain-killing drugs: Paper by Anne
    Stamper at the Second International
    Conference on the History of
    Voluntary Action, University of
    Surrey, September 2003.
the weeks are incorrect: Orwell, Diaries,
    pp. 29–30.
I shall have done this year: Ibid.,
    p. 305.
out of the kitchen: Diaries 1939–72,
    p. 84.

said the vet: All Hands to the Harvest,
   p. 144. Gwen McBryde's fifteenth-
   century farmhouse, Dippersmoor,
   stands on a high knoll. Its spooky
   atmosphere appealed greatly to M.
   R. James, the former Provost of
   Eton, who wrote several of his ghost
   stories there.
dropped down the mine: Memoirs,
   p. 242.
used for feeding poultry: They Can't
   Ration These, p. 65.
permanent home and career: Ibid.,
   pp. 11–12.
our national defence: Ibid., p. 13.
'Oh – five bob!': BBC PW 3943389.
performing a useful service: Members
   of the Women's Institutes used
   rabbit fur to line thousands of coats,
   waistcoats, hoods and caps for
   export to Russian women via the
   Red Cross. They also bred rabbits
   and cured the skins.
it becomes a bush again: BBC PW
   A2792036.
nuzzling his hands: Ibid.
a couple of onions: CL, 7 October 1939.
kitchen had been opened: Abberley
   Lives website.
during the year: FW, 7 March 1941.
from 25,532 barrels to 32,667: The
   Brewers' Almanack, 1955, p. 56.
   Specific gravity here refers to the
   density of beer compared with the
   density of water.
and three the next?: Orwell, Diaries,
   p. 352.
where a dahlia might grow: Unnamed
   colleague on the Sunday Express.
will the roses be with us again: Digging
   for Victory, p. 5.
you can't swat them all: Ibid.,
   pp. 17–18.

snow to get into it: Ibid., p. 62.
pleasant and profitable pursuit: London
   at War, p. 257.

Nine: Girls to the Fields
Trudie's biographer Gervas Huxley:
   Lady Denman, p. 156.
I felt so trapped in: BBC PW A3287991.
I had been accepted: Ibid., AD2891955.
added mud to my dungarees too: Down
   to Earth on the Farm, Kindle
   edition, 69%.
by her new uniform: BBC PW
   A3996408.
girls to catch up: Ibid., A3027494.
or 'Oo' (she): A Pullet on the Midden,
   p. 6.
Work without end. Amen: Ibid.,
   p. 240.
level with my ear 'ole: BBC PW
   5705543.
react in this way: Ibid., A2690688.
tea like it since: Ibid., A3054106.
nothing like the real thing: Ibid.
trousers round her ankles: Ibid.,
   A3287991.
and rousing Quicksteps: BBC PW
   A3996309.
for food and shelter: FW, 21 July 1944.
you felt the vibrations: BBC PW
   A3347246.
which formerly they tilled: FW,
   19 December 1941.
on that sunlit morning: Country Notes
   in Wartime, p. 14.
required only two people: BBC PW
   A4060612.
carted off to hospital: Ibid., U526219.
missed it for anything: Down to Earth
   on the Farm, Kindle edition,
   99–100%.
'Keep low on they bushes, won't 'ee': A
   Cackhanded War, p. 18.

wishing myself a Fordson tractor: Ibid., pp. 85–6.

to do, love, would they?: Ibid., p. 29.

the way they're going: Ibid., p. 47.

'full of harpies': Ibid., pp. 122–3.

a rare labour of love: The box is now in the museum at Edenbridge, Kent.

Ten: In the Woods

no place for debating societies: Newfoundland Overseas Forestry Website.

an orderly and law-abiding manner: Ibid.

a few people living there: Ibid.

all the cutting day: New Zealand Journal of Forestry, February 2001.

wearing nothing underneath: Ibid.

with 'any man in the woods': BBC PW A4682568.

and nearly killed her: Ibid., A4115585.

and very pleasant: Ibid., 4181988.

as 'beings from another planet': BBC PW A4311037.

for a whole night and a day: Don't You Know there's a War On?, p. 80.

on my face and leg: Ibid.

taking a Spit up to Prestwick: Ibid., pp. 80–81.

the plane would not explode: BBC PW A2064917.

heavier than we knew existed: Wartime Britain, 1939–1945, p. 61.

Eleven: Laying Up Treasure

and connected to it: During the 1950s a complete Cold War city was built 100 feet beneath Corsham.

the stocks had gone up: Grass, shrubs and trees have grown to soften the outlines of the crater, but it is still immediately obvious, seventy years after the explosion.

but in a haughty way: Daily Telegraph, 21 September 2008. Martin Davies became Director of the National Gallery in 1968 and was knighted in 1972.

should wait upon them: Second World War Secret Bunkers, p. 8.

solved itself for the moment: The National Gallery in Wartime, p. 24.

shall leave this island. W.S.C.: The Other Half, p. 5. In a letter to a colleague Clark gave a slightly different version of Churchill's utterance. 'Hide them in caves and cellars, but not one picture shall leave this island.' The National Gallery in Wartime, p. 31.

We brought them down and set them: Saving Britain's Art Treasures, p. ix.

nicknamed 'the Cathedral': The blue-grey roofing slates produced by the quarry were known as Empresses, Small Duchesses, Broad Countesses and Wide Ladies.

hellish town of Blaenau Ffestiniog: The Other Half, p. 5.

packing case passed through: Ibid., p. 6.

cleared of its contents stop: The National Gallery in Wartime, p. 83.

a few pictures: The Other Half, p. 7.

by Raphael had hung: After 1945 the repository at Manod remained in much the same state until the early 1950s. Then, in the depths of the Cold War, when a nuclear strike by the Soviet Union seemed all too likely, the Government ordered an exercise over one weekend in which pictures from the National Gallery were again taken to the quarry.

Twelve: White Elephants

monasteries in the sixteenth century: *Brideshead Revisited*, Penguin Books, 1960 edition, p. 8.

the more desirable it has seemed: CL, 30 September 1939.

fancy brick chimneys: *Evidence in Camera*, p. 107.

in position for launching: Ibid., p. 223.

each twenty-four hours: Ibid., p. 224.

overwhelming victory for the Allies: Ibid., p. 225. In 1942 Constance Babington Smith was mentioned in dispatches, and in 1945 she was awarded the MBE.

Allied photographic reconnaissance: Ibid., p. 232.

unfocused and incomprehensible: *The Secret Life of Bletchley Park*, p. 34.

miles away in thought: Ibid., p. 13.

suffered from hay fever: In 1952 Turing was prosecuted for homosexuality, and submitted to chemical castration, rather than to prison; but in 1954 he died from cyanide poisoning. Although the inquest recorded his death as suicide, his family believed it had been accidental. In 2009 the Prime Minister, Gordon Brown, apologized on behalf of the Government for the appalling way in which he had been treated, and in 2014 the Queen granted him an official pardon.

manor pets were buried: There were two other main bombe locations, in north London, each with about 100 machines, separated from Bletchley to preserve them if the Manor site were bombed.

came through unscathed: After the war the establishment was used for training telephone engineers, but later the house fell into disrepair and the huts began to disintegrate. Then in 1991 the Bletchley Park Trust was formed, with the aim of converting the whole site into a national museum and preserving as many as possible of the wartime facilities. In this the Trust has succeeded triumphantly: such is the fame and fascination of this once top-secret place that it now attracts more than 200,000 visitors a year.

Thirteen: Rescue Operations

ancestral white elephant: *People and Places*, p. 217.

the country house enterprise: Today the National Trust has nearly 4,000,000 members and employs almost 5000 staff. It owns 200 historic houses open to the public, and 630,000 acres of land. It also owns or protects 700 miles of coast in England, Wales and Northern Ireland.

descended the perron and mounted: Ibid., p. 9.

… I agree: Ibid., p. 80.

shortly be called up: *People and Places*, p. 73.

Only a char left: Ibid.

passed to the Trust: Ibid., pp. 68–83. In 2012 Stourhead attracted 350,000 visitors.

laundry maids, lamp-men: *The Destruction of the Country House*, p. 172.

favour of Lord Sackville: *People and Places*, pp. 166–83.

spoke with a peevish lisp: Ibid., p. 94.

tiresome and stupid: Ibid., p. 100.

his demise very much: Ibid.

on a modest scale: Ibid., p. 125.

May Day 1946: Ibid., pp. 122–33.

subordinates as barbarians: Ibid.,
p. 34.

peas-in-a-pod likeness: *The Estate
Magazine, Winter 1941*, pp. 717–18.

scarcely boil an egg: private
reminiscence.

'not at all the thing': Queen Mary,
p. 596.

Mary, Duchess of Beaufort: The
Duchess's father, the first Marquess
of Cambridge, was Queen Mary's
younger brother.

delight of the family: King George V,
p. 202.

'So that's what hay looks like': Queen
Mary, p. 600.

proverbial at Sandringham: Ibid.

one never knows: Ibid., p. 601.

without the Queen's knowledge: Ibid.,
p. 602.

enemy's land advance: Badminton
archive.

churches and private houses: Details
from the Badminton archive.

does not remember seeing it:
Badminton archive.

smiled a glorious welcome: School Days
at Chatsworth.

a punishable sin: Ibid.

in the cleared areas: Details from the
Chatsworth archive.

empty for years: In 1945 an oak in the
Old Park was blown down. When
sawn up for timber, the trunk
revealed a ball shot enclosed by 400
rings of annual growth.

other side of the house: Details from
the Queen Margaret's School
archive.

in the antiques corridor: Soon after the
fire Anne Hollis left school to join
the WRNS. After the war she

married Robert Warin, who was
training to be a consultant
dermatologist, and they had five
children. When all five had been to
university, she decided it was her
turn to get a degree, and obtained
first class honours in Humanities at
the Open University. She wrote
poems and children's stories, and
put together a book called *Dear Girl,
I Escaped* from her father's diaries
and her mother's letters from the
First World War. She then wrote a
life of the eighth-century Abbess
Hilda of Whitby, and she had almost
completed a study of Hilda's arch-
rival Wilfrid of Hexham when she
and her husband were killed in a car
accident in 1992.

'firm and sound': Private conversation.

our great meeting hall: Ibid.

carefully-controlled 'accident': Ibid.

Fourteen: Plane Fields

at our expense: Lincolnshire Airfields in
the Second World War, p. 167.

US Air Force moved in: The land has
now reverted to agriculture, but a
few wartime buildings remain.

a large model ship: community.
lincolnshire.gov.uk/
bardneyvillagehistory/

hardly a lavatory door left: Lincolnshire
Airfields in the Second World War,
p. 178.

successes of the war: Bomber
Command, p. 183.

tranquil once more: BBC PW
A2204326.

airmen and women: Lincolnshire
Airfields in the Second World War,
p. 272.

the invasion had begun: Ibid., p. 49.

scarlet women from the cities: Bomber Command, p. 241.

numerous others wounded: Yorkshire Airfields in the Second World War, p. 89.

the airfield boundary: The Wartime Memories Project – RAF Marston Moor.

of one of the dead: Yorkshire Airfields in the Second World War, p. 240.

a head inside it: Ibid.

in hospital for months: Ibid., p. 209.

anyone else about it: Ibid., p. 236.

when the fog had cleared: The Wartime Memories Project – RAF Marston Moor.

Fifteen: American Invasion

pleading for handouts: During the war the annual consumption of meat was 140 lb per head, but GIs averaged 234 lb.

distrust between them: Instructions for American Servicemen in Britain. Introduction. Pages unnumbered.

It's an even swap: Ibid.

like a shot: Rich Relations, p. 49.

far from their minds: BBC PW A2742860.

the search for fun: Rich Relations, p. 54.

a natural state of affairs: BBC PW A2935749.

the Brown Bomber: World History Connected, Vol. 5, No. 1. 'Black and Asian Involvement'. When Joe Louis went to a cinema in Salisbury in 1944, he was told by the manager, who knew who he was, that he would have to sit in a section reserved for black troops.

in the near future: NARA, RG 107, Box 36, File 291.2

with money to spend: Rich Relations, p. 218.

cruelly betrayed: Wycombe Abbey School, p. 106.

forty different schools: Among the foster-schools were Headington (in Oxford), Benenden (which had been evacuated from Kent to Cornwall), Queen Anne's, Caversham, Malvern Girls' College and Cheltenham Ladies' College.

'If mistress is desired, ring bell': Rich Relations, p. 115.

would have been impossible: Wycombe Abbey School, p. 121.

landed at Polebrook: The Mighty Eighth, p. 7.

marshalling yards at Rouen: The pilot of the lead B-17 was Major Paul W. Tibbets, who, on 6 August 1945, was at the controls when B-29 *Enola Gay* dropped the Little Boy atom bomb on Hiroshima.

105 combat missions: Ghost Fields of Suffolk, p. 51.

from one of the planes: Rich Relations, p. 284.

in only eight seconds: www.recordinguttlesford history.org.uk/

up and down the river: BBC PW 235141.

grazing in the green meadow: hethersett.org.uk/wars.htm

or "It's only a Lancaster": Action Stations, p. 21.

sought the thinner air: The Mighty Eighth, p.153.

to white US soldiers: Life, 23 August 1948.

Sixteen: On the Wing

was the heron: British Birds, Vol. XXXVI, 1942, p. 126.

the rest driven away: Caerlaverock is now a National Nature Reserve, managed by Scottish Natural Heritage, and some 24,000 Barnacle geese over-winter there.

the strongest possible terms: The colony of gannets has grown to about 34,000 pairs, and the northern side of the island where the birds breed, is so plastered with droppings that from a distance it looks as though it is covered in snow.

breeding British pigeons: NA KV4/10.

It will take off at day-break: NA CAB 154/35.

severely reprimanded: BBC PW AD4017809.

Seventeen: Fun and Games

on that strange contradiction: The Lost Seasons, p. 40.

the English sports clubs: The Times, 10 July 1940.

except RAIN!: The Lost Seasons, p. 65.

had been sounded: War Games, p. 98. Stallard was expelled from the British League of Racing Cyclists which he had helped found; but he is still regarded as an important force in the development of the sport, and was instrumental in planning the Tour of Britain.

Martlesham Heath in Suffolk: Such was Obolensky's renown that a building is named after him at his school, Trent College; a statue of him stands in Cromwell Square, Ipswich (where he was buried in the cemetery); an annual Obolensky Lecture is given in his honour; the stadium at Twickenham has an Obolensky restaurant, and an annual Prince

Obolensky award is presented by the Prince Obolensky Association at Rosslyn Park Football Club, for which he played.

to face unpleasant facts: The History of the Derby Stakes, p. 527.

immune from attack: Ibid.

a division of troops: Orwell, Diaries, pp. 306–7.

were in uniform: Mervyn Jones was killed in action two years later.

very large sums indeed: The History of Steeplechasing, p. 157.

its very life?: Hansard, 13 June 1940.

available to the workers: Ibid.

cannot get supplies?: Ibid., 5 June 1940.

Penalty one stroke: War Games, p. 82.

importance to the war effort: Ibid.

Eighteen: Field Sports

or anyone in particular: NA MAF 44/25.

'the most blimpish peer imaginable': People and Places, p. 218.

We then went on hunting: Wyndham and Children First, p. 63. When the Queen went down to inspect Canadian troops stationed on the Petworth estate before D-Day, Lord Leconfield declined to meet her, on the grounds that he was too busy.

for Brain of Britain: Raoul Millais, p. 40.

did conform to the Rules: Badminton archive.

'a large increase of cur-dogs': Ibid. Master's obsession with foxes lasted until his death. It is said that one day at the end of January 1984, when he was eighty-three, in the graveyard of St Michael and All Angels' Church at Badminton he saw three foxes apparently predicting his demise.

One was sitting on the grave of his grandfather, one on that of his father, and the third on the spot under which he proposed to be buried. He died a week later, on 5 February 1984.

into the nearest field: *Wartime Diaries*, p. 152.

not lectured them upon: CL, 9 December 1939.

as soon as possible: *Come Dawn, Come Dusk*, pp. 111–12.

coming from one engine: Ibid., p. 114.

few people left to fish: FG, 9 September 1939.

what tactics to employ: FG, 16 September 1939.

'a first-rate season for flatfish': Ibid.

trying their luck: Ibid.

for ever in peace: *Fishing and Flying*, pp. 22–3.

absolutely FULL OF GRAIN: NA MAF 44/48.

to be of any use: NA MAF 44/29.

absence of manpower: Information contributed by grouse moor managers.

but in hundreds: Private source.

seems rather drastic: NA MAF 44/27.

to initiate culling: Twenty years passed before the Deer Act (1963) set close seasons and laid down minimum calibres of weapons for shooting deer. Paradoxically, as the human population of Britain has expanded to sixty million, and more and more land is taken up by houses, roads, industrial sites, airports and so on, deer numbers have grown to over one million – easily the highest total in recorded history. Some 50,000 deer are involved in traffic accidents every year, and more and more

stalkers are being trained by the British Deer Society and the British Association for Shooting and Conservation; yet numbers are still increasing.

Nineteen: Animals Under Fire

they were very high: Huxley, *Memories*, p. 248.

not a kicker: Ibid., p. 255.

to survey the damage: *The Story of Bristol Zoo*, p. 78.

to "our gallant ally": Ibid., p. 80.

one of a panda: Clifton College had been evacuated to Bude, in Cornwall.

break the barriers instantly: *Diaries 1939–72*, pp. 82–3.

destroyed overnight: *Bertram Mills Circus*, p. 128.

Twenty: Slate Country

finding people for work: *Anglesey and Gwynedd in the War Years*, p. 132.

assembling aircraft components: By 1943, when conscription was extended to include women up to fifty, more than half all Welsh war-workers were female.

seek out his enemy: Sniping Manual, p. 3. In 1956 Wills succeeded his father as the second Baron Dulverton. A skilled forester and naturalist, he became President of the Timber Growers' Organisation, Chairman of the Forestry Committee of Great Britain, and President of the British Deer Society.

training and practice: Sniping Manual, p. 8.

great sport of sniping: *With British Snipers to the Reich*, p. 284.

'a bag of something like fifty Huns': In 1946 Major General G. H. A. MacMillan, Director of Weapons and Development at the War Office, wrote to Wills's father saying, 'He did an extremely good job when in command of the Sniping School, and the Army owes him a great deal more than is known generally.'

blowers in the dining halls: During the war Billy Butlin was recruited by the Ministry of Supply as an unpaid morale-raiser in Britain, and in Europe, at the invitation of General Montgomery, he set up leave centres for the 21st Army Group. After the war he opened many more holiday camps in England, and in 1964 he was knighted for his charitable work. In 1973 the Rank Organisation launched a takeover of his empire for £43 million – over £400 million in today's figures.

Twenty-One: Evictions

we enjoyed ourselves: Rich Relations, p. 122.

roared over the heath: The training carried out at Stanford was realistic enough to cause several deaths, but must have contributed to the success of Operation Overlord. Families were told that men who died on exercises had been killed in action.

Britain for the British: Farming on a Battleground, p. 32.

to land his planes on: Ibid.

more specially the tanks: Ibid., p. 63.

way of life were to go: BBC PW AD3258362.

when the war was over: Hansard, 4 July 1946.

ever discovered in Britain: The treasures found at Sutton Hoo are now in the British Museum.

to live in Imber: Imber's buildings survived the war more or less intact, but many of them were damaged by shellfire or explosions when British troops trained on Salisbury Plain in the 1940s and 1950s.

In October 1961 2000 people gathered on the site, demanding that the villagers be allowed back, but in January 1962 the Ministry of Transport announced that the closure of rights of way on the ranges would be permanent, and a public inquiry found in favour of Imber's continued use by the army. During the 1970s several dummy houses were built, to make the place a more realistic scenario for street fighting. Military training continues, but the village is open to the public on specified days.

Public attachment to Imber has remained exceptionally strong. Concerts and festivals have been staged in the village. In 2008 St Giles's Church was restored (after being struck by lightning five years earlier); annual services are still held there, and there is a carol service on the last Saturday before Christmas.

Southern Command: Dorsetshire.com website.

over the ridge: Tyneham: A Lost Heritage, p. 2.

aged ninety-three: Tyneham was never reoccupied. In spite of vigorous and sustained protests by local people, the Government reneged on its promise of allowing the inhabitants to return, and in 1948 compulsorily bought the whole valley for £30,000. By then the weapons being fired on the gunnery ranges at Bovington, five miles to the north, were so powerful that Tyneham had become a danger zone, and it has remained a military training area ever since. Strange to relate – in view of the frequent explosions – the valley has proved a haven for wildlife, and is frequented particularly by Sika deer.

In 1967 the Ministry of Works demolished the Manor House, which had become unsafe; but the church and schoolhouse have been repaired and preserved as museums. Tyneham is now open to the public at weekends and in August – the mysterious and melancholy remains of a village peopled only by ghosts.

on 20 December: Reg Hannaford's story appeared in *The Wartime News*, Vol. 4, 2nd edition, May 1999.

had been destroyed: FW, 11 August 1944.

Twenty-Two: Far North

or anyone representing me: Cameron-Head papers L/D27, The Highland Archives, Lochaber Archive Centre, Fort William.

roof over my head: Ibid.

and down steep hills: Paramilitary Training in Scotland, p. 3.

weapons is first class: Gavin Maxwell: A Life, p. 55.

with a Colt .45: Ibid., p. 57.

most beautiful place in the world: Ibid., p. 61.

eels floating on the water: Paramilitary Training in Scotland, p. 69.

have been collected: Cameron of Lochiel Papers (CL), The Highland Archive Centre, Fort William.

without a permit: After the war timber merchants became reluctant to buy wood from the estate, because so much shrapnel was embedded in the trees. Live mortar bombs and hand grenades are still being found in the peat. In 2011, before excavation started for a new water system, an electronic sweep of the ground revealed seven bombs and a hand grenade.

with automatic weapons: Private information.

on the South Forest: Private archive.

Lieutenant Tony Younger: Blowing Our Bridges, pp. 83–5.

were incinerated in 1945: Gruinard was finally cleaned up in the 1980s at a cost of £500,000. Nearly 300 tonnes of formaldehyde diluted in seawater were sprayed on the land, and the worst contaminated soil was taken away in sealed containers. A flock of sheep put onto the island remained healthy, as did rabbits, black and brown, which had survived throughout, and in May 1990 the original owners were allowed to buy the island back for £500.

however good it was: www. rememberingscotlandatwar.org.uk

its master returned: www. WW2inthehighlands.co.uk

on his conning tower: The wreck of the battleship still lies on the bottom of Scapa Flow, almost upside down in 100 feet of water, with her hull only sixteen feet beneath the surface. As the bodies of her crew could not be recovered, she is a designated war grave, and at annual ceremonies Royal Navy divers place a White Ensign on her stern. In Germany Günther Prien became a national hero, but not for long: in March 1941 he and his submarine *U-47* were lost.

to play for them: BBC PW A2692811.

Twenty-Three: On the Springboard

we were imitating: Fortitude South, pp. 63–5.

the hours of daylight: Ibid., p. 46.

more ambitious programme: The Double-Cross System, p. 142.

deception campaign: Double Cross, p. 175.

a campaign of assassination: Ibid., p. 186.

"hide the facts in order to trick us": Ibid., pp. 290–91.

bottom of the English Channel: King's Counsellor, pp. 224–9.

in the past four years: Ibid., pp. 224–30.

drop in the barometer: The Times, 5 June 1944.

excluded from the area: www.qe2activitycentre.co.uk/hms%20Cricket.htm

vehicles of every description: Past Forgetting, p. 162.

with the Lord's Prayer: www.qe2activitycentre.co.uk/hms%20Cricket.htm

fingers crossed: Evidence for the Crown, p. 139.

landing in Normandy: Ibid.

we would later regret: Double Cross, p. 325.

'extraordinary merits': After the war MI5 spirited Garbo away to Venezuela, where he became a Spanish teacher and opened a bookshop. In 1984 he came to England to receive his MBE, and he died in 1988, content in the knowledge that his machinations had saved hundreds of lives and casualties on the Normandy beaches. In the words of Ben Macintyre, 'he was a warrior who fought to save lives, not to take them, using words as his only weapons'.

Twenty-Four: Flying Bombs

destroyed by Allied bombers: Hansard, 6 July 1944.

talking to all and sundry: King's Counsellor, p. 243.

poor, defenceless London: Ibid.

driven partridges: Ibid.

outside Tunbridge Wells: Eden Valley Museum archive.

before anyone came: War in the Countryside, p. 151.

to ruin tomato crops: FW, 7 July 1944.

with a bang!: Evidence for the Crown, p. 141.

a fanatical suicide: Ibid., p. 144.

rather striking: Ibid, p. 145.

'almost with affection': Hertfordshire Mercury, 18 September 1998. The last V-1 of the war also landed in the Hertfordshire countryside, on the morning of 29 March 1945.

of the London region: The Double-Cross System, p. 181.

Twenty-Five: Unfinished Business

moving off to the kill: I Am My Brother, p. 269.

will derive benefit: The Battle of the Land, p. 140.

'united the nation as never before': Ibid.

dug up in the fields: Details from Roald Dahl's *The Wonderful Story of Henry Sugar*, pp. 52–81. In April 1946 he read a newspaper report of the find, and was so excited that he immediately drove 120 miles to Mildenhall, where he talked to Gordon Butcher at length. Ford closed the door in his face. Dahl embroidered his account of the discovery with extra detail, but insisted that all the main facts were accurate.

stiff East Anglian clays: FW, 28 July 144.

the black earth of Suffolk: The silver is now exhibited in the British Museum.

what had been lost: The Times, 6 June 1944.

foxes or trees: FW, 11 August 1944.

blackbird and robin: All Hands to the Harvest, p. 207.

carried indoors and unloaded: FW, 29 September 1944.

they needn't bother: FW, 8 September 1944.

and West Perthshire: Ibid., 7 July 1944.

effaced and forgotten: Ibid.,18 May 1945.

the amount blown out: Ibid.

concrete and modern materials: Ibid.

to wander about them: The Country Gentleman's Estate Magazine, June 1943, p. 156.

twice on Sundays: FW, 19 January 1945.

orchard and dairy: Lady Denman, pp. 178–9.

general-maid-of-all-work-and-no-initiative: FW, 11 August 1944.

our post-war policy: FW, 11 March 1945.

any politician departs: Ibid., 3 November 1944.

Heavy rain in afternoon: John Alsop's diary is now in the library at Newquay Zoo.

a fireworks display: www.lgchronicle.net/WW2.html

relief and thankfulness: FW, 11 May 1945.

the medical service: The Lady, 14 June 1945.

marvellous capacity for greatness: Evidence for the Crown, p. 148.

time to stiffen: Orwell, *Diaries*, p. 339.

as being 'the enemy': Richard Moore-Colyer in the *Agricultural History Review*, quoted in www.bahs.org.uk/AGHR/ARTICLES/54n2a8.pdf

one's stride and enjoyed: Ibid.

equally strange: Action Stations, p. 32.

to be properly exploited: Country Notes in Wartime, p. 18.

List of Illustrations

Plate Section 2

Page 1: (clockwise from top left) World War II poster – 'Dig For Victory Still' (*The National Archives/SSPL/Getty Images*); World War II poster offering guidance on how to grow cabbages, tomatoes, leeks and onions. Issued by the Ministry of Agriculture and Fisheries (*Heritage Images/Corbis*); 'Dig For Victory Now' Home Front food propaganda poster (*Topfoto*); 'Plough Now!' Propaganda poster published in *Farmer's Weekly*, March 1940 (*Museum of English Rural Life, Reading*)

Page 2: (top) Art treasures from the National Gallery are moved to Manod Quarry slate caverns in Merionethshire, Wales, for safekeeping during World War II, September 1942 (*Fred Ramage/Keystone Features/Hulton Archive/Getty Images*); (bottom) Paintings from the National Gallery undergo their daily dusting in a subterranean chamber at Manod Quarry, September 1942 (*Fred Ramage/Keystone Features/Hulton Archive/Getty Images*)

Page 3: (top) Storemen stack 250-lb MC bombs in one of the tunnels at No. 21 Maintenance Unit at RAF Fauld, near Hanbury, Staffordshire (© *IWM, CH 3043*); (bottom) Shot-down German plane in rural setting, 1940 (*Museum of English Rural Life, Reading © Keystone Press Agency*)

Page 4: (top) Photograph of Penrhos College schoolgirls skating on the Canal Pond at Chatsworth, 1940 (© *Devonshire Collection, Chatsworth. Reproduced by permission of Chatsworth Settlement Trustees*); (bottom) The Allied Central Interpretation Unit at RAF Medmenham. D-Day forces were briefed with the aid of 340 synthetic rubber models of the landing sites based on aerial reconnaissance photographs (© *IWM, CH 16106*)

Page 5: (top) Winston Churchill with his wife Clementine, holding a lion cub during a trip to London Zoo, July 1943 (*Topical Press Agency/Getty Images*); (bottom) Ming the giant panda at London Zoo attracting a crowd, March 1940 (*A. Cook/London Express/Getty Images*)

Page 6: (top) British World War II anti-landing devices. Old cars are strung across a field so that it could not be used as a landing ground by enemy aircraft (*Topfoto*); (bottom) World War II double agent, Juan Pujol García, codename 'Garbo' (*The National Archives, UK. KV2/70*)

Page 7: (top) Blacksmith's forge bombed and damaged in Sidcup, 1941 (*Topfoto*); (bottom) WLA moving trees with Fordson tractor after an enemy incident (*Museum of English Rural Life, Reading*)

Page 8: (top) Italian POW marching to work in the field, 1941 (*Museum of English Rural Life, Reading © Topical Press Agency*); (bottom) inflatable rubber tanks

Index

443

Masterman, J. C. 367, 368, 388
Matthews, Stanley 291
Mau Mau 162
Mauduit de Kervern,
  Georges, le Vicomte de
  142–4
  Private View 142
  They Can't Ration These 142
Maxwell, Captain Eustace 86,
  87
Maxwell, Gavin 86, 349–50
  Ring of Bright Water 349–50
Medoc II (race-horse) 290
Mee, Frank 101, 241–2
Melville, Flight Lieutenant
  Richard 274–5
Melville House, Monimail
  (East Fife) 86–7
Merritt, Betty 162
Merseyside 34
Merton Hall, Norfolk 333
Meteorological Office 374–5
Metropolitan Police piggery,
  Hyde Park 139
MI5 75, 274, 277, 319, 368
MI6 204, 369
Microbiological Research
  Centre, Porton Down 357
Middleton, Cecil Henry
  149–52
Midhope Moor, Yorkshire
  307, 396
Midwinter, Eric 281
Mildenhall hoard 393–5
military training 321, 323–7
  in East Anglia 330–4
  on farm-land 329–30
  local reactions to 331–4
  requisitioning land for
  329–43
  Sutton Hoo 334
Millais, Raoul 297
Miller, C. H. 336
Miller, Glen 265
Mills, Bernard 318–19
Mills, Bertram 318
Mills, Cyril 318, 318–19
Mills, John 264
Milton, John, *Paradise Lost*
  379

Ministry of Agriculture 17,
  20, 22, 23, 70, 135, 140, 287,
  296, 305, 308–9, 395, 398,
  410
Ministry of Defence 185
Ministry of Food 112, 130,
  132–5, 138
Ministry of Health 397
Ministry of Information 58,
  59
Ministry of Labour
  Instructional Centre,
  Cairnbaan (Argyll) 172–3
Ministry of Works 204
Möhne Dam 307
Moidart 345
Moll, Richard 246
Monks Risborough Women's
  Institute 136–7
Monkton Farleigh Quarry,
  Wiltshire 184
Monnickendam, Albert 322
Montacute House, Somerset
  187
Montgomery, General
  Bernard 82–3
Montgomery-Massingberd,
  Field Marshal Sir Archibald
  Armar 215–16
Montreal (ship) 279
Morar 345
Moreton-in-Marsh,
  Gloucestershire 21
Morley Hill, nr Newcastle
  403–4
Mortimer, Roger 287, 288
Moscow 62
Mosley, Sir Oswald 331
Moss, Alan 113
Moss, Dennis 113
Mottershead, George 317
Mt Snowdon 46
Much Marcle Watchers 67
Muller, George 396
Munich Crisis (1938) 188, 204,
  236
Mursell, Norman 300–1
Museums and Galleries Air
  Raids Precautions
  Committee 187

music and entertainment
  100–1
Music While You Work (radio
  programme) 99
Myles, Sandy 300

NAAFI 164, 217
Nanking University 133
Napoleon Bonaparte 142
Nash, Sergeant 223
Nashleigh Hill, Chesham
  385–6
National Air Raid Precautions
  Animals Committee 51, 112
National Allotments Society
  133
National Anthem 30
National Camps Corporation
  47
National Cyclists' Union 285
National Farmers' Union
  (NFU) 92, 97, 392–3, 398
National Federation of
  Anglers 302
National Federation of
  Women's Institutes 146–7,
  154
National Fishing Association
  303
National Gallery, London 187,
  188–9, 192, 193
National Health Service
  (NHS) 407
National Hunt 289, 290
National Maritime Museum,
  Greenwich 334
National Pigeon Service 273
National Savings 100
National Stud 288
National Trust 187, 211–17, 229
Nazis 73–4, 75, 86, 112, 143,
  165, 204, 205, 248, 355, 376
Nevett, William 288
New British Broadcasting
  Station 73–4
New Forest 22
New Romney, Essex 384
New Statesman and Nation 412
New Zealand Corps of
  Engineers 173